THE QUILTERS *Ultimate* VISUAL GUIDE

From A to Z—Hundreds of Tips and Techniques
for Successful Quiltmaking

Ellen Pahl, Editor

Rodale Press, Inc.
Emmaus, Pennsylvania

OUR PURPOSE

We inspire and enable people to improve their lives and the world around them.

The authors and editors who compiled this book have tried to make all of the contents as accurate and as correct as possible. Illustrations, photographs, and text have all been carefully checked and cross-checked. However, due to the variability of materials, personal skill, and so on, neither the author nor Rodale Press assumes any responsibility for any damages or other losses incurred that result from the material presented herein. All instructions and illustrations should be carefully studied and clearly understood before beginning any project.

Printed in the United States of America
on acid-free ∞, recycled paper ♲

Editor: **Ellen Pahl**

Cover and Interior Designer: **Carol Angstadt**

Cover and Interior Illustrator: **John Kocon**

Fabric Pattern Illustrator: **Carole Ann Kocon**

Alphabet Letter Illustrator: **Frank Rohrbach**

Cover and Interior Photographers: **John Hamel and Mitch Mandel**

Layout Assistance: **Robin Hepler**

Technical Artist: **Dale Mack**

Copy Editor: **Jennifer R. Hornsby**

Manufacturing Coordinator: **Patrick T. Smith**

Indexer: **Nanette Bendyna**

Editorial Assistance: **Susan L. Nickol and Jodi Rehl**

RODALE HOME AND GARDEN BOOKS

Vice President and Editorial Director: **Margaret J. Lydic**

Managing Editor: **Suzanne Nelson**

Art Director: **Paula Jaworski**

Associate Art Director: **Mary Ellen Fanelli**

Studio Manager: **Leslie M. Keefe**

Copy Director: **Dolores Plikaitis**

Book Manufacturing Director: **Helen Clogston**

Office Manager: **Karen Earl-Braymer**

We're always happy to hear from you. If you have any questions or comments concerning the editorial content of this book, please write to:
Rodale Press, Inc., Book Readers' Service, 33 East Minor Street, Emmaus, PA 18098

Look for other Rodale books wherever books are sold. Or call us at (800) 848-4735. For more information about Rodale Press and the books and magazines we publish, visit our Web site at:
www.rodalestore.com

Library of Congress Cataloging-in-Publication Data

The quilters ultimate visual guide : from A to Z—hundreds of tips and techniques for successful quiltmaking / Ellen Pahl, editor.
     p.   cm.
  Includes index
  ISBN 0–87596–710–8 hardcover
  ISBN 0–87596–987–9 paperback
  1. Quilts—Encyclopedias. 2. Patchwork—Encyclopedias. 3. Quilting—Encyclopedias. 4. Appliqué—Encyclopedias. I. Pahl, Ellen.
TT835.Q5214 1997
746.46'03—dc20   96–27757

Distributed to the book trade by St. Martin's Press

    18 20 19 17   hardcover

14 16 18 20 19 17 15   paperback

CONTENTS

ACKNOWLEDGMENTS

I want to extend a huge thank you to all the many talented quilters who have contributed to this book. It has been such a privilege and pleasure for me to have worked with each of you. I have learned an incredible amount and can't wait to share all these words of wisdom with other quilters. During the course of editing this book, I was continually impressed by the willingness of each contributor to share tips and techniques that make her or him successful, going above and beyond the call of duty to provide information and inspiration.

Special thanks go to Cyndi Hershey, owner of the Country Quilt Shop in Montgomeryville, Pennsylvania, for supplying batting, marking supplies, needles, pins, and thimbles for the photo shoots. Sharee Dawn Roberts, owner of Web of Thread, sent us a wonderful array of threads and embellishments to photograph.

Also, thank you to Dawn Hall of Cherrywood Fabrics, who supplied the luscious hand-dyed fabrics to make the striking biscuit quilt shown on page 53. Thank you to Doris Carmack for making it.

I wish to thank the following people for graciously loaning quilts, samples, or other projects to be photographed: Doris Adomsky, Cheryl Greider Bradkin, Karen Kay Buckley, Rolinda Collinson, Carol Doak, Philomena Durcan, Lynne Edwards, Anna Eelman, Susan Faeder, Jane Hall, Dixie Haywood, Jeanne Jenzano, June Kempston, Roxanne McElroy, Susan McKelvey, Karen Phillips, Caroline Reardon, Susan

Ellen Pahl

Stein, Suellen Meyer, Sharee Dawn Roberts, Eileen Sullivan, Debby Wada, and Hari Walner.

For allowing the reuse of photos of their quilts, I would like to thank Shelly Burge, Gwen Marston, Judy Martin, Judy Miller, Julie Silber, and Edith Zimmer.

Many of the fabrics photographed throughout the book were supplied by Virginia Robertson, who designs for FabriQuilt. The lamé shown on page 139 was generously donated by Rosebar Textiles.

The following manufacturers and suppliers donated or loaned tools and equipment that were used in the photographs: Bernina, Cottage Tools, Wholesale Cutlery (Dovo/Solingen), Fiskars, Gingher, Olfa, Omnigrid, and Pfaff.

I am very grateful for the help and support received from my coworkers, the Rodale quilt book editors, and Managing Editor Suzanne Nelson. Their assistance, encouragement, and comic relief were much appreciated. For vastly improving the text and adding the final polishing touches, thanks go to Jennifer Hornsby.

I would also like to acknowledge and thank Carol Angstadt for her stellar book design and John Kocon for his incredible illustrations. Together they have made this ultimate visual book live up to its title.

Lastly, thanks to my family for putting up with a great deal of chaos, neglect, and junk food while I was working on this book.

INTRODUCTION

Welcome to a visual feast of quiltmaking techniques, tips, definitions, and inspiration! In this comprehensive A-to-Z volume, 60 well-known quiltmakers share their knowledge and expertise about basic quiltmaking, specialized techniques, tools, supplies, quilt genres, and just about anything you ever wanted to know about quiltmaking.

Our goal in creating this book was to make sure it would be extra easy to use. The entries are organized alphabetically, so you can flip through and quickly find your topic; you'll find the topics listed at the top of each page for easy access. Or, use the index as a shortcut route to the subject of your choice. (You'll also find other references to a subject.) To see at a glance who the author of a particular entry is—who's speaking or expressing an opinion—look at the name that appears at the top of each page. There is also a postmark logo at the end of each person's entry. That's your signal that someone else will be writing the next section. Any Try This, Taking the Trouble Out of, Skill Builder, or other boxes have bylines if they are written by someone other than the main author.

One of the many wonderful characteristics these quilters have in common is their willingness to share knowledge and information. Throughout the book, you'll find that not all quilters do things the same way or have the same preferences. I have always believed that what works for one person doesn't necessarily work for someone else. I have tried to stay true to that belief, presenting the writer's opinions and the methods and techniques that work for that individual. Someone else may do things differently, and that's fine. My advice is to experiment and test them all. Eventually, you'll have your own set of "best ways" to do every technique you need for quiltmaking.

Quilters often mention products that they prefer, and whenever they are unusual or hard to find, I have included a source for them in the Resource Guide, which begins on page 274. Most other products and tools should be readily available in quilt shops and mail-order catalogs.

The cast of quilters who have contributed to this book includes professional quilters, quilt book authors, technical writers, quilt historians, textile specialists, quilting teachers, quilt shop owners, quilt designers, quilt show judges, and my colleagues, the quilting editors at Rodale Press. In the Contributors section, which begins on page 275, there's a bit more information about each one of this extraordinary group of quilters.

As you page through this book, you'll probably have the same reaction I did as I worked on the manuscript. Every day I'd read something that made me say, "Wow! I didn't know that! I can't wait to try that out." If you love quilts and can't get enough of new techniques, ideas, and inspiration, you'll love this book!

Ellen Pahl

ALBUM QUILTS

"The Buckley Album Quilt," 74" × 74", made by Karen Kay Buckley, with help from her husband, Joe. Each block contains dates, places, and things that have special meaning in their lives.

An album is a collection of images or objects meaningful to the owner, such as a scrap book of cherished photographs, sketches, pressed flowers, poetry, or other mementos. An album quilt is a collection of quilt blocks, each one different from the others. The blocks are usually equal in size, with the exception of center medallion blocks, which can be up to four times the size of the other blocks.

Both patchwork and appliqué are popular for album quilts, and many contain interesting combinations of both techniques. Settings vary greatly, and sashings can be solid-color, pieced, appliquéd, printed, or striped. The borders usually contain designs that relate to the blocks in the center portion of the quilt.

In the nineteenth century, album quilts were popular as friendship and presentation quilts, made in honor of special people and occasions. Some contained simple botanical shapes with a folk-art quality; others had more realistic appliqué designs.

A unique style of album quilt was developed in Baltimore, Maryland, during the 1840s through the mid-1850s. A typical Baltimore Album quilt contained intricate, pictorial images such as flowers, wreaths, leaves, animals, buildings, and ships, or figures of men, women, and children. Broderie Perse was a popular technique for these quilts, in which whole or partial motifs were cut out of printed chintz fabrics and appliquéd onto background squares. Another classic style that was often included in Baltimore Album quilts was a snowflake-like block, similar to Scherenschnitte, or cutwork. To complement the formal elegance of these quilts, the quiltmakers of Baltimore frequently embellished their work with delicately inked inscriptions, friendship verses, dedications, and signatures.

Twentieth-century album quilts cover a wider range of styles, from traditional samplers featuring mainly patchwork to whimsical country-style quilts that include folk art shapes like chickens, roosters, or cows to more formal appliqué quilts that are similar to album quilts of the nineteenth century.

Jane Townswick

AMISH QUILTS

If ever a quilt makes a statement about the maker, it is an Amish quilt. An Amish quilt allows a glimpse into the orderly, methodical, and productive way an Amish woman lives. More so than any other quilt genre, Amish quilts represent a lifestyle—one that's simple, uncomplicated by social trends, and undistracted in its goal of serving God.

The Amish did not bring quiltmaking with them when they immigrated to America in the eighteenth century. It is believed they learned the skill from their neighbors in the Pennsylvania communities they settled.

Amish quilts are easily recognizable by their vivid colors and distinctive, yet uncomplicated patterns. Most quilts contain bits of fabric left after dresses and shirts have been made for the family. While modest black is perceived as the color of choice by outsiders, closer examination of antique Amish quilts reveals an appreciation for colors. Colors, however, were and are limited to the availability of dyes and fabrics in the market and to the parameters set by the church and community at large. The jewel-tone colors are most typical of Lancaster County, Pennsylvania, quilts, while midwestern Amish quilts contain black and more muted or pastel colors.

Squares, rectangles, diamonds, and triangles form the basis for most quilts. Curves and other "fancies" are reserved for hand-quilted details. Each Amish community has set its own standards, and quiltmaking styles can be easily traced to an area. Historically, Lancaster County, Pennsylvania, quilts are almost always square and feature wide borders and corner squares. Quilts from other communities, such as the ones in Ohio and Indiana, are usually rectangular and have narrower borders; corner squares are only occasionally incorporated into a design. Mitered borders are rarely used, since they require more fabric. In keeping true to their faith, the quilts the Amish

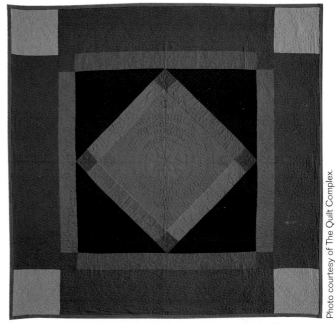

This Center Diamond quilt, 79 ½"× 81½", is made of dress-weight wools. An Amish woman from Lancaster County, Pennsylvania, stitched this classic beauty circa 1920.

Photo courtesy of The Quilt Complex.

make are simple in design and fulfill a utilitarian need of providing warmth.

Lavish hand quilting is, perhaps, the most recognized aspect of Amish quiltmaking. Tiny stitches, as many as 20 to the inch, are the hallmark of an experienced Amish quilter. Even though quilting stitches add depth and beauty to a quilt, the Amish view hand quilting as purely functional—it serves to hold the layers of the quilt securely together. Borrowing from everyday life, the Amish have incorporated recognizable objects into their quilting. Typical designs include feather, cable, basket, star, and pumpkin seed.

To understand the lives of the Amish is to understand the stark nature, yet incredible beauty, of many of their quilts. The Amish see quiltmaking as functional; those outside their community have come to appreciate it as art.

Karen Bolesta

These solid colors make up the Lancaster Amish color palette.

APPLIQUÉ

Appliqué is best known as "fancy quiltmaking" or as a method reserved for formal quilts. It was traditional in the nineteenth century to use appliqué on "Sunday-best" or special occasion quilts. These were often bridal quilts, made by young women in anticipation of marriage. They were stitched to display a young lady's skill with a needle and her readiness for mature responsibility. Red and green fabrics were typically used for the repeated appliqué pattern.

Another type of nineteenth-century appliqué quilt was the album quilt, made to honor a special individual. Each block was designed, stitched, and signed by a different person and then presented as a whole to the recipient. (See "Album Quilts" on page 6.)

Appliqué is misunderstood as advanced and difficult work. Unlike patchwork, where precision is important to achieve success, appliqué is very forgiving. Slight changes in appliqué shapes or shifting of the pieces during stitching make no difference as long as the finished result is pleasing. So relax and get started. Just remember that practice makes perfect, and the more you do, the better your stitches will look!

Supplies

Small scissors
Long, thin needles
Silk pins (with very thin shanks)
Thimble (optional)
Thread to match the appliqué fabric
Pencil to mark stitching lines

Note: I use size 10 or 11 straw needles. They are extra long, thin, and glide through fabric easily.

Try This I prefer a tailor's thimble with an open end that allows the finger to protrude. This frees the finger to manipulate the needle while still giving the finger protection.

TAKING THE TROUBLE OUT OF

Thread Color

When the correct shade of thread is unavailable, choose a shade lighter than the appliqué piece if the background fabric is light. When the background fabric is dark, choose a shade darker than the appliqué piece. This eliminates the possibility of the thread being the most contrasting color on the surface and keeps the stitches from standing out.

Making Templates

To avoid the extra time it takes to trace each piece of an appliqué design, make photocopies of the master pattern and cut them apart for templates.

Step 1. Cut the paper templates the *actual size* of the finished motif. The seam allowance will be added when the motif is cut from fabric.

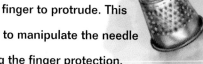

Paper template

Step 2. Place the paper template on the right, or printed, side of the appliqué fabric. Position the template to use the fabric print most effectively.

Note: Straight of grain is unimportant on appliqué motifs since the stability of the entire block is established by the much larger background fabric, which is cut on the straight of grain.

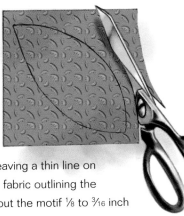

Step 3. Trace around the template with a mechanical or very sharp pencil, leaving a thin line on the right side of the fabric outlining the motif's shape. Cut out the motif ⅛ to ³⁄₁₆ inch beyond the pencil line.

Note: Seam allowance for appliqué is less than the ¼ inch used for piecing. It is proportional to the size of the piece you are stitching. The maximum seam allowance for large pieces is ³⁄₁₆ inch, and the minimum for the smallest pieces is ⅛ inch.

Preparing Background Fabric

Step 1. Cut background fabric generously larger than the finished size. For a 16-inch finished block, cut the background fabric at least 18 inches square. It is cut down to 16½ inches square once the appliqué is complete and before joining the blocks together.

Step 2. Fold the background fabric and then the master pattern in half twice to find the center and one-quarter positions.

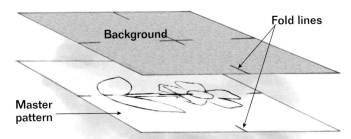

Step 3. Layer the master pattern and the background fabric together with the pattern on the bottom. Line up the one-quarter-folded markings and pin.

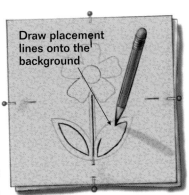

Draw placement lines onto the background

Step 4. Trace a "skeleton," or abbreviated version of the appliqué design, onto the background to serve as placement lines. Mark the stems with a single line in the center. Mark the lines of the other motifs a seam allowance width inside the actual shape. This marks a guide for appliqué placement without the risk of pencil marks showing on the finished piece.

Needle-Turn Appliqué

Needle-turn is an appliqué method in which you use the needle to turn the seam allowance under as you stitch. Right-handers, stitch counter-clockwise. Left-handers, stitch clockwise. (There are exceptions to this, but it's easier to get good results if you go in these directions.)

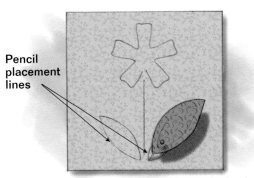

Pencil placement lines

Step 1. Position and pin the appliqué onto the background over its marked position.

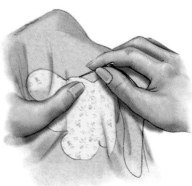

Step 2. Hold the block with your nonsewing hand. Use the side of the needle's point to turn the seam allowance under. Hold the turned-under edge in place with your thumbnail and a corresponding finger underneath the background.

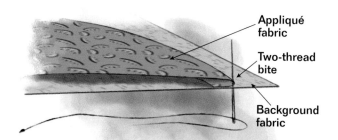

Appliqué fabric

Two-thread bite

Background fabric

Step 3. With knotted thread, guide the needle through the background, the turned seam allowance, and out through the top. As the needle travels upward through the fabric, bring it up about two threads away from the fold of the appliqué, taking a "two-thread bite" into the fold.

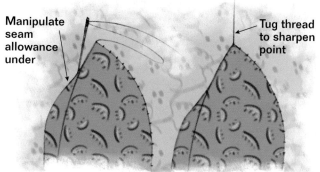

Manipulate seam allowance under

Tug thread to sharpen point

Step 2. Beginning at the tip, manipulate the seam allowance under and tug the thread to sharpen the motif's point. Continue stitching down the side.

1/16"

Step 4. To complete the stitch, insert the needle into the background fabric next to where the needle just came up. Then move the needle forward, traveling approximately 1/16 inch while under the background. Bring the needle up through the appliqué fabric, taking another two-thread bite.

Step 5. Pull the needle and thread through the fabric and give the thread a little tug. The tug will secure the stitch. Appliqué stitches are taken one at a time. There is no speed method for appliqué stitching. However, once you get the feel for taking these stitches, you'll establish a smooth rhythm.

Inside Points

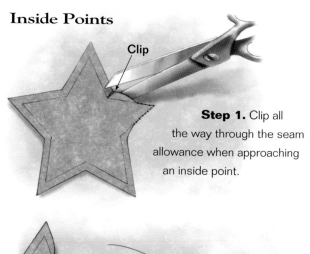

Clip

Step 1. Clip all the way through the seam allowance when approaching an inside point.

Step 2. Stop stitching one stitch short of the point. Turn under the seam allowance.

Trim excess

Outside Points

Step 1. Stitch all the way to the tip of the point, leaving the last stitch unsecured. Trim the excess that sticks out to the side once the fabric has been folded over. Leave at least 1/8 inch for the seam allowance.

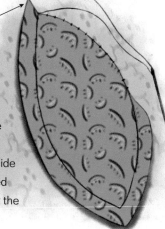

Step 3. Finish the previous stitch and come up for a "four-thread bite" inside the center of the point. Insert the needle under the edge of the appliqué and into the background fabric with the needle point out of sight.

Four threads deep

Rotate needle and begin next stitch

Step 4. Continue on to the next stitch by rotating the needle and moving forward. The needle then comes up to begin the next stitch.

Reverse Appliqué

Reverse appliqué is a technique in which an upper layer of fabric is turned back to expose a lower layer. You can do an entire block this way or add detail to a simple appliqué piece. See also "Channel Appliqué" on page 20.

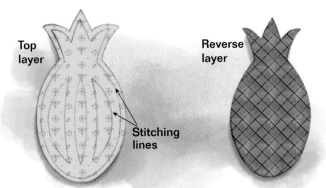

Top layer

Reverse layer

Stitching lines

Step 1. To add details to a piece that will be appliquéd to a background, mark the stitching lines on the top layer of fabric and the part of the design to be cut away. Cut the reverse layer—the fabric that will be exposed after cutting—the actual size of the finished appliqué.

Cut slit

Step 2. Cut a small slit in the top layer where the fabric will be cut away. Align the top layer and the reverse layer together, making sure the right side of the reverse fabric is facing up. Appliqué the top piece to the background, encasing the reverse layer between the two.

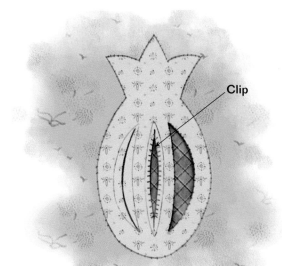

Clip

Step 3. Insert sharp scissors into the slit in the top layer and cut away any excess fabric, leaving a seam allowance. Clip all the way to the inside points but only halfway through the seam allowance on concave curves. Fold back the top layer and stitch, exposing the reverse layer.

SKILL BUILDER

Toothpick-Turn Appliqué
by Jane Townswick

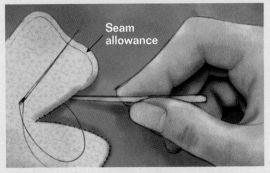

Seam allowance

One of the most indispensable tools in my sewing box is a round wooden toothpick. I use it for appliquéing smooth curves and crisp points. Here's how it works. Place a threaded needle underneath an appliqué piece and bring it up through the fabric, exactly on the turning line. Place the shank of the toothpick at the edge of the fabric and turn under approximately ¼ inch of the seam allowance, using a sweeping motion. Finger press the fabric, stitch the ¼ inch, and stop. Repeat this process around the entire appliqué piece.

An easy way to establish the order of stitching the appliqué pieces for floral designs is to mimic the way the plant grows: stems first, leaves, then the buds or flowers. Analyze other designs piece by piece until you get to the bottom layer.

Appliqué Borders

An appliqué border should complement the quilt center by repeating shapes and fabrics already included. There are several types of appliqué borders, but perhaps the most popular is a flowing vine that surrounds the quilt center. Another that is my favorite is an appliquéd dogtooth border.

To determine the border width, divide the finished individual block size by two, and add two inches. For example, a quilt with 12-inch blocks would have an 8-inch-wide border (12 inches ÷ 2 = 6 inches + 2 = 8 inches).

Vine Border

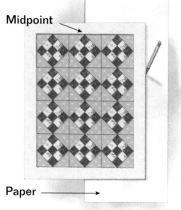

Midpoint

Paper

Step 1. Make an actual-size paper pattern that equals one-half of the finished-size border area. Use any large sheet of paper that can be cut and pasted together. You can trace around the quilt to get the outer dimensions.

Step 2. First, fold the corners of the pattern to create a folded corner square. Then fold the sides into equal sections, leaving a one-half fold on the pattern ends to allow the vine to flow evenly. Do this by gently folding back and forth like a fan until you get equal folds and a one-half fold on the end. Then crease the folds. For a full-size quilt, the sections will be 7 to 10 inches long.

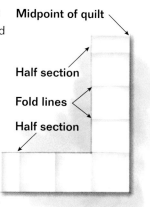

Midpoint of quilt

Half section

Fold lines

Half section

Step 3. Draw a line through the center of the length of the pattern. Next, draw a U-shape at the corner and continue to draw a flowing line that undulates across the folds and the center line evenly. Fill the open areas evenly with your chosen leaves and flowers.

Dogtooth Border

This border treatment is traditionally placed along the outside edge of the quilt, and the quilt is then bound in the same fabric. Any size dogtooth border can be created by using the following method. A finished size of 2 inches is used below as an example.

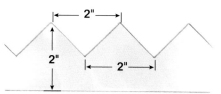

Step 1. Determine the dogtooth size you wish to use. The height, base, and spacing between points are all equal.

Step 2. Cut four fabric strips on the straight of grain to match the length of the outside edges of the quilt. The strip width is the finished dogtooth size plus ½ inch (2 inches + ½ inch = 2½ inches). Pin the first strip to the outside edge of the quilt.

Interior of quilt x = **Finished dogtooth size** y = ½ **finished dogtooth size**

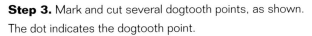
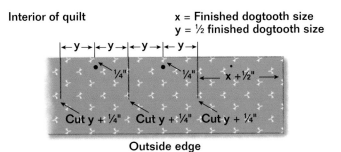

Cut y + ¼" Cut y + ¼" Cut y + ¼"

Outside edge

Step 3. Mark and cut several dogtooth points, as shown. The dot indicates the dogtooth point.

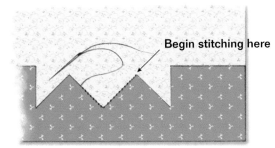

Begin stitching here

Step 4. Fold excess fabric from cut to dot, forming the first half of the dogtooth point. Begin stitching where shown. Fold excess fabric down the other side and continue stitching.

Step 5. Continue to mark, cut, and stitch along the dogtooth strip until you are within 18 inches of its end. From the unfinished edge of the strip, measure a distance equal to the finished dogtooth plus ½ inch (2½ inches for the example) and cut the same depth as all the other cuts (1¼ inches). This will allow for a mitered corner. Measure all the remaining dogtooth points on that strip. Slight "fudging" adjustments—slightly lengthening or shortening the distance between points—will need to be made to each measurement. These will not be noticeable on the finished quilt, and they make it possible for all corners to be mitered the same way.

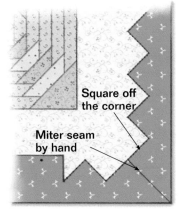

Square off the corner

Miter seam by hand

Step 6. Miter the corner by hand with a diagonal seam joining the two strips. Then trim off excess fabric, "square off" the corner by folding it under to make a straight edge, and hand appliqué the corner, as shown.

There are many techniques for successful appliqué. Experiment with several to determine which works best for you. Do not pass judgment on a technique because of the time factor. Make a decision based on how smooth your curves look and how sharp your points are. It is very beneficial to know different appliqué techniques because some techniques will work better on some shapes than others.

—Karen Kay Buckley

Freezer Paper Techniques

Reynolds freezer paper works best for these techniques. It is available in most grocery stores. In the Freezer Paper Up method, seam allowances are pressed onto freezer paper and the paper is removed after stitching. This gives a nice, crisp shape to stitch. In the Freezer Paper Down method, the seam allowances will not stick to the paper, but you will get very good creases in the edges of your appliqué shapes. The paper is removed before stitching. Try both methods to see which works better for you.

Freezer Paper Up

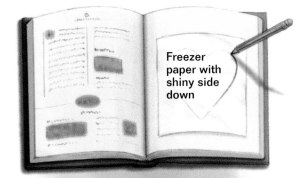

Freezer paper with shiny side down

Step 1. Place the freezer paper over your pattern with the shiny/waxy side down and the paper side up toward you. You will be able to see through the freezer paper. Trace the shape with a pencil. Cut on the lines you just drew. Do not add a seam allowance.

Step 2. Trace the freezer paper template. Cut the shape from your fabric, adding a ⅜-inch seam allowance.

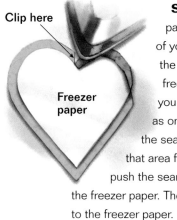

Clip here

Freezer paper

Step 3. Center the freezer paper template over the back of your cut fabric shape, with the shiny/waxy side of the freezer paper facing up toward you. If there are inner points, as on a heart, make a clip into the seam allowance, and press that area first. Use a dry, hot iron to push the seam allowance up and over the freezer paper. The seam allowance will stick to the freezer paper.

Step 4. To make nice sharp points, pull the point straight up and in. Press it to the freezer paper. With the iron, push one side up and over the freezer paper. Repeat on the other side, making sure to push the second side up tightly, to ensure a sharp point.

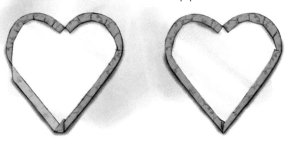

Read This Before You Cut

by Jeana Kimball

I do not cut away the background fabric behind my appliqué. Doing so compromises the strength of the quilt. Most nineteenth-century quilts did not have the background fabric cut away. Appliqué stitching is the weakest point of the quilt. If it loosens and there is a hole in the background fabric, it is almost impossible to repair. I quilt through the layers, often doing stab stitches, but there is usually minimal quilting through the appliqué. If you have a heavily layered flower or other design, you can assemble the item separately and then cut away some of the layers before appliquéing it to the background.

Step 5. Pin the shape in place and blind stitch the edge.

Step 6. Remove the freezer paper in one of two ways. You can stitch the entire way around the shape and then slit the backing fabric using a pair of sharp pointed scissors. Make the slit in the back at least ½ inch from your sewing line and remove the freezer paper. Or, you may prefer to stitch around the edge until you have a 1-inch opening. Reach in and remove the freezer paper, then stitch the opening closed. Both methods work well, so try each to determine which you prefer.

Remove freezer paper through slit

Remove freezer paper through 1" opening

Freezer Paper Down

Step 1. Follow Step 1 under Freezer Paper Up on page 13.

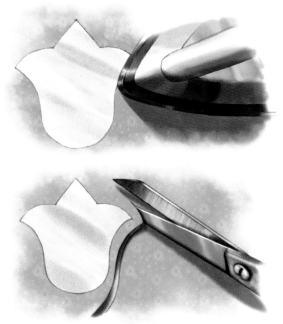

Step 2. Place the freezer paper shape, shiny side down, on the wrong side of your fabric. With a dry, hot iron, gently press the shape to the fabric. Cut around the shape, adding a ⅜-inch seam allowance.

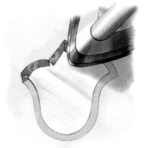

Step 3. With a dry, hot iron push the seam allowance up and over the freezer paper. Begin at an inner point, if possible. Handle the points as in the Freezer Paper Up method on page 14.

Step 4. After all the edges, curves, and points are creased, remove the freezer paper. Pin or glue the shape in place, and appliqué.

 When using pins to hold appliqué shapes, use one pin on the top to position the shape. Turn the piece over and place remaining pins in from the back. Turn the piece back over, remove the original pin, and your thread will not get caught on pins while you stitch.

Dimensional Appliqué
by Susan Stein

Appliqué that stands out from the surface of the quilt can add wonderful interest and texture to a wallhanging or quilted garment. Raw edge and faced appliqué are examples of techniques that give a three-dimensional look. Try this faced appliqué technique—it's an excellent method to use for flowers, leaves, butterflies, and bird wings. (See also "Raw Edge Appliqué" on page 26.)

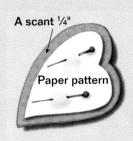

A scant ¼"

Paper pattern

Step 1. Choose a simple flower shape and draw it finished size. Layer two pieces of fabric, right sides together, and pin the flower pattern through all the layers. Cut the fabric a scant ¼ inch larger than the pattern.

Step 2. Sew around the fabric with short stitches, overlapping the stitches where they meet. Remove the pattern. Clip the inside corners and trim points.

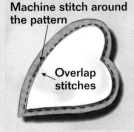

Machine stitch around the pattern

Overlap stitches

Step 3. Cut a slit in one layer of the appliqué, just long enough to turn the flower right side out. After turning the appliqué, run a crochet hook or point turner around the inside of the appliqué to push out all the edges smoothly. Press.

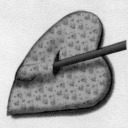

Step 4. Pin the flower to the background and sew the center parts of the flower over the appliqué to hold it in place. The center can be a dimensional stamen, a button, smaller petals, or machine stitching, as shown here, to represent flower parts such as the center of a hibiscus blossom. Leaves can be secured with machine quilting to look like veins.

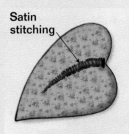

Satin stitching

Spray Starch and Templar for Appliqué

by Karen Kay Buckley

This is my favorite technique for doing appliqué. The spray starch gives a crisp, clean edge, and it holds the seam down really flat. After pressing, simply remove the Templar. Your stitching is effortless since the edge is already turned under.

This technique works well for leaves, flowers, circles, and many animal shapes. It does not work for intricate cut-away shapes, reverse appliqué, or very tiny shapes.

Supplies
Spray 'N Starch
Templar heat-resistant plastic
Q-Tips or a stencil brush

Note: I recommend Spray 'N Starch because some brands of spray starch can leave a thick residue on the fabric, making it too stiff to sew. I prefer the Templar brand of heat-resistant plastic—other brands are too thick, making it difficult to cut an accurate shape.

Step 1. Place Templar over the appliqué design. Trace the shape with a pencil.

Step 2. Using paper scissors, cut the Templar on the lines you just drew. Do not add a seam allowance.

Step 3. Place the Templar shape on the back of your fabric, and trace around the edge of the Templar with a pencil. Cut outside those lines, adding a 3⁄8-inch seam allowance.

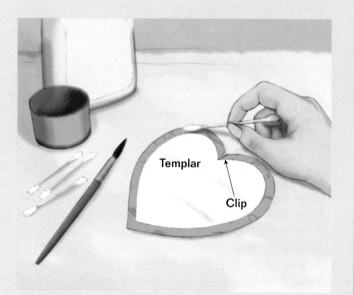

Templar

Clip

Step 4. Place the fabric shape on your ironing surface and center the Templar template over the wrong side of the fabric shape. With a Q-Tip or stencil brush apply spray starch to the seam allowance. Work in 3- to 4-inch sections at a time.

Step 5. Using a dry, hot iron push the seam allowance up and over the Templar. You will hear a sizzling sound, which means the spray starch is drying. You must keep the iron in place long enough for the spray starch to dry. When you remove the iron, the seam should lie flat. If the seam pops up, you have not allowed the iron to sit long enough. You will have to find the "happy setting" on your iron. Every iron is different. The iron needs to be hot enough to dry the spray starch but not so hot that it warps the Templar. If the Templar warps, it will not damage your iron, but you will have to make a new template. If there are inner points, iron them first. It is usually best to handle outer points last.

Step 6. After all of the edges are pressed flat, gently remove the Templar and appliqué the design in place.

To protect your ironing board cover from starch stains, layer some pieces of muslin or other scrap fabric on your ironing surface. I use ¼-yard pieces of muslin folded in half. It is much easier and less expensive to wash these scraps than it is to replace an ironing board cover.

Machine Appliqué

For all of these stitches use an open embroidery foot. This makes it easier to see the edge of the appliqué work. When you can more clearly see where you're stitching, it's easier to be as precise as possible.

Straight Stitch

In this machine appliqué method, you are simply stitching appliqué shapes onto the background fabric with a straight machine stitch.

Thread: Use cotton thread on the top and in the bobbin. The top thread color should match the appliqué. The bobbin thread can be a neutral color. Cotton machine embroidery thread is best, since it is thinner than regular cotton thread. You can also use nylon thread on the top and cotton embroidery thread in the bobbin. You may need to adjust your tension when using nylon thread; this is normal. A good tension setting will not show any of the bobbin thread on the top. YLI is the best nylon thread to use; some are too thick. Use clear thread on light and medium colors and smoke-color on dark fabrics.

Needle: Use a size 60/8 needle in your machine. This is a very thin needle that goes down into the fabric easily and will not make big holes; too large a needle can distort the appliqué.

Step 1. Turn the seam allowance under. I like the spray starch and Templar method on the opposite page.

Step 2. Pin or glue the shape in place. If using glue, be sure that it is fabric safe and water soluble.

Step 3. Begin on a curve or straight edge, not an inner or outer point. If portions of the shape have a raw edge because they will be covered by another shape, start at the raw edge. Do not stitch the raw edge itself.

Step 4. Set the stitch length at 0 and make 2 to 3 stitches. The stitch should be about 1/16 inch from the folded edge of your appliqué shape. This will anchor the end of the thread. As you are stitching, gradually increase the stitch length until you are sewing approximately 15 stitches per inch.

Pivot at the dots

Step 5. To stitch inner and outer points, drop the needle down, lift the presser foot, and pivot. Put the foot back down and resume stitching.

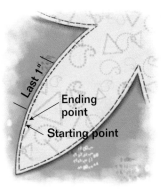

Last 1"

Ending point

Starting point

Step 6. To finish, gradually reduce your stitch length to 0 in the last inch. The last two to three stitches should be next to the stitches where you started. The goal is not to backstitch or overlap, because that area would become very thick and more noticeable.

Try This

Use silk pins when pinning appliqué shapes in place. They are thin and have very sharp points. They do not push the shape out of place and work better than larger sewing or quilting pins.

Satin Stitch

To do satin stitch appliqué, you need to be able to adjust the stitch width and length on your machine. Begin by doing a test on some scraps of fabric. Set your machine on zigzag. Reduce the stitch length until the stitches lie side by side. You do not want the stitches to stack on top of

SATIN STITCH

each other. Choose the width that you like based on the size of your appliqué shapes. Generally, for small shapes it is better to keep your stitches narrow.

Thread: Use a cotton machine embroidery thread or a rayon or metallic thread on the top, depending on the look you prefer. Use cotton machine embroidery thread in the bobbin regardless of your top thread.

Satin stitching is done on the raw edge so no seam allowance is needed. It works well on regular appliqué and reverse appliqué edges. To add stability and keep the edges from fraying, use fusible web on the back of the shape. (See "Quick-Fuse Appliqué" on page 27 and "Fusible Web" on page 118.)

Use a stabilizer such as tear-away paper or freezer paper underneath the background fabric when stitching to eliminate puckers or pulling. Carefully remove the stabilizer after stitching.

Beginning: Bring the bobbin thread up by inserting the needle down and holding on to the top thread. Gently tug on the top thread to bring the bobbin thread to the surface. This prevents tangled threads underneath, also known as "bobbin barf" or "thread throw-up!" Begin stitching just slightly beyond the edge

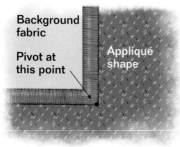

of the appliqué. Satin stitch should be approximately half on the appliqué and half on the background. This gives more leeway to manipulate slightly as you stitch around the shape.

Begin on a curve or straight edge, not an inner or outer point. If portions of the shape have a raw edge because they will be covered by another shape, start at the raw edge. Do not stitch the raw edge itself.

Pivoting on Curves: Keep the needle on the outside edge for outer curves and on the inside for inner curves.

Inner Points: Stitch beyond the inner point for a distance equal to the width of the stitch. Pivot and stitch down the edge. These stitches will overlap the previous stitches.

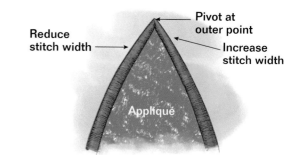

Outer Points: As you approach the point, reduce the stitch width. Pivot and gradually increase the stitch width.

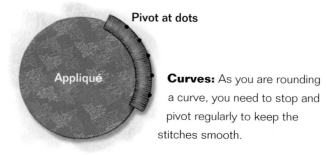

Curves: As you are rounding a curve, you need to stop and pivot regularly to keep the stitches smooth.

Ending: To secure the end stitching, switch to a straight stitch and do four to five stitches along the inside edge of the satin stitching. The stitch length is so close that these stitches are side-by-side and will appear to sit almost on top of each other. Clip the threads, leaving a tail on both the top and the bobbin threads. Pull on the bobbin thread to bring the top thread to the wrong side, and clip both threads.

Blind Stitch

Using a blind stitch on your machine will give you a look that most closely resembles hand appliqué. It is often referred to as mock hand appliqué.

Needle: Use size 60/8. This thin needle will go down into the fabric easily and will not leave big holes.

Thread: Use nylon on the top and in the bobbin. YLI nylon is the best. Other brands can be too thick and stiff. Use clear thread on light and medium-color fabrics and smoke-color thread on dark-color fabrics.

Stitch setting: Refer to your machine manual. Select a stitch that does three to seven straight stitches and then one zigzag or straight stitch over to the left—often called a blind hem stitch. After you have selected the appropriate stitch, adjust its length

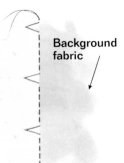

and width. The stitch length should be about 22 stitches per inch. Adjust the width so the zigzag takes a small bite into the appliqué shape, about one to two threads.

Background fabric

Step 1. Turn under the edges of your appliqué. I like to use the spray starch and Templar method on page 16, but the freezer paper methods would work, too. Glue or pin the shape in place.

Step 2. Bring the bobbin thread up on top, as for satin stitch. Insert the needle right along the folded edge of the appliqué, but into the background fabric only. The straight stitch should enter the background, and the zigzag should enter the appliqué. Begin on a curve or straight edge, not an inner or outer point. If portions of the shape have a raw edge because they will be covered by another shape, start at the raw edge. Do not stitch the raw edge itself. Stitch around the shape.

Step 3. To finish a complete shape, overlap where you started by about ½ inch. This stitch is so tight it will be very secure simply by overlapping, and the nylon thread will not show.

Karen Kay Buckley

Step 1. Cut each piece of the spiral design and baste it onto the block you are making.

Step 2. Make enough ⅛-inch bias strips to cover the raw edges of the basted design. To do this, cut ¾-inch bias strips with a rotary cutter and ruler. Each strip should be long enough to cover the curved raw edge from the inner starting point to the outer ending point. Fold each strip lengthwise with wrong sides together, and machine sew down the center. Trim the raw edges almost to the sewing line to make a tube of fabric.

Step 3. Insert a ⅛-inch metal Celtic bias bar into the tube and roll the seam to the center of a flat side. (Other bias press bars may be used, but I find that the aluminum Celtic bias bars give better results.) Steam press the fabric with the bar still inserted so that the seam is pressed to one side down the center of the strip. Push the bar forward through the tube until the entire strip is pressed. There is no need to sew the strips together into one piece, as they are tucked under one another during the appliqué.

Celtic Appliqué

Celtic appliqué is a technique that adapts ancient Celtic art forms, such as Celtic interlace and spiral patterns, to quilting. The over-and-under use of bias strips and layering of pieces coupled with dramatic use of color give Celtic appliqué a rich, three-dimensional quality.

The basic Celtic shapes of diamonds, zigzags, spirals, and interlace would have been almost impossible to appliqué prior to the introduction of the "bias bar" technique of making the appliqué strips. This technique makes a very difficult task easy, so that even beginners can achieve professional results. Follow these steps to create a Celtic spiral design.

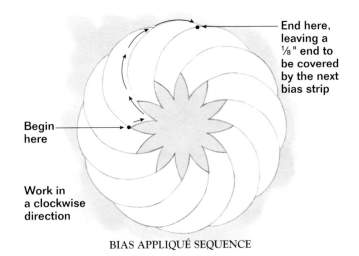

End here, leaving a ⅛" end to be covered by the next bias strip

Begin here

Work in a clockwise direction

BIAS APPLIQUÉ SEQUENCE

Step 4. Follow the Bias Appliqué Sequence to add the bias strips. Leave a ⅛-inch tail at the beginning. It will be covered by the last strip in the design.

Step 5. Pin the bias strip along the contour of the basted spiral design, leaving a ⅛-inch tail at the ending point. The end will be covered by the next strip to be added. The raw seam on the underside of the bias strip should flare outward on an outward curve; the strip will lie flatter and be easier to manipulate.

Step 6. Sew down the inside curves first, then sew the outside edge. Continue to work your way around the design in a clockwise direction until the design is completed.

Use interlace designs to border or accentuate the spiral pattern or blocks.

Channel Appliqué

Technically, channel appliqué is a type of reverse appliqué. However, with this new concept, you appliqué lines only, not whole areas. To create a channel appliqué design, transfer a line drawing of any degree of difficulty you choose to the background fabric, or top layer of fabric.

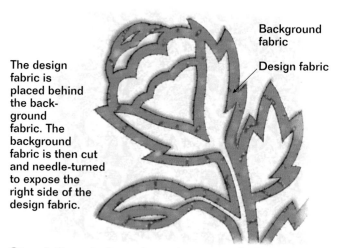

The design fabric is placed behind the background fabric. The background fabric is then cut and needle-turned to expose the right side of the design fabric.

Background fabric

Design fabric

Step 1. Trace the lines of your design onto the background fabric using a light box or by using pencil carbon paper (available in office supply stores). It is much softer and marks with less pressure than ordinary carbon paper. Place the background fabric over the design fabric, with right sides of both fabrics facing up.

Step 2. Run lines of basting stitches through the two fabrics ½ inch from every line, on both sides, so pieces don't move or fall away when you cut through the background fabric.

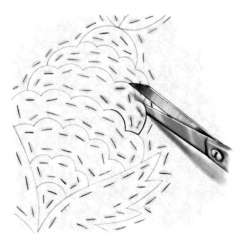

Step 3. Clip and sew by cutting the background fabric on the line, just for a couple of inches, or around one small island, and then needle-turn appliqué the raw edge under about ⅛ inch. You will be stitching the raw edges on either side of the cut line.

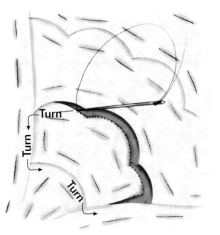

Whenever you come to an intersection, always turn left around the "island" to get back to where you started. (Left-handed stitchers should turn right.)

Channel appliqué is easy and fun! You can use the other raw or stitched edge as a guide to know exactly how much raw edge to turn under. The object is to turn all the lines of your drawing into ¼-inch "channels" formed by the design fabric behind the background fabric.

You don't have to be an artist to come up with a line drawing. A picture from a coloring book, a comic strip character, and even traditional appliqué designs can be used. Just remember to keep parallel lines at least ⅜ inch apart, or they will be too close to turn the seam allowances under.

Roxanne McElroy

Hawaiian Appliqué

The appliqué design distinguishes Hawaiian quilts from other forms of quilting. Large symmetrical designs depict elements in nature, in history, and in the heart of one's own imaginings. Quilters today use both 100 percent cotton and cotton blends, but early Hawaiian quilts were made with silks, satins, jacquards, and even cotton calicoes (a coarse weave fabric) in solids and prints. White thread was used for appliqué and quilting until colored thread became more readily available on the islands in the early- to mid-twentieth century.

Traditional One-Eighth Fold Technique

Prepare the background fabric and appliqué fabric in the same manner, following Steps 1 through 3 below. Note: Adjust seams so that appliqué background and backing seams do not overlap.

Step 1. For quilts that are larger than 45 inches, piece widths of fabric together to get the desired size. Stitch together using ½-inch seams. After stitching, trim selvages and leave ¼-inch seam allowances. Press the seams open; there will be less bulk to appliqué and quilt through.

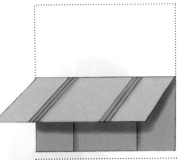

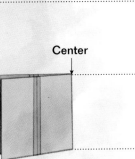

Step 2. Fold the fabric in half with right sides together. Press the fold lightly. Fold the fabric in half again, and press lightly. Make sure that the folds are even.

Center

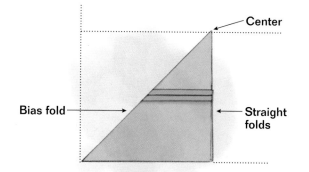

Step 3. Bring the folds together with a diagonal fold. Press lightly. Again, make sure that the folds are even. The point where the folds meet will mark the center of both appliqué and background fabrics. Unfold the background fabric.

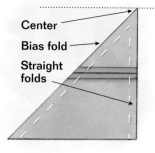

Step 4. Baste the folds of the appliqué fabric together to prevent slippage when cutting. Use white thread, as colored thread may bleed.

Step 5. Place the pattern on the folded appliqué fabric (pin, thread baste, or draw in place). Match the center and folds of the pattern to the center and folds of the folded appliqué fabric.

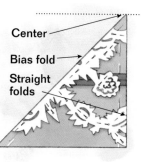

Step 6. Cut the design out of the fabric, making sure to cut through all thicknesses. Do not cut through the fold edge unless indicated. Many Hawaiian patterns have slashes or intricate details. You don't have to cut these. They can be embroidered or quilted. Let your level of expertise and the fabric determine what you do. Intricately cut designs can also be appliquéd with an embroidery stitch over the cut edge. If you do cut something that you're not pleased with, appliqué or embroider something wonderful over it. Be inventive!

Step 7. Remove any pins and basting. Unfold the appliqué onto the background fabric using the fold lines as guides. Pin in place. Baste the appliqué securely about ¼ inch from the cut edges using white thread.

Step 8. Appliqué with your favorite thread in a color that suits your needs. Use an overcast stitch or a blind stitch for the needle-turn appliqué. Be creative. This is your expression of *love*. Enjoy!

Designing the Pattern

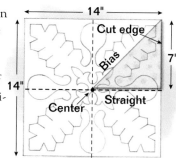

The traditional Hawaiian pattern is one-eighth of the whole. When designing using the eighth-fold technique, determine the size of the finished appliqué and divide by two. That will be the length of the two sides of a right triangle in which to draw your design. When you create a design, be sure to have a connection on all folds, no matter how small. If you don't, you will have pieces instead of a whole design. You will be turning the edges under about ¼ inch, so keep the design bold enough that it won't lose its definition.

Elizabeth A. Akana

Tahitian Appliqué

The people of Tahiti generally design their quilts to be approximately 90 × 108 inches, so they start drawing their design 45 × 54 inches, only putting onto paper one-quarter of the whole design. The designs may often be similar to Hawaiian appliqué, but Tahitian quilts are based on a quarter-fold technique and were traditionally never quilted.

The technique for making Tahitian quilts, called Tifaifai, has its roots in the artistic amusement of German paper cutting (Scherenschnitte) and in the knowledge of general quiltmaking passed to Tahitians by members of the London Missionary Society in the early nineteenth century.

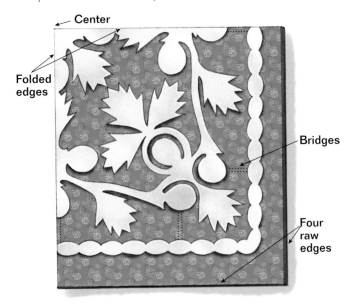

Step 3. Carefully peel the cut appliqué fabric layers apart. Do not stress or stretch the fibers. Match the center cross fold of the appliqué design with the center cross fold of the background fabric. Pin matched folds in all four directions to generally straighten the design. Gently pat with your hands in the direction of the grain in all areas to finalize the total flattening of the appliqué fabric design on the background fabric. Baste the Tifaifai about ½ inch from the raw edges and then appliqué.

Step 1. Fold the appliqué fabric into fourths and iron so the fold lines are crisp. Place the paper pattern on the folded appliqué fabric with the center pattern corner matching the center fabric folds. Pin heavily and then cut out through all four layers. Keep any borders and "island" areas attached to the design by cutting "bridges" of fabric to hold them in place. These will aid in laying out the piece after it's cut. Cut the bridges off after the design is basted down.

Step 2. Prepare the background fabric by folding and ironing in the same manner as the appliqué fabric. Unfold and center on a very large flat surface. Remove the pins from the appliqué cutout and set the paper pattern aside.

Missionary wives taught the royal Tahitian women how to quilt, but they soon eliminated that process. The tropical conditions made it uncomfortable to sleep under a heavy quilt. They simply hemmed all the edges of the completed quilt top and used it just as we use a summer spread. Because no traditions were ever established on quilting designs for the Tifaifai, we are totally free to be as creative as we want when quilting our quilt tops.

There are only two rules to making a Tahitian quilt. The first is to fold the fabric into fourths, cut out, and appliqué. The second rule is that if you design a Tifaifai of your own, it must be based on something that either influences you in your daily life or it must honor a thing or an event. Instead of being locked into established traditional designs, any printed or plain fabric can be used. The door is wide open for new contemporary designs not necessarily tropical in subject matter.

Roxanne McElroy

APPLIQUÉ TECHNIQUES

The iris block is an exquisite example of machine appliqué, done by Caroline Reardon.

This is a beautiful example of Tahitian appliqué by Roxanne McElroy.

This grapevine wreath is needle-turn appliqué, impeccably stitched by Karen Kay Buckley.

Wonderfully unexpected fabrics are combined in this channel appliqué by Roxanne McElroy.

Raw Edge Appliqué

Raw edge appliqué is a perfect choice for quilt-makers who like to be spontaneous and not get bogged down with tedious techniques. It is particularly suited for wallhangings and quilts that won't be receiving a lot of hard wear. The creative stage of quiltmaking is extended right into the sewing stage.

Shapes are usually cut to their finished size so there's no seam allowance to distract you as you're composing a quilt on a design wall. Stitching may be done anywhere from ¹⁄₁₆ inch to ¼ inch in from the outside edge, depending on the fabric used for the appliqué shape and the desired finished appearance. Select an inconspicuous color of thread if you want the stitches to blend in.

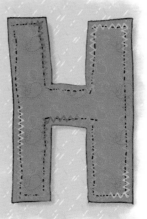

Firmly woven fabrics that don't fray easily can be stitched close to the edge, using a smaller than normal straight stitch on your machine. Stitch around twice for added security. The second set of stitches doesn't have to fall directly on top of the first line. Wash the finished piece to make sure the sewing will hold up under stress.

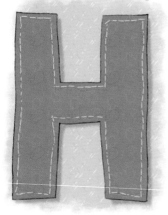

For fabrics that are likely to ravel, I suggest sewing from ⅛ to ¼ inch from the edge. First, stitch around with a regular length straight stitch. On the second go-round, use a widely spaced zigzag stitch or randomly curve back and forth over the original line of stitching. It usually looks more artful when you think of the stitches as machine doodling.

Change the color of the thread; even try stitching with a shiny rayon, variegated, or metallic thread the second time around. Fraying can be considered surface embellishment.

If the appliqué shape is large, you may want to temporarily stiffen it with a wash-away fabric stabilizer like Perfect Sew (follow directions on the bottle). You can also bond the appliqué shape to the background with a spot here and there of the stabilizer and a touch of your iron. Rinse the finished project in lukewarm running water to remove stiffness. Smaller shapes not requiring stiffening can be secured to the background with a fabric glue stick.

Usually you will want to place a lightweight, tear-away stabilizer between the background fabric and the feed dogs of the machine. This will keep the project flat as you do your decorative stitching. The stabilizer is then torn away when your sewing is completed. Make a small test sample with your fabrics, desired threads, and stitches to determine if the stabilizer is necessary before you proceed with the project.

Roberta Horton

Quick-Fuse Appliqué

This is a wonderful, quick-and-easy technique that gives the look of appliqué in a fraction of the time. It is perfect for designs with small details and projects that you want to make for last-minute gifts. Fusible web is the time-saving material that allows you to apply appliqué designs to the background fabric with the touch of an iron instead of needle and thread. If you want to add decorative stitching (such as blanket stitches) around the shapes, be sure to use a light-weight fusible web. For other projects, a heavier-weight fusible web works well. (See also "Fusible Web" on page 118.)

Step 1. Trace the design onto the paper side of the fusible web. Since you can see through the fusible web, you can lay it directly over the design for tracing. The finished appliqué design will be a mirror image of what you are tracing. Numbers and letters *must* be traced in reverse.

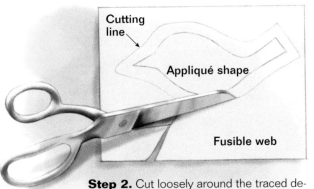

Cutting line
Appliqué shape
Fusible web

Step 2. Cut loosely around the traced designs using sharp paper scissors. You won't want to use your best fabric scissors for this task. Do not cut exactly along the lines at this point.

Step 3. Follow the manufacturer's instructions for proper iron setting and the time for fusing. Fuse each piece of fusible web to the *wrong* side of your selected fabrics. The paper side should be up and the webbing side against the fabric.

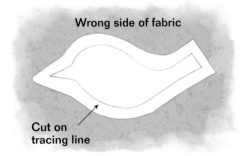

Wrong side of fabric
Cut on tracing line

Step 4. When the pieces are all fused, cut out the shapes along the tracing lines. Remove the paper backing. A thin fusing film will remain on the wrong side of the fabric.

Step 5. Arrange and center all the pieces of the appliqué design on the background fabric. When everything is arranged, fuse the pieces in position with your iron. Now you're done!

Try This

If you used a lightweight, sewable, fusible web, you can add decorative stitches, such as blanket stitch, by hand or machine. Or add pseudo-stitches, what I call Penstitch, with an extra-fine point, permanent felt-tip pen if you like. Use Penstitch on smaller projects that have a lot of detail but won't have a lot of stress put on them. This technique is great if you want quick results. After all, the pen is much quicker than the needle! (See also "Decorative Stitches" on page 87.)

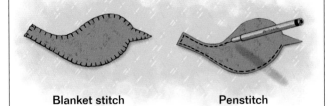

Blanket stitch   **Penstitch**

Debbie Mumm

BACKING

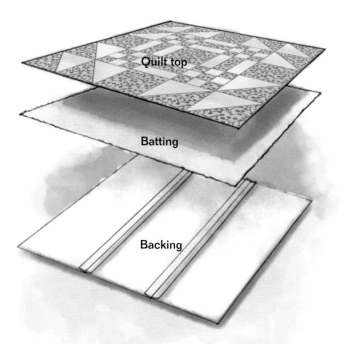

Quilt top

Batting

Backing

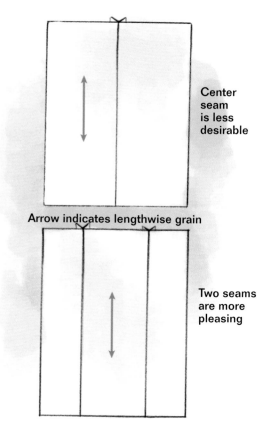

Center
seam
is less
desirable

Arrow indicates lengthwise grain

Two seams
are more
pleasing

PIECED BACKINGS

The backing, also called the back, or lining, of a quilt is the third, or bottom, layer of the quilt "sandwich."

The quilt top features the main design, and most backings use regular yardage—fabric that has no patchwork or appliqué designs. For large quilts, backings must be pieced. If possible, plan to have two equally placed seams rather than one seam down the middle. It is more pleasing visually, and the quilt will wear better over time. Quilts are frequently folded down the center where a single seam would add bulk and cause extra stress. Fabric for the back should be similar in quality, color, and pattern to that used for the front of the quilt.

The backing should be at least 2 inches larger than the front in every direction for ease when basting.

Since the lengthwise straight grain of the fabric is the strongest, it is best to have it follow the length of the quilt. This is especially important on wall quilts where vertical grain will help prevent sagging when they are hung.

The selvages may cause seams to pull or pucker. Cut them off before sewing. Use a walking or even feed foot to help prevent any slight gathering that may occur when sewing long seams.

A good stitch length is one that is about 10 to 12 stitches per inch. Seam allowances are usually ½ inch and, for quilts that will be hand quilted, they should be pressed open.

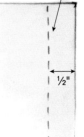

10–12 stitches per inch

½"

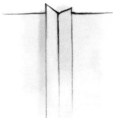

Press seam open for hand quilting

This gives one less layer to quilt through in the seam area. For machine quilting, seams may be pressed open or to one side. Before the quilt is basted, press the backing carefully, as this will be the last opportunity to do so.

Try This Selvages cut from a long piece of fabric are strong and can be used like string. Some are very pretty and give a fresh look to gift packages.

Selecting Fabric

When selecting fabric for the backing, there are several factors to consider. Since your quilt will be around for a long time, it's worth the best quality fabric that you can afford.

How will the quilt be used? Will it be hung on the wall only? Will it be draped over furniture? Will it serve as a lap quilt? Is it going on a bed for daily use or on a guest bed? If the back is likely to be seen, you may want to splurge on a fabric you love. If not, you can choose something functional or economical.

Is it a fabric you like? Are you happy with the fabric, and does it harmonize with the quilt top?

What will it cost? For a full-size quilt, you'll need a lot of yardage. The ideal is to find your favorite fabric on sale, but that rarely happens.

What is the quilting design? For simple designs and outline quilting, you may not necessarily want the design to be prominent on the back, so a print

would be fine. If it is elaborately quilted and you want your stitching to stand out, choose a solid.

Will it be hand or machine quilted? Do you want your stitches to show up or blend in? Prints will disguise less-than-perfect quilting, while a solid will highlight the stitches.

Do you want the back to be pieced? If not, you'll need to look into extra-wide fabrics for a large quilt.

For functional quilts such as bed or lap quilts, it is important to coordinate the back with the front since both the back and the front of the quilt will often be seen at the same time. The backing fabric should be at least equal to the quality of the front of the quilt so that it will hold up as well as the front during use. A good quality 100 percent cotton fabric is ideal.

For wallhangings, the choice of a backing may not be as important visually. The quality and type of fabric is less critical—it should be sturdy enough to lend support to the quilt while it is hanging.

TAKING THE TROUBLE OUT OF
Wide Backings

Fabric for backings can be purchased in widths up to 108 inches. There is little variety in the wide fabrics available. They are usually natural or white muslin or a white on white print muslin. These extra-wide fabrics are not always top quality, so check carefully before buying.

Bed sheets are sometimes considered for the back of a quilt because they are seamless and relatively inexpensive for the amount of fabric they contain. They may, however, present problems. Their quality can be rather poor, and it may be difficult to find one that coordinates with the front of the quilt. They are often difficult to quilt through, which could be a problem for handwork but not for machine quilting.

Print vs. Solid

Prints used as backings do not show the quilting design or stitches well and may be a good choice for those who have not yet mastered fine quilting techniques. They will also help hide the starts and stops when machine quilting.

If the quilt is to be heavily quilted, it is difficult to find anything better than a 100 percent cotton, solid-color fabric. The elaborate quilting shows up well and the back can be as lovely as the front, looking much like a reversible quilt. It is also easier to coordinate a solid with the front.

Back Art

In recent years some quilters have been making backs that are pieced in either simple or very elaborate patterns. Such "back art" can add a lot of interest to the quilt and may be as complicated as a completely pieced back. As these require much more planning and extra work, you must decide if the resulting two-sided quilt will be used in a way that will justify your effort. Pieced backs also increase the number of seams you have to deal with. Lots of piecing on the back is fine for machine quilting, but if you plan to hand quilt, think before you piece!

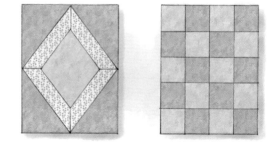

Try This If the cost of plain yardage for the back is a consideration, leftover fabric from the front could be used to make a simple pieced back.

SIMPLE PIECED BACKS

The Final Touch

If the quilt has not been signed on the front, don't forget one final step. Be sure to add a signature or label to the back of the quilt. (See the "Labels" on page 136.)

Becky Herdle

BASTING

Basting, sometimes called "sandwiching," is the process of securing together the three layers of the quilt—the quilt top, batting, and backing. It's important to do this task carefully to assure that the layers of the quilt do not shift, which could cause puckering, bunching, crookedness, and general aggravation. A tidy job of basting will make quilting a pleasure.

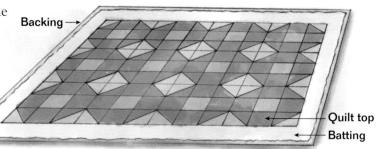

QUILT SANDWICH

Basting is like the half-time of a football game. It leads from the first half of the project, making the quilt top, to the second, the actual quilting. Basting doesn't take as long as what comes before or after it. It can be every bit as entertaining as (or at least a welcome break from) the main activity. Best of all, no one keeps score, and you're on your way to the goal—a finished quilt. Touchdown!

There are three techniques for layering the backing, batting, and quilt top together: basting the quilt with running stitches, pinning, and tacking.

Find a Place to Work

One secret to success is a suitable and comfortable space to work. You can use a spotless floor, although it is awkward and uncomfortable. A better way is to use a large bed. When using either a bed or a carpeted floor, place a layer of cardboard or a cutting mat under the quilt. A large table is best. This will take much of the strain off your back. A Ping-Pong table (with the net removed) is perfect for basting. You could also contact a quilt shop, library, school, or church. These places may allow you to use their tables.

Prepare the Quilt Sandwich

Step 1. Prepare the batting. It may or may not need to be prewashed. Read the packaging for recommendations. At the very least, unroll and unfold the batting to allow it to relax for a day or two before basting to help remove fold lines that could remain in your quilt. The batting should be at least 2 inches larger than the quilt top on all sides.

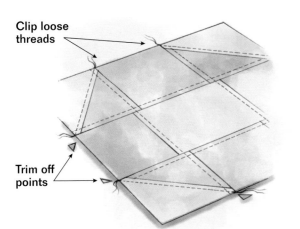

Clip loose threads

Trim off points

Step 2. Press the quilt top carefully. Clip any loose threads and trim any points so they won't show through the quilt top. After pressing, mark the quilting design if necessary.

Step 3. Press the backing and make sure that it is at least 2 inches larger than the quilt top on all sides.

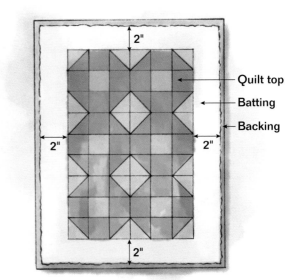

Quilt top
Batting
Backing

Step 4. Spread out the quilt backing, wrong side up, on your work surface. Smooth out all wrinkles. Gently unroll the batting and center it over the backing. Work out any wrinkles in the batting so it is smooth. Place the quilt top right side up on the batting, checking that backing seams and edges are straight with the top. Gently pull on the quilt top, pat it, and smooth it until it is flat and positioned exactly as you want it.

Step 5. Enlist a friend's help. As you hold one end of *just* the backing, ask your helper to pull on the backing at the opposite end. Check again that the seams are straight with the quilt top. Repeat this gentle pulling in the opposite direction. Any time you need to move the quilt during the basting process, repeat this step. This should make the backing sufficiently taut. If you tape or pin the backing in place, it could be overstretched, causing puckering when the tape or pins are released.

Step 6. Use long, straight quilting pins to hold the layers in place, pinning every 12 inches or so. The pins allow you to move the quilt or even fold it if necessary.

Basting with Running Stitches

You'll need a thimble, white thread (dark or colored thread could leave marks), long straight pins, scissors, and long needles such as milliner's or sharps.

Basting stitches are simple running stitches, with the underneath stitches about ½ inch long and the stitches on top about 2 inches long. Try to avoid basting stitches where quilting stitches will go. Your basting stitches can meander and still be effective.

Try This Use a long darning needle to make quicker work of the tedious task of thread basting. The point of the needle is sharp and the length of the needle allows you to make a nice large running stitch. The needle itself is thicker, making it sturdier and easier to hold than a regular sharp needle. —*Karen Kay Buckley*

Step 1. Gently slide the quilt so that one end lies next to the edge of the table or bed. Support the quilt with chairs if it hangs over the edge.

Step 2. Thread a needle with a long piece of white thread (up to 48 inches), and tie a knot in the tail. Sit in a comfortable chair facing the quilt. Thread several needles at a time.

Step 3. Make the first line of basting about ⅛ inch inside the edge of the quilt top. This will help stabilize the edges and allow a smoother binding. Baste from right to left if you are right-handed, or from left to right if you are left-handed. It is not necessary to baste from the center out since you have already done a good job of checking for excess fullness and securing the layers. When ending a basting thread, make one or two large (½- to 1- inch) backstitches. The basting threads (except those at the quilt edges) will be pulled out later, and this will make removal easy.

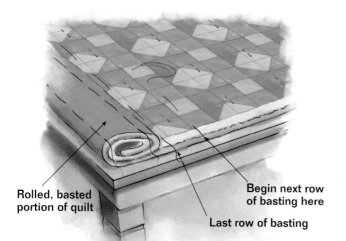

Rolled, basted portion of quilt

Begin next row of basting here

Last row of basting

Step 4. Make the next line of basting 5 to 6 inches away from the first. Continue basting in more-or-less parallel rows. As you stitch, gently roll the quilt so that you can easily reach the area being basted. Always leave the last line of basting

lying flat on the table so that the layers will not shift. Continue across the quilt, ending with a line of basting ⅛ inch inside the opposite edge of the quilt.

Step 5. After basting across the quilt in one direction, rotate the quilt a quarter turn or move your chair to an adjacent side. Repeat the process, working across the quilt in the other direction, beginning and ending the lines of basting ⅛ inch from the edges of the quilt top.

Step 6. Remove the pins, and fold the extra backing and batting over to cover the raw edge of the quilt top. Baste in place. If you will be using a floor frame, you might want to leave these outer edges flat.

TAKING THE TROUBLE OUT OF Basting

- Mark quilting designs on the quilt top *after* the final pressing—heat from the iron may permanently set the marks.

- Keep equal tension on the three layers of the quilt as you baste.

- Place basting stitches, pins, or tacks where they won't interfere with the quilting.

- Cover the edges of the quilt top and batting with the backing to prevent fraying during quilting.

- Insert pins into print patches rather than solid ones. Pin holes will show less.

- Store safety pins open after removing them to save time during the next round of pin basting.

Basting with Safety Pins

Baste with safety pins if you plan to quilt by machine so that you can remove them just before quilting an area. (Sewn basting is not a good idea because the presser foot could get caught in the basting stitches.) You'll need pins that are rustproof and will not tarnish. Use brass or nickel-plated steel pins in size 00, 0, or 1. Brass is more flexible than nickel-plated steel. Buy plenty—a bed-size quilt could require 500 or more pins.

Step 1. Prepare the quilt sandwich on your work surface. Begin at one end of the quilt and insert safety pins along the edge, spacing them 3 to 6 inches apart. (Pinning with straight pins first is not necessary.) Keep both hands on top of the quilt.

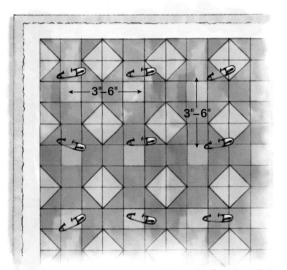

Step 2. Continue pinning across the quilt. Gently roll the quilt as necessary so that you can easily reach the area being basted. Pin basting will be complete after one pass across the quilt. Fold the backing and batting over the edge of the quilt top and pin them in place.

 **Wait until all pins are in place to begin closing them. To avoid sore fingers, use the serrated tip of a grapefruit spoon to grip and close the pin shaft. Or purchase a quilting tool called Kwik Klip made especially for that purpose.** —*Janet Wickell*

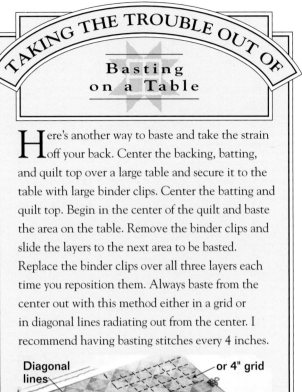

TAKING THE TROUBLE OUT OF

Basting on a Table

Here's another way to baste and take the strain off your back. Center the backing, batting, and quilt top over a large table and secure it to the table with large binder clips. Center the batting and quilt top. Begin in the center of the quilt and baste the area on the table. Remove the binder clips and slide the layers to the next area to be basted. Replace the binder clips over all three layers each time you reposition them. Always baste from the center out with this method either in a grid or in diagonal lines radiating out from the center. I recommend having basting stitches every 4 inches.

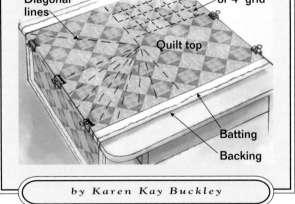

by Karen Kay Buckley

Basting with a Tacking Tool

QuilTak is one brand name for a relatively new tool on the market. It has a gunlike appearance with a very sharp needle. (Store it out of reach of children and handle very carefully.) It uses plastic tacks that have a ¼-inch shank to hold the layers of the quilt together (similar to the plastic tacks that hold price tags on garments in stores). It can speed your basting time considerably. Ask for a demonstration of the tool and ideally try it out before deciding if you want to purchase one.

Step 1. Prepare the quilt by fastening the layers with long, straight pins.

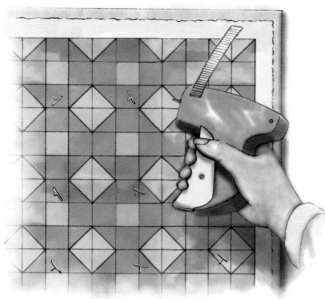

Basting with a tacking tool

Step 2. Place one hand underneath the quilt to support the area being tacked, and poke the needle of the tool straight down through all layers. Be careful not to stab your fingers, and squeeze the handle. The plastic tack will pop through the layers easily.

Step 3. Work across the quilt in rows and roll the quilt as you go. Fold the edges of the quilt over and secure with tacks or running stitches.

Once your quilt is successfully basted, you can fold it, carry it around, or drape it over the sofa to enjoy your work in progress, no matter how long it takes you to quilt it!

Marie Shirer

TAKING THE TROUBLE OUT OF Basting

Change a basting chore into a social event by having a "Basting Bee." Get your friends together, make tea or coffee, baste the quilt, and have lunch together afterward.

by Becky Herdle

When you have to press bulky areas against another seam allowance, it is worth taking the time to baste the seam allowance in the direction that you would like it to lie. Make a quick pass with some long stitches using basting thread. It is not necessary to knot the thread; just leave long tails on the front of the quilt for easy removal after the quilting is finished.

by Beckie Olson

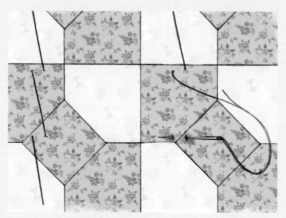

Tailor's basting stitch

I recommend using a tailor's basting stitch to keep the front and back of the quilt flat without the channels that a running basting stitch makes. Take a horizontal stitch about ½ inch long, then drop straight down about 2½ inches and take another horizontal stitch. Continue in this manner until you reach the outside edge of the quilt. The horizontal stitches are on the back of the quilt, while the diagonal stitches are on the front. An additional benefit is that most of the thread remains on the top surface of the quilt so you can easily avoid it while quilting.

by Beckie Olson

Make Your Own Basting Frame

Cyndi Hershey

Here's a simple basting frame that will get you off the floor and ease strain on your back. Anyone can make it—it's so easy!

Materials

Four 1 × 2-inch boards, 10 feet long

Four C-clamps

30 (or more) Bull Dog clips or large binder-style clamps to fit over edge of boards

Step 1. Place the four boards at right angles to each other so the quilt backing just extends over the edges. (The backing should be several inches larger than the quilt top in all directions.)

Step 2. Use a square ruler to make sure the corners are 90 degree angles. Clamp each corner firmly with a C-clamp.

Step 3. Place the frame over the backs of four chairs, one at each corner. High-back chairs work really well for this, as they provide a comfortable height at which to work. (Sawhorses or TV trays can also serve as supports.)

Step 4. With the frame balanced on the supports, place the backing over the frame. Pull the backing taut and attach it to each side of the frame, using the Bull Dog clips or binder clamps. Work on one set of opposite sides and then the other. Spread the batting evenly over the backing, and finally, spread the quilt top over the batting.

Step 5. Releasing one clamp at a time, pull the batting and quilt top to join the backing. Then reclamp.

Now you can stitch, pin, or tack your layers together in a much more comfortable way. To reach the center of a large quilt, baste as far as you can, then unclamp one piece of wood and move it toward the center. Reclamp the quilt, and continue basting.

BATTING

Once your quilt top is completed, you will feel a great sense of accomplishment—maybe even relief! But now you're faced with deciding which batting to use. Ask yourself some basic questions:

How much time or interest do I have in quilting this project? This is the most important question. Being honest and realistic when you answer will help you decide whether you will hand quilt, machine quilt, or tie/tack your quilt. This will help determine which battings are most appropriate. Some battings are easier to needle than others and are preferred for hand quilting. Another batting may be more difficult to needle but has more "grip," making it better for machine quilting. Also, some battings are more stable, requiring less quilting (of any type), while other battings require more extensive quilting to keep them stable.

How do you want the finished item to look— flat or fluffy? Flatter batting is usually preferred if the item is being displayed against the wall or needs to be drapeable. Fluffier batting is generally used if greater dimension is preferred to highlight the quilting. The fluffiest batting is reserved for tied projects like comforters. Loft refers to the thickness or thinness of a batting. Light or low loft battings are the thinnest while high loft battings are the thickest. Cotton batting gives a flatter look, as it is considered to have a low loft.

Do you need or want a natural or synthetic fiber batting? While polyester has been the choice of quilters in the past, cotton and other natural fiber battings seem to be just as popular now. Cotton is non-allergenic; polyester and even wool may be a problem for people prone to allergies. Cotton batting tends to be denser than some polyester types, while wool tends to be lighter and fluffier.

Polyester Battings

Polyester battings are very lightweight, inexpensive, simple to wash and care for, and easy to needle. However, synthetic fibers are not considered "breathable," meaning they have a low level of air permeability. A polyester batting can contribute to a buildup of body heat if used in a bed quilt. Synthetic fibers are also more sensitive to heat. They can melt and are more flammable than natural fibers. You would not use such a batting inside pot holders or any other item that comes in contact with heat. Polyester battings also tend to "beard," which refers to the migration of tiny fibers out through the fabric layers. Unfortunately, this is a natural static reaction of polyester.

Some battings are treated to resist this condition better than others through glazing or bonding. These processes seal the loose fibers to the surface of the batting with the use of chemicals or heat. Hobbs makes a charcoal gray batting that was developed to hide these loose fibers against the fabric of a primarily dark quilt.

Needlepunched batting refers to a process in which needles are used to mesh or interlock the polyester fibers to create stability. This type of batting is not generally glazed or bonded, so there may initially be more bearding. However, these fibers eventually wash or rub off, and the resulting project is actually more stable with this type of batting.

Natural Fiber Battings

Natural fiber battings are breathable and tend to be cool in summer and warm in winter. They are not sensitive to heat and are less flammable.

Cotton batting has been "reinvented" in recent years. Older cotton batting was basically matted or compressed cotton fiber or lint. It was necessary to quilt projects at extremely close intervals in order to provide stability, as the batting tended to shift and lump between quilting lines. It was also very difficult to needle. However, we now have a variety of improved cotton battings. Some are natural (unbleached), while some are pure white (bleached). This alone could be a consideration, depending on how light the background fabric is in a particular project.

Stability is provided to these newer types of batting in several different ways:

- Needlepunching breaks up the density of the cotton fiber, allowing for easier needling, as well as interlocking the fibers.

- Some cotton batting is needlepunched into a micro-thin polyester scrim (base) to make the batting even more stable. This type of batting is the most stable available, as it allows you to quilt or tie at 8- to 10-inch intervals.

- There are also blended fiber cotton battings that are 80 percent cotton and 20 percent polyester. This amount of polyester is just enough to stabilize the cotton fibers, allowing you to quilt at 3- to 5-inch intervals on most of these batts.

Wool batting is another natural fiber batting that is now readily available. Hobbs makes a wool batting that is easy to use and affordable. The advantages of wool are many. It is lightweight, breathable and very easy to hand or machine quilt. Due to static, it may beard to some degree, but this shouldn't be a major problem.

To Wash or Not to Wash

Washing cotton batting has become an issue of sorts for many quilters. The purpose of washing this batting before use was to preshrink as well as to release any cotton seed flecks that may be remaining in the fiber. Follow the *specific* directions on a package of batting to see if you need to wash it, and if so, what the recommended procedure may be.

Most quilters use cotton batting as it comes from the package since the current battings are very clean and shrinkage is minimal. If you choose not to prewash your batting and it does shrink somewhat, you will get a nice "puckery" look as in an antique quilt. This look is actually preferred by many quilters. However, the deciding factor is how you want your project to look.

Batting Tryouts

The best way to learn about battings is to make several batting "sandwiches" consisting of two layers of muslin or other cotton fabric with different types of batting in the middle. If your project contains fabrics other than cotton, you would also want to try this exercise. Since new battings are always being introduced, it's a good idea to check with a quilt shop to see what's new.

A fun and easy way to test battings is to join together with several friends or members of your quilt guild. As a group, purchase baby or craft-size batts of different types and divide them among yourselves.

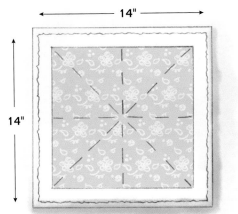

14"

14"

Step 1. Cut the batting and fabric into 14-inch squares. Use old rotary blades to cut the batting especially when cutting synthetic fibers so you won't dull your good blade.

Step 2. Layer the batting between the fabric and pin, baste, or use a tacking gun to hold the layers together.

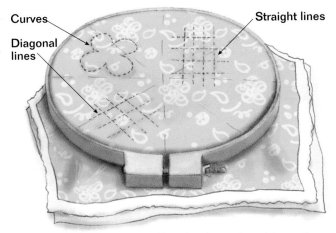

Curves

Diagonal lines

Straight lines

Step 3. To test it for ease of hand quilting, place this sandwich in a hoop or frame and quilt straight, diagonal (on the bias), and curved lines. Also, try using different types of thread such as 100 percent cotton, polyester-cotton blend, rayon, and metallic. You may need to use a different size needle for some of the combinations. If it's difficult to push the needle through the layers, or if the thread is shredding, try a larger needle.

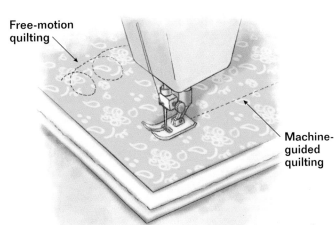

Free-motion quilting

Machine-guided quilting

Step 4. Test machine quilting, using different techniques and threads. File the different sandwiches along with your notes in file folders, plastic notebook sleeves, or large resealable plastic freezer bags. Write directly on the sandwich to record the batting type in case the sandwich ever becomes separated from its notes. This is a terrific reference tool for you to keep and share.

You could also wash your batting sandwiches one or more times to check for shrinkage, bearding, appearance, and drape.

Piecing Batting

Sometimes it becomes necessary to piece batting, either to get a required size, or simply because you want to use up some leftovers. It's best not to overlap the batting when stitching as it creates a welt which may show through the quilt. Most quilters choose instead to cut clean edges on the batting and butt them together, joining them with a simple whipstitch.

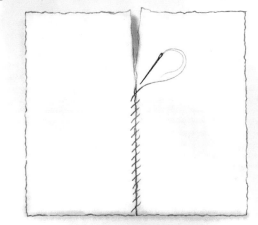

Whipstitch cut edges together

(continued on page 40)

BATTINGS COMPARED

Brand	Fiber Content	Quilting Interval	Characteristics	Suggested Uses
Hobbs Wool	100% Wool Bonded with resin	up to 3"	Low loft, soft, drapeable. Very warm.	Clothing, quilts of all sizes.
Wool Naturally	100% Wool Needlepunched	up to 10"	Soft, drapeable, very warm. Costly.	Quilts of all sizes, crafts.
Hobbs Heirloom Cotton	80% Cotton/ 20% Polyester	up to 3"	Easy to hand or machine quilt. Soft, drapeable. Some shrinkage.	Quilts of all sizes, items with direct heat contact.
Fairfield Cotton Classic	80% Cotton/ 20% Polyester	up to 3"	Flat. Minimal shrinkage. Can be split in half for thinner layer.	Wallhangings, quilts, clothing, place mats, table runners.
Warm & Natural	100% Cotton Needlepunched into a Polyester scrim	up to 10"	Flat and dense, yet soft. Extremely stable. Manufacturer recommends prewashing.	Wallhangings, quilts, items with direct heat contact, crafts, dolls.
Fairfield Soft Touch	100% bleached Cotton Needlepunched	up to 2"	Soft, drapeable. No need to prewash. More difficult to hand quilt.	Quilts of all sizes, clothing, crafts, items with direct heat contact.
Morning Glory Old Fashion	100% Cotton Needlepunched into a Polyester scrim	up to 6"	Flat and heavy. Will shrink. Gives a nice, old-fashioned look.	Quilts of all sizes, crafts, items with direct heat contact.
Mountain Mist Blue Ribbon	100% Cotton	up to 2"	Thin and flat. Minimal shrinkage. Difficult to hand needle. Use to give an old-fashioned look.	Wallhangings, quilts, items with direct heat contact.
Morning Glory Clearly Unbleached	100% Cotton Needlepunched	up to 6"	Soft, stable.	Quilts of all sizes, clothing, crafts.
Hobbs Polydown & Polydown DK (DK = Dark)	100% Polyester	up to 4"	Made to reproduce the look of down. Extremely easy to hand needle, yet has nice loft.	Bed quilts, comforters, some clothing, jackets.
Fairfield Traditional	100% Polyester Needlepunched	up to 4"	Dense. Gives "heavy" look of cotton.	Bed quilts, wallhangings.
Hobbs Thermore	100% Polyester	up to 6"	Lightweight, drapeable. Doesn't beard.	Clothing, miniatures, quilts of all sizes.
Mountain Mist Regular & Quilt-Light	100% Polyester	up to 3"	Thin to mid-loft. Easy to hand needle. Lightweight.	Quilts of all sizes.
Fairfield Extra & High Loft	100% Polyester	up to 4"	Puffy, but may flatten with time.	Tied, comforter-style quilts.
Mountain Mist Designer's Choice	100% Polyester Needlepunched	up to 5"	Lightweight. May be layered to produce the loft you desire. Layers stick to each other.	Quilts of all sizes, some clothing.

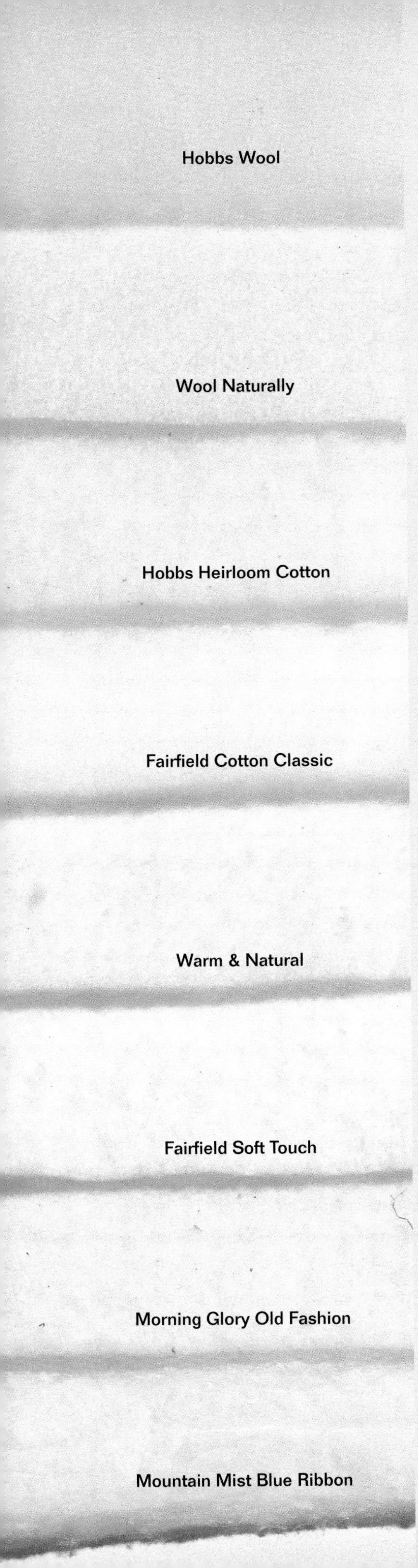

Hobbs Wool

Wool Naturally

Wool Battings

Wool has a low loft and is very warm. According to many quilters, it "quilts like butter."

Hobbs Heirloom Cotton

Fairfield Cotton Classic

Cotton/ Polyester Blend Battings

Polyester adds stability to the cotton. The battings are still breathable and give the look of antique quilts.

Polyester Battings

Polyester battings are lightweight and easy to hand quilt. Loft ranges from very low in Thermore to the high loft Polydown, which mimics the look of down.

Warm & Natural

Fairfield Soft Touch

100 Percent Cotton Battings

Cotton battings give a more traditional, flat, antique look to quilts. They are soft and drapeable with low loft.

Morning Glory Old Fashion

Mountain Mist Blue Ribbon

Hobbs Polydown DK

Hobbs Polydown

Fairfield Traditional

Hobbs Thermore

Mountain Mist Quilt-Light

Fairfield High Loft

Mountain Mist Designer's Choice

Mountain Mist Regular

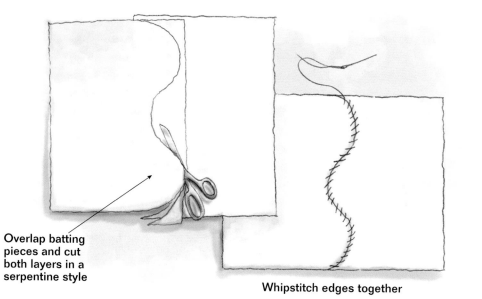

Overlap batting pieces and cut both layers in a serpentine style

Whipstitch edges together

Other quilters cut a serpentine edge on both pieces to be joined and then whipstitch. The curved lines are thought to distract the eye from any joint that may be apparent through the quilt. As with every other aspect of quilting, there are as many different thoughts on this as there are quilters!

Cyndi Hershey

BEESWAX

To bee or not to bee, that is the current quiltmaker's dilemma. Beeswax has long been a quilting staple, but nowadays, most people don't really use it or even know what to do with it. Molded in  pretty decorative shapes or small round cakes within plastic holders, beeswax is recommended most often to help keep regular sewing thread from tangling.

Some hand quilters still use it when they can't find the exact color of quilting thread they want. Regular sewing thread in the desired color can be coated with beeswax to strengthen it. It was probably used more often for quilting before quilting thread became available in such a wide variety of colors.

Quilters who do hand appliqué often use beeswax to help keep thread from twisting and knotting. One quilter who uses it for hand appliqué recommends that you remove any excess wax by running your thumbnail down the thread.

 Before sitting down to do your hand sewing, cut several lengths of thread. Draw each thread back and forth several times over the cake of beeswax to coat it. Remove excess wax by ironing the thread on scrap fabric or paper towels. It may seem like a lot of preparation, but it really helps the thread glide through fabric.

Ellen Pahl

BIAS PRESS BARS

Bias press bars make the construction of bias stems and Celtic appliqué easier by eliminating the need to press under the seam allowances on a bias-cut fabric strip. By making a tube and pressing it with heat-resistant bars that flatten the tube, you can avoid the burned fingers and crooked, irregular edges usually associated with making your own bias. You may also use any fabric to match your project rather than being limited to the shiny polyester bias tapes available in fabric stores. Bias press bars are available by mail and in quilt shops and are packaged with several widths included. The original Celtic Bias Bars introduced by Philomena Durcan are made of aluminum, but they may also be made of plastic.

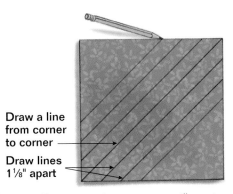

Draw a line from corner to corner

Draw lines 1⅛" apart

Step 1. To prepare the strips you will use to make the bias tubes, draw a line from corner to corner on a square of fabric. The size of the square depends on how much tubing you need. (The easy formula for figuring this is in the Try This box, at right.) If making ¼-inch-wide finished bias, draw lines out from your first line spaced 1⅛ inches apart.

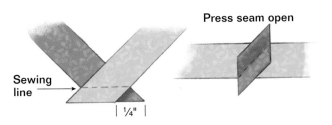

Press seam open

Sewing line

¼"

Step 2. Cut on the pencil lines and join the strips end to end, with diagonal seams if a long piece is needed. To do this, place two strips right sides together, offsetting the seams by ¼ inch. Stitch and press the seams open.

Fold

¼" seam

Trim seam allowance for narrow-width bias

Step 3. Fold (do not press) the strips lengthwise, wrong sides together. Sew the raw edges together with a ¼-inch seam. For narrow-width bias, trim the seam allowances.

Bias press bar

Press seam allowances in one direction

Step 4. Insert the appropriate bar into the end of the tube with the seam in the center on top of the bar. Press the seam allowances in one direction, using water or starch if the tube does not want to lie flat. Move the bar along the inside of the tube until you reach the end. Remove the bar and lightly press the bias again.

Try This

To determine how wide to cut your bias strips for any width of bias stems, double the finished size, add ½ inch for seams and ⅛ inch for ease.

To determine what size square to cut, multiply the length needed by the width. Take the square root of this number (it's easiest to use a calculator), and this will give you the size of the square needed. Add 2 or 3 inches to this number and cut a square that size.

Susan Stein

41

BIAS STEMS

Bias stems are used primarily in appliqué whenever a design includes curved flower stems or vines. The techniques covered here can also be used to make bias for Celtic appliqué or anywhere a narrow outline is needed around a curved shape. You can use commercial bias tape or make your own. The advantage to making your own is that you can match the fabric to the others in your quilt, have unlimited color choices, and use 100 percent cotton.

Double-fold bias tape

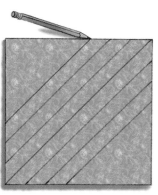

Step 1. Draw a line corner to corner on the square of fabric and draw lines out from the first line at the intervals that will give you the finished size you need.

If you choose to use commercially packaged bias tape, you will get a very consistent product and you will save some time. For a small project, choose double-fold bias tape and cut off the narrower of the two sides, leaving a ¼-inch width of single-layer tape with two turned-under seam allowances.

This eliminates the shinier of the two sides, something that occurs during the manufacturing process. Be sure to test a piece of the tape before using it, as some colors will bleed. For wider stems choose ½-inch-wide single-fold bias tape.

Trim off the narrower side

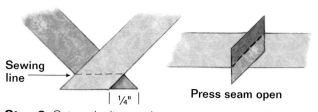

Sewing line → ¼"   **Press seam open**

Step 2. Cut on the lines with a rotary cutter and ruler or scissors. Sew the strips end to end by pinning the strips right sides together, offset ¼ inch. Sew the pieces together until you have the length you need for your project. (Do not sew the ends together if you will be using short pieces and hiding the ends under leaves and flowers.) Press the seams open to reduce bulk.

Making Bias Stems

To figure the width of strips to cut, double the finished size of the stems, and add ½ inch for seams. If you are using bias press bars, add ⅛ inch more. Determine how many inches of stems or vines you will need for your project. For a smaller project, start with an 18-inch square of fabric; for larger projects, start with a 36-inch square.

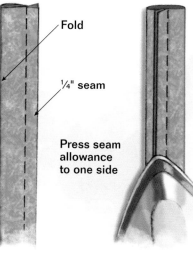

Fold

¼" seam

Press seam allowance to one side

Step 3. Fold the strips wrong sides together and sew the raw edges with a ¼-inch seam. Trim the seam allowance if you are making narrow stems. Position the seam in the center of the tube and press the seam allowance to one side. Bias press bars can make this easier (see page 41).

Susan Stein

42

BINDINGS AND OTHER EDGE FINISHES

The success of any quilt, no matter how beautiful, is influenced by how skillfully the edges are finished and how well that final touch complements the top in both design and color.

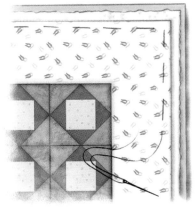

There are many ways that the edges of a quilt can be finished—the choice depends on the quilt and the wishes of the person making it.

Applied binding

The most common finishes are bindings. Applied bindings use additional material for the binding, while edge-turned bindings are made by folding the fabric from one side of the quilt, usually the backing, over to the

Edge-turned binding

other side, to encase the edge and serve as the binding. Other less common finishes include facings, knife edges, corded edges, and prairie points. Lace, ruffles, and fringe, though frequently seen on crazy quilts, are not often found on most quilts made today.

Baste around the entire edge of the quilt to help prevent the top from being pulled out of shape during the binding process. This is especially helpful if there is minimal quilting near the edges. Basting can also help solve the problem of rippled edges.

Baste around the edges before binding

TAKING THE TROUBLE OUT OF
Rippled Edges

If the edges of your quilt are slightly rippled, baste around the quilt with stitches about ⅛ inch long. Then lay the edge on a flat surface and gently gather it until it lies flat. Stay stitch by hand or machine to hold the gathers in place and to keep the edges flat.

Prepare the Quilt

Check to make sure the quilt lies flat and the corners and edges are accurate. Square corners should be 90 degrees; if they are not, trim them, if possible, with a square (90 degree) ruler to be as close as possible. The edges should be straight (or smoothly curved) and without ripples. The more care that is taken at this point, the better the edge finish will turn out.

Binding Options

Double-fold applied binding, or French-fold binding, consists of two layers of fabric and is probably the most durable edge finish you can use. This is the binding most commonly used today; it's easily applied and looks good.

Single-fold bindings, in my opinion, are justified only where a straight, rather than a mitered, corner is to be used, or to conserve a very small amount of fabric. Though they can be neatly sewn, they do not wear as well as double-fold bindings.

Edge-turned bindings are also easy and attractive, but since they too are a single thickness, they will not wear as well as double-fold bindings. They may be an easy answer for a wall quilt that will get little wear on the edges.

Commercial binding tape is not recommended since it is generally of poor quality and can rarely be found in a color that really matches the quilt.

Decorative bindings can be made by several methods. One of the simplest is to use striped or plaid fabrics and either cut them straight across or diagonally. They can also be pieced, in which case the piecing seam should be on the diagonal to reduce bulk after it is applied. (See "Sewing and Pressing the Strips" on page 45.) Small, evenly spaced geometric or floral-patterned fabrics can also be cut to create interesting bindings.

Grain

Bias binding is preferred by some people, but I do not like to use it. I find it harder to handle and to apply and feel it has a tendency to pull out of shape on straight edges. Many people feel that bias must be used on curves, but I have found that a cross-grain binding has enough stretch to easily handle all but the sharpest of curves.

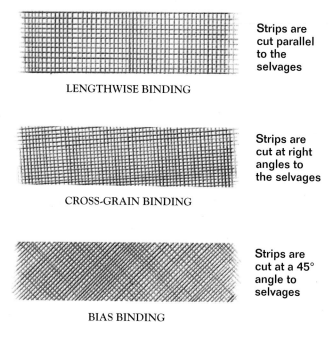

Strips are cut parallel to the selvages

LENGTHWISE BINDING

Strips are cut at right angles to the selvages

CROSS-GRAIN BINDING

Strips are cut at a 45° angle to selvages

BIAS BINDING

Quilters who prefer bias believe it wears better than straight-grain bindings because the fibers in the fabric are not aligned with the edge of the quilt. A straight binding cut exactly on grain would have one thread running right along the edge; this thread would get the bulk of the wear and stress. While this would be true for bindings cut on the lengthwise grain, which is very straight and strong, it is rarely true with bindings cut across the fabric on the cross grain. Most crosswise threads in today's fabrics do not run straight across from selvage to selvage, so there would not be one single fiber running exactly along the edge of the binding. They would wear almost as well as bias.

Double-Fold Bindings

How Much to Cut

Width: For a double-fold binding that will finish to be a scant $\frac{3}{8}$ inch, cut strips that are 2 inches wide (using a $\frac{1}{4}$-inch seam allowance). For a different width binding, add two times the width you want the binding to be plus the width of the seam allowance. (Choose a seam allowance that you are comfortable using—$\frac{1}{4}$ inch, the width of the presser foot, or $\frac{3}{8}$ inch.) Multiply the result by 2 to get the width to cut. (If using a very thick batting, add $\frac{1}{4}$ inch to allow for extra fullness.)

| 2 × Finished binding width | + | Seam allowance | = | | × 2 = | Width to cut |

Length: For binding cut cross-grain, measure around the outside edge of the quilt and add 12 inches. (This allows for mitering corners and overlapping where the binding starts and stops.)

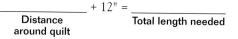

| Distance around quilt | + 12" = | Total length needed |

Number of cross-grain strips: Measure the width of the fabric and subtract the width of the strip being cut to get the maximum width available. (This allows for seams in the strips.)

Divide the total length needed by the width available to give the number of strips needed.

| Total length needed | ÷ | Maximum width available | = | No. of strips |

Cutting for Straight-Grain Bindings

Fold the fabric from selvage to selvage. Fold again by bringing the fold up to the selvages. Be sure that the fabric lies flat and smooth. Square up your fabric with a rotary cutter and ruler following instructions in "Rotary Cutting" on page 197. From this cut, measure the desired width of the binding strip and cut again. Continue cutting strips until you have the number needed. If you prefer to use scissors, mark the cutting lines and be very careful not to let the fabric slip while cutting.

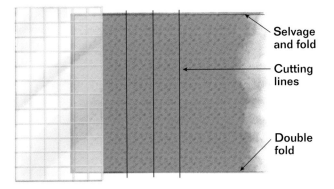

Selvage and fold

Cutting lines

Double fold

If you have a long, narrow, lengthwise piece of fabric you wish to use for the binding, you can cut it lengthwise for a quilt with straight edges. The binding will have less give and may be harder to work with, but that is better than having numerous seams resulting from many short strips.

Cutting for Bias Bindings

For a true bias, fold the fabric on the 45 degree diagonal and mark the fold by pressing, being careful not to stretch it out of shape. Use the fold line as a guide for marking and cutting strips of the desired width.

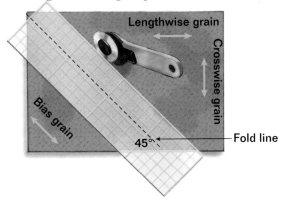

Lengthwise grain

Crosswise grain

Bias grain

45°

Fold line

TAKING THE TROUBLE OUT OF Cutting Patterned Fabrics

Geometrics and other prints may have a definite line that does not always follow the grain line of the fabric. When using these for bindings, cut them so that the cutting line follows the design line. Otherwise they will make the edges of the quilt look crooked.

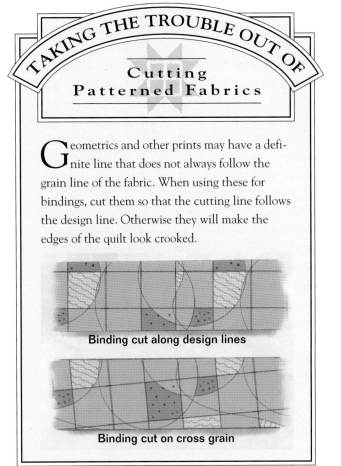

Binding cut along design lines

Binding cut on cross grain

Sewing and Pressing the Strips

Trim after sewing

Sewing line

Step 1. Sew the cut strips together on the diagonal using a short stitch length (about 14 stitches per inch). You may want to draw a diagonal line as a guide to ensure a straight seam.

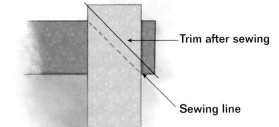

Step 2. Trim the seams to ¼ inch and press open.

Press seam open after trimming

Step 3. Fold and press the binding lengthwise with the wrong sides together.

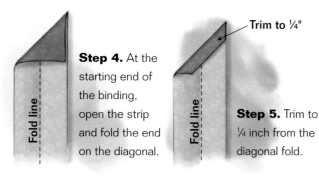

Step 4. At the starting end of the binding, open the strip and fold the end on the diagonal.

Fold line

Trim to ¼"

Fold line

Step 5. Trim to ¼ inch from the diagonal fold.

Applying Double-Fold Bindings

Follow these guidelines exactly, and your bindings should turn out perfect no matter how wide the binding or what seam allowance is used.

- Do not trim backing or batting before applying binding. Trim them after the binding is applied.
- Start the binding on a side, top, or bottom, not at a corner.
- Plan the placement of the binding so that seams do not come at the corners. Do this by laying out the binding along the edges of the quilt before sewing.
- Use the same seam allowance that was used when calculating the width of the binding.
- Keep all the layers of the quilt smooth while you work to prevent any pulling.
- Be careful not to pull or stretch the binding while sewing it. A walking foot may help feed the layers through evenly, but it is not essential.

SKILL BUILDER

Continuous Sew-and-Cut Bias Binding

A fast way to make bias bindings is to sew and cut them in one continuous process.

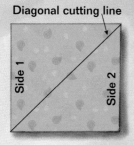

Diagonal cutting line

Side 1

Side 2

All corners 90°

Step 1. Start with a square, making sure that the corners are right angles (90 degrees). Mark the two opposite straight edges as shown.

Step 2. Mark the diagonal carefully with a long ruler or yardstick, and cut on this line.

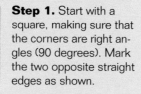

Sides 1 and 2

Step 3. Using a short stitch length (about 14 stitches per inch), sew the two marked straight edges with right sides together.

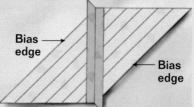

Bias edge

Bias edge

Mark lines on wrong side of fabric

Step 4. Press the seam open and mark lines on the wrong side of the fabric parallel to the bias edges, making the space between the lines equal to the width of the desired bias strips.

Step 5. Bring the right sides of the non-bias edges together to make a tube of fabric. Shift the edges so that the top of one aligns with the first marked line of the other. Be sure the edges are in the proper position for stitching. Sew the edges together in this position and press the seam open.

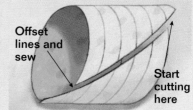

Offset lines and sew

Start cutting here

Step 6. Start cutting at one uneven end along the marked line. As you progress, you will be cutting one long continuous length of bias.

Note: To estimate the amount of binding a square will produce, multiply the length of two of the sides together. Divide the result by the width of the binding you want. For example, using a 30-inch square, multiply 30 × 30 to get 900. Divide 900 by 2 to get 450, the length of 2-inch binding you would get from a 30-inch square.

• Sew the binding first to the front of the quilt by machine. Then fold it over to the back and sew by hand using a blind stitch.

Starting and Ending the Binding

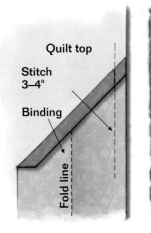

Quilt top

Stitch 3–4"

Binding

Fold line

Step 1. Starting: Begin on one side of the quilt. Start sewing the binding to the quilt with the fold open. Sew through one binding thickness for about 3 to 4 inches, keeping the raw edge of the binding lined up with the raw edge of the quilt top.

First stitching

Start stitching all layers

Step 2. Lift the presser foot, fold the binding into the doubled position, and continue sewing around the quilt.

Step 3. Ending: After you have sewn the binding around the whole quilt and have returned to the starting point, leave the needle in position and place the end of the binding over the single thickness sewn at the start. Cut off any excess length and tuck the end into the pocket formed at the starting point. Continue to stitch through all thicknesses.

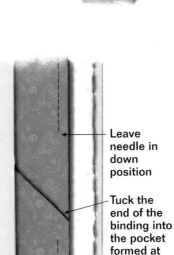

Leave needle in down position

Tuck the end of the binding into the pocket formed at the starting point

Mitered Corners

This system will give perfect miters for any width binding and any seam allowance you choose, as long as you are consistent in sewing and accurate in measuring.

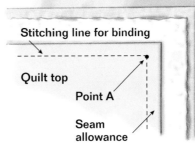

Stitching line for binding

Quilt top

Point A

Seam allowance

Step 1. Determine the exact point where the seam should turn at the corner, Point A. This is where the seam allowances on both sides intersect.

Step 2. Sew the binding exactly to Point A and backstitch. Remove the quilt from under the presser foot.

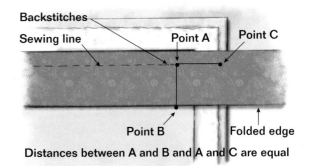

Backstitches

Sewing line

Point A

Point C

Point B

Folded edge

Distances between A and B and A and C are equal

Step 3. Measure the exact distance from Point A to the folded edge of the binding, Point B. Measure this exact same distance from Point A out onto the unsewn binding. This becomes Point C, as shown.

Step 4. To make the corner fold, insert the tip of a pin down through the binding at Point C. Hold the pin while turning the binding enough that the point of the pin can be inserted into the quilt at Point A underneath the binding that is already sewn on. Keep the pin snugly in place to hold Point C over Point A while the unsewn binding is placed in position to continue down the next side of the quilt.

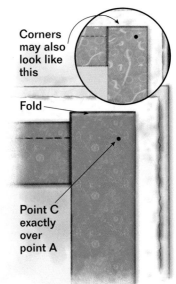

Corners may also look like this

Fold

Point C exactly over point A

Step 5. Insert the machine needle at Point C without catching the fold of the binding. (The needle should go as closely as possible into the point where the pin was holding Point C and Point A together.)

Step 6. Sew with a shortened stitch length for a few stitches, then continue with a regular stitch length down the next side.

Inside Corners

Double Wedding Ring and other quilts have inverted corners. Prepare and attach the bindings for these quilts in the same way as for straight-sided quilts, except at those inside corners.

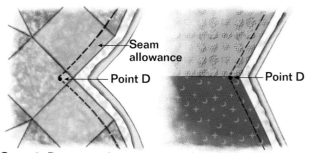

Step 1. Determine the exact point where the binding seam should turn, Point D, as indicated by the width of your seam allowance.

Step 2. While stitching the binding to the quilt, shorten the stitch length for ½ inch on either side of turning Point D.

Step 3. Stitch exactly to Point D, stopping with the needle in the quilt, and raise the presser foot.

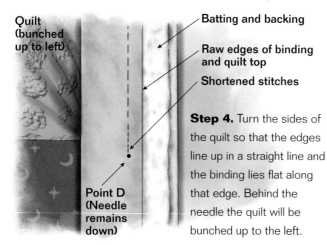

Step 4. Turn the sides of the quilt so that the edges line up in a straight line and the binding lies flat along that edge. Behind the needle the quilt will be bunched up to the left.

Step 5. Lower the presser foot and continue stitching, being careful not to catch the bunched-up quilt or to stretch the binding. Use fine stitches before lengthening them again.

Step 6. After you finish stitching the binding to the quilt, trim away the batting and backing fabric, leaving enough to completely fill the finished binding.

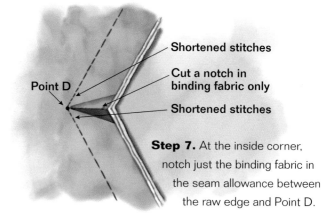

Step 7. At the inside corner, notch just the binding fabric in the seam allowance between the raw edge and Point D.

Step 8. When the binding is turned to the back and stitched down, the miters will fall into place on both the front and back. Blind stitch them as you go along.

Finishing Double-Fold Bindings

Step 1. Trim away the excess batting and backing. Be sure to leave enough of the batting and backing layers to completely fill the finished binding.

Step 2. Stitch the diagonal overlap closed at the starting/ending point outside of the binding.

Step 3. Turn the binding to the back and stitch into place, just covering the machine stitching line. Use small, inconspicuous stitches and a thread color that matches the binding.

Step 4. At the corners, sew right up to the turning point before folding the miters into position and they will then fall easily into place.

Step 5. Blind stitch the mitered folds on both the front and the back and then continue around the quilt.

Single-Fold Binding for Nonmitered Corners

To reduce bulk of nonmitered corners, use a single-fold binding. To prepare a single-fold binding, cut and sew strips together in the same manner as for a double-fold binding. Press down the center with wrong sides together. Open the binding and press each raw edge in just to the center fold.

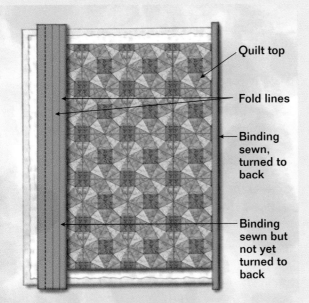

Quilt top

Fold lines

Binding sewn, turned to back

Binding sewn but not yet turned to back

Step 1. Open the binding strips and sew them to two opposite sides of the quilt, sewing along the outer fold line.

Step 2. Trim the batting and backing fabric as needed, turn the bindings to the back, and blind stitch. (The thread color should match the binding color.)

Step 3. Trim the ends of these bindings exactly even with the unbound sides of the quilt top.

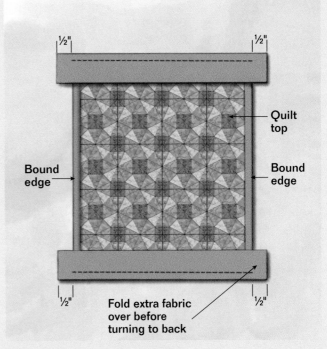

½" ½"

Quilt top

Bound edge

Bound edge

½" ½"

Fold extra fabric over before turning to back

Step 4. Sew the binding to the other two sides, leaving a half inch of extra binding at each corner.

Step 5. Trim off the remaining batting and backing fabric and then fold the extra binding in so that it is even with the previously bound sides of the quilt.

Step 6. With the folds in place, turn the binding to the back of the quilt and blind stitch.

Edge-Turned Bindings

Some quilts are bound by folding the fabric from one side of the quilt around to the other side, thus encasing the edge and serving as a binding. These are called edge-turned bindings. Edge-turned bindings have only one thickness of fabric so they are less durable than double-fold bindings but, if well done, they can be just as attractive.

Unfortunately, in some quilts bound this way, the binding seems loose and shifts along the edge even though it has been well sewn. This happens because the edges have not been secured through all three layers of the quilt. To prevent this on a hand-quilted quilt, add a row of quilting right along the edge of the binding. On a machine-quilted or tied quilt, an edge-turned binding is sewn by machine through all the

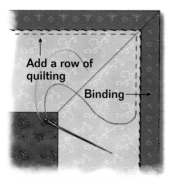

EDGE-TURNED BINDING

layers, giving a firm, neat edge that closely resembles an applied binding.

Since these bindings are most often done by folding the back of the quilt to the front, it is very important to plan for the back at the same time that the quilt top is designed and the fabrics are chosen. This assures that the backing fabric will coordinate in color and design with the front of the quilt. Plan for enough backing fabric on all sides to allow for the width you want for the binding. This allowance should be at least twice the width of the finished binding. Before basting the quilt, be sure that each corner of the quilt top is square (90 degrees).

Step 1. Trim the batting even with the quilt top, being careful not to cut the backing fabric.

Step 2. Baste all around the quilt ¼ inch from the edge to prevent the edges from slipping.

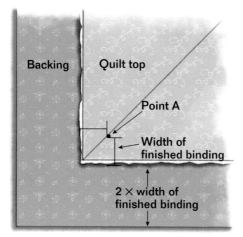

Step 3. Trim the backing fabric so that its distance from the edge of the quilt top equals twice the width of the desired finished binding.

Step 4. Mark the point (Point A) where the finished binding will turn at the corner. Determine this point by measuring the width of the finished binding in from each side.

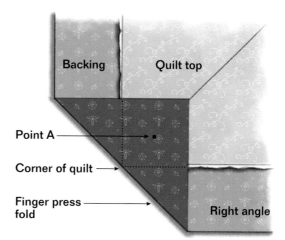

Step 5. Fold the corner of the back exactly across the corner of the quilt top, forming a right triangle. Finger press, being careful not to stretch the bias fold.

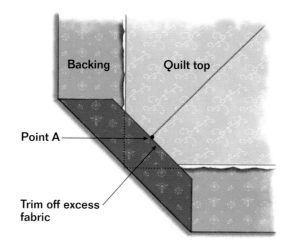

Step 6. Cut off the excess fabric between the fold and Point A.

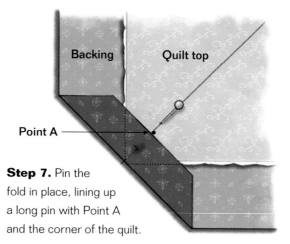

Step 7. Pin the fold in place, lining up a long pin with Point A and the corner of the quilt.

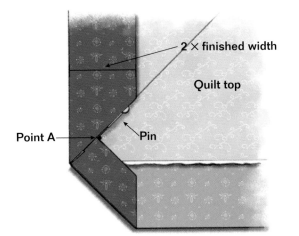

Step 8. Bring the back over to the front so that the folded edge at the corner lines up with the pin. When turning, be careful not to pull the fabric off-grain. Repeat for the other side of the corner.

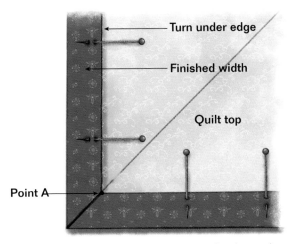

Step 9. Turn the raw edges under on all sides and pin securely.

Step 10. Sew the binding in place by hand or machine as desired. If sewn by hand, add a line of quilting close to the edge of the binding. Blind stitch the miters at the end or as you get to them.

Step 11. Remove the basting from Step 2.

Knife Edges

Some quilts are finished without a binding, and a knife edge finish is one method used to do this. I don't recommend using a knife-edge finish on bed quilts, but it is fine for wall quilts, small quilted projects, and special items such as pillows or potholders. Knife edge finishes can be used for unusual shapes when you don't want to add a binding. For this technique, you are simply sewing the front and the back of the quilt together with a blind stitch. Here's how to make a successful knife edge.

Step 1. Trim the batting so that it is a little smaller than the front and back of the quilt.

Step 2. Turn the top of the quilt under ¼ to ½ inch.

Step 3. Turn the back under so that it is exactly the same size as the front and is folded over the batting.

Step 4. Baste all the layers together.

Step 5. Blind stitch the front to the back.

Step 6. Complete the edge by adding a row of quilting ¼ to ½ inch from the edge. This stabilizes the edge and keeps it from shifting so that neither the back shows on the front nor the front on the back.

Step 7. Remove the basting stitches.

Facings

Faced edges are sewn in the same way that a facing is sewn when making clothing. They are particularly useful for quilts that have very irregular edges, such as scallops or hexagons. The fabric for the facing should be wider than the edge to be faced—wide enough to stitch to the curve.

Step 1. Sew the facing to the top of the quilt with right sides together. You will be sewing through all layers. Use a short stitch length for curves and at corners.

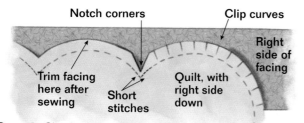

Notch corners   Clip curves

Right side of facing

Trim facing here after sewing

Short stitches

Quilt, with right side down

Step 2. Clip the seam allowances of the curves and at the corners through all layers before turning the facing to the back so that the facing will lie flat.

Step 3. Trim the facing even with the seam allowance, and turn the facing to the back of the quilt. Baste in place.

Step 4. Turn under the raw edge of the facing and slip stitch it to the back of the quilt.

An easy way to finish irregular edges such as sharp curves or hexagons is to appliqué them to a long straight border before layering and basting. Quilt and then bind the straight edge.

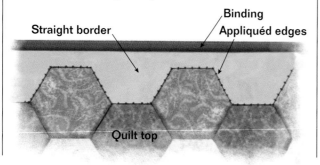

Straight border

Binding

Appliquéd edges

Quilt top

Step 5. To keep the edge from rolling or shifting, add a row of quilting ¼ to ½ inch away from the edge after the facing has been completed.

Step 6. Remove the basting stitches.

Special Finishes

Special finishes include laces, ruffles, fringe, cording, and prairie points. (See "Rose Petal Trim" on page 98 and "Prairie Points" on page 176.) They are usually sewn on after the quilt has been quilted, and for this reason, the quilting stitches should not be closer than ½ inch from the edge.

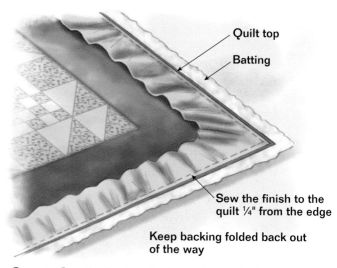

Quilt top

Batting

Sew the finish to the quilt ¼" from the edge

Keep backing folded back out of the way

Step 1. Sew the finish to the front of the quilt about ¼ inch from the edge, stitching through both the front of the quilt and the batting. Be sure to hold the back of the quilt out of the way.

Step 2. Trim the batting close to the seam line.

Step 3. Turn the seam allowance in toward the center of the quilt so that the finish will turn outward. Turn the seam allowance of the backing fabric under and baste or pin it to the back side of the trim, covering the seam allowance and the row of stitches from Step 1.

Step 4. Slip stitch or blind stitch the back in place.

BISCUIT QUILTING

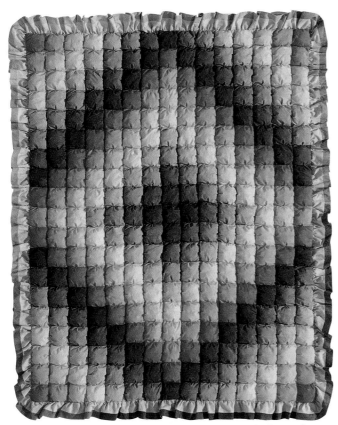

Here's a striking, updated version of the old-fashioned biscuit quilt, measuring 45" × 57", and made by Doris Carmack from luscious hand-dyed cottons by Cherrywood Fabrics.

Biscuit quilting, or puff quilting, is a form of patchwork in which a piece of fabric is sewn to a smaller background piece and stuffed to form a biscuit shape. The origin of biscuit quilting is unknown, but a few examples have been located dating back about 150 years. Usually made for warmth rather than beauty, these quilts were used and worn out, so it's rare to find an antique biscuit quilt.

Biscuits by Machine

Biscuits are made with two squares of fabric, one of which is ½ inch larger than the other. The smaller backing piece does not show in the finished quilt. A good size for a quilt is a 4-inch top square and a 3½-inch square for the backing. The finished biscuit will be a 3-inch square.

You should establish a layout or color plan on graph paper before you begin so you can determine how many biscuits you need of each color. Keep your biscuits in rows as you stitch them.

Step 1. Match the four corners of each biscuit and backing fabric, placing wrong sides together. Use a ⅛-inch seam allowance and sew around three sides, stitching a pleat in each side to take up the extra fullness. Without breaking the thread, pick up another pair of squares and again sew around three sides. Continue until the first row of blocks has been sewn.

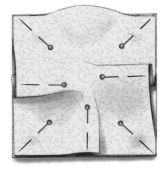

Step 2. Stuff each block with a soft, good quality fiberfill. Note that too much filling will make it difficult to sew the blocks together. Begin with a small handful so that the biscuit puffs up but is not too firm. Experiment until you get a feel for the right amount.

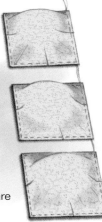

Step 3. Sew the fourth sides together, pleating again and using a ⅛-inch seam allowance. Do not stop to break the thread between blocks, and do not cut them apart until you are ready to sew the blocks together.

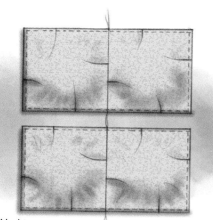

Step 4. Working on one row at a time, cut the blocks apart. Sew pairs of blocks together using a ¼-inch seam allowance and having right sides together.

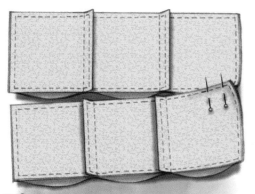

Step 5. Sew the rows together, matching seam allowances to complete the quilt top. The direction of the seam allowances should alternate from row to row.

Finishing the Quilt

Step 1. Spread the quilt on a flat surface and measure the length and width *without stretching* the quilt. This is the exact measurement to cut the backing. Pin the backing to the quilt with right sides together, distributing the excess fullness in the top evenly. The biscuits contract because of the stuffing and make the back too loose if not done this way.

Step 2. With the backing on top, sew around the quilt. Leave an opening for turning. Turn right side out and sew the opening closed.

Step 3. Lay the quilt out flat, and put a straight pin at each intersection where you want to have a tie, at least every 6 inches. Place a zigzag bartack, three or four closely spaced zigzag stitches, wherever there is a pin.

Try This

- **Sew a 3-inch piece of ribbon with each tacking stitch, then tie a knot in it.**
- **Put a ruffle or lace around the quilt before tacking.**
- **For invisible tacking, use monofilament thread in the needle and match the bobbin thread with the backing.**

Design Your Own Quilt

Measure your bed and determine the total dimensions you want your quilt to be. Make your final measurements divisible by three if you are making 3-inch blocks. For a large quilt, you will lose as much as 3 to 6 inches in the process of making the biscuits, so be generous when estimating.

Plan the quilt design on graph paper. Let each block of the graph paper equal one block of the quilt. Color in the design and follow it when sewing the rows together. You can use any quilt design made of squares. You can also use pieced triangle squares for biscuits, greatly expanding the design possibilities. Or make a completely scrappy quilt requiring no plan at all!

If your quilt turns out to be smaller than you need, add border rows.

TAKING THE TROUBLE OUT OF **Large Biscuit Quilts**

- For a large quilt, divide the project into sections of about five or six rows. Complete these sections and sew them together.
- When finishing the quilt, space bartacks closer together because of the weight of the quilt.

Doris Carmack

BLIND STITCH

This stitch is most often used for hand appliqué and is sometimes called the "appliqué stitch." It may also be used for bindings and other edge finishes or for stitching a label to the back of a quilt. It offers secure anchoring, but as the name implies, the stitches are nearly invisible. These directions are for appliqué, but use the same technique for other applications.

You may want to try using an appliqué needle for this stitch—many quilters feel it makes the stitch much easier. Use a single strand of thread that matches the color of your appliqué fabric or other fabric to be stitched, not the background.

Background fabric

Step 1. Knot the end of your thread. Bring the needle and thread up from under the background, through the background and edge of the appliqué shape. Keep the needle very close to the folded edge. For appliqué, it is best if you do not start on a point.

Stitches are straight on top

Step 2. Take the needle down into the background fabric, straight across from where you started. Bring the needle up into the appliqué fabric ⅛ inch or less away from the preceding stitch and keeping it close to the folded edge. The stitch on the top is straight and the back will be at a slight angle. Keep the stitches close together. You should have seven to ten stitches per inch.

Angled stitches on the back

Step 3. To finish the stitch, take the needle and thread through the background fabric, and knot the thread on the back. Make sure the knot is behind the appliqué fabric and will not show on the front. For bindings and quilt labels, make a knot and bury it in the batting layer as for hand quilting. (See "Hand Quilting" on page 124.)

Karen Kay Buckley

BORDERS

Borders add a finishing touch to your quilt. You can think of them as the frame or mat around a painting, as something to set off or complement the patchwork or appliqué. You may plan the borders when designing your quilt, or wait until most of the quilt is together before deciding. No matter when you plan your borders, they provide another opportunity for creativity.

Designing Your Borders

You may add simple borders to your quilt, multiple borders, or borders that repeat an element of your quilt design. The borders should balance the design and color of your quilt and be proportional to the

block size in your quilt. A very wide border may overpower the design in your quilt, and a very narrow border may give an unfinished look.

Too narrow

Too wide

Many quilters design their borders according to the size of the blocks in the quilt: full-size, three-quarter size, or half the size of the blocks. All of these combinations give pleasing results, but the border you choose will depend on your specific quilt and your special tastes. Choose a border that complements the design in your quilt.

Same size as blocks

Three-quarter size

Half-size

If you have not chosen a fabric for your quilt border, it is fun to "audition" border fabrics. Take the center of your quilt to your favorite quilt shop and lay it on different fabrics to determine the ones you like the best. One suggestion is to choose one of the dark fabrics in your design to add a dynamic frame to your quilt.

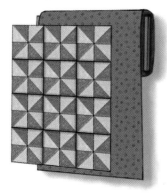

using. Check the size by measuring the quilt through the center of the patchwork in two directions. Measure lengthwise to determine the side borders and widthwise to determine the top and bottom borders.

Length measurement   Width measurement

Sometimes the edges stretch, and a measurement through the center will be accurate. Cutting the borders following the center measurements of the quilt helps avoid stretched and rippling borders. When you sew, ease the edge of the quilt to fit the borders, as needed.

Try This One of my favorite border techniques is to add a narrow ½- to 1-inch border between the center of the quilt and the wide border. This frames the design, adds an accent similar to the mat around a picture, and often repeats one of my favorite colors from the quilt.

Measuring Your Quilt for Borders

If you are making a large quilt or a quilt with many patchwork pieces, the size of the quilt can change slightly because of all the seams involved. For this reason, it's always a good idea to cut the borders to match your actual quilt rather than cut the size specified in the book or pattern directions you may be

Cutting Your Borders

Always cut borders on the straight grain of the fabric, never on the bias, because they will stretch out of shape. If possible, buy enough fabric and cut the borders on the lengthwise grain (parallel to the selvage). Before you cut your borders, trim the selvage from your fabric. If you have to piece the border fabric, sew together with a diagonal seam. It will be less noticeable than a straight seam.

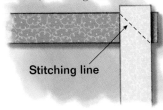

Stitching line

Overlapped Borders

Overlapped borders are the easiest to design and apply to your quilt. To make overlapped borders, two of the borders are cut the length of the patchwork design, and the other two borders are cut the width of the total design (including the first two borders).

Step 1. Measure through the center of the quilt to determine an accurate width and length for your quilt. The side borders are cut the length of the quilt. The top and bottom borders are cut the width of the quilt plus the width of two borders, minus 1 inch for seam allowances.

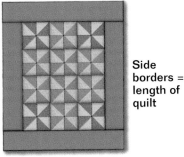

Side borders = length of quilt

Top and bottom borders = width of quilt + two borders

Step 2. To sew overlapped borders, stitch the side borders first. Pin the outer ends of the border and quilt, right sides together, and match the center of the border to the center of the quilt. Ease the quilt to fit the border. Use ¼-inch seam allowances and backtack at the ends of the seams. Press the seam allowances toward the border.

Step 3. Attach the top and bottom borders, overlapping the two side borders. Match the centers and ends. Pin and ease the quilt to fit the borders as you did for the sides. Stitch the seam, backtacking at the beginning and end. Press the seam allowances toward the borders.

Mitered Borders

Mitered borders are a little more difficult, but they are well worth the effort when using a striped fabric or other fabric that you would like to make a more continuous pattern around the quilt. This is my favorite technique, and will take all the fear out of mitering borders!

Step 1. Estimate the finished outside dimensions of your quilt, including borders. Determine these numbers by measuring across the center of the quilt and adding two border widths to both the lengthwise and widthwise dimensions.

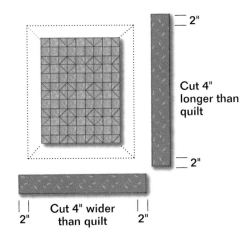

2"

Cut 4" longer than quilt

2"

2"   **Cut 4" wider than quilt**   2"

Step 2. Cut two border strips, each 4 inches longer than the quilt width as estimated in Step 1, and two border strips each 4 inches longer than the quilt length estimated in Step 1.

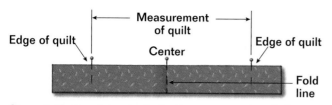

Edge of quilt — Measurement of quilt — Edge of quilt
Center
Fold line

Step 3. Fold each border to find its center, and mark the center with a pin. Mark the size of the quilt on the border, placing pins to designate the edge measurements.

Step 4. Match the center fold of the border with the center of the quilt top, having right sides together. Sew the borders to the edges of the quilt, backtacking and leaving ¼ inch of the quilt un-stitched at the beginning and end of the seam. Press the seams toward the borders.

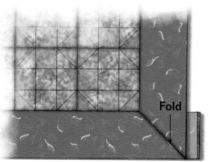

Border
Stop stitching ¼" from edge of quilt

Step 5. To miter the corners, lay the first corner to be mitered on your ironing board, pinning the quilt to the ironing board as necessary to keep it from pulling and to keep the corner from slip-ping. With the quilt right side up, fold one of the borders under at a 45 de-gree angle. Work with the fold until the seams meet properly.

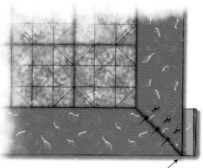

Fold

Step 6. Place pins at the fold. Place a square ruler over the corner to check that the corner is flat and square. When every-thing is straight and square, remove the pins and press the fold.

Corner should be flat and square

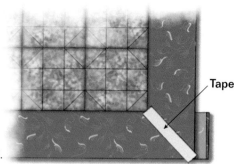

Tape

Step 7. Carefully center a piece of 1-inch masking tape over the mitered fold.

Step 8. Unpin the quilt from the ironing board and turn it over. Draw a light pencil line on the crease created when you pressed the fold. Fold the center section of the quilt diagonally from the corner, right sides together, and align the long edges of the border strips.

Tip: Draw your line slightly away from the crease to prevent sewing through the masking tape.

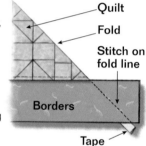

Quilt
Fold
Stitch on fold line
Borders
Tape

Step 9. Beginning at the inside corner, stitch on the pencil line, backtacking at the beginning of the seam. Remove the tape. Check to make sure the borders lie flat, then trim the ex-cess fabric, leaving a ¼-inch seam allowance. Press the seam open for a mitered corner.

Step 10. Repeat these steps for the three remaining corners.

Multiple Borders

Multiple borders are often designed to use two or more of the quilt's colors to frame the design. Usually the borders graduate in size with borders becoming

wider toward the edge of the quilt.

You may choose to add the borders one at a time, or you may sew them together before applying them to the quilt.

If you want to add the borders one at a time, use the overlapped technique described above. Complete each border before adding the next, pressing the seam allowance toward the new border.

If you want to sew the border strips together before you add them to the quilt, use the mitered-corner method. Sew the border strips together to form four complete borders (one for each side). Treat them as one border as you stitch them to the quilt. Carefully match the individual border seams as you miter the corners.

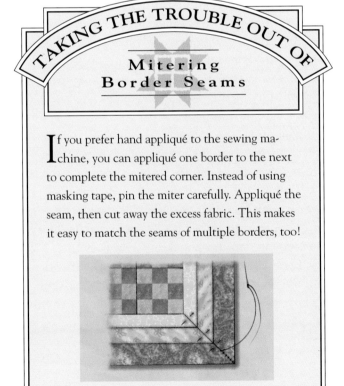

TAKING THE TROUBLE OUT OF

Mitering Border Seams

If you prefer hand appliqué to the sewing machine, you can appliqué one border to the next to complete the mitered corner. Instead of using masking tape, pin the miter carefully. Appliqué the seam, then cut away the excess fabric. This makes it easy to match the seams of multiple borders, too!

Cornerstone Borders

Cornerstone borders give a special look to your quilt and offer a chance to add a splash of color if needed. Select one of the fabrics from the quilt or use an accent color or print in the corners of the border. The cornerstone is usually square, and its size is determined by the width of the quilt borders.

Cornerstone

Step 1. Measure your quilt through the center to determine the border lengths and widths. Cut four corner squares using the border width as the dimension.

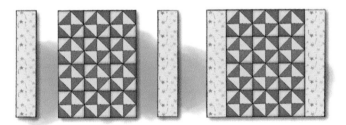

Step 2. Sew the side borders to your quilt.

Step 3. Sew the cornerstones to the sides of the top and bottom borders.

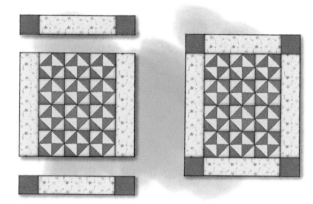

Step 4. Sew the top and bottom borders on to complete your quilt.

Add cornerstones to multiple borders for an extra accent.

If the borders are the same size as the blocks, try incorporating a special block design from your quilt as a cornerstone. This repeats a design from the quilt and adds balance between the quilt center and the border.

Pieced Borders

Pieced borders look complicated, but can be easily designed to complement the look of your quilt.

First, determine the finished dimensions of the quilt. Measure the length and width of the quilt through the center and subtract ½ inch for seam allowances. If your quilt is square, divide the measurement by a number that can easily be used for the pieced units. For example, if your quilt measures 42 inches, you can use 3, which will result in 14 patchwork units along the edges of the quilt. The finished size of each unit is 3 inches.

If your quilt is rectangular, you will have two measurements. Find a number that will equally divide both the width and length. If you cannot find the perfect number, use close numbers. If the patchwork units vary no more than ½ inch, they will appear the same. For example, you could have 2½-inch patchwork units on one side and 3-inch units on the other.

When you determine the size of the patchwork unit, use graph paper to sketch some ideas for your pieced border. You may want to repeat a pattern from the quilt or use a new shape.

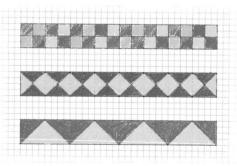

60

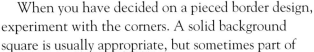
Experiment with the width of the design: you will have squares if the border is the same size as the repeated measurement of the pieced unit, or rectangles if the border is narrower or wider.

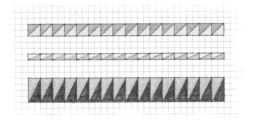

If the shape is irregular and cannot be cut easily with a rotary cutter, use your graph paper drawing to create templates for your design. Trace each piece for your border onto template material, and add ¼-inch seam allowances. (See "Templates" on page 238.) If you have a computer and a quilt design software program, you can quickly and easily try different ideas around your quilt and print out templates.

Add ¼" seam allowance

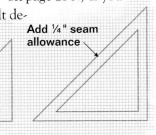

If you cannot find an easy number to divide the measurement of your quilt by, try using a narrow border to increase the size of your quilt to a workable number.

When you have decided on a pieced border design, experiment with the corners. A solid background square is usually appropriate, but sometimes part of the patchwork design will look great. Try a few different ideas on graph paper to help you decide.

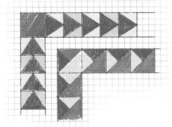

Scrap Borders

For a quick border with a scrappy look, try using all of the fabrics from your quilt in a strip-pieced border.

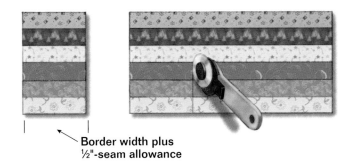

Border width plus ½"-seam allowance

Step 1. Sew several fabric strips together. The strip sizes can vary or they can be cut the same width. Cross-cut the strip sets using the desired width of the border plus ½ inch for seam allowances.

Units cut from strip set

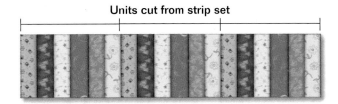

Step 2. Sew the pieces together to create the border length needed.

Mimi Dietrich

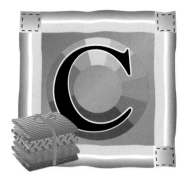

CALICO

This medium-weight, plainly woven fabric is usually printed in a small, closely repeating design. The name comes from Calicut (Calcutta), India, where cotton wood-block prints have been made for hundreds of years. Early calicoes, which featured elaborate animals, birds, trees, and flowers, were also made by painting and resist printing.

CATHEDRAL WINDOW

"Peacock Windows," 38" × 38", made by Lynne Edwards, 1994. This handsome quilt features classic Cathedral Windows in the corners and the Secret Garden variation in the center area. It is made of blue and green silk and hand-dyed cotton fabrics.

Cathedral Window is a traditional folded patchwork technique that first appeared in the United States in the 1930s. My research suggests that it originated in Asia, with earliest examples found in China and Korea.

 Choose the size of folded square that you want. Multiply this measurement by two and add ½ inch. Cut your square this size.

Classic Cathedral Window: Making the Folded Squares by Hand

This method is more time-consuming than machine construction, but the end result is a window with nice flat corners.

Turn in edges ¼"

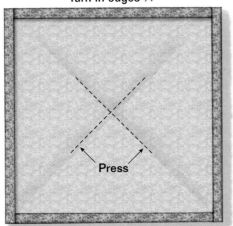

Press

Step 1. Mark the center of each fabric square by folding diagonally and pressing the center one way and then the other, making a small X in the center. With the wrong side of the fabric up, turn in each edge ¼ inch, pressing firmly with a steam iron.

← **Aim for sharp points at outside corners**

Step 2. Fold each corner to the center in turn, pressing firmly. The outside corners should have really sharp points.

TAKING THE TROUBLE OUT OF Cathedral Windows

If an outside corner is blunt, pull the two center corners together across the middle until that outer corner makes a sharp point. Press well. If the center points now overlap each other, don't worry. Readjust them to look like the Step 2 illustration. Any nasty puffy areas will be lost in the next stage of folding.

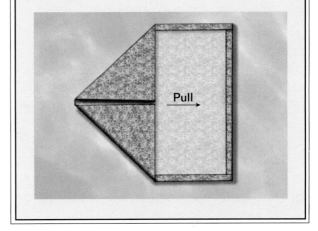

Pull

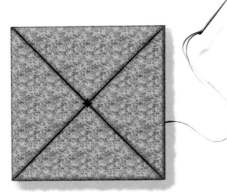

Step 3. Secure the center points with two tiny crossed stitches through all layers, starting and finishing at the back. The thread is left there, ready for the next step.

Step 4. Re-press the four outside corners to keep them sharp. Bring each point in to the center, easing any fullness into the folded areas as you do so. Press firmly. Stitch the center down through all layers using the original thread. Make a tiny cross with the stitches, pulling very firmly. Repeat to make another pair of stitches. Finish by tying a knot and burying it within the fabric layers, as for hand quilting.

Making the Folded Squares by Machine

This is quicker than the hand method, as it eliminates the first stages of folding and pressing. It is also more secure. The disadvantage is the bulkiness in the corners, but there are strategies to reduce this bulk.

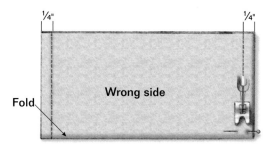

Step 1. Fold the fabric square in half with right sides together. Pin and stitch a ¼-inch seam at both ends.

Trim corners after stitching

Step 2. Pull the two open edges apart and refold, matching the seams and raw edges. Pin and stitch from each corner to about 1 inch from the center. Work first on one side, then repeat for the other.

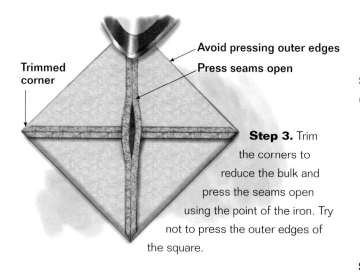

Trimmed corner

Avoid pressing outer edges

Press seams open

Step 3. Trim the corners to reduce the bulk and press the seams open using the point of the iron. Try not to press the outer edges of the square.

Step 4. Turn the square right side out through the center opening and press. It is now at the same stage as Step 3 of the hand method. (See page 63.)

Step 5. Bring the open edges together in the center with two tiny stitches through all layers. Continue to fold and stitch the center a second time, following Step 4 of the hand method. (See page 63.)

Joining the Squares

Once two folded squares are prepared and stitched in either method, place them right sides facing, and whipstitch together, matching corners carefully. When assembling several squares, work in rows, and then stitch the rows together. For large projects, you may find it easier to work in sections and complete all the windows that you can before joining all the sections of squares together.

Adding the Windows

Step 1. Measure from the center to a corner of one folded square. Cut a window square to those dimensions.

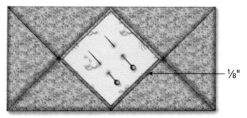

⅛"

Step 2. Pin the window on the joined squares, and trim it until ⅛ inch of background fabric shows all around.

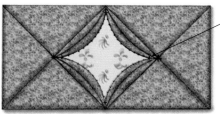

Double bartack

Step 3. Roll the surrounding border over the window, stretching it into a curve and stitching it with appliqué stitches or tiny spaced backstitches close to the folded edge. Secure the window fabric with a double bartack ¼ inch from each corner.

The Secret Garden Variation

Only one folded square is needed to make this four-petaled shape.

Step 1. Prepare the folded square, using either the hand or machine method. Bring the final four corners to the center. Press well, but do not stitch them down.

Step 2. Unfold the corners. The fold lines will be clearly visible. Cut a square of window fabric measuring the same as the finished folded square. Place this on the fold lines, trimming if necessary, and stitch it down with small running stitches ⅛ inch from the edge.

Step 3. Bring the four outside corners to the center, then press and stitch, following Step 4 of the hand method. (See page 63.)

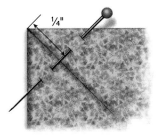

Step 4. Insert a pin ¼ inch from each corner through all the layers.

Step 5. Roll back and stitch down the edges of the background square to make the four petal shapes. Remove each pin as you reach it and make two bartacks through all layers to secure the corners.

Lynne Edwards

CHARM QUILTS

A charm quilt is a quilt in which every single piece is cut from a different fabric. Hundreds—or even thousands!—of fabrics may be used. The key is to avoid duplication. Most charm quilts feature one simple geometric shape, such as a triangle or square, which is repeated over the entire surface to form the quilt's design. Occasionally, however, the traditional block format appears.

The earliest documented charm quilts can be traced to the last quarter of the nineteenth century, when the craze for amassing a vast variety of fabric patches coincided with similar contemporary fads—such as collecting and swapping buttons, bottles, and other "charms." A common goal was the acquisition of 1,000 different pieces. The search contained an element of intrigue and romance, especially for the young girl who dreamed of finding the final swatch in the coat of her "one true love." With needlework such

There are several options for charm quilts based on a single shape—the rectangle.

a universal female pastime in the nineteenth century, it is little wonder that these carefully collected fabrics would be incorporated into quilts.

The appeal of the charm quilt has been cyclical, with periods of intense interest followed by years in which popularity wanes. The complete cycle spans

approximately 50 years. The first revival came in the 1920s and 1930s, when muslin or another unifying background was introduced to blend the hundreds of busy, pastel prints of that era. A second renaissance occurred in the mid-1970s, when quiltmakers were once again drawn to the excitement and challenge of collecting the wide variety of fabrics necessary for a true charm quilt. This current interest shows little sign of fading.

Not every charm quilt contains 1,000 fabrics. Some contain fewer; some, many, many more. Regardless of

"Simply Charming," 75" × 97", made by Edith Zimmer of San Diego, California. A 60° diamond divided in half creates Six-Pointed Stars among the traditional tumbling blocks in this well-executed charm quilt.

whether a charm quilt contains 500 or 5,000 different pieces, the prerequisite that no two pieces be cut from the same cloth requires an extensive collection of fabrics.

A charm quilter is always searching for new swatches to add to her stash, and is historically quite enterprising in acquiring them. In the nineteenth century, charm quilts were sometimes called "beggars'" quilts, as a result of the quiltmaker "begging" fabrics from the scrap bags of family and friends to round out her own collection.

Today's quiltmaker continues this custom, often relying on modern technology to supplement the quest. Quilt publications regularly feature swap columns and classified advertisements for enthusiastic quiltmakers to exchange charm squares with other interested quilters. The search has naturally moved into the computer age, with international fabric swaps engineered on the information superhighway by fabric-loving, computer-literate quiltmakers.

Darra Duffy Williamson

CHEATER CLOTH

If you need a true shortcut to a finished quilt, you can use cheater cloth, which looks amazingly like a pieced quilt from a distance. The cloth is printed to look like many small pieces of different fabrics combined into a popular quilt design. Although the designs have changed, cheater cloth has been around since the 1850s.

Although this fabric appears to be a quilt top, it is really a length of cotton printed to mimic the Dutch Mill pattern. Each "patch" duplicates a fabric popular when the cloth was printed in the 1880s. It would probably have been used for the back of a quilt, though some quiltmakers did use it for the front; hence its name, cheater cloth.

The first cheater cloth (also called printed patch-work or faux patchwork) mimicked chintz blocks and calico squares, designs popular in the mid-nineteenth century. In the 1880s, textile manufacturers made fabric resembling pieced stars. By the 1890s, quiltmakers could buy cheater cloth with patterns imitating crazy quilts, charm quilts, or Log Cabin cheater blocks. The 1933 Sears Roebuck catalog offered Grandmother's Flower Garden, Dresden Plate, and Double Wedding Ring, the three fads of the 1930s. Today you can find many of these same patterns.

If you look at cheater cloth carefully, you will see a cross section of popular fabric designs. For instance, in the photograph at left, the designer set this variation of Dutch Mill on point so the whole piece looks like a field of stars. As she drew the blocks, the designer combined large and small plaids, solids, florals, and small geometrics, just as a quiltmaker would have. Since this cloth was produced in the 1880s, it tells you what colors and prints were popular then.

Like most cheater cloth, the design carefully places full blocks in the center of the yardage and partial blocks at the selvage. By sewing together the half-blocks at the selvage, you can fool the viewer into thinking you have a full-size pieced quilt.

While you could sew two or three lengths of cheater cloth together to make the top of a whole-cloth quilt, most traditional quiltmakers used them for the backs of quilts (for instance, pairing a Log Cabin cheater cloth with a Log Cabin pieced quilt). Some contemporary quiltmakers use cheater cloth for small projects, such as table mats, Christmas stockings, and baby quilts. In such projects you can quilt around the design or use a diamond or square grid.

suellen Meyer

COLOR AND FABRIC SELECTION

The Color Wheel

Learning about color is one of the most useful gifts we as quilters can give ourselves. Just as knowledge about the correct tools and techniques helps us make precise and accurate blocks, knowledge about color helps us avoid mistakes, solve problems, and achieve beautiful, colorful quilts.

The color wheel is a wonderful tool. It provides a colorful way to learn and then share information about color. The example shown on the next page is a 12-color wheel. Each color is distinct from the 11 others. It is by varying these 12 colors—making them darker, lighter, or combining two colors—that all other colors are formed. Join me for a spin around the color wheel to discover the basic color terms you need to know.

Pure, Intense Colors

The 12 colors on the color wheel are *pure* colors, or *intense* colors. They are the truest, purest versions of themselves: the reddest red or the greenest green available. That is why they are called pure colors.

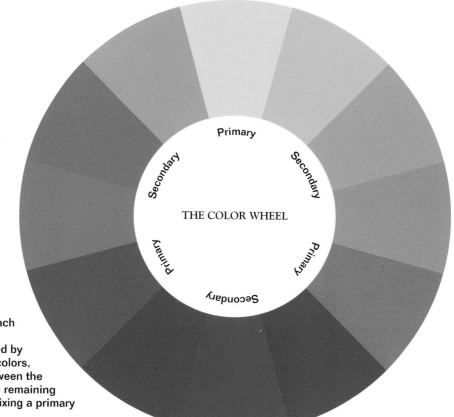

THE COLOR WHEEL

The primary colors, red, blue, and yellow, are set at points on the color wheel that are equal distances from each other. All pure colors are derived from them. The secondary colors are created by combining equal parts of the primary colors, and secondary colors are halfway between the primary colors on the color wheel. The remaining colors are tertiary colors created by mixing a primary and an adjacent secondary color.

Value

We can make these colors lighter or darker. This is called changing their *value.* Lighter values are called *tints* and darker values are called *shades.* The idea of value is not a new idea for quilters. We are used to including many values in our quilts, but we usually don't use the term value. We say we used several shades of a color.

Tint

Pure color

Shade

Intensity

We can change the *intensity* of the colors on the color wheel. They are brilliant and strong, but we can dull them by toning them down or diluting their intensity. A *tone* is a grayed version of a pure color. Quilters use grayed versions, or tones, of colors all the time. (See "Tones, Tints, and Shades" on page 70 for further discussion of value and intensity.)

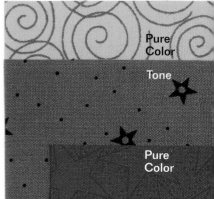

Pure Color

Tone

Pure Color

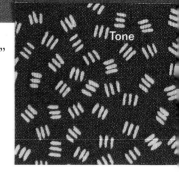

Tone

Temperature

Colors are either warm or cool in feeling. On our color wheel, the cool colors—the blues and greens of the sky and the sea—are on the left side of the wheel. The warm colors—the reds and oranges of fire and the sun—are on the right side of the wheel.

Colors Advance or Recede

Once we know these color ideas of value, intensity and temperature, we can use them to create beautiful quilts. Let's see how.

Colors behave differently when used together. Some stand out, advance, and catch the eye of the viewer. Some recede or fade into the background. How they behave depends on their value, intensity, and temperature.

Colors advance if they are dark, pure, or warm.

Colors recede if they are light, toned down, or cool.

Knowing that colors appear to advance and recede is the most powerful information quilters can possess. It allows us to design quilts in which the pattern does what we want it to do. We can control which part of a design stands out by putting the advancing colors there. We know that we should place cool colors and tones in the background because they will fade into the background despite our efforts to make them advance. Understanding how colors behave frees us to use the colors we love, but we can place them where they will do what we want them to do.

"Summer's End," 79" × 90", made by Judy Miller of Columbia, Maryland. The cool blues, purples, and greens recede in this straight furrows setting of Nine Patch blocks, while the warm yellows advance.

How I Plan a Quilt

When planning a color scheme, I choose colors by what they will do in the quilt. I ask myself several questions.
• What mood do I want the quilt to convey?
• Where do I want it to lie or hang?
• For what purpose am I making it?

When I have answered these questions, I choose fabrics. If I want a bold, striking quilt, I pull fabrics from my stacks of pure colors and warm colors. If I want a peaceful, quiet quilt, I pull out cool colors, tones, and pale colors. I always pull out more fabrics than I will use, knowing I can eliminate them later.

I then sort the fabrics by their power. Within every set of fabrics, some will advance and some will recede. I want a balance of advancing and receding colors—I don't want everything to advance! Color is a long-distance illusion, so the best way to see how colors interact is to lay the fabrics out or pin them on a wall and step back to view them. I stand at least 5 feet away from the fabrics to see their colors and relationships. If I see that I have too many strong or weak fabrics, too many light, dark or pure fabrics, I return to my shelves and pull out more of whatever I need for variety and balance.

Then I look at the design of the quilt and decide which parts I want to stand out or recede. I know what colors to use where because I know how colors behave.

Colors Create Moods

Just as colors advance or recede because of their value, intensity, and temperature, they create a mood or atmosphere because of these same characteristics.

Light values, low intensity tones, and cool colors create a quiet, soothing mood.

Dark values, pure intense colors, and warm colors create a strong, vibrant mood.

Building a Fabric Collection

I collect fabric with color considerations in mind. I search for variety in everything—print style, print scale, and of course, color. Although I always buy fabric I love, I also try to force myself to buy colors I don't like much but will probably need some day. Most of us have our favorite colors, and our quilts usually reflect these preferences. The way to learn about color and to expand our minds is to force ourselves to use the colors with which we are uncomfortable. Incorporating them into our quilts and our lives is good for us. Despite this warning, my fabric shelves, which are sorted by color, are still loaded with some colors and weak on others!

It is easy for me as a professional quilter to talk about a fabric collection, but I began just as every quilter does, buying a limited amount of fabric for a specific project. When I discovered that other quilters bought fabric with no project in mind, it was a great relief!

If you are a beginning quilter buying just enough for the current project, your collection may begin and end with each quilt. Don't worry. It will grow if you remember this simple rule: It is the leftovers from each project that make a collection. Don't fret about buying more than you need for a quilt. If you like the fabric enough to spend months working with it,

chances are good that it will be a welcome addition to your collection.

Whenever you can, buy extra fabric, and watch your collection grow. As you add fabrics, sort and store them by color. You will see immediately where your collection has color holes. Of course, you know how to fill those holes! Just make a list and take it with you next time you go to the fabric store.

Tones, Tints, and Shades

Tints and shades are created by mixing black or white with one of the 12 color wheel hues. A tint is created by adding white to a hue, which lightens the color. A shade results from adding black to a color, which darkens the value. Adding both black and white makes a tone, which dulls the color.

A tint has white added to the color wheel hue.

A shade has black added to the color wheel hue.

A tone has both black and white added to the color wheel hue.

These three elements of color are very important to the understanding of how color works in a quilt. Most quilts are made of tones, tints, and shades, rather than pure colors from the color wheel spectrum. Pure, bright color wheel hues are used most often in wall-hangings, children's quilts, and art quilts. Since most quilts are created for use in the home, decorating trends influence color choices. Tones, earth tones, and tea-dyed prints are popular fabrics used today to create nostalgic folk art quilts and crafts.

Pure color wheel hues include primary, secondary, and tertiary colors.

When white is added to a color, the value is lightened to create a tint. These tints feel sweet, light, and airy and work well as background fabrics in quilts. Sometimes we call them pastels. Tints are often used to create a Victorian theme and to make children's quilts. The tints tend to recede and do

This block is composed of tints.

not dominate other colors. Light tints help to create contrast in a quilt. Adding white to yellow intensifies and brightens the color while adding white to blue softens the hue.

Adding black to a color darkens the hue to create a shade. Shades are rich, saturated, sometimes intense hues that create depth in a quilt. The darkest shades are very dramatic and help create shapes in a quilt when contrasted with lights. Red becomes extremely vivid when darkened, but loses its

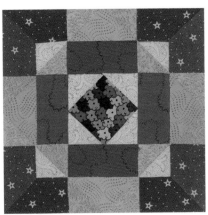

This block is created from shades.

power when white is added. Yellow becomes brilliant when white is added, but dull and dirty when mixed with black. The darkest darks are the blues and violets. Shades are often used in country and folk art style quilts.

This block is made of tones.

Tones are the result of adding both black and white to a color wheel hue. Tones pose special problems to the quilter because the value is so muted and muddy that good contrasts are difficult to achieve. If only tones are used in a project, the result is rather flat. The quilt may lack movement, dimension, and visual interest. For best results, use tones in moderation to give visual relief to stronger areas of a quilt. Tones are often included in country, folk art, and darker Victorian theme quilts.

Tea-dyed fabrics are in a special category of tones. A yellowish over-dye stain is used to mute the value and hue of the fabric. The result has the appearance

71

of aged, yellowed antique textiles that are charming and reminiscent of Grandma's quilts. Tea-dyed fabrics have the same flattened values as tones. These hues are grayed so that the brilliance and color saturation is lowered. Tones and tea dyes lack the vibrancy and lasting visual interest of pure colors, tones, and tints. However, they are safe and easy to live with when used in home decorating.

Virginia Robertson

Intuitive Color in Quilt Design

Color is what puzzles quilters most. I am asked more questions pertaining to color and fabric choices than anything else. During my 25 years as a quilt-making teacher and 21 years as a quilt shop owner, I have developed some ideas and techniques that have helped others gain more confidence in color planning and fabric selection. Here I will share them with you.

Be an observer! Become mentally aware of color and design around you. Keep a journal of your impressions of colors. Really study your flowerbed, the scene out your living room window, the flower stand on the way to work, the vegetables in your refrigerator. Note the colors that you are seeing. Is it a grass green, a sage green, a yellow green, a blue green? Notice how nature uses every color of green, and they look good together. Look at the different shades of color that you see in one flower blossom compared to what happens in a whole bouquet.

Don't forget stores and commercial buildings. Lots of money is spent on interior designers and decorating for these structures. Make notes in your journal. If there are fabrics that contain colors you especially like, clip swatches and paste them in your journal.

Collect inspiration everywhere you go. Be on the lookout for anything that sparks your creativity. Learn to look at everything with color in mind. Take snapshots of anything that catches your fancy—a wood pile that is artfully stacked, the design on a manhole cover, window boxes filled with flowers. Here are

some things that help stimulate my imagination:

- Greeting cards are great for color combination ideas.
- Magazines are filled with color and inspiration. The car in the picture may not excite you, but the colors in the rocks and sky behind it do. You may want to tear the ad out and put it in your journal or inspiration box.
- Walking. I see things when I am walking that I wouldn't ordinarily see. It might be a pile of rocks at the edge of a stream, or tall grass, dried flowers, and foliage in the fall. Keep notes and sketches in a journal.
- Gardening is a passion of mine. Seeing plants close-up allows me to see color and interesting shapes.
- A change of scenery is always inspiring. When I go to the city to see my children who are in college, the buildings fascinate me. Be an observer; fill up your soul with images and colors around you. Record them in your journal and when you are ready to make a quilt, you will have a frame of reference to work from.

Planning a Quilt

Here are some questions that will help you get started. Remember, it's all right to make a quilt just because you want to or because you want to have fun with a set of colors.

- Is there a quilt size range that you want to work in?
- Is it for a particular person, event, holiday, or celebration?
- What mood do you want the quilt to project?
- Why are you making it?
- Are there particular colors that you want to work with?
- What designs are you considering?
- Will you be challenging yourself on this project?
- Do you have a deadline? Does it have to be done quickly?

By jotting down answers to the above questions, you will end up setting parameters to work in. Within those parameters, stretch yourself as much as possible so you gain experience from the project. Form a basic plan for the quilt that answers the questions above.

Gather up any fabric that might be a contender for the quilt. I take the attitude that my fabrics are auditioning for the quilt. We all know that in an audition not everyone makes it. By taking that approach, I think you will be more open to possibilities. The number one rule is "please the quilt!" Plan to take some time collecting fabric—then you won't be disappointed if you don't find everything at the first store you visit.

Theme Fabric

If you don't have a theme fabric, find one that evokes the mood of the colors you want or a print that suggests the theme of the quilt. Take your cues from this fabric as you search for others. This fabric can be just a frame of reference for the fabric selection or may play a major part in the quilt. It is your security. It will

help you begin the selection process. Pull out any other fabrics that you think might work in the quilt. It is always better to have more and eliminate than to be looking for just one fabric. Display all of the fabrics where you can walk away and glance at your choices.

Be sure to have enough contrast. Contrast is the difference between light and dark. You will need contrast for the shapes in the patchwork or appliqué to show. Find lights, mediums, and darks.

Light   **Medium**   **Dark**

Choose a variety of sizes of print designs. This is scale. All the same size prints are boring. Look for small, medium, and larger prints. Differences in scale make a more interesting quilt.

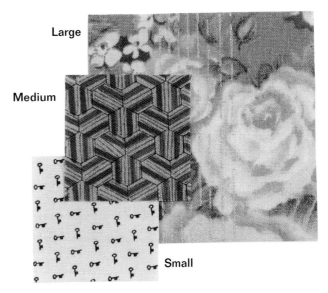

Large

Medium

Small

A theme fabric and coordinating colors

Use a variety of styles

palette as a group of friends—they all have something in common. Your fabrics are the same. The theme is what gives them something in common. In a group of friends, there is always one person who is a little crazy or wears wild clothes. He or she stands out, but is still part of the group. This is what the accent fabric does.

Proportion

Some fabrics will be used in the quilt more than others. Let's say you are making a Log Cabin quilt using two color families—blue and green. When the blocks are assembled into the quilt top, looking at it may give you an unsettled feeling. This is because the quilt is half blue and half green. Your eye can't determine whether this is a blue quilt or a green quilt. Once you add the binding or a border, then the quilt will be more of one color than the other, having a more balanced look.

Opt for variety in the style of fabrics. There are tiny repetitive prints, small florals, large florals, stripes, plaids, large swirls, bulky geometrics, and "blenders," which look like solids from a distance, but have a subtle, low-contrast design.

You may want to use mostly florals and blenders and add a small, high-contrast stripe to make the quilt interesting.

Select at least one fabric that will act as an accent. The accent is brighter, darker, or lighter than the rest of the palette. It sets the others off and adds energy to the design. Think of the fabric

To apply this principle to fabric selection, mentally divide the colors in the proposed quilt into percentages. For example, use 60 percent blue, 20 percent red, 10 percent yellow, 5 percent white, and 5 percent black. Fold the chosen fabrics so that color shows in the same relative proportions as above. Slip in the accent fabric so that only a small portion shows.

Now walk away from the fabrics, turn around, take a quick glance at the palette, and turn

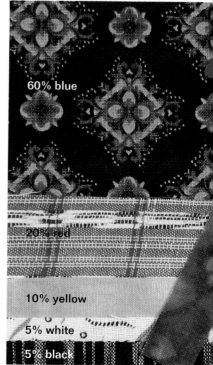

60% blue

20% red

10% yellow

5% white

5% black

away. Your mind will register what it sees. If one of the fabrics jumps out at you now, then it will do the same thing in the quilt. Try making adjustments. Let a smaller amount of the fabric show. Usually this fixes the problem. Too much of some fabrics can be overpowering.

Try florals with a stripe

If this doesn't work, then maybe that fabric needs some new friends. Look for other possibilities. Be open to making adjustments in the palette. Most of my quilts become a collection of fabrics from different places, even though I own a quilt shop. I like the collecting process and enjoy seeing a palette develop over time.

It may take a while to make adjustments in the fabrics until you are completely happy with the palette. Remember to choose lots to start with so you have plenty of possibilities to audition. As you work with the colors, prints, and textures, I will bet that you go back and look for more. In the process, you will become more open to possibilities. Many times I end up choosing something that I don't love as a single fabric, but I know will work in the quilt. Please the quilt!

In your quiltmaking journey, try to challenge yourself once in a while, not only with technical skills, but with color and fabric. Never dismiss a fabric as ugly—every fabric has potential. You just haven't discovered it yet!

Jean Wells

Be Unpredictable!

by Roberta Horton

The secret to combining colors and fabric patterns in a quilt is to work with fabrics that *don't* match each other! When small pieces of fabrics are joined to make a quilt, individual fabrics must read differently than their neighbors if they are to show in the composition. Most of us work in an opposite fashion. We select fabrics that go together, or blend. The result can be a predictable, safe quilt.

The key to color usage is to have a variety of choices available. Buy, and use, as many versions of a color as you can find. You need light, medium, and dark examples so that you will have the needed ammunition to make your selected quilt pattern show through value contrast.

Also pay attention to the variations of a color. When buying reds, for example, make sure you have some reds with blue in them, such as magenta, as well as those that are red-orange, such as peach. Most of us think of these variations within a color as clashing with each other. In reality, that's where the excitement comes from. Think of all the versions of green, some of which you like and some of which you dislike. You need them all, just as Mother Nature does. Feature those you like the best, and use the others in smaller amounts.

Use a variety of greens.

These greens match too closely.

When evaluating the patterns on your fabric, remember that you can achieve visual contrast and interest through variety. The more your fabrics resemble each other, the more the viewer will scan over them instead of really looking at them. First, make sure that there's a difference in the scale of the patterns. You have a favorite size that you naturally select, but you need to go beyond that preference. Size controls visual activity; smaller scale is calmer, while larger scale reads as busier. Contrast in scale will add visual excitement.

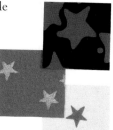
These fabrics resemble each other—the eye scans and doesn't notice the individual fabrics.

Make sure that there's also a mixture of subject matter on your patterned fabrics: florals, geometrics, textures, plaids, and stripes. Designs with curved lines will seem busier than those that feature straight lines. Some of the patterns should be more eye-catching; some should serve as accents.

Lastly, don't be predictable in how you combine your fabrics. Don't make all your blocks the same, but instead have some blocks seem more important or exciting than others. Also think in terms of majority and minority. The accent fabrics will give the finished quilt excitement. Make viewers scan your whole quilt because they don't want to miss anything!

In this mixture of subject matter, the eye will see and appreciate each piece.

The Color Yellow

Poor yellow! Whenever quiltmakers talk about color, yellow seems to merit the "shadiest" reputation on the color wheel! It is often dismissed completely, considered the most difficult color to use successfully in a quilt. "Yellow is so strong…powerful…dominant," quilters have been heard to complain. "It just—well, it just takes over!"

There is no denying that yellow *is* the brightest color on the color wheel. It engages the eye with ease and—if not carefully harnessed—can lead the viewer on a merry chase. Even when paired with purple, its natural complement, it is recommended that yellow be used sparingly. Three parts purple to one part yellow is generally considered a pleasing and harmonious proportion.

In addition to being naturally strong and bright, yellow is also a warm color. Like the other warm colors of red and orange, the color yellow suggests heat. Images of the brightly shining sun or an intense roaring flame invariably include a generous dash of yellow. And, like its warm cousins, the color yellow advances toward the eye, seeming to exist on a closer visual plane than its cooler counterparts of blue, purple, and green. These effects can be unsettling if not anticipated!

Once recognized and understood, however, these amazing powers can be considered advantages rather than handicaps. Adding yellow can infuse light and create contrast in an otherwise dark quilt. Use it to add a needed touch of warmth to a cool color scheme, or to introduce a spirit of lightheartedness and buoyancy to a design. Yellow can convey a message— remember those yellow ribbons? And, because of its ability to captivate the eye, it can draw attention to a focal point or lead the viewer's eye across the surface of a quilt just as you intended. Now *that's* power!

Try adding bits of pale lemon or soft buttercup for an ethereal glow, or warm mustards and old golds for a rich, vintage look.

When using yellow, it's important to remember to "spread it around." Placing all of the yellow in the bottom half will make a quilt seem top-heavy. On the other hand, concentrate all of the yellow in the top half of your quilt and it will seem about to float away!

Instead, add a touch of yellow here, a touch there. Unless the intention is to draw the viewer's attention to a particular design element—and keep it there—you'll want to scatter the yellow shapes (or blocks) throughout the quilt. Sparkles of yellow sprinkled across the diagonal line of a quilt add excitement and motion. Scrap quilts especially seem to benefit from the addition of a few yellow patches. All kinds of special effects can be achieved if you use your imagination!

One final note: If you are still skeptical about using yellow, consider that yellow comes from a very large "family." You needn't plunge in with the brightest, purest, hottest yellow first time around. Try incorporating bits of pale lemon or soft buttercup for an ethereal glow, or warm mustards and old golds for a rich, vintage look. Before long, you'll be adding a splash of sunshine without a second thought!

Darra Duffy Williamson

COMPUTERS AND QUILTMAKING

The computer is quiltmaking's hottest new tool. It offers quilters exciting possibilities, not only for designing and embellishing quilts, but for learning about design, networking with other quilters, and teaching this new technology. Yet its potential is only beginning to be understood by the one in three quilters who have access to computers today.

To use a computer to design a quilt, you need design software. You can use either a general drawing software program, or software developed especially for

quilters (called "quilt design software"). General drawing programs offer flexibility, allowing you to draw anything you could draw by hand. Their drawback is their complexity. They require time to master and use. Designing a quilt with a drawing program usually means drawing every line in your design.

Quilt design software, on the other hand, automates many design steps for quilters. You can design a quilt without drawing a line—using the software's ready-made quilt blocks. There are several quilt design programs on the market. All let you draw with straight lines; some include curves for appliqué. Other extras may include fabric prints, quilting stencils, ready-made quilt layouts, multiple borders, yardage calculation, and printing of templates and paper-piecing patterns. For all this automation you trade flexibility. In general, quilt design software is better suited to block-style quilts or pieced central medallions than to large-scale pictorial or abstract designs.

Computers are also great embellishment tools. New computer-compatible Pfaff, Bernina, and Viking sewing machines can hook directly to your computer and embroider out images you design on-screen. These sewing machines are expensive, and often tricky to master, but offer marvelous possibilities.

With a color or black-and-white printer, you can print directly onto fabric or iron-on transfer paper. You would first draw or scan in a design, then color and manipulate it in a drawing or painting software program. This is a great way to make quilt labels or get photos onto fabric. The process you use depends on your fabric, your printer, and the permanence you require.

You can use a computer to help learn about quilt history and design. Using a new block encyclopedia program, you can search through 3,500 quilt blocks by name, read historical notes about each, then color the blocks and print them as patterns. The first CD-ROM multimedia tutorial for quilters is just coming on the market, surely to be followed by others.

TAKING THE TROUBLE OUT OF Buying Quilt Design Software

If you're considering buying quilt design software, ask yourself these three questions before you buy:

1. Am I a novice or a techie? If you're new to computers, then ease of use may be of prime importance. Software features are only useful if you can figure out how to use them. Ask fellow guild members or on-line quilters about a program's user friendliness. Borrow the user manual for the software, if possible, to judge its readability.

2. What are my priorities? Analyze your quilts; then make a wish list, prioritizing the tasks you'd like computer help with. You may not find one program satisfying every wish. But you'll know what features to ask for. Eventually you may find you want several programs, each for different tasks.

3. What kind of computer equipment do I have? Software has system requirements (this means the type of equipment required to successfully run the software). The older your computer, the more important it is to check system requirements. If you're buying a new computer and deciding between Macintosh and IBM-compatible, be aware you'll find more quilting and sewing software available for IBM-compatible models.

Software aside, the computer's greatest impact on quilters has been to link them together, worldwide, via on-line services. Thousands of quilters around the world "meet" in informal on-line "guilds" to share gossip and technical information and conduct block and fabric swaps without ever leaving home. Never before has the quilting world been able to share so much quilting information so instantly!

This fun and sometimes frustrating new technology is already offering something for every quilter, and new class possibilities for every teacher. Just imagine the future!

Penny McMorris

CORNER SQUARES

Corner squares are the separately cut "junction" pieces inserted at the corners of each block in a sashed quilt set. Corner squares serve a variety of purposes. They provide a visual break by introducing a contrasting color or fabric to the longer sashing, or lattice, strips that separate the blocks. They allow for more economical use of fabric by eliminating the need for sashing strips that run the entire length or width of the quilt. (Shorter, easy-to-handle sashing strips make construction of the quilt top more manageable, too!) As an added bonus, corner squares can form wonderful secondary designs over the surface of the quilt, especially when coupled with pieced sashing strips.

To cut corner squares, simply determine the *finished* width of the sashing strips you plan to use. Add ½ inch to this finished measurement. Using a rotary cutter and ruler, cut a strip of this width *crosswise* (selvage to selvage) from the fabric that you have chosen for the corner squares. Square up one end of the strip, and then cut the strip into segments,

using the width of the strip to determine the size of each segment. For example, if the strip measures 3½ inches wide, cut it into segments that also measure 3½ inches. The resulting segments will be perfectly square. Continue cutting strips and segments until you have cut the required number of corner squares for your specific quilt project.

When the quilt blocks are complete and all of the sashing strips and corner squares are cut to the appropriate sizes, you are ready to begin assembling the quilt

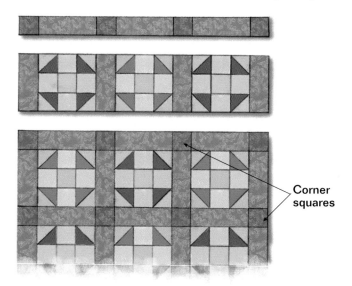

Corner squares

top. Use a design wall or other flat surface to arrange the blocks in the desired number of vertical and horizontal rows. Place the sashing strips so that each block is separated from its neighbor on every side. Insert a corner square in the empty space left at each junction.

Begin by sewing the sashing strips and blocks together to form horizontal rows, pressing the seam allowances away from the blocks. Sew the remaining sashing strips and corner squares together, also in hor-izontal rows. Press the seam allowances toward the corner squares.

Pin carefully to match the seams, then join the rows. Ease as necessary to ensure a perfect fit, and finish by pressing the seam allowances as desired.

See also "Lattice" on page 140 and "Settings" on page 220.

Darra Duffy Williamson

CRAZY PATCH

Perhaps the Centennial Exposition of 1876 in Philadelphia, Pennsylvania, ignited the crazy patch revolution. It was here that the Japanese introduced the concept of mixing fabrics such as silks and velvets together into a fan block and embellishing them with threads. Or maybe it was a home quilter who believed in the "waste-not, want-not" theory of quiltmaking and could not part with her stitching leftovers.

Whatever the case, the crazy patch revolution that broke out at the end of the nineteenth century and ran for some 20 years produced many visually exciting pieces that were more decorative than utilitarian in nature. Women from all walks of life utilized fabric remnants, laces, beads, and embroidery threads to stitch one-of-a-kind masterpieces. Pieces of a mother's wedding gown, a child's birthday dress, a boy's first pair of knickers, and any special occasion fabric rem-nants were lovingly stitched into tangible heirlooms holding memories to be recalled in the future.

Other women created crazy patches for the mere satisfaction of using scraps found through collecting, much like today's quilters who collect fat quarters. Manufacturers hastened to meet the crazy patchers' needs by supplying a variety of fabric collections con-sisting of 6-inch pieces of velvets and silks.

Crazy patching provides the perfect opportunity to use scraps, as it requires no set pattern of fabric place-ment. It is a random piecing of fabrics, encouraging the artists' spontaneity in choosing and placing fabrics.

A beautiful sparkling spider web in metallic threads can be the highlight of crazy patching and, according to Victorian legend, bring the stitcher good fortune!

Crazy Patch Planning

As you begin your project, first decide on a color group, for example, ecrus, whites, beiges, and tans. Separate fabrics into light, medium, and dark shades. Fabrics can be lush velvets, silks, moires, and satins or a mixture of cottons, collected pieces of old fabrics, handkerchiefs, and ribbons.

If you will be embellishing and embroidering after the piecing, decide on special embroidered pictures, initials, baby's hand prints, floral arrangements, stenciled designs, or printed photographs before piecing. Stencil or print any designs or photos on the fabric before piecing.

If you find something that you would like to add later, you can appliqué it onto the finished patchwork as shapes such as hearts or hands with dates and initials of special events. Other last-minute additions can include fans and umbrellas that sport a beautiful ivory button collection or a newly discovered thread that shimmers and shines.

Foundations

There are three foundations used for crazy patching.

1. Muslin-based piecing. Use this for the construction of unquilted blocks and clothing, especially when fabrics such as woolens, velvets, and heavy brocades are used. It lends support to all fabrics, creating an even surface for stitch embellishments.

2. Fleece-based piecing. Fleece is a thin, dense, polyester quilt batting. Use this for crazy patch novelty items such as Christmas stockings, heart-shaped pillows, and teddy bears. It gives a soft touch to the finished product and is an excellent way to hide carry-over threads on the back of a pastel or lightweight fabric article. Fleece also eliminates stretching of pieces, facilitating easier construction.

3. Freezer paper piecing. This method is used primarily when the crazy patch project will be quilted and not embellished. Creating the crazy patch directly on the shiny side of the freezer paper and pressing as you piece stabilizes any bias edges. This allows the crazy patched piece to be used when making quilt blocks, lattice, borders, or articles of clothing. The freezer paper prohibits distortion during construction and eliminates bulk in the finished project. Once piecing is complete and all the edges are secured, the freezer paper is removed by gently tearing it away. Then the crazy patch project, batting, and backing are basted together and quilted as in any traditional pieced quilt.

Crazy Patch Piecing Techniques

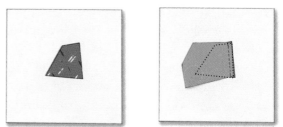

Step 1. Place a three- to six-sided piece of fabric in the center of the foundation block. With right sides together, attach the next piece of fabric along one edge, using a ¼-inch seam allowance. Press flat.

Step 2. Continue piecing clockwise around the center fabric until the block is completely covered. Be sure to maintain

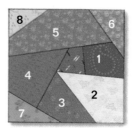

¼-inch seam allowances. This keeps fabric from showing through and can guide the embroidery needle when embellishing. You may need to clip a few stitches to release the fabric for trimming if you have crossed over a previously sewn seam.

Step 3. This is where you can "fix things." If there are any raw edges, pieces of fabrics you don't like, or spaces that are too large, there are remedies. Pieced or unpieced shapes such as hearts, hands, and fan shapes can be appliquéd to these areas to complement the crazy patching.

Appliquéd heart covers raw edges

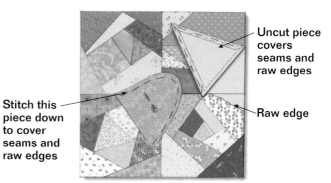

Uncut piece covers seams and raw edges

Stitch this piece down to cover seams and raw edges

Raw edge

Step 4. As crazy patch blocks are pieced, leave some of the fabric along the block edges uncut so that when the foundation of each block is sewn together, the seam formed can be covered by the uncut pieces, thus making the seam less visible.

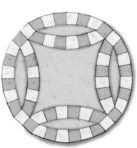

Step 5. Embellishment begins here! Tie-down bows, embroidered flowers, initials, dates, laces, buttons, trims of all kinds, and of course, spider webs, can be added.

Battenburg lace, embroidered doilies (collected or made by the stitcher), flat cotton or nylon lace, folded ribbon points, or appliquéd dimensional silk flowers tied with bows are just a few of the decorations that can enhance the crazy-patched piece.

Embellishing the seams adds the finishing touches that pull the project together and can be quite simple (using just one favorite embroidery stitch throughout) or can become well-orchestrated thread, ribbon, bead, and button frenzies, depending on the time and talent you want to devote to the project. See also "Decorative Stitches" on page 87 and "Embellishment" on page 95.

Karen Phillips

Embellishments

Once the crazy patching is finished, the fun of embellishing the surface with stitchery can begin!

CURVED PIECING

The Drunkard's Path, Double Wedding Ring, Clamshell, and Apple Core are the most recognized blocks requiring curved piecing. Although often perceived to be difficult, the piecing is similar to attaching a collar or sleeve in dressmaking, and can be done either by machine or hand.

Cutting the Shapes

Templates for most curved designs are available for either scissors or rotary cutting. When using scissors, remember to hold the scissors in one place and turn the fabric, cutting around the curve, not into it.

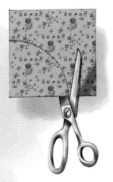

DRUNKARD'S PATH BLOCK

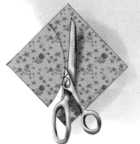

DOUBLE WEDDING RING

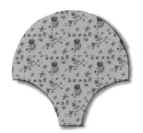

CLAMSHELL

APPLE CORE

Try This A small rotary cutter works best for cutting curves. It's a good idea to use a separate cutting mat for curved cutting. Most cutting mats have ruts from straight cutting, and it is bumpy and less accurate to cut across them. Instead of buying a second mat just for curves, try the reverse side of the mat you normally use.

For the Drunkard's Path, I prefer Easy Curve templates. They allow cutting around the curve, never into the template. Cutting around the template is easier on the wrist, and the rotary-cutting blade does not hit the template. The Easy Curve template set has three quarter-circle pieces that are ¼ inch apart in size. Use the smallest template with a square of fabric ½ inch larger than the finished patch size, cutting the corner out of the square. Use the square for the patch, not the quarter circle. The largest of the three templates is used with a rectangle of fabric, cutting opposite corners to give two pieces. The middle template is used to mark the sewing line on either piece. (See the Resource Guide on page 274 for a source of Easy Curve templates.)

EASY CURVE TEMPLATES

Use this piece

Cut the background square

Cut the quarter circles

Mark the sewing lines

The leftover fabric under the smallest template can be used in a smaller patch or made into a square, rectangle, or triangle to be used in a border or another quilt.

Template sets that include the concave and convex pieces are fine to use if you already own them. It's easiest to cut strips into squares for the concave piece and to cut rectangles for the wedge or convex shapes. You can also make your own templates for the Drunkard's Path. See "Drafting Curves" on page 93 and "Templates" on page 238.

Try This Here are some hints to help you remember terms. Concave—the curve "caves" in. Convex—the curve is out.

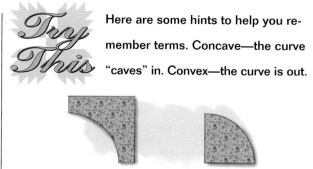

CONCAVE   CONVEX

Pinning and Sewing

It is your choice to pin or not. When pinning, fold the pieces in half and finger press to find the center. If you fold one piece with right sides together and the other piece with wrong sides together, you will find they nest into each other easier. Pin in the center.

Note: I use silk pins, which are thin and long. Pin through twice. I sew over the pins, although some sewing machine companies do not recommend this.

Another way to pin is to place the quarter circle on the concave background, lining up the curved edges and making sure the points are aligned. Keeping the fabric on the table, pin the center. Turn the piece over so the quarter circle is on the bottom.

Holding it in your hand, pin the edge, then pin between that pin and the center pin. Repeat on the other half. Clipping the seams is usually not required because of the bias edge.

Most Drunkard's Path blocks are four patch construction, with the top half rotated 180 degrees to make the bottom half. I prefer to work in strips across the quilt instead of making individual blocks. This way I can press seams in the first row in one direction, and alternate the pressing direction with each subsequent row.

When you have a few spare moments, match up and pin the center of two pieces. Put the pairs of patches into a basket that's handy when you're watching television, talking on the phone, or waiting in a doctor's office. Complete the pinning, and drop the pinned patches back into the basket. Chain sew the pieces whenever you have a few minutes to spend at your sewing machine. Pinning and sewing can be done in small increments of time. We often look at the clock and say, "I don't have an hour, I can't get any sewing done," instead of saying, "I have five minutes; what can I do?"

Before sewing, make certain that you have an accurate ¼-inch seam. This is important to prevent distortion of the final pieced square.

Step 1. Sew with the quarter circle (the flat piece, now that it has been pinned) on the bottom. Use your fingertip to smooth the fabric before it goes under the needle, and apply a small amount of pressure to straighten the seam. Small puckers can be smoothed, but pleats do require the frog stitch—rippit, rippit, rippit!

¼" seam

Step 2. Press gently on the right side to prevent small pleats. Press the seams in either direction, usually toward the darker fabric. The curve is on the bias, so be careful not to stretch it as you press.

SKILL BUILDER

Creating Your Own Drunkard's Path Variation

For an easy, dynamic variation to a traditional Drunkard's Path block, alter the proportions in the patch. This can be accomplished by using the same size templates as in a regular patch and making the starting square smaller. In this variation, press all seams toward the quarter circle. Be sure that your seam allowances are accurate; it will be evident in the finished block if they are not.

Create new designs by alternating two blocks.

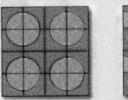

Betty Kiser

CUTTING MATS

A cutting mat is essential when using a rotary cutter, both to avoid dulling the blade and to protect the surface on which you are cutting. There are several brands of mats on the market, made of three different materials. Most can be used on both sides.

Soft Plastic Mats

The least expensive mats are made of white translucent soft plastic, usually with one smooth side and one textured side. These mats can be used with a light table for drafting, and are the only ones that can be rolled. They do take time to flatten after rolling, but weighting the surface will speed the process. Pins can be stuck into this plastic to hold difficult-to-handle fabric.

Because the plastic is soft, a rotary cutter will leave marks on the surface, which may affect cutting accuracy when making small cuts for miniature quilts or when trimming blocks. Use an emery board or very fine sandpaper to smooth cuts in the mat.

Hard Plastic Mats

Mats made of a single layer of hard plastic are thinner than the soft plastic mats, and are not as easily scuffed. The June Taylor brand mats are not supposed to warp, crack, or peel. Some generic mats, usually made of green plastic, will.

Mat Care

- Store your mat flat and away from heat. Heat will cause permanent warping. If the mat cannot be left on the cutting surface, hang it or store it flat under a bed or chest.
- Do not set anything hot on your mat.
- Wash when necessary with lukewarm soapy water.

Three-Layer Mats

The most expensive mats are made of three layers, with a softer layer in the center. Several have contrasting colors on each side of the mat. Choose sides based on the color of fabric that you are cutting. These mats, made by Omnigrid and Olfa, are self-healing, so cuts do not remain on the surface, ensuring accuracy in cutting. They are long-lasting if the mats are kept flat and not exposed to heat.

Mat Features

Mats are available in sizes from 5 × 7 inches to 48 × 96 inches. Most have a 1-inch grid on one surface of the mat, with ¼-inch markings along the outside. Some mats have centimeter markings on two edges, and all-metric grids are available. The gridded mats include a 45 degree angle; some also have a 60 degree angle.

Although the grids are generally accurate, they are more useful for squaring up fabric or quilt blocks than for measuring cuts. The grids are printed on the plastic and will wear away with use. In addition to a grid, some mats have template shapes printed on them. Some quilters find these useful; others find them distracting.

See also "Rotary Cutters" on page 196 and "Rotary Cutting" on page 197.

Dixie Haywood

DARNING FOOT

The darning foot was originally designed to mend small holes or tears in fabrics. In quiltmaking, it is used for free-motion machine quilting.

Because of its unique purpose, the foot has a very distinctive look. There are as many shapes of darning feet as there are brands of machines. The foot can be made of metal or plastic, and it may have an arm or extension that interacts with the needle clamp. The base of the foot is usually a small oval or square.

No matter how they are shaped, all darning feet work according to the same principle. The foot is designed to allow free movement of the fabric as you stitch. The feed dogs are lowered or covered and the foot only rests on the fabric when the needle is lowered. As the needle approaches its highest point, the foot lifts off the quilt, allowing you to stitch in any direction. The stitch size and placement are determined by your quilting skill. You are moving the fabric and controlling the length and direction of the stitches.

There are a number of variations to the basic foot that have been developed to adapt the foot to quilting. One is an open darning foot. A small portion of the metal foot has been removed for better visibility. It changes the foot from a closed circle to a C shape. Another variation is the Big Foot, a generic foot that has a large clear plastic base to hold the layers of the quilt flat and to help you see where you are stitching.

If your sewing machine does not have a darning foot, you may want to try a Big Foot. I prefer the open-toe darning foot, but many of my beginner students do like the Big Foot.

See "Free-Motion Quilting" on page 154.

Debra Wagner

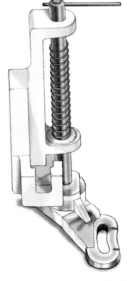

GENERIC DARNING FOOT

OPEN-TOE BERNINA DARNING FOOT

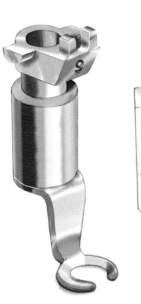

BIG FOOT DARNING FOOT

DECORATIVE STITCHES

Decorative stitches are usually associated with the Victorian style of crazy quilting. Contemporary quilt-makers, though, can use the stitches as embellishment for any type of quilt. Use them for a touch of dimension or color on the front, or use embroidery stitches to add flair to a quilt label. Do any stitching before layering and basting your quilt.

The stitches included here are some of the most widely used. They can be done in pearl and cotton flosses, metallic threads, rayon and silk ribbons and threads. Let your creativity loose!

Chain Stitch

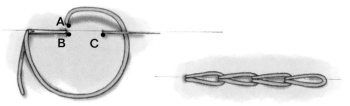

Bring the thread up at A. Insert the needle at B, which is one thread away from A, and bring the needle up at C over the loop. Gently pull the thread through. Insert the needle down one thread from C and continue to finish.

Blanket Stitch

With the edge of fabric to the left, bring thread up at A. Take the needle down at B and up at C, over the loop formed. Work the stitch toward yourself.

Detached Woven Chain Stitch

Lay chain stitches leaving a small space in between. Weave the second thread as shown.

Buttonhole Stitch

Bring the thread up at A. Take the needle down at B and up at C, pulling thread through the loop toward D to make a raised edge. If you are stitching over the raw edge of an appliqué, keep the edge to the right.

Feather Stitch

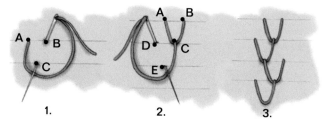

1.   2.   3.

Bring the thread up at A. Insert the needle at B and up at C over the loop. Insert the needle at D, and bring it up at E over the loop. Continue to finish.

 *Try This* Draw pencil lines lightly on fabric as guides to practice the stitches first. Quilter's ¼-inch masking tape is handy to mark straight lines on your actual project.

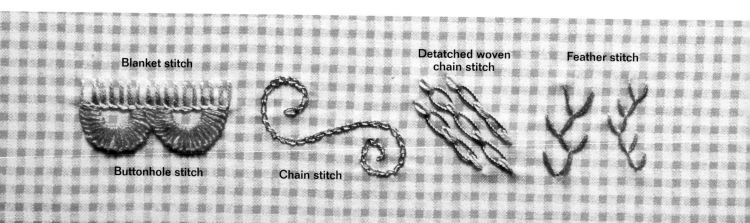

Blanket stitch

Detached woven chain stitch

Feather stitch

Buttonhole stitch

Chain stitch

Fly Stitch

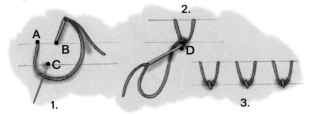

Bring the thread up at A. Insert the needle at B, and bring it up at C over the loop. Insert the needle at D. Bring the needle up a thread away from B to start the next stitch for a continuous row, or bring the needle up wherever you want to begin a new stitch.

French Knot

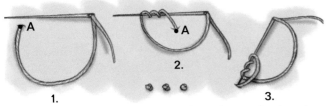

Bring the thread up at A. With the left hand, wrap the thread around the needle three times. Insert the tip of the needle just behind the thread at A. Pull the needle down through the fabric.

Herringbone Stitch

Bring the thread up at A. Insert the needle at B, and bring it up at C, pulling through. Insert the needle at D, and bring it up at E. Repeat to finish.

Couched Herringbone Stitch

Stitch the herringbone stitch. With a separate thread, couch at the cross (a small stitch to hold the cross in place).

Outline Stitch

Bring the thread up at A. Insert the needle down at B, which is ⅛ inch away from A. Bring the needle up at C, down at D, and up at B. Repeat to finish.

Satin Stitch

For a circle, bring the thread up at A. Insert the needle down at B, pulling through. Bring the thread up at C. Insert the needle down at D. Continue to the top of the circle. Bring thread up at E. Insert the needle down at F. Continue to fill the circle.

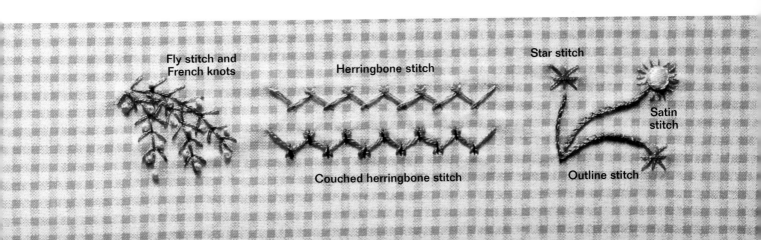

Fly stitch and French knots

Herringbone stitch

Couched herringbone stitch

Star stitch

Satin stitch

Outline stitch

Spider Web

This is the "good luck charm" for Victorian crazy patch.

Place the rays of the web using the outline stitch. Stitch curved webbing using the chain stitch. Place the spider's drop thread using a running stitch. Use two beads for the spider and two straight stitches for each leg.

Star Stitch

Make one cross stitch by bringing the thread up at A. Take the needle in at B and up C. Take the needle in at D. Cross with a second cross stitch. You can vary the lengths of the stitches for different effects.

See also "Crazy Patch" on page 79 and "Embellishment" on page 95.

Karen Phillips

DESIGN WALL

A design wall is a wonderful addition to any sewing room. It allows you to preview all of your quiltmaking steps, from fabric selection to the layout of finished blocks.

To make a simple design area, pin or tack a large area of flannel, low-loft batting, or felt to a flat wall. Most fabric patches will stick readily to these materials. Special flannel, printed with grid lines, is nice—it can help to keep pieces properly aligned as they are positioned. (See the Resource Guide on page 274.)

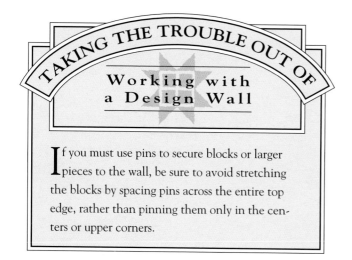

TAKING THE TROUBLE OUT OF

Working with a Design Wall

If you must use pins to secure blocks or larger pieces to the wall, be sure to avoid stretching the blocks by spacing pins across the entire top edge, rather than pinning them only in the centers or upper corners.

Audition individual fabrics side by side on your design wall to help determine how they will look in the finished quilt. Move them around, or add and subtract fabrics until the combination is pleasing to you. Cut out the pieces for a block and arrange them on the wall. Is the combination what you envisioned? If not, now is the time to make changes.

A design wall is a valuable tool for assembling scrappy quilts. Since we often cut all pieces randomly before the layout process begins, the wall gives you an overall view of the quilt as you shuffle the shapes around to create that perfect layout.

It's also handy to sort fabrics into like color values, an important aspect of many quilts, especially those that resemble watercolor paintings. Pin fabrics side by side and step back. Do they all blend together? Remove those that do not.

Even if your quilt is sewn in a limited color scheme, a design wall will help you keep track of where you are in the assembly process. I find it lifts my spirits to have visual proof that something has really been accomplished. Seeing all of the elements coming together after many hours of cutting and sewing always motivates me to continue the project.

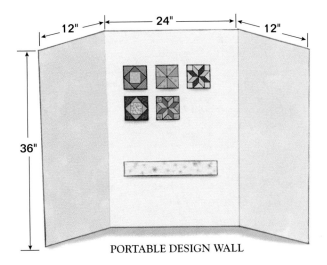

PORTABLE DESIGN WALL

For small, portable projects, you can purchase a 48 × 36-inch tri-fold cardboard panel from an office supply store—students often use these to display school projects. Fold flannel snugly around the board and secure it on the back with duct tape or electrical tape. Its table-size dimensions make the board a useful accessory for a quilt class or at home. It can stand on a table for small projects or lean flat against the wall. You can also attach it to a wall with Velcro. The two narrow sides of the panel fold inward to cover the center section, helping to keep your pieces from shifting around during transportation or storage.

Janet Wickell

Make An Instant Design Wall

by Liz Porter and Marianne Fons

Here's another option for an inexpensive and portable design wall that is great to use at home or take to workshops. Purchase flannel-backed vinyl by the yard at a variety or fabric store, or buy a picnic tablecloth at a discount store. Pay attention to the flannel side of the material—look for a nice fuzzy flannel on the back side. Don't get caught in the trap of being too discriminating about how the printed side looks!

Place the vinyl side of the material against the wall with the flannel side facing you. Use a generous amount of masking tape to secure the material to the wall. If you do not tape the material adequately, you run the risk of having it fall off the wall as you add your fabric pieces.

To help you position squares and patches in straight lines, use a permanent marking pen (such as a Sharpie) and a yardstick to draw a grid on the flannel side. If the plastic side of the material you purchased is printed in a geometric design such as a plaid or checks, you may be able to see the design faintly through the flannel and to use these lines as guidelines for placement.

If it becomes necessary to take the design down off the wall, you can usually transport it successfully without pinning all the pieces in place. Have a friend help you turn up about 6 inches of the material along the bottom edge. Continue to turn up the material so you always have plastic against your fabric pieces. The fabric will not adhere to the plastic and will tend to stay in place against the flannel. When you have

folded all the way to the top edge, loosen the masking tape and remove the folded piece from the wall. Fold the outside edges to the middle and fold again to make a small packet. To rehang your portable design wall, unfold the packet to its full width. Have someone help you hold the folded piece against the wall, securely tape the top edge in place, and carefully unfold the length of your project.

INSTANT DESIGN WALL

DRAFTING

Don't let the word *drafting* intimidate you! Even if the mere word at the top of the page makes your eyes glaze over and your fingers poised to flip on through the book, you should realize that it's not hard. Before the myriad of patterns and books that are now available, quilters nearly always drafted their own patterns. Accurate piecing depended upon a carefully drawn, full-size draft of the design. From such a drawing, templates were made for hand or machine piecing.

If you are designing your own original blocks, you must draft. You can also resize any block to suit your needs, or get accurate dimensions for rotary cutting any block. Drafting allows you to get inside a block design and truly know it. Because you have drawn it, you know how the pieces must fit together, and that helps you sew the pieces in the proper order. Because the designs are drawn in full, finished sizes, you can also make scale judgments on the size of the pieces. Are they too big or too small? Is this the proper scale for the quilt you want to make?

Easily half of all patchwork designs are based on grids of squares and subdivisions of squares. A grid is simply a set of small squares that make up a larger square. Each smaller square can be subdivided into smaller shapes to make a design. These block designs lend themselves nicely to the graph paper approach to drafting.

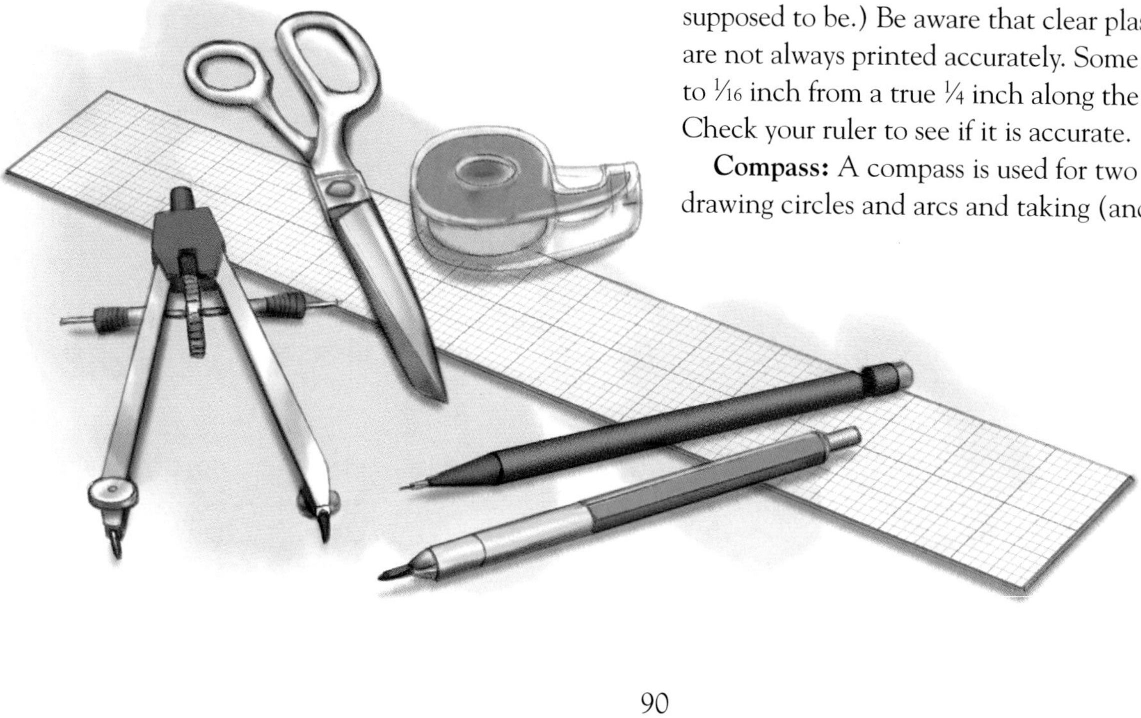

The Basics

Graph Paper: Use the most accurate graph paper you can find. Usually stores that sell art or drafting and engineering supplies will have a good variety. The large sheets (17 × 22 inches) come in several grids: ¼ inch, ⅕ inch, ⅙ inch, ⅛ inch, and ⅒ inch. If you can, buy the kind with the heavier lines at 1-inch increments—it is easier to work with, especially if you wear bifocals. Expect to pay from 25 to 85 cents per sheet. Some papers will be accurate in one direction but not the other, so check dimensions with your ruler. Smaller sheets and tablets are handy for drafting blocks 8 inches and smaller and for quilt design and planning.

Pencils: A fine-tipped mechanical drawing pencil is ideal for drafting, but an ordinary number 2 pencil and a good sharpener will do just fine. Keep your pencil sharp. Lines drawn with a dull pencil have extra width and will make your drafts inaccurate. Colored pencils are handy for identifying which shapes need to be cut.

Rulers: The drawing ruler (C-thru B-85) used for drafting full-size designs and making templates is thin, has a red grid of ⅛-inch squares, and measures 2 × 18 inches. (It is best not to use a rotary-cutting ruler for drafting; these are usually ⅛ inch thick and tend to cast a shadow on the paper just where the pencil line is supposed to be.) Be aware that clear plastic grid rulers are not always printed accurately. Some rulers vary up to ¹⁄₁₆ inch from a true ¼ inch along the long sides. Check your ruler to see if it is accurate.

Compass: A compass is used for two things—drawing circles and arcs and taking (and

90

keeping) measurements. The dime-store variety is not good enough; it slips. A bow compass with a 6½-inch radius and a roller stop to hold a setting is sufficient for most operations encountered while drafting patchwork patterns.

Scissors: You will need scissors for cutting paper.

Removable Tape: Most stationery stores and art supply stores carry this great product. Use removable tape to hold paper in place while you work. It is especially useful for tracing. This kind of tape will not harm the paper underneath when the tape is removed.

DECIMAL EQUIVALENTS					
0.1	=	$\frac{1}{10}$	0.6	=	$\frac{3}{5}$
0.125	=	$\frac{1}{8}$	0.625	=	$\frac{5}{8}$
0.166	=	$\frac{1}{6}$	0.666	=	$\frac{2}{3}$
0.2	=	$\frac{1}{5}$	0.7	=	$\frac{7}{10}$
0.25	=	$\frac{1}{4}$	0.75	=	$\frac{3}{4}$
0.3	=	$\frac{3}{10}$	0.8	=	$\frac{4}{5}$
0.333	=	$\frac{1}{3}$	0.833	=	$\frac{5}{6}$
0.375	=	$\frac{3}{8}$	0.875	=	$\frac{7}{8}$
0.4	=	$\frac{2}{5}$	0.9	=	$\frac{9}{10}$
0.5	=	$\frac{1}{2}$			

Basics of Drafting

To begin, study the design and determine the type of grid needed. How many squares are in the larger square—9, 16, 25, or some other number? A Nine Patch design has three divisions on each side of the square; a 16-patch design has four divisions on each side of the square, and so on.

Decide on a finished size for the design block. Divide the side of the square by the number of divisions on each side to determine the size of the grid squares and the type of graph paper to use. For example, if you want a 9-inch block, and the design has nine grid squares with three divisions per side: divide 9 inches by three and the result is 3-inch grid squares. Sometimes the resulting number will be a whole number plus a fraction. The fraction will tell you what kind of graph paper to use. For instance, if your grid square measures 1¼ inches, use graph paper with four squares to the inch; if it measures 1⅖ inches, use graph paper with five squares to the inch. Use six squares to the inch for measurements that end in thirds or sixths; use eight squares to the inch for measurements in eighths, fourths, halves, and so on. If you use a calculator for this simple math, your answers will be in decimals. Use the decimal equivalent chart provided here to translate the decimals to fractions.

To draft a patchwork design based on a grid, follow these steps. The Whirligig block is used as an example.

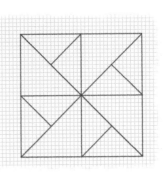

WHIRLIGIG

Step 1. Draw a square the finished size of the design on the proper graph paper.

Step 2. Draw the grid squares inside the larger square.

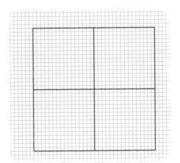

Step 3. Subdivide the grid squares to create the design. Note that not every line in the draft will be a seam line. Some lines need to be dropped out to simplify piecing.

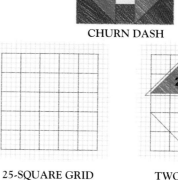

Step 4. Identify those shapes that need to be templates and color them with colored pencils. Add the ¼-inch seam allowances around each shape to bring them out to cutting size.

Step 5. Make traditional templates or use this drafting as a guide for rotary cutting dimensions.

Here are examples of blocks based on other grids.

CHURN DASH

25-SQUARE GRID   TWO TEMPLATES

QUAIL'S NEST

NINE-SQUARE GRID   THREE TEMPLATES

Drafting the LeMoyne Star

The LeMoyne Star is one of the most basic patterns in patchwork. It is based not on equal grid squares, but on equal triangles that radiate from the center of the square.

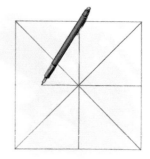

LEMOYNE STAR

The eight star points are equidistant. It can be drafted on graph paper or plain unlined paper. The following directions apply to any size square.

Step 1. Draw a square of any size on a sheet of paper. Graph paper lines can sometimes be distracting because the grid lines will not always line up with the lines on the graph paper. You can draw a square on graph paper first and then trace it onto an unlined sheet.

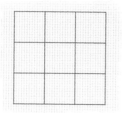

VARIABLE STAR

16-SQUARE GRID   FOUR TEMPLATES

Step 2. Draw two diagonal lines to find the center of the square. Then draw two more lines vertically and horizontally to divide the square into eight triangles.

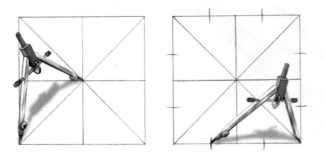

Step 3. With a compass, take a setting diagonally from the center of the square to one of its corners. Keeping this setting, move the point of the compass consecutively to each corner of the square, making two marks from each corner on each side of the square. These points will be the points of the star.

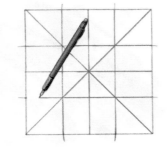

Step 4. Draw four lines, joining the eight points across the square.

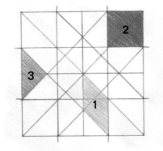

Step 5. Draw four more lines, joining the points diagonally across the square. Identify the diamond, square, and triangle that will be templates and color them in.

Step 6. Add the ¼-inch seam allowances around each shape to bring them out to cutting size.

Step 7. Make traditional templates or use this draft as a guide for rotary cutting dimensions.

Drafting with Curves

A popular traditional pattern, the Drunkard's Path is based on squares with curved elements added. It has only two templates and they are drafted as follows. A number of different blocks can be made from the basic unit.

Step 1. On ¼-inch graph paper, draw two 3-inch squares 1 inch apart.

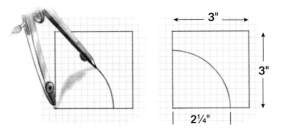

Step 2. With a compass setting of 2¼ inches (an arbitrary number—you can use whatever you think is attractive), draw identical quarter-circles in each 3-inch square.

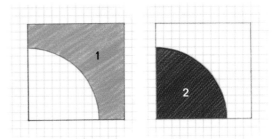

Step 3. In each square, color in the shape that will be a template, and number it.

Step 4. To add the ¼-inch seam allowance to the curve of Template 1, reduce the original compass setting (2¼ inches for this example) by ¼ inch. Draw

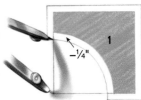

a second quarter-circle inside the first. Add ¼-inch seam allowances to the remaining four sides with a ruler.

Step 5. To add the ¼-inch seam allowance to Template 2, increase the original compass setting by ¼ inch and draw a second quarter-circle outside of the first. Add seam allowances to the remaining two sides with a ruler.

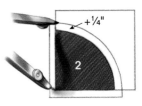

See "Templates" on page 238 for instructions on making templates.

TAKING THE TROUBLE OUT OF
Drawing a Grid without Graph Paper

If you are unable to find graph paper with the right grid, proportional drawing is another way to draw a gridded square in any desired size. The example here is a 4-inch square divided into a nine-square grid. When 4 inches is divided by three, the result is 1⅓ inches. This could easily be drawn on graph paper with six squares to the inch, but if that paper is unavailable, here is what to do.

Step 1. Draw a 4-inch square on a sheet of paper. Graph paper lines can sometimes be distracting in this operation because the grid lines will not line up with the lines on the graph paper. Draw a square on graph paper first and then trace it onto an unlined sheet.

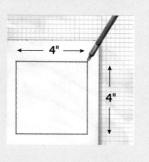

Step 2. Select a measurement on your ruler that is longer than the side of the square (4 inches), shorter than the diagonal (about 5⅝ inches), and easily divisible by the number of divisions desired (in this case, three). In this situation, 4½ inches is a good number. So divide 4½ inches by three to equal 1½-inch intervals.

Step 3. Hold the point of your pencil on the exact corner in the lower left of the square. Place the 0-inch or end of the ruler against the pencil point and pivot the ruler until the mark for your chosen number (4½ inches) on the ruler touches the right side of the

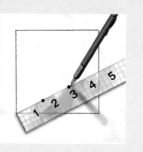

square. Make a fine dot at the calculated interval (every 1½ inches—that is, at the 1½- and 3-inch marks on the ruler).

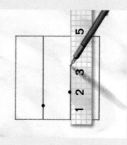

Step 4. Use a gridded ruler or right angle to draw a vertical line through each dot. Make sure each line is perpendicular to the top and bottom and is absolutely parallel to the sides. These lines divide the square into three equal sections.

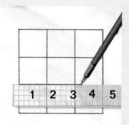

Step 5. To make the horizontal divisions, place the ruler with the 0-inch at the same lower left corner, but this time pivot until the mark indicating your chosen number (4½ inches) touches the top of the square. Again, make dots at the calculated interval (1½ inches) and use a ruler or right-angle tool to draw horizontal lines to complete the grid.

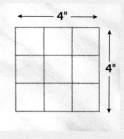

You can use this grid to draw triangles or other shapes needed for your design. For each size and shape of patch, add ¼-inch seam allowances. Make traditional templates or use the draft for rotary cutting dimensions.

EMBELLISHMENT

The Chinese began embellishing textiles as early as 3000 B.C., but ancient Egyptians, Babylonians, Assyrians, and Persians were the first needle artists to employ lavish embellishment. Later, in Europe during the sixteenth and seventeenth centuries, few articles of clothing escaped the embroiderer's needle. Elaborate needlework also covered chair cushions, screens, fabric-covered boxes, draperies, and bed curtains.

In America, quiltmakers embraced a variety of materials and techniques to adorn their quilts and became especially noted for extravagant embellishment during the Victorian Era.

Today's quiltmakers may attach charms, beads, buttons, lace, decorative threads, cords, ribbons, and braids, as well as all sorts of "found" objects, such as bark, feathers, paper, plastic, and jewelry to quilts. They may be sewn, embroidered, painted, glued, fused, or stamped. Embellishment may be subtle or extravagant. The objects may have sentimental meanings or symbolic messages, but the most effective embellishments enhance, rather than cover, what exists on the surface of the quilt.

before layering and basting. Bulky items such as dangling tassels and fringe are easier to apply after the quilt is assembled.

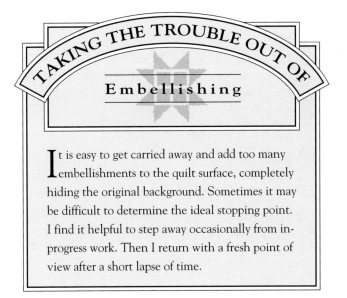

TAKING THE TROUBLE OUT OF Embellishing

It is easy to get carried away and add too many embellishments to the quilt surface, completely hiding the original background. Sometimes it may be difficult to determine the ideal stopping point. I find it helpful to step away occasionally from in-progress work. Then I return with a fresh point of view after a short lapse of time.

Planning for Embellishments

Consider the embellishments for a quilt during the planning and design stage. Some may need to go on the quilt top before it is layered with the batting and backing, while others are better added after the quilt is completed. Paint is easy to dab on a completed quilt as an afterthought, but embroidery should be added

Inspiration

Embellishments should emphasize the original inspiration for the quilt—the fabric print, the weave or texture of the quilt top, a pieced pattern, or an appliqué design. Fabric prints themselves provide a wealth of ideas to embellish cloth for quiltmaking.

My favorite fabrics are geometric, animal, and tropical prints. I like to study the printed design to decide how to embellish the fabric. A checked fabric might look sensational by couching along the linear outline with metallic yarn, and a tropical flower print would appear vibrant and realistic by filling in the leaves and petals with machine embroidery. The print itself will suggest ideas for embellishment, so examine your fabric for inspiration. Take a trip to a quilt shop, fabric store, or quilt show and you will come away with many ideas to add touches of embellishment to an interesting cotton print.

The dynamic geometric pattern of this print seems to be pulsating because of the free-motion embroidery that emphasizes the printed design. The gold metallic couching sets apart the embroidered disc as a focal point, and beading and machine quilting with decorative threads create a feeling of movement.

Machine Embroidery

Machine embroidery is accomplished by dropping the feed dogs of the sewing machine and moving the fabric beneath the machine needle to "thread sketch" designs using decorative threads. A design may be outlined and accentuated with linear patterns, or for a more painterly effect, fill in areas with built-up stitches. Here are the general guidelines:

- Use a Schmetz embroidery needle for rayon threads and a Metafil needle for metallic threads.

- Fill the bobbin with a lightweight polyester thread, such as Madeira Bobbinfil or Sulky Bobbin Thread.
- Lower the feed dogs, or use your cover plate.
- Lower the top tension slightly.
- Remove the sewing foot. A darning foot is optional.
- Stretch your fabric as tight as a drum in a wooden machine embroidery hoop.
- Bring the bobbin thread up to the top by taking one stitch with the needle and drawing up the thread.
- Practice moving the hoop beneath the needle to doodle. Do not pivot, but slide the hoop in all directions. You can use either a straight stitch or a zigzag stitch. Change thread colors often to mix colors next to each other.

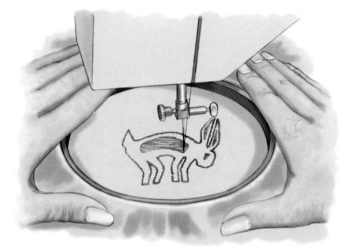

Machine embroidery is easy! With a little practice, you will be filling in shapes and embellishing designs on your cotton prints. It's a beautiful and fast way to add texture to fabric.

Couching

Applying beautiful cords, yarns, and braids to the background fabric by couching with my sewing machine is one of my favorite forms of embellishment. Couching is best suited for linear designs without sharp points or tight curves.

Machine embroidery and couching are
the techniques used to accentuate the swirling
design of this cotton print. A combination of metallic and
rayon threads were selected to match the colors of the print,
creating a beautiful mix of textures.

Machine couching is accomplished by using the
zigzag setting to stitch over a pretty cord that is placed
beneath the sewing foot. Use either a transparent
nylon thread or a decorative machine embroidery
thread in the needle to stitch over the cord. If you
want only the decorative yarn to show, use nylon
thread—clear for light-color yarns, and the smoke
color over dark yarns. I like to contrast thread textures
and colors. To couch over gold metallic cord, I will use
red silk thread, and to stitch over black silk ribbon, I
might choose a bright variegated rayon thread.

Set up your machine for couching and give it a try!

- Fill the bobbin with lightweight polyester thread.
  Thread your machine with your chosen decorative
  or invisible thread.

- Use an all-purpose sewing foot, or a single-groove
  cording foot.

- Adjust the zigzag stitch width setting to just clear
  the yarn you have chosen.

- Lower the top tension slightly, and set your machine's stitch length to normal.

Step 1. Pull about 6 inches of the couching cord behind the
presser foot to leave a tail. Lower the presser bar, with the
foot centered over the yarn. Lock the start by taking one complete zigzag forward, then reverse for one stitch, and continue
forward again. Keep the yarn centered beneath the foot.

Step 2. Stitch forward, keeping the foot centered over the
yarn. As you stitch along the couching path, the foot will keep
the yarn in position.

Step 3. When you reach the end of your line of stitching, cut
the yarn, leaving a tail about 6 inches long.

Step 4. Thread the tail end of the yarn through a crewel embroidery needle, and pull it to the wrong side of the fabric. Tie
it together with the bobbin thread. Repeat this at the start of
the stitching line.

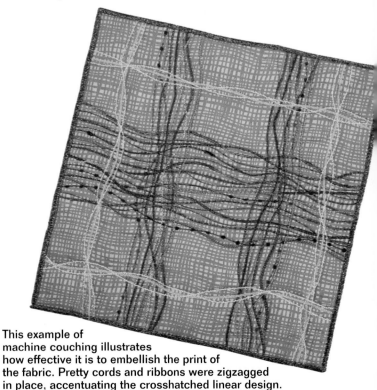

This example of
machine couching illustrates
how effective it is to embellish the print of
the fabric. Pretty cords and ribbons were zigzagged
in place, accentuating the crosshatched linear design.

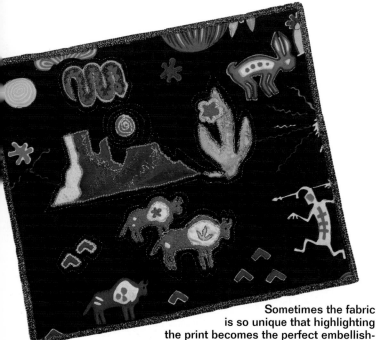

Sometimes the fabric is so unique that highlighting the print becomes the perfect embellishment. These whimsical folk art figures are touched with dashes of fabric paint then simply filled in with free-motion straight stitches using metallic, silk, and rayon threads.

Bobbin-Drawing

Bobbin-drawing is a technique in which a heavy, decorative thread, such as ribbon floss or metallic yarn, is wound on the bobbin and stitched with the right side of the print facing down. Bobbin-drawing may be stitched with the feed dogs up using the all-purpose presser foot, or it may be stitched free-motion with the feed dogs dropped. Use free-motion bobbin drawing when you have tiny curves or sharp maneuvers.

The same type of heavier weight yarns and cords used for couching may be used for bobbin-drawing, as long as the yarn is smooth enough to feed evenly from the bobbin case. It is not necessary to wind the bobbin by hand; however, the yarn will be too heavy to thread through the normal bobbin-winding tensions. Loosen the flywheel, set the empty bobbin on the winding pin, and place the spool of yarn in a cup to allow it to feed freely. To provide manual tension, pinch the yarn between your thumb and forefinger as you press the foot pedal to wind the bobbin.

Because these yarns are much thicker than regular-weight sewing thread, loosen the bobbin tension to allow the yarn to feed freely. It is easier to adjust the bobbin tensions of sewing machines that have

removable bobbin cases than those that have a drop-in bobbin case. Check your sewing machine manual for the correct way to adjust the bobbin tension; loosen the tension until the yarn pulls easily from the bobbin case.

Jazzy Techniques

Jackets and other wearable art have been my medium for embellishing, but the techniques can also be incorporated into quiltmaking by anyone who would like to be a bit adventurous.

Rose Petal Trim

This ruffled trim works as an outside finished edge of a quilt or garment.

Step 1. Determine the length of trim needed and allow 1½ times that length for gathering. Cut enough 1½-inch bias strips to get the necessary length. Stitch them together with diagonal seams as needed.

Step 2. Fold the bias strip in half lengthwise, but do not press. Stitch ¼ inch from the raw edges of the strip and pull the threads up to gather.

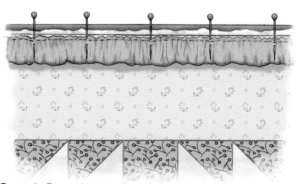

Step 3. Pin and stitch the trim to the right side of the quilt along the edges to be trimmed. See "Special Finishes" on page 52 and follow Steps 1 through 3.

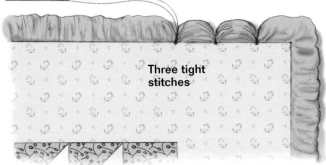

Three tight stitches

Step 4. Thread a needle and insert it into the backing. Use a double strand of thread. Bury the knot in the batting and bring the thread through to the quilt top. Stitch over the shirred ruffle three times. Pull the thread up tightly with each stitch. Take the thread to the backing side again. (You will be stitching the backing down at the same time you are making the rose petals.)

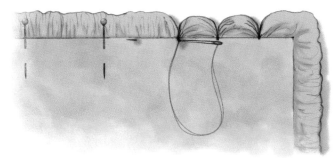

Step 5. Slip the thread through the batting and come out on the quilt back ½ inch away. Make a small stitch to secure the backing and take the needle to the front to begin the next petal. Stitch over the ruffle three times as before. Continue until the rose petal edge is complete.

Stitch and Slash

The multiple layers of fabric used with this technique will add weight to a quilt, along with a wonderful dimensionality that mimics chenille.

Use equal yardage of four fabrics. I usually work in ¼-yard pieces, but you may work with pieces as small or large as you like. The end result will be only slightly smaller than what you started with, after stitching and shrinkage. A 100 percent cotton fabric will give better fraying for this technique. Try to select fabrics in which the dye is concentrated through to the back rather than those that are white on the back.

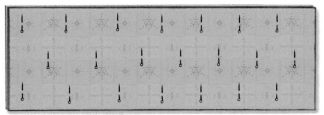

Step 1. Stack the four layers of fabric with the dominant fabric on top. Pin together.

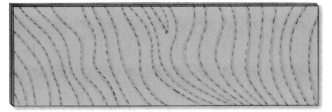

Step 2. Starting from the outside edge on any of the four sides, create a design and stitch through all four layers. It works best if you stitch from a raw edge to a raw edge without stopping in the middle. The design is free-form, but you can mark it if you wish. Sew with a slightly longer stitch length than normal, using a decorative thread if desired. Keep the stitching lines approximately ¼ inch apart to create the channels for cutting. Do not cross over threads. Continue stitching until you reach another edge.

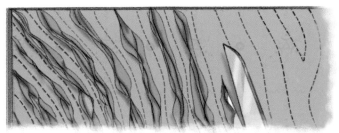

Step 3. Using small scissors and starting from the outside edges, cut between every stitching channel in the top three layers of fabric. Take care not to cut through to the fourth layer of fabric.

Step 4. When slashing (cutting) is complete, wet the fabric, if it has been prewashed. If the fabric has not been prewashed, wash it with detergent to get the sizing out. Put the piece in a dryer on medium heat. Remove when completely dry, and shake off the excess threads.

Judy Murrah

ENGLISH PAPER PIECING

English paper piecing is the construction of a quilt on precut paper shapes. This technique has been used over several centuries for its accuracy. One of the earliest American quilts in existence, the Saltonstall quilt (a quarter-square design made of silk brocade and velvet), dated 1704, still contains the papers from the Harvard College catalog of 1701. Today's quilters find English paper piecing to be the perfect "on the go" project.

Paper templates cut to the exact size of the finished quilt pieces are used as a guide to cut the fabrics and also as part of the construction. The paper template acts as a stabilizer and will not allow the fabric to stretch on bias seams. Seam allowances are folded over and basted to the paper, eliminating any error in sewing. Since the paper remains in until construction is complete, all the pieces fit together perfectly and the quilt blocks turn out exact.

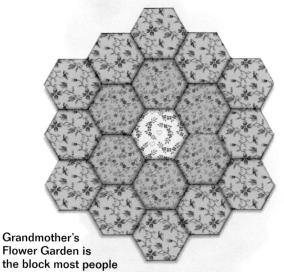

Grandmother's Flower Garden is the block most people associate with English paper piecing.

Cutting

Cut your fabric by using the paper template as a guide. You can purchase accurately precut paper pieces for templates or make your own.

To make your own, create an accurate master template, and mark it "master." Trace around it onto paper that is heavier than typing or bond paper. Cut the shapes out on the inside of the tracing line. Doing this and using one master template prevents the quilt

from "growing" as you get to the outside edges. If the paper is of good quality, you can use each template several times.

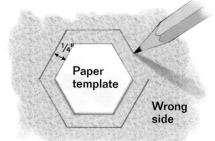

Cutting Individually: Mark a ¼-inch seam allowance with a pencil around each piece, on the wrong side of the fabric. You can use a seam guide or ruler to mark the cutting line, or just eyeball it. You can always trim to ¼ inch or less if you will be quilting ¼ inch away from the seam. Cut each piece out with scissors. You can selectively cut parts of your fabric this way, capturing specific designs or centering them within the template.

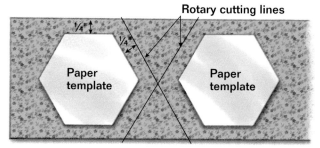

Quick Cutting: To cut large numbers of pieces at one time, it is easiest to work with strips. Use a rotary cutter to cut strips the width of the template plus seam allowances. For example, if your hexagon is 2 inches measured across the paper piece, cut your strip 2½ inches wide. Center the template and use a ruler and rotary cutter to cut ¼ inch away from the template.

Basting and Sewing

Step 1. Center the template over the fabric and pin. Fold the seam allowance over the paper with your fingers. Using a number 5 or 7 quilting needle and a contrasting thread, baste the fabric to the paper template with one or two stitches on each side of the hexagon.

Step 2. When you have two pieces basted, place the pieces right sides together and sew with a whipstitch through the folded edge of the fabric along one side. Use a quilting or appliqué needle and a single strand of quilting thread or a double strand of regular thread. Do not sew through the paper when joining the pieces. There is no need to pin the hexagons together; pinning can actually cause them to shift.

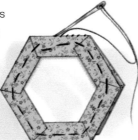

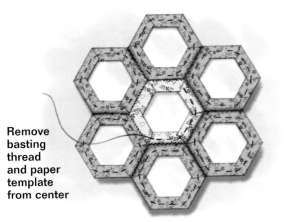

Remove basting thread and paper template from center

Step 3. When a piece is sewn around all the edges and completely stabilized, you may remove the paper. Clip and pull the basting threads, and remove the paper template from the back. The template can be reused many times.

Handling Points

Points on diamonds should be basted with the seam allowance extended for pieced blocks.

Step 1. To baste a diamond, start just above the center point on one side, and baste to the point. Finger press the seam allowance that extends beyond the point of the paper.

Step 2. Fold the seam allowance from the second side over the foundation and continue basting down the next side. The seam allowance will extend beyond the basted template at the point.

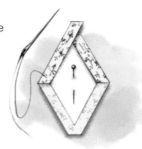

Step 3. When joining the pieces, hold the extended seam allowance out of the way and sew through only the folded edge of the fabric. This will produce less bulk when the points connect. The extended seam allowances will spiral around at the center.

Try This The paper shapes used for this technique can be used for appliqué as well as piecing. You can get sharp points and smooth curves by basting the fabric onto a paper shape. Appliqué the shape to the background without removing the paper. Turn to the back side and cut the background fabric away ¼ inch *inside* your appliqué stitching line. Remove the background fabric. Clip and pull the basting stitches from the shape, and remove the paper template from the back.

Tess Herlan

ENLARGING AND REDUCING PATTERNS

Patterns and quilting motifs printed in books and magazines are not always the size that you need. You can adapt patterns to your desired size by enlarging or reducing them.

Appliqué and Quilting Designs

Using the enlarging/reducing option on a photocopier is the fastest way to enlarge or reduce these types of patterns. Appliqué pattern pieces do not generally fit together as precisely as patchwork pieces do, so if the copier creates a bit of variation in the pattern, it's usually not noticeable. Quilting designs can easily be enlarged or reduced on a copier without any problems caused by distortion. Enlarging by 150 percent on a copier means that you increase the size of the original by one half.

If you prefer, you can use graph paper to alter pattern sizes. Trace the original pattern onto graph paper. (A light box will help you see the pattern lines.) To enlarge the design, draw a larger grid on another piece of plain or graph paper. For instance, if the original grid is composed of ¼-inch squares, and you want to double the size of the pattern, darken lines on the graph paper to create a ½-inch grid. Evaluate each square occupied by the original pattern, and duplicate the lines in the corresponding square of the larger grid. To reduce a design, duplicate the lines in each square onto a smaller grid.

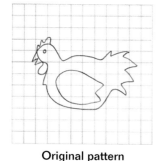 

Original pattern   Enlargement

Patchwork Patterns

To reduce or enlarge patchwork patterns that you will be rotary cutting, choose a finished block size based on the number of units in the block—not necessarily a size you feel is standard. Since our rulers are marked at ⅛-inch intervals, that should be the smallest increment you must measure and cut.

Four common types of patchwork blocks are illustrated below.

FOUR PATCH

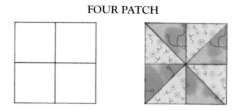

A Four Patch block is initially divided into 4 equal units, 2 across and 2 down

NINE PATCH

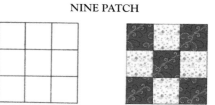

A Nine Patch block is initially divided into 9 equal units, 3 across and 3 down

FIVE PATCH

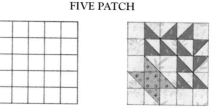

A Five Patch block is initially divided into 25 equal units, 5 across and 5 down

SEVEN PATCH

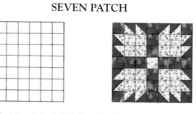

A Seven Patch block is initially divided into 49 equal units, 7 across and 7 down

To determine block size, consider these factors:

- What is the approximate finished block size required for the quilt you need to make?
- How many units does the block contain across and down? If original units have been subdivided, consider them in your calculations.
- Are two or more types of blocks being used in the same quilt?

To determine the unit size, divide the desired finished size of the block by the total number of units across or down. For a 12-inch square Nine Patch block, each unit would equal 4 inches.

12 inches ÷ 3 units = 4 inches per unit

Note: Don't worry about seam allowances, since they add length in ⅛-inch increments and are automatically "rotary cuttable!"

For blocks that must be a specific size, enlargements and reductions can be made using graph paper, in a manner similar to that given for appliqué patterns. Draw a square the desired finished size of your block, then divide it into a grid of squares based on the number of units in the block. Fill in each square of the grid by duplicating the lines in the original pattern. Trace shapes, add seam allowances, and make templates to construct the quilt using that method. (See "Templates" on page 238.)

Original pattern

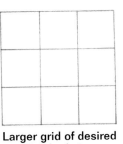

Larger grid of desired finished size

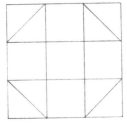

Lines duplicated

TAKING THE TROUBLE OUT OF
Uneven Dimensions

To make a 12-inch square Five Patch block, each unit would equal 2.4 inches—not a size you can accurately cut with rotary equipment. The same is true for a 12-inch square Seven Patch block, since each unit would be 1.71 inches square.

To solve the problem, alter the size of the units, rounding them up or down to the nearest "cuttable" size. For example, the five patch units can be rounded up to 2½ inches each, and the seven patch units to 1¾ inches each, with little change in the final size of the block. For a quilt that must finish at a specific size, the difference can be easily compensated for by altering the width of borders or sashing.

If two different types of blocks are being used in the quilt, be sure the chosen size works well for each one. For example, you've seen that the 12-inch block is suitable for both the Four Patch and Nine Patch blocks, but not the Five Patch or Seven Patch blocks. If no one size will allow you to rotary cut all blocks in a quilt, determine a size that will be best for most, and construct the others using the template method.

Photocopiers can distort patchwork patterns, so be very cautious in using them to alter sizes. A good quality copier may give satisfactory results, but be sure to measure carefully for accuracy first.

Janet Wickell

FABRIC GRAIN

Most of us have seen a craftsperson demonstrate the art of weaving fabric on a loom, passing a shuttle of thread back and forth through threads attached to the loom ends. The quilting cottons we purchase from bolts of fabric are made in a similar way, although much of the process is automated and done on a large scale.

First, long threads are stretched across a loom and attached securely to both ends. These threads are referred to as *warp* threads and create what we call the lengthwise grain of the fabric. More threads, called *weft* threads, are woven across the warp threads, moving repeatedly from side to side along their entire length. We call the direction of the weft threads the crosswise grain of the fabric. Both grain types are referred to as the straight-of-grain. At the outer edges of the weft threads are the selvages, bound edges that develop as the weft threads reach the edges of the warp and are turned around to make another pass through the warp threads.

Think of the warp threads as the stabilizers in a piece of fabric. Cut a small square from one of your cottons, making sure its sides are parallel to the lengthwise and crosswise grains. Leave the selvage in place on one side of the square. (It runs parallel to the lengthwise grain, so will help you differentiate between the two grain directions.) Pull on the square in the direction of the lengthwise grain. It probably won't have much give. One reason for this is that the warp threads gained stability by being firmly attached to the loom during weaving. Their stability is further enhanced by the interlacing of the weft threads, which run perpendicular to the lengths of the warp threads. A third stabilizing factor is the number of threads per square inch. Although thread counts vary from fabric to fabric, there are usually more warp threads than weft threads per square inch.

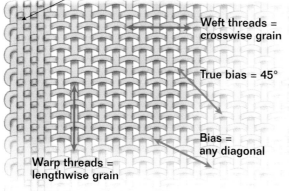

Selvage

Weft threads = crosswise grain

True bias = 45°

Bias = any diagonal

Warp threads = lengthwise grain

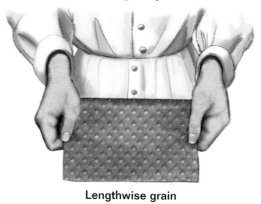

Lengthwise grain

Now stretch your square in the direction of the crosswise grain. It will likely have a bit more give, but shouldn't stretch permanently out of shape unless you handle it roughly. The weft threads themselves act as the stabilizers for this grain.

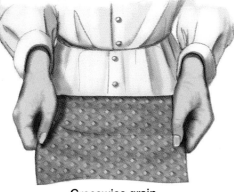

Crosswise grain

The true bias of a fabric is a 45 degree angle from the lengthwise and crosswise grains. However, any cut not parallel to one of the grain lines is called a bias cut. Tug on your square along the true bias, from corner to corner, and notice how much more stretching occurs than when you pulled it in the directions of its threads. With no straight threads to stabilize it, the fabric stretches easily.

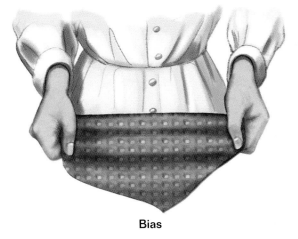

Bias

Edges cut along the bias lose the stability provided by the straight-of-grain, and must be handled with care to keep them from stretching permanently out of shape; stretched edges are difficult to match up with adjacent patches.

In most cases, when we cut patches for quilting, our goal is to cut them with their edges parallel to the straight-of-grain. This is not a problem for squares and rectangles—their 90 degree corners allow their sides

to fit naturally into the pattern of the woven threads. It's when we introduce a cut at anything other than a 90 degree angle that decisions must be made.

A triangle is an example of a commonly used shape that must be cut with at least one bias edge. Take a look at the block the triangle will be used in, and try to cut the patch so that its bias edge does not end up on the outer perimeter of the finished block. The sooner that bias edge is sewn to another patch, the less handling it will receive, so the less chance there will be to stretch it. When possible, a bias edge should be sewn to a straight grain edge to help stabilize it.

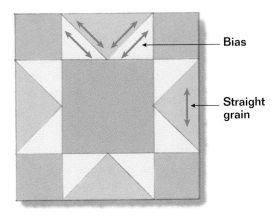

Bias

Straight grain

Once you understand the basic properties of your fabrics, you can put them to work for you. For instance, a bias edge is sometimes desirable. Its natural stretchiness makes long bias strips the perfect choice for applying binding around a quilt with curved edges. Bias strips are used in appliqué for the same reason, when vines must be woven into graceful curves around a floral design. Lengthwise-grain strips are a good choice for the outer borders of a quilt you feel needs added stability.

Take some time to get to know your fabrics. You'll have a better understanding of the instructions that accompany quilt patterns, and you'll have the confidence to make your own decisions when cutting.

See also "Preparing Fabric" on page 179.

Janet Wickell

FEEDSACKS

Feedsacks are not defined in most dictionaries, but whether you say textile bags, sack cloth, or chicken linen, all of these terms refer to the bags purchased with products like flour, grain, feed, seed, or sugar in them. Since the nineteenth century, these bags were made of cotton or burlap, and when the product inside was used up, the cloth was recycled into garments, household articles, and quilts.

Someone once observed that when the prairie wind blew the skirts of little girls, you could see brand names on the seats of their feedsack underpants. Hints and tips for removing the lettering were exchanged just as food recipes were at teas or quilt patterns at sewing bees of the past.

Considering how successful the print bags ultimately were, it seems amazing that the Percy Kent Bag Company had to be convinced to bring bright prints to the bag trade. Richard Peek of that company is credited with being the first to "sack it to them" in color prints. He even visited New York City to enlist name designers to develop appealing motifs that would keep the buying public coming back for more. The first print bags went to Crescent Flour and Feed Company of Springfield, Missouri.

Soon there were feedsack curtains, slipcovers, bathing suits, table covers, handbags, dresses, and men's shirts in American homes. The bags were cut, stitched, embroidered, and smocked. Some were even used for pulled and drawn threadwork designs. The National Cotton Council directed a campaign featuring feedsack wardrobes. Four-H Clubs did feedsack projects. In 1944, *Business Week* reported that 30 million yards of printed cotton material were used annually for feed bags in the United States.

However, by the 1950s, the frugal feedsack era had faded, though a few were marketed in the Southwest until the 1960s. The farm wife had become more sophisticated and was drawn to the attractive yardage available at the local dry goods shop.

Feedsacks have a place in the history of the American way of life of the nineteenth and twentieth centuries. For many, they evoke remembrances of home and childhood. Today, collectors, many of whom belong to the Feedsack Club, keep the mystique alive by trading, buying, and selling whole sacks and small squares to make new quilts out of the old fabric. Old quilts or tops made of feedsacks are treasured. There are few fabrics that can give a home such an instant sense of country and warmth as well as a feedsack.

Anna Eelman

"Feedsack Patches" (top left), circa 1940, and "Hearts and Gizzards" (center bottom) are both full-size bed quilts that were purchased as tops and recently quilted by Anna Eelman. "Hearts and Gizzards" includes red gingham feedsacks and plain sugar sacks.

FLOOR FRAMES

The full-size frame is sometimes referred to as a *stretcher frame* because the quilt is stretched out fully when the quilting begins. This differentiates the full-size frame from the roller frame, in which the quilt is rolled up on two long boards, creating a rectangular arrangement. I will explain how both of these frames work and what I think are the advantages and disadvantages of both.

The Full-Size Frame

The full-size frame is made up of four long boards held together with C-clamps and something to rest the frame on. The quilting boards are 1 × 2-inch boards with duck or twill fabric stapled along the edges. The boards need to be at least 4 inches longer than the measurements of the quilt.

In the old days, quilters sometimes rested their frames on ladder-back chairs, and that still works. I have a set of quilt "legs" that hold my frame. These can be very simple in design—just four legs sturdy enough to hold the quilt frame. If you have a carpenter make a set for you, they should be about 29 inches high so the frame is held at a comfortable working height.

How to Put a Quilt in the Frame

Make the quilt backing about 2 inches larger than the quilt top on all four sides. For example, if your quilt is 60 inches square, make the quilt backing 64 inches square.

Step 1. Place two boards on the chairs parallel to each other with the stapled fabric on top and toward the middle. Rest the other two boards across them. The boards on the bottom are called "stretchers;" the ones on the top, "rollers."

Step 2. Pin the backing to the rollers, making sure it is centered. Use just enough pins to hold it in place. With a single strand of thread, sew the backing to both rollers using overcast stitches ¼ inch long. Remove the pins, and clamp the crossed boards on one side with two C-clamps, one at each intersection. When pulling the second roller tight, brace the stretcher end against your thigh to keep the whole thing from clattering to the floor. Pull the board tight and position the clamp.

Step 3. Pin the backing to the stretchers.

Step 4. Spread the batting smoothly over the backing and trim off the excess batting. Trim so that the batting is about ½ inch smaller than the backing on all sides.

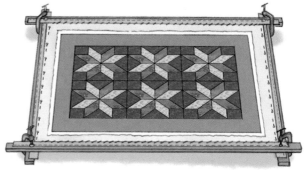

Step 5. Center the quilt top over the batting. Start in one corner and pin with quilting pins through all three layers, every 2 inches, near the edge of the quilt top. Pull the top taut but not so tight as to distort it. The pins will be removed during the quilting process.

Unlike hoop quilting, where you always start in the center of the quilt and work outward, frame quilting is done from the outside inward. Quilt all the way around the outside as far as you can reach on all four sides. To reach the middle, roll up the quilted part on the rollers like a scroll. Unclamp one side and unpin the sides as far as you need to roll. Roll the quilt under, reclamp, and repin. Repeat on the other side.

Advantages and Disadvantages

The advantage of this frame is that you do not have to baste the layers of the quilt together. You simply put the quilt in the frame and begin to quilt. Once the quilt is in the frame, even tension is maintained throughout the entire process, resulting in a finished quilt that lies perfectly flat with no puckers or uneven fullness. If you quilt in a hoop, a roller frame, or a Q-Snap floor frame, the full-size frame is definitely the best way to baste quilts.

The only disadvantage is that it takes a lot of room to have a full-size frame set up. Because of this, the full-size frame has almost become extinct.

Roller Frames

There are two types of roller frames available on the market. Originally, all roller frames had two long rollers upon which the quilt was rolled, and two short side boards, called stretchers, that held the sides of the quilt.

Sometime in the 1980s, the three-roller frame was introduced, sporting three long boards instead of two. The three-roller frame was designed to eliminate the need to baste the top and to eliminate any fullness when the quilt was rolled onto the long boards. There are a number of differences in how these two frames work. Roller frames work basically like floor frames with a few exceptions.

The Two-Board Roller Frame

If you roll the three layers onto the two long boards without basting, the backing will sag. There are two ways to eliminate this problem. One is to baste the three layers together first, roll the quilt onto the long boards, and pin the sides to the shorter boards.

If you want to skip the basting (and who doesn't!), roll only the backing and the batting onto the two long boards. Pin the backing to the sides. Lay the quilt top over the exposed area of backing and batting. Smooth out the top and attach it with pins to the side boards. Make sure there are no wrinkles. Quilt as far as you can, unpin the sides of the quilt, roll the quilted area, repin the sides, and continue quilting. I know a number of quilters who use this method very successfully.

TWO-ROLLER FRAME

The Three-Board Roller Frame

Attaching the backing and batting to two rollers and the quilt top to the third roller eliminates sagging and the need to baste. The sides of all three layers are pinned to the fabric on the short side boards.

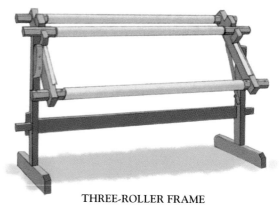

THREE-ROLLER FRAME

Advantages and Disadvantages

The advantage of a roller frame is that it has many of the benefits of the full-size frame without taking up so much room. The disadvantage is that there is a little more fussing with the roller frames, either in the basting or in coping with three rollers.

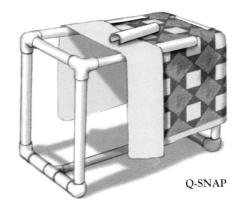

Q-SNAP

The Q-Snap Floor Frame

Q-Snap frames are made of lightweight PVC tubing. Many quilters like this frame because it is easy to use and easy to handle. Putting the quilt in the frame requires that you first baste all three layers of the quilt together. Then it is a simple matter of laying the basted quilt over the frame, putting the clamps on, and tightening. The ribbed inner surface of the clamps holds the tension just where you want it.

This frame is lightweight and very portable. It fits through a standard-size doorway without needing to be taken apart. These frames come with their own carrying cases and can be easily disassembled and taken on vacations or put away when not in use. Extensions are available that double the work space, making it possible for six quilters to sit around the frame.

Gwen Marston

FOUNDATION PIECING

Long used for crazy quilting, string piecing, Log Cabin, and pieced Pineapple quilts, foundation piecing is regaining popularity as quilters realize its potential. It is versatile, precise, and exciting to work with.

Foundation piecing involves the use of a separate material as a base to aid in the piecing process. It can be pieced on, it can serve as a guide to stitch along, and it can be used to prepare fabric or create pre-sewn units for subsequent piecing. The two major techniques used in foundation piecing are pressed-piecing, often called "sew-and-flip," and single foundation piecing, based on traditional English paper piecing.

The biggest advantages of using foundations are precision and stability. You can achieve absolute accuracy of shapes, points, and lines. Fabric will not shift, even when using off-grain or slippery fabrics, small pieces, and fabrics of differing weights. Blocks will all be the same size, with the same points at the same places, whether made by one quilter or by many.

In addition, a design can be drawn directly on a foundation, with color placement, piecing order, and registration marked to avoid confusion and piecing errors. Speed is often a function of foundation piecing because no templates are needed.

The disadvantages of foundation piecing are few. Preparation time is an extra step, some foundation materials can add unwanted bulk, and the extra expense of pre-printed foundations may be a consideration. These are negligible compared to the advantages and can be easily overcome.

Materials

Foundations can be permanent or temporary. Permanent foundations, such as fabric, batting, and interfacing, remain in the piece. They are useful when extra body is needed and can act as a lining or stabilizer. They can be sewn on either by hand or machine.

Temporary foundations are removed after piecing. They are most often made of paper or removable interfacing and are pieced on by machine. Quilters can choose from a wide variety of paper types and weights. We strongly suggest using lightweight paper, such as tracing paper or freezer paper. Typing or copy paper is thick and, when removed, will distort the stitches unless they are extra small (20 per inch). Lighter weight paper allows the use of a more moderate (12 to 14 per inch) stitch length, which is easier to remove if an error needs to be corrected. Easy Tear is a lightweight interfacing that is an excellent choice as a temporary foundation. It is opaque, can be drawn on, is less apt to tear than tracing paper, and is easily removed.

We prefer a temporary foundation most of the time. This avoids the extra layer and weight of a permanent foundation, which can make hand quilting difficult.

Marking Foundations

Depending on the material used, foundations can be marked with pencil, pen, needle-punching, or computer printing. In most cases, we do not recommend printing foundations on a copy machine because of the inherent distortion and potential inaccuracy of the final stitching lines.

If a pattern is traced, the best tool to use is a fine-point pencil. It is important to position the ruler so that the traced line is exactly the same as the printed line. Needle-punching is done by stitching through a marked pattern placed on a stack of paper with an unthreaded sewing machine. Identical, accurate, and inexpensive foundations can be quickly created in this manner.

Number the piecing order directly on the foundations. If you have color and fabric changes, mark them, too. Realize, however, that you will be working with a mirror-image if you are using under pressed-piecing, and arrange the colors accordingly.

Pressed-Piecing

The most widely used foundation piecing technique is pressed-piecing. Pressed-piecing has been around for a long time. The name comes from the technique. Fabric is stitched and then pressed on a foundation. Pressed-piecing can be done in two ways.

For either method, place the first piece of fabric right side up on the foundation. Position the second piece of fabric on top of the first, with right sides together, and stitch through all layers, using a ¼-inch seam allowance. Open out the second patch, press firmly, and pin it to the foundation. Add the next fabric patch, right side down, matching the cut edge of the previous piece. Stitch, open, press, and pin as before. Continue until the foundation is covered with fabric.

Sewing ¼-inch seam using top pressed-piecing.

Top pressed-piecing involves stitching and pressing with the fabric on top of the foundation, using a ¼-inch seam allowance. Use the edge of the opened-out patch to position the next piece of fabric.

Under pressed-piecing is done with the fabric placed under the foundation. Sewing lines are drawn on the top of the foundation and the fabric is positioned on the undrawn side. Turn the foundation over so the fabric lies against the feed dogs of the sewing machine. The stitching is done on the line. Since the sewing line is clear while stitching, precision is achieved effortlessly.

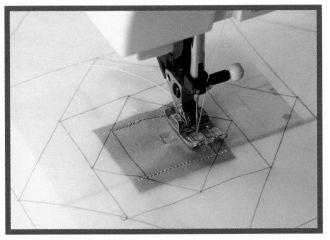

Sewing on the line using under pressed-piecing.

Row trimmed and pinned. Next pieces ready to be positioned for stitching, on opposite sides of the block.

The fabric pieces must be correctly placed with adequate seam allowances on all sides since they will not be visible during stitching. After stitching, open out the piece sewn, and trim any excess seam allowance to provide an accurate placement edge for the next patch. It is easiest to do this by folding back the foundation at the line of stitching and trimming the fabric to ¼ inch. Use scissors or a rotary cutter and ruler.

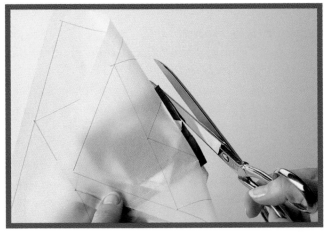

Trimming excess seam allowance with foundation folded at the seam line.

Continue to add pieces of fabric in sequence until the design is completed. It is often possible to position more than one piece of fabric in the same sewing step, stitching one seam and moving to the beginning of the next without cutting the threads.

Once you have mastered stitching "upside down," under pressed-piecing becomes an easy, almost foolproof method for precise piecing. It provides accuracy and consistency with simple patterns and allows construction of more difficult patterns often considered beyond the reach of many quilters.

We use top pressed-piecing for any design where matching exact lines is not required, such as crazy quilting, string piecing, and other types of random piecing. We use under pressed-piecing for designs where angles, lines, and joinings must be precise.

Try This When press-piecing around a center-based design, stitch patches on opposite sides of the center to help combat the circular influence of piecing in a clockwise manner. This is particularly important with Log Cabin and Pineapple patterns, where the center should remain square.

Pressing, trimming, and pinning are essential when press-piecing to ensure that the block will lie flat and be the desired size.

• Pressing must be done firmly to smooth and flatten the fabric taut against the foundation. It's best to use a dry iron, especially with freezer paper.

- Trimming excess seam allowances after stitching prevents them from being trapped under subsequent cross-seams.

- Pinning prevents shifting of the piece in place, as well as folding or crumpling of the piece being added.

TAKING THE TROUBLE OUT OF
Under Pressed-Piecing

Sometimes when the fabric patch is sewn and opened, it doesn't cover the area with adequate seam allowances. Care must be taken to use appropriately sized pieces of fabric. To cover the area completely, we prefer to cut shapes with a little more seam allowance than necessary, rather than using large "chunks" of fabric. This "rough-cutting" provides ample seam allowances and preserves the integrity of the fabric grainline and print (not the case with chunks or large squares of fabric).

- For strips and squares, cut fabric ½ inch larger on all sides.

- For half- and quarter-square triangles, cut squares ½ to ¾ inch larger than the usual added measurement.

- For angled shapes, make a rough template and cut fabric ½ inch larger on all sides, creating a rough-cut piece. The angles of the shape will be replicated and the patch will cover the area amply.

Don't forget to trim the excess seam allowance after the patch is pressed open, so the next piece of fabric can be positioned accurately.

which is then cut out with ¼-inch seam allowances on all sides. The patches are sewn together by stitching along the cut edges of the foundations. If set-in seams are involved, the edge of the foundation marks the exact spot to begin and end stitching. (See also "English Paper Piecing" on page 100.)

Single foundation piecing can be used alone or in combination with press-pieced units or conventional piecing. It can be done by hand, machine, or both. It is the technique of choice when piecing patterns such as birds, animals, flowers, or scenic designs that involve many different shapes, often used only once. Many contemporary quilters use single foundations to construct their innovative designs, avoiding templates and designing directly on the foundations.

Foundation Removal

The stabilizing effect of a foundation maintains the accuracy of the piecing and keeps the block size consistent. This is invaluable when assembling a quilt of multiple blocks and when adding borders. We do not remove temporary foundations until the edges of all blocks have been contained by other blocks or a border. You can remove foundations on the interior blocks to lighten the weight of the quilt top, but it is essential to keep foundations on the outer blocks until the borders are added.

Single Foundation Piecing

Single foundation piecing requires a separate foundation for each piece in the block. The idea is based on English paper piecing, often used with mosaic-type designs. Freezer paper or adhesive-backed paper foundations are attached to the wrong side of the fabric,

Formats

Historically, foundations have been used for whole blocks with pressed-piecing, and for mosaic-type designs with single foundation piecing. The whole blocks were center- or side-based patterns such as Log Cabin, string, and crazy quilt designs, which could be sewn by adding strips or patches until the foundation was covered. Patterns in which the next patch to be added involved a cross-seam presented geometric impossibilities for continued pressed-piecing, and

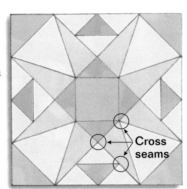

were not considered for foundation piecing.

These patterns can be foundation pieced, however, if they are divided into sections that can be press-pieced and then joined, using the edges of the foundations as stitching guides. A block may be composed of all press-pieced segments, or it can be press-pieced, made of single foundation segments and conventionally pieced patches. Using this combination, the entire repertoire of patterns becomes open to the possibility of foundation piecing, with all its advantages.

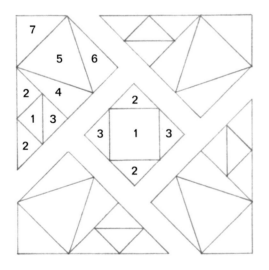

These kinds of segment divisions are applicable to most patterns, traditional or innovative. Foundation piecing may not be practical for all parts of some patterns. For instance, curves are sewn more easily with conventional piecing, but they can be accurately and easily joined to foundation-pieced segments, using the edge of the foundation as a stitching guide.

Some designs are easy to piece with quick piecing, but some quick piecing can benefit from using a foundation. Strip sets can be press-pieced on freezer paper foundations to control curving or stretching. When

sheeting (the grid method) half- or quarter-square triangles, it is easier and more accurate to draw sewing and cutting lines on a paper foundation than to draw on the fabric, as is usually done. The two fabric layers are then positioned under the foundation for sewing. The resulting squares will be identical, with no bias distortion. (See also "Triangle Squares" on page 251.)

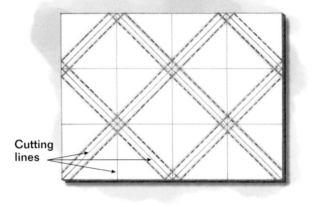

Hands-On Foundation Piecing

We have included three types of blocks on the next page to illustrate using foundations in different formats. We suggest enlarging each block to at least 6 inches, using graph paper rather than a copy machine. (See "Enlarging and Reducing Patterns" on page 102.) If you wish to make multiple blocks, try needle-punching the drawn pattern by stitching through several layers of paper with an unthreaded sewing machine.

24 Triangles Variation: This can be constructed as a whole block, using under pressed-piecing. To make the triangles, cut squares for half-square triangles, adding 1½ inches to the right-angle side measurement of the triangle. We suggest tracing paper or Easy Tear for the foundation.

Step 1. Pin the center square, right side up, onto the wrong side of the foundation. Stitch a triangle onto each side. Press each triangle open and flat; trim excess seam allowance.

Step 2. Pin the next row of triangles in place, wrong side up. Stitch, press, and trim as before. After the final row is added and pressed, sew a line of stay stitching a scant ¼ inch outside the outer drawn line, to stabilize the loose edges of the block. Trim fabric and foundation just outside the stay stitching.

Rambler: This is constructed in segments (marked by dotted lines) using under pressed-piecing. For A and C triangles, cut squares for quarter-square triangles, adding 2 inches to the long side measurement of the triangle. For B triangles, cut squares for half-square triangles, adding 1½ inches to the right angle side measurement. Note that a directional print fabric may require cutting the triangles as half-square rather than quarter-square, and vice versa. Use tracing paper or Easy Tear for the foundation.

Step 1. press-piece each segment, following the numbered piecing order. Place patch 1 on the foundation, and pin the first triangle on top, matching seam allowances. Stitch, press, pin, and trim the excess seam allowance. Add the next piece.

Step 2. When all segments are pieced, trim edge seam allowances to ¼ inch. Pin segments together, matching the cut edges of the foundations.

Step 3. Sew, using the foundation as a stitching guide. Press seams open and stay stitch a scant ¼ inch outside the outer drawn line of the foundation. Trim the fabric and foundation just outside the stay stitching.

String Star: This pattern and its variations are constructed with top pressed-piecing for segment A, and with single foundation piecing for segments B and B reverse. Use freezer paper for the foundations. To avoid the seam between the B triangles, cut as one foundation and set into the angles formed by piecing the star.

Step 1. press-piece segments A, using random size strips and chunks of fabric. Trim the outside fabric to ¼ inch from the edge of the foundation.

Step 2. Press the B freezer paper foundations to the wrong sides of the fabric and cut out with ¼-inch seam allowances. Stitch a B on either side of each A, matching beginning and ending points and the cut edges of the foundations. Join the four segments. Press seams open.

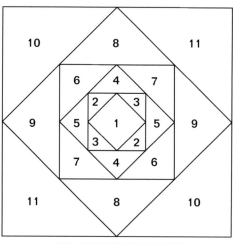

24 TRIANGLES VARIATION

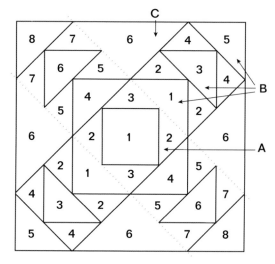

RAMBLER BLOCK

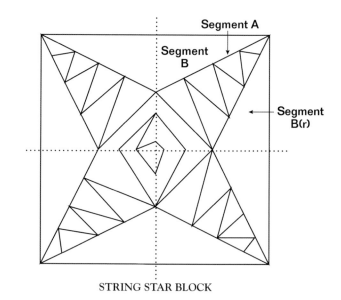

STRING STAR BLOCK

Top Ten Tips for Machine Paper Piecing

by Carol Doak

When machine piecing with paper as your foundation, here are my tips for success:

1. Use a size 90/14 needle. The larger hole helps to perforate the paper for easier removal later.

2. Set your sewing machine at 18 to 20 stitches to the inch. The smaller stitch length secures the seam when the paper is removed, makes the paper easier to remove, and permits smaller seam allowances.

3. Make copies using a copy machine from an original drawing only. Making a copy from a copy compounds any distortions. Check copies for accuracy.

4. Use a small clip-on lamp as a light source near your machine to aid in seeing through the paper and the layered fabrics for proper placement.

5. Make notations for fabric placement on the blank side of the paper. This is how the finished block will appear.

6. Use a press board and a small travel iron with no steam near your sewing machine for pressing the patchwork.

7. Cut oversize pieces of fabric. This will ensure that the fabric piece will cover the area adequately.

8. Place the next fabric to be joined right side up first on the blank side of the paper over the area it will fill, before you flip it right sides together with the previous pieces along the seam line. This will guarantee that the piece will open to cover the intended area.

9. When joining blocks, machine baste the beginning of the block, across any matching points, and the end of the block. Open and check for a good match. Should you need to redo a particular area, the thread can be easily removed by pulling it from the bobbin side. Baste that area again, and then stitch with smaller stitches to join the blocks.

10. Keep the paper intact until the blocks are surrounded by other blocks or fabric pieces.

FRIENDSHIP QUILTS

Friendship quilts are signature quilts that were made to be given to friends or loved ones. There are two main categories: quilts of one block repeated throughout, and album quilts, which contain different blocks. The common denominator of friendship quilts is their purpose, to convey affection to people we care about.

History

The friendship quilts being made today are descendants of the friendship quilts popular in the mid-nineteenth century. The friendship quilt fad was at its height from 1840 to 1865. During those years, thousands of signed quilts were made to be given to friends. We believe their popularity is tied in to America's westward expansion, at its peak from 1840 to 1865. Millions of people made the difficult trek westward, leaving families and friends forever. Women made friendship quilts as gifts for the loved ones who were leaving. They also made quilts on the trails and after settling in the West, exchanging fabric and blocks by mail with those who had stayed home in the East.

Many of the mid-nineteenth-century friendship quilts have survived because they were treasured too much to be used. They contained fabrics contributed by friends and relatives, scraps from their clothing, and, of course, the signatures and messages from loved ones.

"Cardinals in Friendship Pines" is a friendship quilt pieced and signed by a block-by-mail group of 16 quilters and other close friends and relatives of Rolinda Collinson of Friendship, Maryland. Rolinda supplied the pattern and red fabric for the "cardinal" and hand quilted the bed-size quilt.

Planning a Friendship Quilt

As you begin to plan a friendship quilt, you must make some organizational decisions. First, consider how many people you want to participate. If you have many people to include, use small blocks so the finished quilt doesn't become unwieldy.

There is no correct friendship block. Almost every block has been used successfully in friendship quilts. Any block may be signed if the fabric is light enough in color for the ink to show. On most blocks, you can create a place to sign by replacing one piece with a light piece. Consider traditional blocks whose titles match the theme of your quilt; for example, use the Freedom block for a graduation quilt or state blocks for a friend who is moving. Many blocks have the words *memory* and *friendship* in their titles and would complement the theme. A glance at a list of quilt blocks should provide more inspiration than you need.

Decide who will make the blocks. This will affect the signing procedure. Do you want to make the blocks and have your friends just sign them? If so, you might want to send out the fabric to be signed before piecing the blocks, to preclude mistakes. Do you want your friends to make as well as sign the blocks? If so, provide an accurate, pretested pattern for them. You need to decide further whether you want a controlled color scheme or a potpourri of colors. If you want a color focus for the quilt, either tell the block makers several main colors you want or provide each of them with a piece of fabric to incorporate into the block.

How to Sign Friendship Quilts

The easiest way to sign a friendship quilt is to use a permanent pen. The Pigma Micron pen is permanent on cotton and doesn't bleed much as you write, making it perfect for friendship quilts. The Pigma .01 imitates the delicate, spidery writing we see on antique quilts. The ink of the nineteenth century was black, but on antique quilts it has often faded to brown. Either black or brown pens produce the look of aged writing. The Pigma .05 is slightly thicker than the .01, making it more comfortable for the unpracticed writer to use. The points of both Pigma pens are so tiny and fragile that you need to write lightly. Never press hard. The ink flow is slow, so you need to write slowly and give the ink time to penetrate the fabric.

The Pigma .01

The Pigma .05

The fabric you choose to write on must be high quality 100 percent cotton in a color light enough for the ink to show. Always prewash and iron the fabric. Then test it for permanency with the pen you plan to use. To do this, write on the fabric, let it dry for 24 hours, and wash it briefly in a gentle detergent (just as you would wash the finished quilt). If the ink doesn't wash out, it means it is compatible with the fabric. If it washes out, try another fabric.

Organize the Signing

If you are preparing the blocks to be signed by different people, make it easy for them. Supervise the signing if possible, but if you can't get your signers together, make a kit to send with the blocks or fabric.

First, stabilize the fabric to be signed by ironing the pieces onto the shiny side of freezer paper. For your own writing, just placing the fabric over another piece of cotton fabric usually anchors it enough.

Provide the stabilized fabric, several pens, some practice muslin, at least two pieces to sign in case they make mistakes, and a direction sheet on how to sign. This sheet might include:

- A statement about what you are doing and why

- A note of thanks for participating

- An invitation to get fancy and do more than sign if you are comfortable with that

- A deadline for returning the block (include whether you want the pen back, too)

- These specific directions:
  Write lightly.
  Never press hard.
  Write slowly.
  Practice on muslin first to find the correct speed for you.

When You Get the Blocks Back

Depending on how you organized the friendship quilt, you may face a challenge when the blocks are returned. You may need to get the blocks to the same size by adding on to or subtracting from some of them. Perhaps you will have to live with some points cut off, or add a narrow border to some.

You will need to coordinate the colors. To do this, lay the blocks out on the floor and rearrange them until you have a satisfactory layout.

You will have to decide how to set the blocks. Some considerations might include whether to use a sashing between them, whether to set them straight or on point, and whether to add connecting blocks. You may have to add some blocks, but you probably shouldn't leave any out. (See "Settings" on page 220.)

A friendship quilt is the product of love and not always the product of talent. When you ask many people to make or sign blocks, the results are not always perfect. But a friendship quilt makes up for any deficiencies in workmanship by the sheer power of the contributors' love. Treasure it for the symbol it is and the memories it holds.

Susan McKelvey

FUSIBLE INTERFACING

Fusible interfacing is a staple in most sewing rooms, and now quilters have discovered a practical use for it. This lightweight, nonwoven stabilizer with a heat-activated coating is ideal for positioning appliqués on blocks or quilt tops. Using it doesn't give the same heirloom-quality results as traditional needle-turn appliqué, but it helps to keep appliqués from moving or bunching as you stitch them in place.

To appliqué with fusible interfacing, cut out the appliqué shape from both the appliqué fabric and fusible interfacing, adding a ¼-inch seam allowance. Place the right side of the fabric and the fusible side of the interfacing together. Pin and sew around the appliqué shape, using a ¼-inch seam allowance and leaving an opening for turning. Clip the curves and trim the corners as necessary to reduce bulk in the finished design. Turn the appliqué right side out, then finger press the unsewn seam allowances inside the appliqué "pocket." Do not iron the appliqué at this point or you will activate the bonding material. If necessary, use a point turner, awl, or stiletto to push out corners or small areas if your appliqué isn't quite flat.

To fuse your appliqué in place, position it interfacing side down on the background fabric, then lightly press, holding the iron on each spot about three or four seconds. Stitch the appliqué by hand or machine.

Karen Bolesta

FUSIBLE WEB

Fusible web is one of many new products designed to help today's quilters find time to be creative. It is a paper-backed adhesive that bonds fabrics together. It eliminates the need to turn under the raw edges of a shape when appliquéing. For projects that aren't intended to become heirlooms, fusible web is an option. See "Quick-Fuse Appliqué" on page 27 for the basic steps to complete a fusible web appliqué project.

Supplies

Fusible web (Aleene's Hotstitch, Heat n Bond, Steam-A-Seam, and Wonder-Under are just a few)

Design pattern or preprinted motif

Tracing paper if the pattern is not printed in reverse

Iron, ironing board

Scissors

Appliqué pressing sheet (optional)

Sewing machine (for securing edges of appliqué if the project is to be worn or laundered)

Embellishments as desired: buttons, embroidery floss, pearl cotton, and charms

Tips for Successful Fusing

• Read and follow manufacturer's instructions carefully.

• Use good quality, sharp scissors to cut "clean" shapes.

• Experiment with different brand-name webs. Some have a "shelf-life," some tend to coat a sewing machine needle, and some require a cool iron. Try several and compare.

• Always prewash fabrics to remove coatings, such as sizing, that may interfere with the adhesives. *Never* use fabric softener when prewashing!

• Arrange your pieces on the background or appliqué sheet directly on the ironing board. You can press without moving the pieces.

• If adhesive gets on your iron, Iron-Off, a commercial iron cleaner, will usually remove the residue.

• If using an appliqué sheet, let the pieces cool completely before removing them, or the adhesive will stick to the sheet.

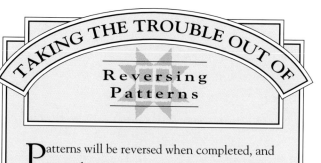

TAKING THE TROUBLE OUT OF

Reversing Patterns

Patterns will be reversed when completed, and it may be necessary to reverse the pattern for tracing. Trace each design onto tracing paper or thin white paper with a black felt-tip pen. Flip the paper over and, if necessary, retrace on the flip side. Clearly label the side to trace, and use this to trace the designs onto the paper side of the web.

If a project requires many of the same shapes, it may be more efficient to make a plastic template of that shape. Reverse the template, if necessary, and mark the top.

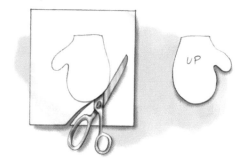

Securing the Edges

If projects done with fusible web are to be worn or laundered, the edges should be secured with hand or machine stitching. A narrow zigzag stitch using mono-filament or matching thread works well. Or use satin stitch, a buttonhole stitch, or another decorative stitch.

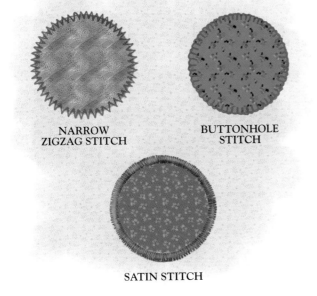

NARROW ZIGZAG STITCH

BUTTONHOLE STITCH

SATIN STITCH

Tips for Stitching the Edges

- Use a tear-away stabilizer underneath your project when securing edges by machine.

- Choose a neutral color bobbin thread to use throughout the stitching, and loosen the top tension slightly.

- When stitching around a curve, stop with your needle down on the outside of the curve, lift the pressure foot, and pivot. Pushing the fabric too much will distort the shape.

- When satin stitching, first sew the edges of the pieces that go underneath. Generally, a satin stitch is most attractive when the thread matches the fabric on which it is stitched.

- Use a black 40 weight machine embroidery thread with the buttonhole stitch to add a "folk art" touch. You can also add the buttonhole stitch by hand, using either embroidery floss or lightweight pearl cotton. The thread can contrast or match the fabric shape. (See "Buttonhole Stitch" on page 87.)

Using an Appliqué Sheet

An appliqué pressing sheet is not essential, but it is designed to make fusing easier. It protects the ironing board cover, and a more complex pattern may be placed under the transparent sheet for easy placement.

Step 1. Place the pattern *under* the appliqué sheet.

Step 2. Peel off the paper on the individual shapes and arrange them *over* the appliqué sheet with the rough adhesive side down.

Step 3. Press the shapes together *on top of* the appliqué sheet. Let cool. Lift the unit off the sheet.

Step 4. Apply to the background fabric.

If you are arranging a complex design involving many overlapped edges, it may be best to trace the design on transparent paper. Lay the paper on the background or appliqué sheet in the appropriate position, and secure one edge with masking tape. Use the tracing paper as a flip sheet. It is then easy to place the individual pieces.

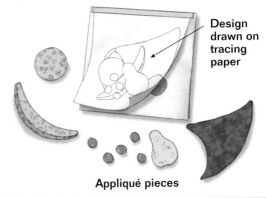

Design drawn on tracing paper

Appliqué pieces

Decorate fused projects with buttons, permanent markers, embroidered stitches, charms, or found objects to add personality and a bit of whimsy.

Toni Phillips & Juanita Simonich

HAND PIECING

No matter how many zippy-quick tools and techniques come along to help quilters speed toward a finished quilt, there will always be a time and a place for hand piecing. In fact, depending on your lifestyle and schedule, hand piecing might actually be more convenient, faster, and more conducive to a happy home and a completed quilt! How can this be?

Hand piecing is the ultimate take-along sewing. I have pieced my way through many conferences, plane trips, and evenings away from home. Even when I sew at home, I often find hand piecing more relaxing than machine work. I can always find enough energy to hand sew some patches, whereas the thought of hunching over my sewing machine is too daunting. Plus, I can be sociable or watch (listen to) television while still working steadily on my quilt. The end result? I can get a lot of piecing done and "sew" can you!

Making Templates

Templates for hand piecing are exactly the same size (and shape, of course) as the finished patch. You could draw your block on a sheet of template plastic, cut the pieces apart on the drawn lines, and have a template for every patch in the block. But if your block has pattern pieces that are repeated, you will need only one template for each different patch. Published patterns usually label patches with letters. Reversed, or mirror-image, patches usually have an *r* after the letter. If you are drafting your own pattern, identify and label each different shape.

Trace pattern pieces accurately onto template plastic or paper and cut them out. Glue paper templates to a heavier-weight paper. The template should match the pattern exactly, so use a fine pencil or pen and cut exactly on the line. Mark each template with its patch letter and add the grain line arrow, if there is one.

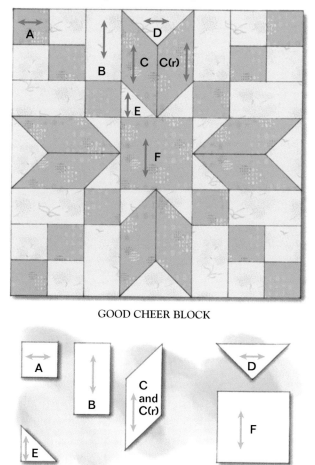

GOOD CHEER BLOCK

TEMPLATES FOR GOOD CHEER BLOCK

Marking and Cutting Patches

Smooth your fabric, wrong side up, on a convenient, non-slippery work surface. Turn the template wrong side up and align the grain line with the threads of the fabric. Using a fine pencil (a mechanical pencil is perfect), mark around the template. Mark adjacent patches, leaving ½-inch spaces between marked patches. These marked lines will be the sewing lines. The spaces between markings will become the seam allowances when the patches are cut out.

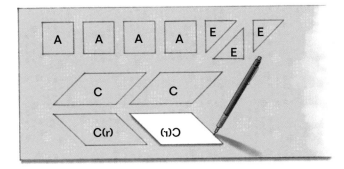

Once all of the patches from one fabric have been marked, use either fabric scissors or a rotary cutter and ruler to cut them out ¼ inch outside the marked lines.

Getting Ready to Sew

With all your patches cut out (for at least one block, if not the entire quilt), you are almost ready to begin sewing. Gather these few items first, perhaps putting them in a self-closing plastic bag if you will be sewing on-the-go.

Besides your patches, you will need thread. I use a good quality thread that matches the darker of the two fabrics I will be joining. If I am sewing navy fabric to pink fabric, I choose navy thread.

I keep a card of needles handy—sharps, sizes 5/10—so that I can select one with an eye I can thread at the time (depending on the amount of available light). You'll need a few pins with fine, sharp points, such as silk pins. I like to use my prettiest embroidery scissors for snipping threads. Your large fabric scissors can take a rest, but they will work fine if that's all you have. If you wear a thimble for quilting, you might want to use it for piecing.

Sewing Patches

Lay out the patches for one block to determine the sewing order. (Many quilt books and magazines "explode" block diagrams to indicate the sewing order.) Blocks are usually assembled in units, then rows, and then the rows are joined.

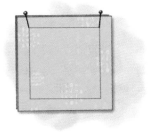

Step 1. Pick up the first two patches to be joined and place them right sides together. The marked seam lines will be visible. Insert a pin through the beginning of the marked line on both patches. Insert another pin at the end of the marked line. For small patches (3 inches or less), two pins will probably be sufficient to hold the patches together and to align the seam lines. Larger patches will require another pin or two.

Step 2. Thread a needle with about 24 inches of thread. Make a knot in the longer thread tail, if you wish. Remove the pin at the beginning of the seam line and insert the needle in the same hole. If you have made a knot in the thread, simply pull the thread until the knot holds. If you have not knotted, leave a tail of about 1 inch and make two tiny backstitches to hold the thread secure.

For a portable lap "table," use a large, cloth-bound book that has a slight texture to it. Fabric will not slip and slide on such a surface. If your personal library does not include such a book, visit a used-book store or library book sale. Enjoy letting people wonder why you are feeling the books instead of studying their titles!

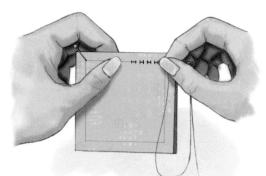

Step 3. Use a running stitch for hand piecing. Insert the needle exactly at the beginning of the marked line. Check to be sure the needle hits the marked line on the "behind" patch. Without pulling the needle through, manipulate the fabric to bring the needle point back to the front, making a stitch about 1/16 inch long. Several stitches can be loaded on the needle before the needle is pulled through the patches. Continue to sew to the end of the seam.

Step 4. End the line of stitching at the end of the marked line (not at the edges of the patches) with a couple of tiny backstitches. Continue adding patches.

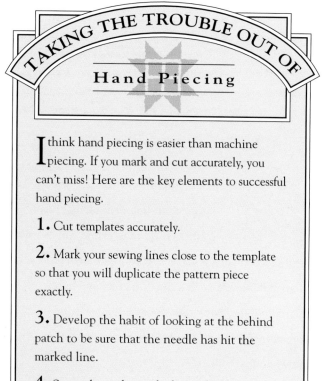

TAKING THE TROUBLE OUT OF
Hand Piecing

I think hand piecing is easier than machine piecing. If you mark and cut accurately, you can't miss! Here are the key elements to successful hand piecing.

1. Cut templates accurately.

2. Mark your sewing lines close to the template so that you will duplicate the pattern piece exactly.

3. Develop the habit of looking at the behind patch to be sure that the needle has hit the marked line.

4. Sew only on the marked seam lines, not through the seam allowances.

Sewing Angles and Curves

Angled seams, such as those required for sewing the D patches of the Good Cheer block on page 120, are perfectly suited to hand piecing if you follow the four key points in "Taking the Trouble Out of Hand Piecing." Sew only on the marked line on one edge of the angled seam. End your thread, then pin the next edge and sew.

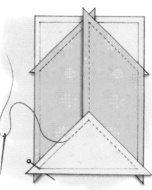

Curved seams also are perfectly suited to hand piecing. Clip halfway into the seam allowance of the concave (U-shaped) curve at 1/2-inch intervals.

Holding the convex (rainbow-shaped) curve toward you, pin the beginning of the seam line and the end. The two seam lines will not match without additional pins to force the alignment. Use as many as are comfortable (at least one pin every inch). For curved seams, it is essential to check that the needle hits the seam line on the behind patch.

Pressing and Tidying Up

Pressing hand-pieced patches is a breeze because the seam allowances are not sewn down. Some quiltmakers like to press after adding each piece or completing each small unit. I prefer to complete a block or large unit before using my iron to lightly steam press the seam allowances to one side. However, after sewing each patch, I "press" the seam allowances to one side with my fingers. Then, if I decide to steam press the seam allowances a different direction, it's no problem.

Marie Shirer

Japanese Hand Piecing

This technique is based on the kimono style of sewing. I am told that Japanese needleworkers developed this way of stitching to keep silk from slipping and sliding. I have found that it also keeps bias edges on cottons from stretching, so every seam will line up. This is not the way Japanese quiltmakers piece with cotton. They generally use traditional American methods. Instead, this is my interpretation of the kimono style for piecing.

There are many advantages to this method. It is very fast because you do not pull the thread all the way through the fabric until you reach an intersection, whether it's 2 inches, 6 inches, or a whole border length. The thread is not being worn by pulling it through the fabric. It is also a very comfortable way to sew as you manipulate the fabric over the needle, rather than moving the needle through the fabric.

Getting Ready to Sew

Mark and cut your patches as for regular hand piecing. A ring thimble or band thimble (*yubi nuki* in Japanese) is essential. It can be either the leather style or the adjustable metal version, available at most quilt shops. I use a number 10 sharp needle and 100 percent cotton thread.

Sewing Patches

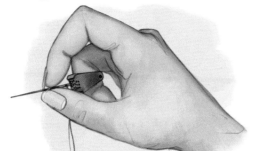

Step 1. Put your band thimble on the middle finger of your right hand if you are right-handed. Put it on your left hand if you are left-handed. Hold on to the tip of the needle with your thumb and forefinger. The back of the needle should be pressed up against the front of the thimble.

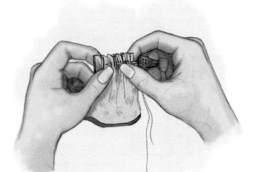

Step 2. Start your needle ¼ inch from the marked intersection and take two or three stitches back toward the beginning intersection. This keeps the knot away from the intersection and backstitches the beginning for you.

Step 3. With your left hand (for right-handed sewers), move the fabric back and forth to manipulate the fabric onto the needle. Slowly push on the end of the needle. When it seems that the stitches are falling off the tip of the needle, move your thumb and forefinger to the tip of the needle again. As the needle fills up with fabric, "brush" the fabric off the needle with the thumb and index finger—somewhat like smoothing out gathered fabric. Do not remove the needle from the fabric until you reach an intersection. The closer you keep your thumb and finger to the tip of the needle, the smaller your stitches will be.

Step 4. When you get to the end of the row of stitching, pull the needle out of the fabric. Smooth out the stitching, and take three backstitches. It is important that your backstitches stay on the sewing line and don't interfere with the finished side of the fabric. If your backstitches leave the sewing line it will appear as though you took a tuck in the block. Tie a knot and cut the thread, leaving a ½-inch tail. This is important for piecing as well as quilting. If you cut the thread too close to the knot, eventually the knot will rub right off the end of the thread.

The stitching may seem awkward in the beginning, but it does get easier. The stitches become shorter and shorter as you develop the ability to wiggle the fabric and push the needle more evenly.

Beckie Olson

HAND QUILTING

Every quilter wants to achieve "that perfect stitch!" There are several techniques for producing exquisite quilting stitches—some work well for some people, but the highest percentage of success still comes with the time-honored method of pivotal stacking, or moving the needle through the quilt with a rocking motion.

Sewing is defined as the act of fastening with a needle and thread. To quilt, you must think in terms of bending the fabrics and batting over the point of the needle. For this reason, it is a bad idea to have the quilt in the frame or hoop drum-tight. Give yourself some "bending" room.

To check the tension of your quilt in the hoop, lay the hoop, with the quilt in it, flat on a table. If you can comfortably lay your hand flat on the quilt and rest it on the table, it is probably loose enough. When putting your quilt in the hoop, pull it on the straight of grain. Pulling on the bias can warp your quilt, and it will be quilted that way.

For ease of learning it is best to start out by quilting toward yourself; later you can practice quilting at other angles and in other directions. With this method it is critical that you wear a thimble on the middle finger of your dominant hand.

I recommend using a size 10 between needle whether you're a beginner or an experienced quilter. I find there is no big advantage to using a size 12, and they are not strong enough to withstand the pressure.

In my own testing of threads, I have found them all to be about equally strong. For hand quilting, I prefer Gütterman quilting thread because it is twisted tighter than many others. This cuts down on the impact of the nap of the thread so that you don't have as much twisting, knotting, and fraying. It is also 100 percent cotton, prewaxed thread. I believe in the "balance of power" in quiltmaking: The thread content should match the fabric content. If you use 100 percent cotton fabrics, use 100 percent cotton thread.

Let's Quilt!

Thread your quilting needle with an 18-inch length of quilting thread. Remember which end of the thread came from the spool last because that is the end you should knot. Doing this will keep your thread from tangling as you are quilting.

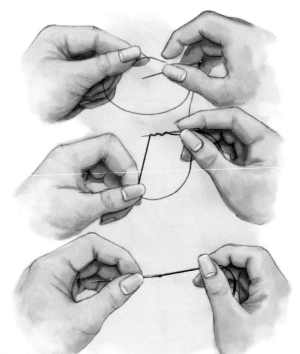

Step 1. Tie a small knot, as shown. Overlap the thread on the needle. Hold the thread down with your fingers. Wrap it around the needle twice. Hold the wrapped thread securely with the right finger and thumb. Pull the needle out of your fingers with your left hand. Pinch the wraps with your right hand. Pull the wrapped thread to the end to complete the knot.

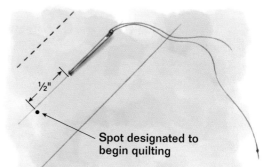

½"

Spot designated to begin quilting

Step 2. Stick the needle through the quilt top and into the batting layer (but not through the backing), about ½ inch from the place where you choose to start your quilting. Bring the needle back up to the surface exactly on the designated marked line. Pull the thread through and give it a tug, popping the knot under the quilt surface and "burying" it in the batting.

Backing

124

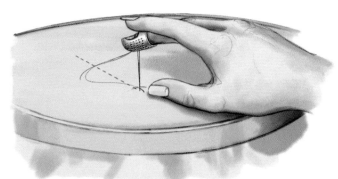

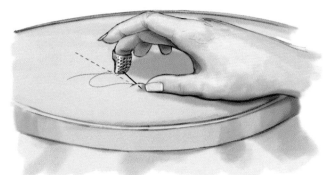

Step 3. Balance the needle between the middle finger of your top hand and the index finger of the hand below, keeping the needle perpendicular to the layers of the quilt. No other part of your hand should be touching the needle! Balance it gently. Do not push on the needle at this time or you will hurt your finger underneath. (I use my index finger underneath, but many quilters use the middle finger.) You should just be able to feel the point of the needle with the finger underneath.

Note: *Do not push down on the needle or you will hurt yourself.* Instead, angle the needle back so that it would lie on the quilt if you were to let go of the needle.

Step 5. If you have done all of the movements in Step 4 correctly, you should be in a position to actually push on the needle for the first time. As soon as you see the shiny point of the needle come through the top of the quilt, or the "peak" of the mountain, *stop pushing.*

Step 6. Gently lift the needle back up to be perpendicular to the quilt. There should be one stitch on the needle. Push on the needle only until you feel the point with your index finger underneath. That will tell you the needle has penetrated all layers of the quilt. Stop pushing immediately! Without letting the needle back itself out, but without pushing either, repeat the three simultaneous movements. Now you should have two stitches on the needle. Repeat the steps until you have approximately four stitches on the needle, then pull the thread through tightly enough to produce a desired lofty look. Pulling with the same tension every time will result in a consistent-looking quilting job.

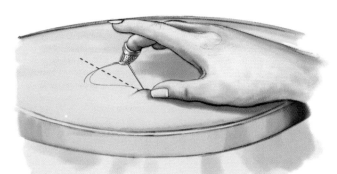

Step 4. This step is a three-part simultaneous movement. The thumb of your top hand should be placed on the quilt about ½ inch in front of the balanced needle. Press down hard on the quilt with the thumb. At the same time, push up with the index finger from under the quilt. The idea is to offset your finger below and your thumb from above, which will form a "mountain." If your finger and thumb are pushing against each other, you are doing nothing but producing a lot of pressure.

 The finger below the quilt will undoubtedly get pricked by the needle during quilting. Try purchasing a product called NuSkin at any drugstore. Use this to help protect your finger until a callous builds up.

Corners, Straight Lines, and Curves

Turning a corner is a simple matter of spacing your stitches so you end your stacking series either right at the corner or one stitch from it. If you end one stitch from the corner, begin your next stacking series by sticking your needle right in the corner.

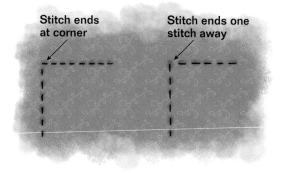

Stitch ends at corner

Stitch ends one stitch away

Quilting a straight line is easy if you begin each stacking series with a reminder to yourself to angle the needle back along that same straight quilting line. This will keep you going on the right track.

A tight curve is a little more difficult to quilt, but only because it limits the number of stitches you can stack on the needle. Try to stack at least two stitches before pulling the thread through the quilt because doing only one stitch at a time will make it more difficult to maintain evenness of stitches and tension.

Quilting with the grain is always harder than quilting diagonally. The stitches are harder to see, and it's more difficult to get them even and neat.

When you reach the end of a line, it is all right to "jump" to another line by running the needle between the layers of the quilt. If you are quilting with a dark thread on light fabric, however, be sure your needle also goes below the batting to keep your thread from shadowing through the top. It's best to keep the length of your "jumps" to no more than one needle length.

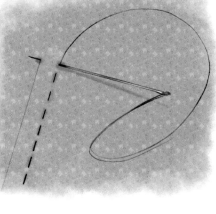

TAKING THE TROUBLE OUT OF

Quilting the Dreaded Seams

Most quilts have seams into which quilting stitches must go. If you have many seam allowances, switch to one size larger needle so you can exert more pressure. This is the one time you should take just one stitch at a time. It will most likely be twice as big as usual because of the extra thickness. Instead of making your next stitch a stitch length in front of where your thread is coming out, start it one normal stitch length in *back*. Repeat this backstitch method until you have crossed the seam allowance and can continue normally.

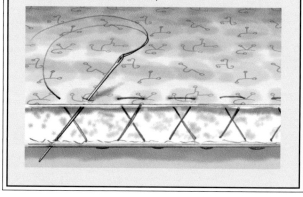

Ending

When the thread in your needle is about 6 inches long, it is time to tie off the thread. Make a circle with your thread and bring the needle up through that circle. Hold the circle down with your finger while reducing its size by pulling on the threaded needle to keep the knot from forming prematurely. The idea is to get the knot to form about ¼ inch from the quilt top so you have some length to bury the knot in the batting.

TYING OFF

Insert the needle back into the same hole from which the thread is emerging. Jump the needle about ½ inch between the layers and bring it to the surface. Pop the knot between the layers and cut the thread close to the quilt top.

When beginning a new thread, bring the needle up in the same hole you vacated when you knotted off. By doing this, you won't have any inconsistencies in the stitches on the back of your quilt.

If Anyone's Counting . . .

The number of stitches per inch is important, but not nearly as important as the evenness of stitches. By even, I mean the stitches and spaces between the stitches on the front of the quilt should all be exactly the same length as those on the back. If you are inclined to count, count only the stitches that show on top of the quilt.

Here's the rating scale:

Average . . . . .6 stitches per inch
Accomplished . . . . .8 stitches per inch
Expert . . . . .10 stitches per inch
Professional . . . . .12 stitches per inch
Microquilter . . . . .14 stitches per inch

If you can quilt 14 stitches to the inch, you are one of a very special group that is off the Quilting Richter Scale! Remember that 8 to 10 very even stitches per inch is considered superior to 12 to 14 uneven stitches per inch.

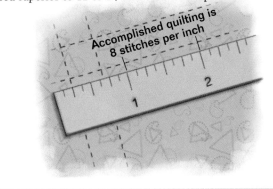

Accomplished quilting is 8 stitches per inch

Roxanne McElroy

SKILL BUILDER

Quilting Feathers

Quilting feathers is fun if you know the progressive sequence. It is most effective to concentrate on one side or row at a time, jumping lines as you go, and then doing the same down the other side.

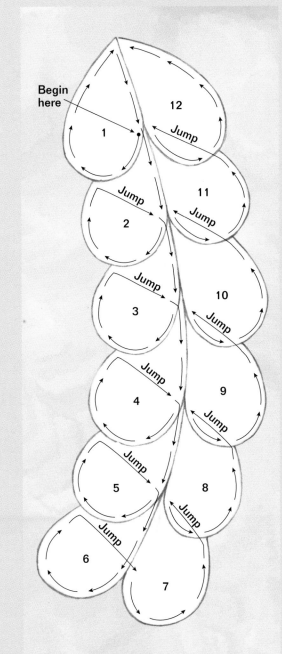

Hand Quilting with Your Thumb

by Carol Doak

Hand quilting with the side of your thumb permits you to quilt away from yourself vertically and to the left and right. When you combine this method with quilting toward yourself, to the right, and to the left with a finger, you will be able to quilt in all directions without turning your work. This is helpful when quilting at a stationary quilt frame. It also saves time when your work is in a hoop because you will not need to turn the work constantly to change quilting direction.

Quilting with your thumb has other benefits. The thumb is a larger, stronger finger, so it is easier to push the loaded needle through the fabric. Changing quilting fingers reduces repetitive motions and relieves stress on the same fingers.

To quilt with your thumb, you will need a thimble that fits your thumb and is designed for pushing from the side. A tailor's thimble is ideal; it has an open top and dimpled sides. A leather thimble will also work. The tailor's thimble should fit the thumb snugly, and the opening should be about level with the top of your thumb.

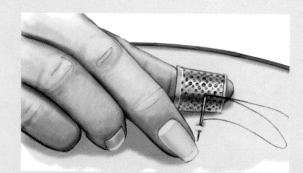

Step 3. Rock the needle level with the quilt, slide the underneath finger back on the shank of the needle, and push up to create a hill. Use your pointer finger to press down just in front of the needle, and push the needle through the quilt. You have just taken one stitch.

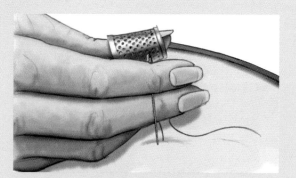

Step 1. Place the needle between your pointer finger and middle finger, and rest the side of the thimble against the eye. Place the pointer finger of your other hand under the quilt in the area where the needle point will be inserted. Push the needle vertically into the fabric.

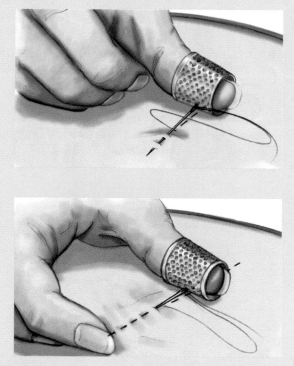

Step 4. To continue, rock the needle back up to a perpendicular position, feel the point with the underneath finger, then rock the needle back flush with the quilt. Push up on the shank of the needle to create a hill, and continue as before.

In the beginning, load just two stitches on the needle. Practice making the two stitches and the space between them straight and uniform in size. As you become accustomed to quilting with your thumb, you should be able to load four or five stitches on the needle before pulling it through the quilt.

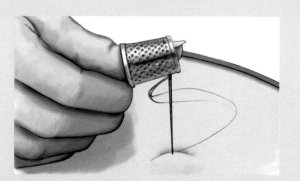

Step 2. Remove the fingers of your upper hand from the needle and balance the needle on your underneath finger.

HANGING SLEEVES

Hanging sleeves, sometimes called pockets, are used either for permanent or temporary display of quilts. Constructed of a tube of fabric, a sleeve provides an excellent means for hanging a quilt and gives it protection from the rod or dowelling used. Permanent sleeves are sewn into the bindings of quilts that will be hung on the wall. Temporary sleeves are used for quilt shows and can be removed when desired.

Sleeves should be made from a tightly woven fabric, and sleeves for large quilts are usually 4 inches wide and 2 to 3 inches shorter than the width of the quilt. Ready-sewn sleeves that measure 4 × 90 inches can be purchased, but you can save money and easily match the backing of the quilt if you make them yourself. Quilt shows usually require a 4-inch hanging sleeve.

Temporary Sleeves

Step 1. Plan the length so that the cut length is 1 inch shorter than the width of the quilt. If seaming is necessary to get the desired length, plan for seam allowances when calculating the length.

Step 2. For the strongest sleeves, cut 9-inch-wide strips across the fabric. Sew them together with ½-inch seam allowances, if necessary. Press the seams open.

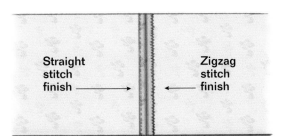

Step 3. Stitch the seams down using a straight or zigzag stitch. Hem each end with a ½-inch hem. The resulting length should be 2 to 3 inches shorter than the width of the quilt.

Step 4. With wrong sides of the sleeve together, sew lengthwise, using a ½-inch seam allowance.

Step 5. Press the seam open and center it on the tube.

Step 6. With the seam of the tube facing the backing, sew the sleeve to the top of the quilt backing along the edge of the binding. Use a thread color that matches the front of the quilt, as the stitches should occasionally catch all three layers of the quilt. This will make the hanging sleeve stronger and put less tension on the back of the quilt, preventing it from pulling out of shape.

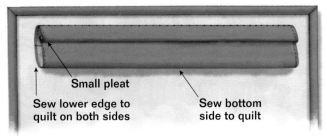

Small pleat

Sew lower edge to quilt on both sides

Sew bottom side to quilt

Step 7. After sewing the top edge of the tube, make a small pleat in the tube to allow space for the rod. Then sew the lower edge and the bottom of each end.

Permanent Sleeves

Prepare permanent sleeves following Steps 1 through 3 under "Temporary Sleeves." The sleeve will be attached after the quilt is quilted but before it is bound. Align the raw edges of the sleeve with the raw edges of the top of the quilt and sew the sleeve through all layers ¼ inch from the raw edges. Sew the bottom of the tube, as shown in Step 7 above.

Align raw edge of sleeve with raw edge of quilt top

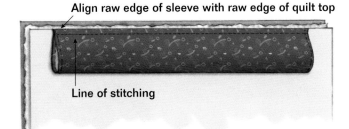

Line of stitching

For large, heavy quilts, make two or three smaller sleeves to be spaced across the quilt. Sleeves for small quilts or wallhangings (no larger than about 4 feet) can be made to finish 2 or 3 inches wide. Cut the fabric 5 or 7 inches wide.

For wall quilts that are not directional, attach sleeves at both the top and the bottom. By occasionally alternating which sleeve is used for hanging, there will be less stress on the fabrics in the quilt.

SLEEVES FOR LARGE QUILT

SLEEVE FOR
SMALL QUILT

Becky Herdle

HANGING YOUR QUILTS

Traditionally thought of as bed coverings, quilts of all shapes and sizes have made the easy transition into the realm of wallhangings. The ongoing popularity of country style in home decor is partially responsible for moving quilts off beds and onto the walls.

Prolific quiltmakers running out of beds to cover quickly discover that hanging quilts on walls gives them another way to display their work. And the smaller size of many of the quick and easy projects quilters love, referred to generically as "wall quilts," lends itself perfectly to hanging. Ranging from the smallest miniature to the largest king-size quilt, any quilt can be hung on a wall safely without the risk of damage. The term "safely" assumes a location out of direct sunlight and away from other harmful environmental factors like excessive heat and moisture.

Kim DeCoste, Manager of Special Exhibits for Quilts, Incorporated, who has supervised the hanging of more than 6,500 quilts at national and international shows, advises that you always use a hanging sleeve sewn to the back of the quilt, and provide a means of support that is sturdy and allows the weight of the quilt to be evenly distributed. (For more information on hanging sleeves, see page 129.)

The type of device you select for hanging your quilt depends in part on the size quilt you have and whether you want the hanging accessory to be visible or not. What follows is a guide to easy and affordable options for hanging quilts. With very little effort you can display your quilts and enjoy the pleasure of their company in every room of the house.

Wooden Dowels

For a simple and inexpensive support for miniatures and small wall quilts, look for ³⁄₁₆- to ⁵⁄₁₆-inch diameter dowels in your local home supply store. To make the means of support invisible, trim the dowel so that it extends about ½ inch beyond each end of the hanging sleeve but not beyond the edges of the quilt. Set the dowel ends on nails to hang.

For a more decorative approach, cut the dowel so it extends an inch or so beyond each end of the quilt. Using decorative cording, or jute for a folk-art flavored quilt, glue-gun or tie the ends onto the dowel, and hang by the cording from a nail. Also check in arts and crafts stores for dowels with decorative wooden motifs on the ends. These are meant to be seen and are fun when the stars or hearts on the dowel ends relate to the designs in the quilt.

Curtain Rods

Another easy option for small to large wall quilts is to slide a thin metal curtain rod through the hanging sleeve. Adjustable rods ⁵⁄₁₆ to ⁷⁄₁₆ inch in diameter can accommodate quilts from 11 to 48 inches wide. Use the sash rod style if you want the support to be invisible. Use the cafe rod style with brass-finish decorative caps on the ends if the decorative motif complements the quilt and fits in with your room style. These kinds of rods can be hung by nails or with the wall-mounted brackets that come with the rods.

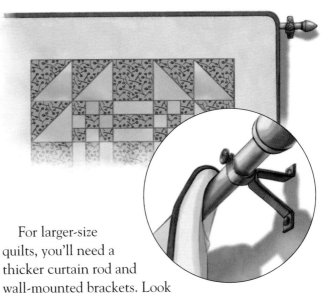

For larger-size quilts, you'll need a thicker curtain rod and wall-mounted brackets. Look for ⁷⁄₁₆-inch-diameter cafe rods that adjust from 48 to 86 inches. These rods can support the weight of a quilt up to full size, plus the brackets offer the advantage of keeping the quilt away from the wall so air can circulate.

Molding

Visit a home supply store and look for strips of flat molding, 1 × ³⁄₈ inches for small to large wall quilts, and 1½ × ³⁄₈ inches for bed-size quilts. Cut these to a length that extends 1 inch beyond each end of the hanging sleeve but doesn't go beyond the edges of the quilt. Use nails to suspend. Molding offers the advantage of not causing a lump or bulge along the hanging edge of the quilt as curtain rods or dowels sometimes can.

Commercially Made Quilt Holders

Quilt shops and mail-order quilt catalogs offer an interesting array of wooden quilt holders that are designed to support quilts safely and attractively. They come in a wide range of woods and are available both finished and unfinished. Most of these holders are variations on this basic design: the quilt slides between two strips of wood that are mounted to the wall. Adjustable screws let you tighten the pieces of wood to grip the quilt and hold it gently in place.

Depending on the style and design, there are quilt hangers available to accommodate anything from a small wall quilt all the way up to a king-size quilt.

HOOPS

For many, many years, most quilting was done on large floor frames that could accommodate several quilters at a time. As quilting became less important and houses became smaller, fewer people were willing or able to give up space in

their homes for a large quilt frame. The quilt hoop became a popular alternative, and today there are probably more quilters who use a hoop than a frame when they quilt.

A quilt hoop is a relatively small, two-part "frame" used to hold the layers of a quilt together, keep the tension even, and prevent slipping while it is being quilted. A screw and bolt attached to the outer circle are used to tighten the hoop around the three layers of the quilt. It is moved from one area of the quilt to another as quilting is completed. Most hoops are made of wood and are either circular or oval, though square frames are also available.

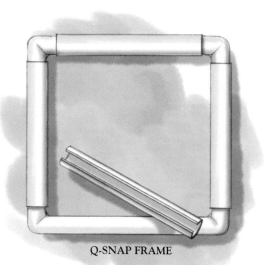

Q-SNAP FRAME

In recent years, plastic piping has been developed and shaped to form into square or rectangular "hoops." Called Q-Snap frames, they are made of PVC plastic, which is easily snapped together for quilting and disassembled for storage or traveling.

Hoops may be very simple and relatively inexpensive, or they may cost several hundred dollars, depending on the kind of wood used and whether they include a support and accessories. Round hoops come in sizes from 10 to 23 inches in diameter and oval hoops are approximately

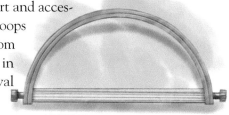

ADJUSTABLE BORDER HOOP

12 × 23 inches. Some hoops have adapters that permit quilting the straight edge of a quilt in a round hoop, or special D-shaped border hoops can be purchased.

As a substitute for an adapter or a border hoop, baste fabric along the edge of the quilt to fill the entire hoop. Turkish towels work well for this purpose.

ADJUSTABLE LAP HOOP

Larger hoops are usually held on stands. A stand support may be rigid, in which case the quilter leans over the hoop, much as when using a quilting frame, or the stand can swivel, tilt, and slant to permit the hoop to go over a person's lap. More expensive varieties often include adapters and different sizes and types of hoops. These can be changed by an easy snap-on process or by loosening a bolt or thumbscrew.

Lap hoops are a variation of ordinary hoops. A simple lap hoop has a base that sits in your lap and upright supports that hold the hoop a few inches above its base. More elaborate, adjustable lap hoops may also be purchased.

SIMPLE LAP HOOP

Lap hoops leave both hands free and are essential for quilters who use a stab stitch, a method in which the needle is inserted straight down through the layers and guided straight back up with the hand underneath.

The choice of a hoop is a very personal decision. If you like to quilt with the work in your lap, choose a hoop no larger than 18 inches in diameter, since it is difficult to hold a larger one in your lap or to reach into the center of it for quilting.

Using a Hoop

The basted quilt is put between the two sections of the hoop with the smaller section of the hoop underneath. The quilt layers are adjusted so that the tension on the top and bottom layers is the same. The tension depends on personal preferences. Some people want the work to be quite loose, as this makes it easier to quilt with a traditional rocking stitch. For quilters who use a stab stitch the work should be very taut.

A person who has never used a hoop for quilting may at first find one difficult to use, but after learning how, most people find their quilting improves by using one.

INSPIRATION

Inspiration isn't always something you can purchase by the yard. It is usually free for the taking, and people find it in many different places. You just have to know where *you* need to look!

inspiration for quilting designs is everywhere—silver tea services, flatware, wallpaper, floor tiles, Greek urns, ancient Egyptian design, pictographs . . . just look around!

Gwen Marston

Antique Quilts and Folk Art

Old quilts have been and continue to be a primary source of inspiration for my quiltmaking. What I know about quilts and quiltmaking I have learned from my continuing study of quilts made in the eighteenth and nineteenth centuries. These quilts exhibit the most incredible and ingenious innovations, which always surprise and delight me. I find ideas so old that they appear new when I borrow them for my own purposes.

As a quilter, I quite naturally became interested in needle arts of other cultures. Over the years, I have amassed a sizable collection of folk art textiles, mainly patchwork and appliqué, from many different countries. Folk art has similar qualities the world over; it is often characterized as primitive, casual, informal, energetic, playful, joyful, asymmetrical, surprising, fun, spontaneous, naive, unsophisticated, ingenuous, innocent, and childlike. These are all wonderful words. I have drawn inspiration for my own work from these refreshing and imaginative textiles.

Most of what I know about classical quilting designs was learned from nineteenth century quilts. But

Fabrics, Techniques, and Tools

For me, inspiration comes from so many areas. I am inspired by a new fabric or groups of fabric—the theme, the colors, or the design speak to me. I can also be inspired by a new garment pattern. The wheels start turning when I envision techniques, manipulations, and embellishments incorporated into the design of the garment. Seeing an unusual design or a different patchwork idea spurs me to incorporate it into something I am currently creating. A new quick-piecing or stitching technique, or a new tool prompts me to learn how to use it.

The excitement, inspiration, and follow-through with the planning of fabrics, colors, textures, and placement are my most favorite parts of the designing process. My energy is at its highest, and I can't move fast enough to keep up with the possibilities that keep popping into my head! I just wish I had the time to execute all the creations that I have imagined!

Judy Murrah

Humor

As a beginning quiltmaker, I was drawn to traditional quilts, especially the lovely two-color beauties. As my experience grew, so did the desire to create original pieces. Since I don't think in mathematical or geometric terms, I experimented with many techniques to find the ones that best translate my ideas.

Now my work is usually pictorial, and often humorous, featuring a theme or specific subject depicted through appliqué and embellishments. There is no grand scheme when I begin—I just pick a subject and beat it to death! My pieces have no political statements or social significance; I'm more likely to be influenced by reading Dave Barry than by the editorial section of the newspaper or by a quilt design book. If I could draw, I'd make Norman Rockwell-like appliqué quilts!

I maintain a journal where I record random thoughts and inspirations that surely wouldn't be retained, as my short-term memory continues to fail and my hectic life marches on. It's not a diary for profound thoughts—I'm not sure I have any of those! Phrases, cartoons, advertisements, line drawings, and sketches are kept there as references to enhance my creativity when gearing up to begin new projects.

Mary Stori

IRON

Quilters of the past probably did not rely on an iron for quiltmaking as much as contemporary quilters do. Today we use an iron as a tool to aid in precise piecing, pressing seams usually to one side as we sew them. Irons come in all varieties from bare-bones models to elaborate irons with nonstick soleplates. Many have an automatic shut-off feature.

Soleplate

For most quilters the automatic shut-off iron is more trouble than it is worth. Each time you go to use the iron, it has shut off and you need to wait for it to get hot again. Also, many shut-off irons make an annoying chirping noise to alert you to the fact they are shutting off. Consider these factors before you make a purchase. Some people do like the safety of the automatic shut-off because they are afraid they will forget to turn the iron off when they leave their sewing area.

Be sure the iron you purchase can be used dry or with steam. Sometimes steam is needed, such as when ironing a newly washed piece of fabric, and sometimes a dry iron is needed, such as when pressing seams. (Steam versus dry is a personal preference that varies among quilters. See also "Pressing" on page 180.)

Any iron should get hot enough to remove folds and creases from 100 percent cotton fabric. Travel irons frequently do not get hot enough, so they are not usually recommended for quiltmaking.

Keep your iron clean and follow the manufacturer's instructions. Starch and residue from sizing on the fabric can be removed from the soleplate with a nonabrasive soleplate cleaner. Check your place of purchase or quilting catalogs for this type of product.

Try This

Use a surge protector or multiple outlet strip with a light on it for your iron. The light indicates when it is on. I keep my iron and a workspace lamp plugged into this outlet right inside my sewing room door. Whenever I go into and out of the room, I know immediately if the iron is on or not by glancing at the outlet strip.

Karen Kay Buckley

135

LABELS

A label provides a record of your handiwork for history. It guarantees that the information on your quilt remains accurate and passes into history *with* the quilt. We owe it to our descendants and to the greater world of interested quilters to provide this information. On a smaller scale, it is a lovely finishing touch for the recipient of the quilt.

Designing Labels

A label may be as simple as a piece of muslin or as complicated as a pieced or appliquéd block. There are also lovely preprinted quilt labels available to make your life easy while making your quilts beautiful.

Consider designing a label that echoes something from the front of the quilt. You might use a block from the front or substitute muslin for a printed fabric in the block so you can write on it. Or take an appliqué motif, such as a flower or vine, from the front, and appliqué it onto a corner or side of the label.

Preprinted labels are a lovely, colorful, and easy option if you are in a hurry.

SPOOL

ANVIL

BASKET APPLIQUÉ

FLOWER APPLIQUÉ

Supplies

Permanent pen

Fabric

Marking Guide (See "Procedure for Writing.")

Paper for rough drafts

Note: Instructions for making the Marking Guide follow in "Procedure for Writing."

Pens

Use any permanent pen you like. I find the Pigma Micron and the Identipen to be good choices. They are permanent, don't bleed very much as you write, and are available in a variety of colors.

With any pen, pretest it on the fabric you will be using for your label. How fast you write will depend on how much the pen bleeds. Write just quickly enough to keep ahead of the bleeding. Always write lightly to protect the delicate felt-tipped pen points.

The Pigma point .01 is delicate for small writing, the Pigma point .05 is broader for larger writing, and the Identipen has two points for large and very large writing.

Fabric

Use 100 percent cotton fabric, prewashed and ironed. Most permanent pens bleed less and are more permanent on cotton than on polyester blends.

Information to Include

- Always include these basics: who made it, when, and where. Use full names for people and places.
- This additional information is nice: for whom or for what occasion it was made.
- Other information that may be applicable: the quilt name or the pattern name.

Procedure for Writing

Make a Marking Guide to keep your writing straight. I designed this simple-to-make tool—you simply draw a series of lines on either paper or muslin, with a thick marker, so they are visible through the label fabric when you lay the label over it. By using the Marking Guide under your label, you will have perfectly straight lines with no marks on the label. I prefer a fabric Marking Guide; it acts as an anchor to keep the fabric from slipping.

Step 1. Decide what you want to write on the label. This will determine how large it will be.

Step 2. Design and make the label. Simply cut out the desired shape, or piece a block to be used. You can also add appliqué as desired.

Step 3. Using the completed label as your guide, figure out how to space the writing. Consider how many lines you will need and what will fit on each line.

Step 4. Make some rough drafts on paper to practice the lettering and spacing. Lay paper over the label to sketch an outline of the actual writing space available.

Step 5. When you are ready to write on the label, lay it over a fabric Marking Guide (to keep it from slipping and to provide guiding lines), place the well-spaced rough draft to your side as a guide, and write on the label.

Attaching the Label to the Quilt

Sew the label onto the quilt backing *before* you layer and baste the top, batting, and backing together. With theft an unpleasant but recurring fact in the quilt world, you want your label quilted into all the layers rather than simply appliquéd onto the back. That way, it can't be detached without cutting into the quilt. We know that you are eager to finish at this stage in the quiltmaking process, but it is worth taking the time to make the label and attach it before quilting. To do this, follow these steps:

Step 1. Make the label and write the information on it. Place the label where you want it on the backing, at least 5 inches in from the probable finished edge—even if you stretch the backing as you quilt, the label will be a few inches from the edge.

Step 2. Appliqué the label onto the quilt backing, using a tiny blind stitch. Trim away the backing from behind the label just as you would under an appliqué so you have only three layers to quilt through.

Step 3. With the label now a part of the backing, layer the top, batting, and backing. Quilt, forgetting the label is there. It will look wonderful no matter what kind of quilting pattern you have on the front, and it will be safely quilted into the quilt.

LABEL DESIGNS
FOR TRACING

A Quick and Easy, Yet Elegant Label

With the same pen you use for writing, you can draw a simple but elegant label. Draw designs in the four corners, on two sides, or on opposite sides. Use different colored pens to add some flair.

If you are not confident of your drawing abilities, try tracing simple designs. Look for traceable designs in copyright-free books in art stores. Three designs are provided for you here. They are corner designs and can be traced easily onto a label in one or more corners. The process is simple.

Step 1. Trace the design lightly onto your label fabric directly from the book.

Step 2. Thicken some lines, and shade gently with the edge of the pen, using a very light touch.

This design was drawn with the fine-point Pigma .01, so that it remains delicate in feeling. Shading is easy with the Pigma .01.

138

LAMÉ

Lamé adds shine, glamour, and elegance to the Celtic appliqué quilt made by Philomena Durcan and to the Christmas table runner made by Cyndi Hershey. Lamé also comes in bright pink and royal blue.

Quilters always seem to be on the lookout for ways to make their projects different and unique. One of the things that has caught their eye is lamé. Lamé is woven with metallic threads in a number of different styles and colors, all of which add sparkle and dimension to a project. Some lamé has a black warp, meaning that half the threads are black, giving this lamé an interesting "smoky" appearance.

Regular lamé is rather delicate and must be fused with a woven cotton fusible interfacing. This fusible interfacing stabilizes the metallic threads so that they don't fray when cut, and it makes the fabric easier to handle when stitching. Fusing also makes it possible for the lamé to be gently washed without falling apart.

Work with the grain lines of the interfacing when marking and cutting your pieces. Be aware that fused lamé may not be as soft or drapable as your other fabrics. This could affect where you choose to use it in your project.

Tricot-backed lamé, also known as knit lamé, is extremely soft and drapable. This type of lamé is commonly used in clothing projects, where those qualities are more important. However, because it is more fluid, it tends to be slippery and may be more difficult to handle.

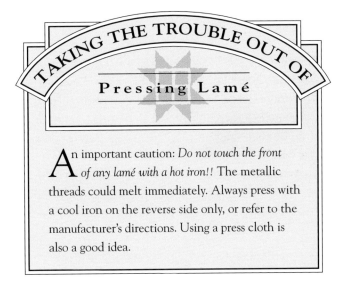

TAKING THE TROUBLE OUT OF
Pressing Lamé

An important caution: *Do not touch the front of any lamé with a hot iron!!* The metallic threads could melt immediately. Always press with a cool iron on the reverse side only, or refer to the manufacturer's directions. Using a press cloth is also a good idea.

Lamé may be stitched by hand or machine. If using a machine, be sure to use the appropriate needle. Size 70/10 or 80/12 sharp needles work well on cotton-fused lamé. Use the same size in a ball point needle when stitching tricot-backed lamé. Cotton thread works well for regular stitching but decorative thread can add even more pizzazz! Use machine embroidery needles for rayon or other embroidery type threads, and use a Metallica needle for metallic type threads. These specialty needles help to prevent fraying of the threads and also protect the lamé.

Cyndi Hershey

139

LATTICE

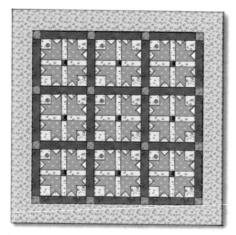

Plain lattice with contrasting squares at intersections

Plain lattice with "busy" blocks

Lattice, also called setting strips or sashing, is used to separate pieced or appliquéd blocks and sometimes adds a secondary design to the overall quilt pattern. It can be used to increase the size of a quilt top and may match or be a different fabric from the border. Lattice strips can help to make irregularly shaped blocks conform to the proper size and are very helpful in unifying the look of a sampler quilt or a friendship quilt. Pieced lattice may also be used with fabric squares or "blocks" that are not pieced or appliquéd.

In some quilts, lattice is not used, such as in Log Cabin, Trip Around the World, or Irish Chain quilts, where the overall design depends on the placement of the blocks next to each other. The blocks for a quilt may be made before you decide whether to use lattice; putting the completed blocks up on a design wall and "auditioning" different lattice patterns will tell you which will highlight the design best.

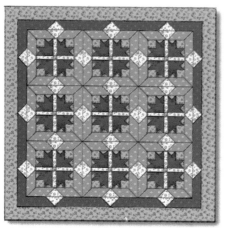

Pieced lattice

Pieced lattice with stars at intersections

Plain lattice strips are often 2 to 2½ inches wide and are frequently accented with squares of a different fabric at intersections. These strips serve as a picture frame around the blocks and are generally a contrasting color. Lattice strips are added between the blocks of a row, and they are sewn to the rows of blocks to separate them. Lattice is usually added around the outside edges, unless the border is made of the same fabric.

Pieced lattice can enhance simple blocks or plain fabric squares by introducing more colors, forming stars or checkerboards at the intersections, creating a

Checkerboard pieced lattice with appliqué blocks

Pieced lattice with appliqué blocks

southwestern flavor through the use of triangles, or adding many other new elements. Often, the use of solid-color fabric for pieced lattice will highlight the piecing and frame the blocks better than print fabrics. You will probably want to draw your design on graph paper if using pieced lattice to make sure all the elements will fit. The addition of a plain outer border will frame and complement the complexity of the pieced lattice.

Susan Stein

LAUNDERING QUILTS

The laundering of a quilt depends on its age and condition. Antique and older quilts are usually treated very differently from those made by today's methods.

A well-quilted, recently made quilt sewn from preshrunk, colorfast fabrics should be machine-washable and machine-dryable. Use gentle cycles, a mild detergent, and lukewarm or cool temperatures. Both polyester and cotton battings are washable. Polyester will not shrink, and prewashed cotton battings will shrink very little. If you prefer a crinkled, antique look, it's not necessary to preshrink either fabrics or batting.

Antique quilts do require special care. Machine washing and drying could be disastrous for them. Fibers weaken when wet and can be damaged easily by agitation or pulling.

Testing for Colorfastness

Before you launder an antique quilt or any quilt you're unsure about, test the fabrics for colorfastness. First, rub the fabric with a dry white cloth or Q-Tip. If no color rubs off, dampen the cloth and repeat. If it still shows no color, repeat with a solution of water and the soap to be used. Even if no color shows here, it is not a guarantee that no running will occur. Agitation sometimes causes dyes to run, but it is usually safe to proceed. If the fabric is not colorfast, you have to decide whether to wash the quilt at all or whether to simply air it or vacuum it lightly. (See "Quilt Care and Storage" on page 185.)

If bleeding occurs while washing a quilt, do not let the quilt dry out. Try treating it with a product called

Easy Wash, and rinse repeatedly to keep the colors from setting in adjacent fabrics. Once dry, it is usually impossible to remove dyes that have bled.

Machine Washing "by Hand"

For laundering, I feel the preferred method is to wash quilts "by hand" in a washing machine. Do not use modern detergents for washing antique quilts. The chemicals are harsh and may adversely affect old dyes. Orvus paste, sold as "Quilt Soap" in most quilt shops, is my first choice. To remove light stains, soaking in Snowy Bleach may help.

Step 1. Fill your washing machine with cool or lukewarm water containing a small amount of a mild soap. Use the large load setting.

Step 2. Add the quilt and move by hand enough to be sure it is wet through with the soapy solution. (Some people feel a gentle lingerie cycle can be used as safely as hand agitation, but that probably depends on the actual machine being used.)

Step 3. Soak the quilt for five to ten minutes, agitating gently by hand once or twice.

Step 4. Spin the water out. Spinning does not agitate the quilt but merely flattens it against the sides of the machine while the water is spun out.

Step 5. After the soapy water has been spun out, add clear water of the same temperature and gently move the quilt around in the water. Two or three rinses may be needed to remove all of the soapy water.

Drying

Carefully lay the quilt out flat on a sheet outdoors. Cover it with a second sheet to protect it from leaves, insects, and fading. Never hang a quilt on a clothes-line while wet since it will not dry straight, and it puts a great deal of stress on the fibers.

If drying must be done indoors, again it should be dried flat; a fan blowing slightly above it will help speed the drying process. Remember to protect the surface under it from moisture with a large sheet of plastic. If a quilt must be folded while drying, refold several times so that fold lines do not dry in.

Sheet of plastic

Hand Washing in a Bathtub

The second laundering method some people suggest is to wash the quilt by soaking it in a bathtub and using gentle hand movements to distribute the water through the quilt. The soapy solution is drained off without lifting the quilt, and it is rinsed several times, letting the water drain well between rinses.

I do not recommend this method because it is slow, requiring many hours for draining between soak periods. Even when carefully drained, there is enough water in the quilt to make it heavy and difficult to handle, putting a lot of strain on the fabrics. Also, if the quilt has fabrics that run, the long time that it is wet and folded against itself can make the problem even worse.

If you prefer this method, place a sheet in the tub first. Use lukewarm water and a mild soap. After the wash and rinse waters have drained thoroughly, use the sheet to very gently lift the quilt and carry it to a flat surface for drying.

142

MACHINE PIECING

Machine piecing is the fast and accurate way to stitch almost any block pattern. There are two basic ways to approach machine piecing. One method depends on accurate ¼-inch seam allowances. The other method uses matching dots to sew accurate seam lines. Each technique has unique advantages. Proficiency in both methods is required to be successful in machine piecing complex quilt blocks.

When you approach a pattern, determine the best way to stitch the pieces by looking at the components of the block. Will you be piecing simple straight lines, or are there complex set-in pieces? This determines how the pieces will be cut, marked, and stitched.

Simple Piecing

Using accurate ¼-inch seam allowances is the best method for beginners and for piecing patterns with large simple pieces. This is the fastest and easiest piecing method. Use it for all straight matches using squares, rectangles, and triangles. It is commonly paired with rotary cut strips and pieces. Your strips and pieces must be cut accurately, and you must be able to sew a precise ¼-inch seam. Refer to "Rotary Cutting" on page 197 and "Seam Allowance" on page 215.

Intricate Set-In Piecing and Stars

Use the matching dots method for set-in piecing and for diamonds such as Eight-Pointed and Six-Pointed Stars. This method goes hand in hand with using templates to mark and cut pieces. Templates need to have ¹⁄₁₆-inch holes punched at each seam intersection to mark the matching dots. This method can be extremely accurate and is unequaled for intricate set-in pieces. The major disadvantage is marking all the dots on every fabric piece. This makes the method slower and more tedious than rotary cutting. You need to know how to make and use templates and to mark your fabric accurately. Refer to "Templates" on page 238.

Constructing Blocks in Units

The best and most logical way to approach stitching any quilt block is the unit method of construction. Stitch the small pieces into larger groups or units. Then stitch these units together to make the block. The purpose of unit construction is to make accurate, easy-to-stitch blocks with straight seams.

In the most basic form of unit construction, the pieces of the block are joined as rows. Look at the simple Four Patch. Two pieces are stitched to make the row. Two rows are stitched together to create the block.

FOUR PATCH CONSTRUCTION

Every block can be stitched with unit construction. Common forms include the 9-patch and 16-patch patterns. Even complex blocks like the Lemoyne Star benefit from unit construction. The eight points are joined in sets of two, then four, to finally make the total eight. The set-in squares and triangles are added last.

9-PATCH CONSTRUCTION

16-PATCH CONSTRUCTION

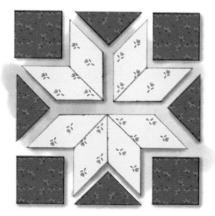

LEMOYNE STAR CONSTRUCTION

Fabric Preparation

Step 1. Prewash all fabrics and check for colorfastness. Press the fabric prior to marking and cutting. Refer to "Preparing Fabric" on page 179.

Step 2. Cut all the fabric pieces needed for a *single* block. I suggest you make one sample block to try the pattern before cutting the entire quilt. This ensures that the pattern is correct and that you understand the piecing process. It also affords a chance to reevaluate color and fabric placement.

 Fabric is easier to handle and accurately cut and piece when it has been starched prior to cutting and stitching. Spray starch adds body and stiffness to the fabric. It prevents the fabric from shifting during cutting and stitching and makes it less likely that points on your cut patches will fray or get caught in the needle hole. I starch every piece of fabric that I use and believe it can greatly increase the accuracy achieved by quiltmakers of every level.

Sewing Machine Setup

- Use a new number 11/70 or 12/80 universal needle.
- Use a fine cotton embroidery thread, size 50 or 60, in a neutral color. Use matching thread in the needle and bobbin. Choose white or beige for pastel fabrics. Choose mid-tone gray for dark fabric.
- Set the machine for straight stitch with a slightly shorter than average stitch length. I recommend a stitch length of about 2 millimeters or 12 to 14 stitches per inch.
- Use the correct presser foot.

Presser Feet

There are two types of presser feet used for machine piecing. One is the true ¼-inch foot. This foot is designed with an accurate ¼-inch guide and is used for simple straight seams.

The second foot is the open-toe or no-bridge embroidery foot. This foot was originally de-signed for appliqué. Its most distinctive feature is the cut-away portion in front of the needle. This foot af-fords an unobstructed view of the needle and is used for intricate piecing, like set-in pieces and eight-pointed stars. It cannot be used as an accurate ¼-inch guide.

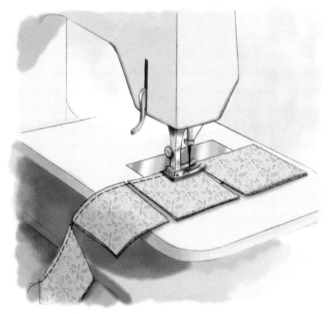

¼" FOOT

OPEN-TOE FOOT

Continue stitching without clipping the threads. The feed dogs will catch the second set of pieces and move them under the foot. A narrow space and short length of thread will divide the two sets of pieces.

Sew all the pieces you can at one time. The chain may be as short as 2 sets or as long as 100 sets. After completing the chain, remove the pieces from the machine and clip the sets apart.

Needle and Thread Choices

The finer the thread and needle, the more accurate the piecing. Thick thread takes up space in the seam. In complex piecing, this extra thickness can affect the completed block. Occasionally the fine thread and needle may cause problems. If the thread is fraying or the machine skips stitches, change to one needle size larger—the next higher number (the higher the number, the larger the needle).

Chain Piecing

Chain piecing is used to conserve both time and thread. As the name implies, chain piecing links sets of patches together with a continuous line of stitching. To chain piece, sew one set of pieces to-gether. Stop a stitch or two before the edge of the fabric. Without lifting the presser foot, slip the next set of pieces under the toes of the presser foot.

TAKING THE TROUBLE OUT OF
Thread That Breaks

If your cotton thread breaks frequently, it may need to be revived. Cotton thread becomes brittle with age or in low humidity. To revive the thread, place it in a plastic bag in the freezer. Allow the thread to freeze for a day or two. Then remove the thread from the freezer and plastic bag, and let it thaw. The frozen thread will attract moisture as it thaws. The increased moisture will restore its pliability.

TAKING THE TROUBLE OUT OF Starting to Stitch

Frequently, students tell me they have trouble beginning a line of stitches. The threads may snarl and jam or the fabric is pulled into the needle hole opening. There are three simple ways to stop these problems:

1. Starch the fabric to give it body.

2. Hold on to the needle and bobbin thread tails as you start to sew.

3. Use a scrap starter.

A scrap starter is a small scrap of fabric that is used as the first piece in a chain of pieces. It can also be used as a spacer between chains. Simply stitch into the scrap as the first piece in the chain. Sew until you can clip the scrap from the chain. Then stitch into it as the last piece, and leave it under the foot, ready to start the next chain line.

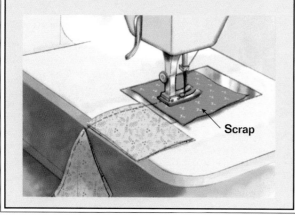

Scrap

Pressing the Seams

Pressing is key to good piecing. Pressing flattens the seam and removes seam wells that can affect the accuracy of the block. Press seams as you sew. Crossing unpressed seams causes inexact matches. Press with care, as overzealous pressing can stretch the pieces and distort the finished block.

The simplest method of pressing is finger pressing. To finger press, pinch the seam between your fingers and thumb. Move your fingers along the seam line. The heat, moisture, and pressure from your fingertips and fingernails will press the seam.

You can also press the seam with an iron. Move the iron in an up and down motion; don't slide it across the fabric.

Traditionally, seams are pressed to one side toward the darker fabric. This is the best choice for simple piecing of squares, rectangles, and triangles. These seams are strong and won't allow the batting to beard along the seam.

Another choice is to press the seams open, as in dressmaking. Pressing seams open has become more popular as quilters have realized the advantages. Open seams produce a smooth quilt top that lies very flat. The open seams facilitate matching points and set-in piecing. Open seams are, however, slightly weaker. There will be more stress on the stitching and fabric. Do not press seams open when you will be quilting in-the-ditch (quilting right next to the seams).

Matching Straight Seams

Straight seams crossing at 90 degree angles are formed by squares and rectangles. This match is commonly referred to as keying a seam. It is the simplest of all matches. The secret to a good match is in the pressing of the block.

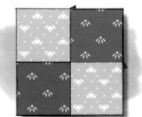

SIMPLE MATCH OF SQUARES

Step 1. Press the seams to one side and in opposite directions. With right sides together, line up the matching edges, and slide the seams toward one another. The slight thickness of the seams will lock the match together.

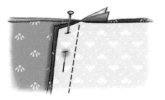

Step 2. Place a pin in the seam allowance that will reach the needle first. The pin should be perpendicular to the seam that will be sewn.

Step 3. Stitch the seam with a ¼-inch seam allowance. Don't sew over the pin; slide it out of the fabric as it moves under the presser foot.

The keyed match will also work with open seams. Keying makes an easy match, while the open seams make a flat match.

Step 1. Simply tip the open seam allowances to one side. Treat the match as a simple keyed match. Place the pins in *just* the block, not the seam allowances.

Step 2. Stitch the seam, keeping the seam allowances open as you stitch across the intersection. Remove the pins as you get to them. Sewing over them can damage your needle.

Matching Multiple Points

One of the more difficult matches is when six or more pieces come together in a single spot. This might be at the center of a Six- or Eight-Pointed Star, or joining four squares made of triangles. I recommend using an open-toe or no-bridge embroidery foot for this match. It gives a clear view of the needle and matching points. As an example in these directions, I will use the center of an Eight-Pointed Star.

Pencil dots

Begin sewing here

Stop ¼" from the edge and take three backstitches

Step 1. Lay out the cut patches with dots marked at seam intersections. Join the eight pieces to make four sets of two. Press the seams open.

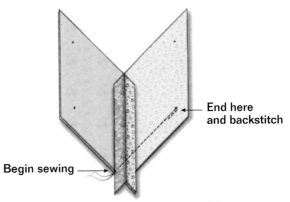

End here and backstitch

Begin sewing

Step 2. Join the four sets to make two units of four pieces. Press the seams open.

Step 3. The final seam will join the two units to make the star. Use a "skewer" or "stab" pin to hold the match. Note how the open seams give a clear view of the matching points on the wrong side of the star. Place the point of the pin through the match on the top piece. Then pin into the match on the lower piece. Leave the pin standing. Don't try to tip the pin or bring the point back into the fabric.

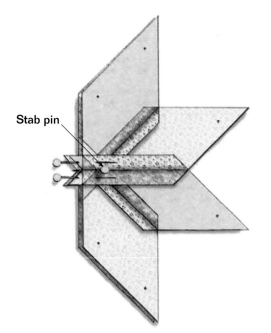

Stab pin

Step 4. Insert a pin on either side of the stab pin, and stitch toward the match and the stab pin. Tip up the pin as you approach the match. Don't remove the pin until it is at the needle. The open-toe or no-bridge foot will allow you to guide the pin right up to the needle. The stab pin will remain skewered through the points until the match is secured with the needle. Once the needle and pin meet, you can pull out the stab pin. Complete the seam, and check the star center.

 To prevent scratches from the stab pin as it is pulled across the bed of the machine, tape a 2-inch square of template plastic on the bed directly in front of the presser foot. Remember to remove the plastic and tape from the machine at the end of every day of sewing. WD-40 is great for removing any tape residue from your machine. Spray it on a soft cloth, and rub the area to remove any gummy tape residue.

TAKING THE TROUBLE OUT OF
Matching Multiple Points

Problem: Center points are cut off.

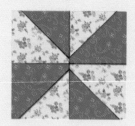

Solution: This is caused by taking too wide a seam at the star center. You can't always trust the ¼-inch seam allowance at this delicate spot. The match is more important than the accurate seam allowance. Stitch toward the match and ignore the seam allowances. Most discrepancies caused by the uneven seam allowances can be pressed away.

Problem: Center points are too far apart.

Solution: This is caused by taking too narrow a seam at the star center. Don't trust the ¼-inch seam allowance. Stitch toward the match and ignore the seam allowances.

Problem: Seam lines don't match in the center.

Solution: This common problem is caused by the feed dogs pulling the lower half of the star as it is stitched. As a result, the vertical seam is straight, but the horizontal seam is not matched. This can be corrected by holding the stab pin straight up and down. Don't let the pin tip toward you as you stitch. Tipping the pin slides the match apart.

Try This Wouldn't it be great if you didn't have to rip out mistakes? I know how frustrating it is to rip out stitches. Eight-pointed stars and other intricate piecing can try the patience of even the most devoted quilter. Try using Wash-A-Way basting thread in the bobbin when stitching difficult matches. Wash-A-Way looks and stitches like regular sewing thread, but disappears when exposed to high levels of steam from your iron. No more ripping! I stitch the complex seam and check the match. If it is incorrect, I simply steam away the seam, pull away the extra needle thread and start again. If it is right, I restitch the seam with my regular sewing thread. Press with steam and remove the extra thread as best you can.

Remember, don't mistake Wash-A-Way for regular thread. Anything you sew with Wash-A-Way will fall apart when exposed to steam or water. To prevent accidents, mark the Wash-A-Way bobbin with a small dot of nail polish. Wash-A-Way is available in quilt shops and from mail-order sewing supply catalogs.

Most seams in quiltmaking are sewn simply from edge to edge, with the exception of set-in seams. These seams must start and stop exactly ¼ inch from the edges of the fabric. The easiest way to know where to start and stop is with a matching dot. To be successful at set-in piecing, each piece will require matching dots. The dots are drawn on the wrong side of the fabric using a plastic template of the pattern piece. A small hole in the template allows you to accurately place the dot. The Attic Windows block is used as an example in the directions below.

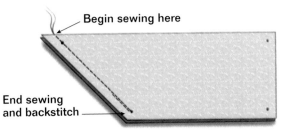

Step 1. Join the two pieces that bracket the inset square. Align the pieces so that you will sew through the dot at the outside corner. The dots are more important than accurate seam allowances. Stop sewing at the dot and take three or four stitches in reverse to knot the stitching line securely.

Step 2. Press the seam open. This will allow you to stitch the inset in one line of stitching.

Set-In Piecing

Set-in pieces occur where three pieces and three seams come together, as in the corners of Eight-Pointed Stars and Attic Windows. Set-in piecing is considered one of the more difficult aspects of machine piecing. It does take more skill than keyed matches, but is surprisingly simple to master. I recommend using an open-toe or no-bridge embroidery foot for this match. It gives a clear view of the needle and matching points.

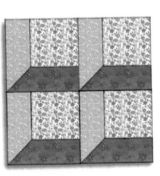

ATTIC WINDOWS

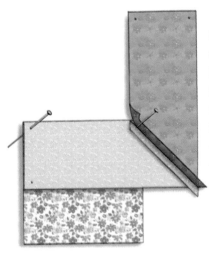

Step 3. Place the single square on the bottom and the two bracketing pieces on the top. The square is right side up and the wrong sides of the bracketing pieces are on the top. The open seam of the bracketing pieces is clearly visible.

Step 4. Line up the edge of the square with the first piece. Don't worry about the second bracketing piece at this time. Use pins at the matching dots on the square and the bracketing pieces to correctly place the square. Note that the corner dot of the square matches the knot on the set-in seam. Use additional pins to secure the match. Align the pieces on your sewing machine so that you will sew through the dot. This is more important than the seam allowances.

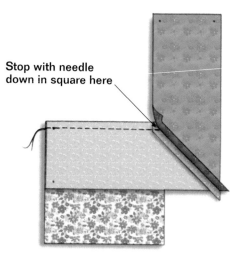

Stop with needle down in square here

Step 5. Stitch toward the open seam of the bracketing pieces. Stitch across the open seam allowance. The last stitch

before turning the corner should fall off the folded edge of the bracketing fabric, as close as possible to the knot securing the opened seam. Stop with the needle lowered in the single layer of the square fabric. The needle is in the *square* only. No other fabric is caught in the needle.

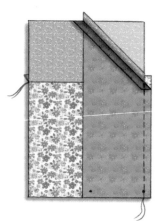

Step 6. Lift the presser foot, and pivot the fabrics to turn the corner. Manipulate the unsewn bracketing piece to line up with the matching dots on the square. Pin if desired. Lower the presser foot and continue sewing.

Step 7. Press the seams toward the bracketing pieces.

Debra Wagner

MACHINE QUILTING

Within the last decade, quiltmakers have realized the speed and technical advantages machine quilting can offer. Rotary cutting and machine piecing allow quilters to create new and exciting quilts at an astonishing speed. Now machine quilting makes it possible to finish them all, too!

Machine quilting can mimic traditional quilting patterns or feature ultra-modern designs. There are two methods, machine-guided and free-motion. For either, you'll need an efficient and comfortable work area.

Organize Your Workspace

Ergonomics (the science of arranging people and things) plays a vital role in workspace organization for the machine quilter. The weight and size of the quilt require special consideration. A poorly designed workspace can contribute to back and shoulder pain, headaches, and repetitive motion injuries, like carpal tunnel syndrome. A few simple changes in your workspace can prevent problems.

The chair: Choose a good secretarial chair. The seat back should be adjusted to hug the small of your back and encourage you to sit up straight. Sitting up straight will prevent headaches and back pain. You can also adjust the height up or down to find the most comfortable position for you.

The table: A work table should be large enough to comfortably hold a large quilt. It is best if the table is not against the wall. This way you can use a second table behind the first to extend your working space. In my workroom, the ironing board and sewing table are placed back to back. The ironing board helps support the quilt and keeps it from falling off behind the sewing machine. For portable machines, consider a free-arm extension table. This will create a large working space around the free arm. These can be an accessory for your machine. Or, you can purchase plexiglass tables to fit around the free arm of most machines through mail-order catalogs.

The sewing machine: Adjust the placement of the machine so you are directly in front of the needle. Move the machine at least 6 inches away from the edge of the table. This gives you extra room to work and rest your arms. Resting your elbows on the table will prevent back and shoulder pain.

The sewing surface: To prevent carpal tunnel syndrome, your arms and hands must be in a neutral position, with the fingers, wrist, and elbow in a straight line. When sewing on a cabinet this happens automatically. When sewing with a portable machine, it is necessary to raise your elbows to the height of the sewing surface. Place a thick book or two on the table for your elbows to rest on.

The relationship between the height of the sewing surface and the height of the chair is critical. Sit up straight, with your arm relaxed and bent at the elbows. Clasp your hands together. Rest your hands and arms on the sewing surface. Now unclasp your hands and place them near the presser foot. The cabinet top (or for portable machines, the thick books on top of the table) should be elbow height or slightly higher. You should be able to rest your arms comfortably on the tabletop without bending or reaching. If the tabletop is too low, you are forced to bend over to sew. If it's too high, you will be raising your shoulders to sew. Switch and replace books until you get it right.

Choose Your Thread and Needle

The thread and needle must be matched for the best stitch quality. Thread is the most important factor in choosing a needle. The hole of the needle must be the right size for the thread you're using. As a rule of thumb, the thread should go through the needle eye without binding or sticking.

Choose the smallest needle size for your thread and fabric choice. A smaller needle will make a less conspicuous hole in the fabric. If the needle is too small for the thread or fabric, the threads may fray as you stitch or the machine will skip stitches. You can use the universal needles or special quilting needles.

As a traditionalist, I prefer threads that are discreet and unobtrusive. I want the quilting design to show, not the threads. Subtle thread colors blend with the fabrics and hide many stitching errors, making them good choices for the beginner. I use two thread types, cotton machine embroidery thread and invisible quilting thread.

My favorite thread is size 50, 60, or 80 cotton machine embroidery thread in a color matching the fabric. I use matching thread in the needle and bobbin. If you use threads with a high contrast, you will always see the other thread on the top or bottom.

Try to make your backing similar to the quilt top so you won't have high-contrast threads, or use a print on the back that will camouflage any knots.

Cotton thread has many advantages. It knots easily at the beginning and end of quilting lines and is well matched to the fibers in the cotton fabrics of the quilt. It is the simplest for a beginner to use. The disadvantage is that the color of the thread must be changed to match the changes in fabric color. It is not possible to quilt across white and red with a single line of stitching.

For multicolor quilts, I recommend invisible quilting thread in the needle and size 30 cotton machine embroidery thread in the bobbin. Invisible nylon thread is available at quilt shops in smoke and clear. Use smoke with dark fabrics and clear for light-color fabrics. Because the thread is transparent, it can be used on any color fabric. It does have disadvantages. It has a slight shine that makes the quilting line sparkle. It is difficult to knot neatly at the beginning and end of stitching lines, and it can cause thread tension problems.

My main concern is with the fiber content. Invisible thread is made of nylon fiber, which is susceptible to ultraviolet light. I worry that the nylon thread may not match the long life expectancy of the cotton fabrics used in the quilt. I use it and love it, but always keep in mind that it does become brittle with age when exposed to light. If you're making an heirloom quilt, you probably shouldn't use it.

THREAD AND NEEDLE PAIRS

Thread	Needle
Size 80	10/65 or 11/70
Size 50, 60	11/70 or 12/80
Nylon (invisible)	11/70 or 12/80
Size 30	12/80

 Keep all the areas of the quilt evenly quilted. Choose patterns that will result in consistent stitching over the entire quilt top. Some patterns, especially heavily stitched fillers like grid or stipple quilting, pucker the quilt. Space these evenly to keep the quilt flat and square.

Machine-Guided Quilting

Machine-guided quilting is most like regular sewing. The presser foot and feed dogs move the three layers of the quilt and determine the size and placement of the stitches. It works well for long, straight or gently curved lines of quilting. Use machine-guided quilting for in-the-ditch quilting, outline quilting, and grid quilting.

Straight stitch is the common stitch choice, but machine-guided quilting can be done with zigzag or any decorative or utility stitches. You can even substitute double needles for the single needle. Double needles stitch two parallel rows of straight stitches on the right side of the quilt and a row of zigzag stitches on the wrong side of the quilt.

Basic How-To

- Select your needle and thread combination, and start with a new needle.

- Use a walking foot. (See "Walking Foot" on page 260.)

- Set your machine for a straight stitch with an average stitch length (12 stitches per inch).

- Use the needle down option on your machine if you have it to help maintain straight quilting lines.

Step 1. Lower the presser foot where you want to start stitching. Hold on to the needle thread tail and take a single stitch. Tug on the needle thread to pull the bobbin thread through the quilt to the top of the fabric. (If you cannot get 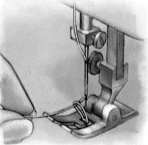 the bobbin thread up to the top, the needle may not be in the highest position. Turn the hand wheel slightly to further raise the needle, and raise the thread take-up to the highest position.) Hold on to both thread tails as you begin to stitch.

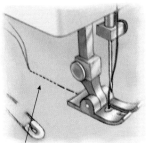

Make seven or eight very short stitches

Step 2. Begin and end each row of stitches with a knot to secure the threads. The best way to knot the thread is with a series of very short stitches. Adjust the stitch length to a shorter stitch as you make the seven or eight stitches that form the knot.

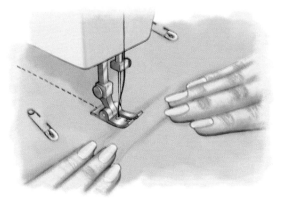

Step 3. Stitch forward. You will need to guide the quilt to ensure uniform feeding of the quilt layers. Place your hands in front of the presser foot, fingertips together and elbows out. Your fingers should be about 2 inches in front of the foot. Slide your fingertips across the top layer of the quilt, toward the presser foot, until there is a small bubble between your fingertips and the presser foot. Use a light touch. Don't move the batting or the backing, just the quilt top.

Start to sew and coax the fabric bubble under the foot. Use your fingertips constantly to help the top layer of fabric feed smoothly under the foot. It is a subtle movement that will become automatic with practice. Doing this nudging action correctly will prevent pleats both on the quilt top when crossing lines of stitching and on the back of the quilt.

 Practice "nudging" by purposely sewing in pleats on a layered quilt sandwich until you get the feel for it. Then lighten up until you are no longer sewing in pleats.

Step 4. Knot the end of the line of stitching by reducing the stitch length for seven or eight stitches.

There is a temptation to stretch and pull the quilt to make smooth lines of quilting. Stretching could remove any pleats on the quilt top, but will cause other problems. The cardinal rule of machine-guided quilting is "How it is sewed is how it stays." Sewing across a stretched area will cause a raised bubble that always pops up where the stitching lines cross.

 A faster, but more advanced, method of knotting stitches at the beginning and end of the quilting line is to gently hold the fabric to inhibit its forward motion. Place your hands directly in front of the presser foot, and gently press down on the quilt layers. The slight pressure will slow the feed of the fabric and will make small stitches. Hold the fabric for seven or eight stitches. This results in a secure knot of tiny stitches that doesn't require adjusting the machine or moving your hands off the fabric. Inhibiting the feeding of the fabric will not hurt the feed dogs or walking foot.

Common Problems and Solutions for Machine-Guided Quilting

Problem: Pleats appear in the backing.

Solution: Stretch the backing taut so that all wrinkles disappear before basting the quilt. This step ensures a flat backing. The backing should be stretched ½ inch to 1 inch for every 36 inches in width and length. Also, proper nudging as described above will help avoid pleating.

Problem: There are diagonal lines or creases between adjacent lines of straight quilting. This is most obvious on long straight lines of stitching like grid quilting or on sashing and is most likely to happen with a higher loft batting. The effect is called "sheering." The presser foot pushes the fabric ahead of the quilting line, trapping the grain line at an angle between the two lines of quilting.

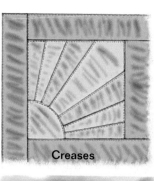

Creases

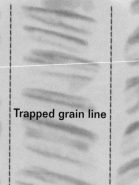

Trapped grain line

Solution: A walking foot can help correct this, but it cannot replace the sense of touch or sight. The key is to correctly nudge the top fabric as you quilt.

Problem: The quilt isn't flat and doesn't hang straight. The quilting lines might dimple or pop up, and the quilt is no longer square.

Solution: Press the seams open as you construct the quilt top. Open seams are less bulky than seams pressed to one side. Thick seam allowances can leave lumps on the finished quilt. They also make the quilt stiff where the quilting crosses the seam allowances.

Open seams also reduce the possibility of the presser foot catching on a thick seam. When the presser foot gets "hung up" or caught on a heavy seam, it can cause the quilt to stretch and dimple.

Free-Motion Quilting

Free-motion quilting is the most exciting and fun part of machine quilting. The darning foot and lowered feed dogs allow the quilter complete control of the stitch placement. Free-motion quilting is more like drawing than sewing. You can do any design, no matter how complex or detailed. Free-motion quilting is the best choice for motifs like feathers, cables, or floral designs. It is also used for echo, stipple, and meander quilting.

Basic How-To

• Use the darning foot or a free-motion quilting foot, such as the Big Foot. Many machines require loosening the pressure on the foot or a special adjustment on the presser foot lever.

• Lower or disengage the feed dogs. On some machines this is done by simply turning or moving a button. On others, there is a needle plate cover that snaps over the feed dogs. See "Try This" on page 156 if your machine has neither of these features.

• Use the needle down option if you have one, to help maintain smooth quilting lines.

• Carefully read your sewing machine owner's manual for further information on using the darning foot and lowering the feed dogs.

Step 1. Lower the presser foot where you want to start stitching. Hold on to the needle thread tail, and take a single stitch. Tug on the needle thread to pull the bobbin thread through the quilt top. If you cannot get the bobbin thread to rise to the top, the needle and

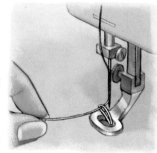

thread take-up may not be in the highest position. Or, you may have forgotten to lower the presser foot. Hold on to both threads as you begin to stitch.

Step 2. Knot the thread with a series of very short stitches. As you start to sew, move the fabric very slowly for the first seven or eight stitches. Then clip the thread tails close to the stitching.

Step 3. Resume stitching. You are in complete control of the stitch size and placement. The fabric will move as you guide it. For best control, place your hands in a C-shape around the presser foot, and press down gently to move the quilt layers.

Step 4. Sew at a moderate speed as you move the fabric. The stitches should be the same size as average machine-guided stitches.

Step 5. Knot at the end of the stitching line.

To move to a new spot, simply lift the presser foot and position it where you want to stitch. It is not necessary to cut the threads. The connecting thread between the two sections should be a taut, straight line. Lower the presser foot, and using the hand wheel, lower the needle into the fabric. Resume quilting. Clip the connecting threads after knotting.

Quilt in Comfort

How you hold and feed the fabric is critical to the quilting stitch and your comfort. You must be aware of both your posture and the way you guide the quilt.

Your elbows, wrists, and fingertips should always be in a straight line. Quilt with your elbows out and fingertips together near the presser foot. Rest the entire length of your forearms and hands on the sewing surface. A common mistake is to quilt with thumbs together and elbows hugging the side of the body. This reduces your control of the quilt. Consciously lower your shoulders by resting on your arms. Sit up straight, and lean slightly forward from the hip.

Common Problems and Solutions for Free-Motion Quilting

Problem: The stitches are too long, and curved lines are square.

Solution: Increase the machine speed, and slow down the movement of your hands.

Problem: The stitches are too small, and the thread frequently breaks.

Solution: Decrease the machine speed, and increase the movement of your hands.

Problem: Stitches are erratic at the beginning of a line of stitching or in the middle of long lines of stitching. It is common to have problems when starting or resuming a line of stitching. At the point where you stop sewing, the needle is lowered in the quilt. You relocate your hands, and resume quilting. It's at this point, when you have just moved your hands and are restarting the machine, that you lose control and one or two stitches make a zig.

Solution: The solution is simple. You can machine quilt only about 4 inches without losing control of the quilt. You are trying to do too many things at once: start the machine, pick up speed, move your hands, and follow a line. Just slow down. Don't do so much at a time. First start the machine running slowly. Don't move your hands until you have taken a stitch or two. Then move your hands slowly as you increase the machine speed.

If you cannot disengage the feed dogs of your machine, cover them with a 2-inch square of template plastic. Cut a small hole in the center of the plastic to match the needle hole opening, and tape the plastic over the feed dogs with vinyl tape. Always remove the plastic and tape at the end of the sewing session to prevent damaging the machine's finish.

Problem: The stitches on the back of the quilt are tiny bumps of thread. This is called "sand" or "sanding" because it looks like a line of sand along the bobbin side of the quilting line. There is only one cause for this effect: too many stitches too close together.

Solution: Try to make longer stitches by reducing your sewing speed and moving your hands faster.

Problem: There are long loops of thread on the wrong side of the quilt, and the machine is jamming.

Solution: Two things can cause these problems. You forgot to lower the presser foot when you started to stitch, or you forgot to raise the presser foot when you threaded the machine. Carefully rethread the machine and start over, paying attention to when you need to raise and lower the presser foot.

Stitching Sequence for Machine Quilting

One of the most difficult aspects of machine quilting can be determining the stitching sequence. Stitching sequence depends on the style of quilting and the pieced pattern of the quilt. Every quilt is different, but these general guidelines can be applied to all quilts:

- Plan ahead to sew the longest unbroken line possible for the design. Lines of stitching may be double or triple stitched to prevent breaking threads. Try to keep duplicate stitching lines exactly on top of each other.

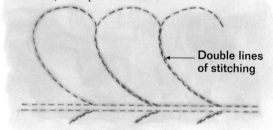

Double lines of stitching

- In general, work from the center of the quilt to the outside edges. This means working the body of the quilt before stitching the borders.
- Work from the longest lines of stitching to the shortest. Start with the sashing or other long lines of stitching. Then move to the designs in the blocks.

- Think of quilting as an extension of basting. If possible, the first two lines of stitching should divide the body of the quilt into quarters. Then work smaller and smaller sections of the quilt.
- For whole cloth or other quilts without strong horizontal or vertical lines, begin stitching in the quilt center and work in a circular motion to the outer edges.

Quilt in the following sequence, which is determined by the style of quilting:

1. Stitch the outline or in-the-ditch quilting. This is simple line quilting that follows the piecing pattern or sashing. This is usually done with machine-guided quilting.

2. Stitch the motif quilting. This includes designs like cables and feathered wreaths. Usually complex motif quilting is done with free-motion quilting.

3. Stitch the filler quilting. Filler quilting "fills" in the background behind motifs. It includes grids, channel, echo, and stipple quilting. Filler quilting can be done machine-guided or free-motion.

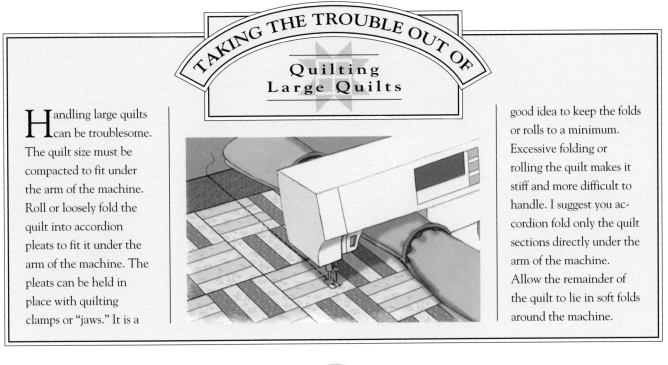

TAKING THE TROUBLE OUT OF
Quilting Large Quilts

Handling large quilts can be troublesome. The quilt size must be compacted to fit under the arm of the machine. Roll or loosely fold the quilt into accordion pleats to fit it under the arm of the machine. The pleats can be held in place with quilting clamps or "jaws." It is a good idea to keep the folds or rolls to a minimum. Excessive folding or rolling the quilt makes it stiff and more difficult to handle. I suggest you accordion fold only the quilt sections directly under the arm of the machine. Allow the remainder of the quilt to lie in soft folds around the machine.

Debra Wagner

COSMOS MINNESOTA

MARKING QUILT TOPS

In the past, marking a quilt was sometimes left to professionals who specialized in marking quilts for others. It is a big job, but having the right tools and knowing how to go about it makes it enjoyable and rewarding.

There are many marking pencils and marking devices on the market. I have tried most of them just to determine for myself which works best. My preference is a pencil made by Berol called the Berol Verithin. You can purchase this pencil at most quilt shops and also at art supply stores. For marking on dark fabrics, I use the white pencil (number 734), and for light fabrics, I use the silver pencil (number 753). The advantage of the Berol Verithin pencils is that they sharpen to a fine point and hold the point well. This ensures that your lines stay narrow and helps you make a light line as well. As you quilt, the markings lighten as your hand rubs over them. The markings are almost invisible by the time you have completed the quilting. This can also be a disadvantage if they rub off too easily. This isn't a problem if you quilt in a floor frame. If you quilt in a hoop where the quilt top is handled more, you may want to mark the designs as you go.

I learned to quilt from a group of Mennonite women. They used regular lead pencils to mark their quilts just as their mothers and grandmothers before them had done. They were very specific about what kind of lead pencil to use. They warned against using a number 2 lead pencil, as it is too soft. It not only makes too dark a line, but it is also likely to smudge. Instead, they suggested a number 3 or number 4 pencil, which has a hard lead and, therefore, makes a light, thin line.

Another good marking pencil is the Dixon Washout. It doesn't lighten or disappear from rubbing your hand against it. The disadvantage is that it has a wide lead, which can make your markings both thick and very dark. But it does wash out easily, so this disadvantage is nothing to worry about at all.

Soapstone markers are fine, as are many other quilter's pencils on the market. I do not recommend the "disappearing ink" type of markers. Some quilters like them, but others have had problems with the ink not disappearing or having it reappear at a later time. Always test any marker on scrap fabric before you use it. This is the best way to see what works well for you. Use a marker that you know is safe.

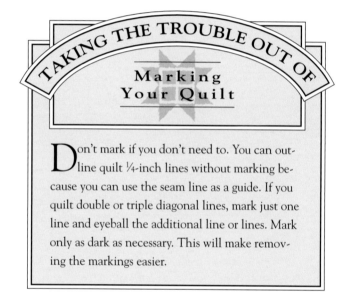

TAKING THE TROUBLE OUT OF

Marking Your Quilt

Don't mark if you don't need to. You can outline quilt ¼-inch lines without marking because you can use the seam line as a guide. If you quilt double or triple diagonal lines, mark just one line and eyeball the additional line or lines. Mark only as dark as necessary. This will make removing the markings easier.

Old Ways of Marking

Traditionally, quilters have been innovative in devising ways to mark their quilts. Here are several methods that have stood the test of time and still work well for contemporary quilters.

Pouncing was a common method for marking quilting designs. Holes were made on the paper pattern and the pattern was pinned in place. The holes were made either with a sharp pencil, a darning needle, or by running the pattern through the sewing machine set at the largest stitch. Cinnamon, cocoa, baking powder, and even snuff, were rubbed, or pounced, through the holes onto the quilt top. Quilters today

usually use cornstarch or baby powder. Place the powder on a 5- to 6-inch square piece of muslin or other cotton fabric, tie it up in a small sack, and gently rub, press firmly, or "pounce" over the holes. You'll need to experiment with this to see what works best. Commercial versions of the pouncer are also available.

Using a thin sliver of soap is another old-fashioned way to mark a quilt. It is fine for marking straight lines, but is harder to control when marking curves or other intricate designs. Some people still like to use soap, because there is never a problem with removing the marks. Use a basic soap without any added moisturizers or creams.

I have also "scratch marked" my quilts for years by running my needle across the fabric to make an impression in the fabric without actually marking on it.

Cookie cutters were sometimes called upon to do dual duty: first to make cookies and then to trace around on a quilt top as a quilting design. I used several of my favorite cookie cutters—a horse, bunny, and a heart—for quilting designs on my "Rose of Sharon" quilt, shown on page 190.

Stencils

Quilting stencils have been around for a long time. In the past, they were made of tin and sold off the backs of horse-drawn wagons. Now they are made of see-through plastic 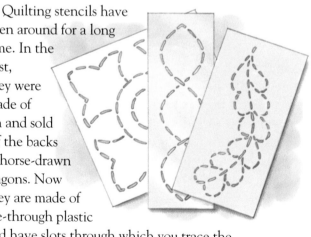 and have slots through which you trace the patterns.

Commercial stencils can be purchased at a quilt shop. Stencils for both block fillers and for borders come in many sizes and designs, so you can find one that fits your quilt. You can also learn how to draft your own quilting designs and make your own stencils. (See "Quilting Designs" on page 189 and "Stencils" on page 232.)

Masking Tape

Sometime in the 1980s, quilters began to use ¼-inch masking tape to guide their quilting lines. Masking tape does work, but for ¼-inch outline quilting, I don't think it is necessary. These lines are easy to eyeball, and it eliminates an extra step.

If you use masking tape, try to keep your quilting needle slightly away from the edge of the tape so your needle does not pick up any of the sticky residue. Be sure to remove the tape immediately after each quilting session, and never leave it in the sun. If left too long, it can leave a sticky residue that is difficult to remove.

Light Table

Tracing a quilting design on dark fabric or a busy print is easy when you use a light table. They are available at most art supply stores, but you can make one yourself. Basically, it is a box containing a light and covered with a piece of glass or plexiglass.

Some quilters take a leaf out of their dining room table, replace it with a piece of glass, such as a storm window, and set a lamp underneath. A glass-top table works well, too. Place your quilting pattern on the glass, the quilt top over the pattern, and trace the pattern onto the top.

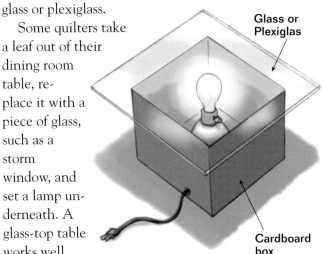

Glass or Plexiglas

Cardboard box

One of the problems with the homemade variety of light table is that sometimes you can see the designs clearly but cannot see the lines as you draw them, so you can't see where you are. The solution to this problem is to diffuse the light by laying one or more pieces of paper over the glass. Then place the quilting pattern on top of the paper, and you should be able to see both the pattern and the lines as you draw them.

Angle Keeper

Marking straight line quilting designs seems easy, but in fact, keeping the lines consistent and straight has been a stumbling block to many a quilter. The fabric can shift slightly and the ruler placement can vary slightly, all adding up to wandering straight lines. Early in my quilting days I invented a little tool to solve this problem. I call it Gwenny's Angle Keeper. Here is how you can make your own angle keeper.

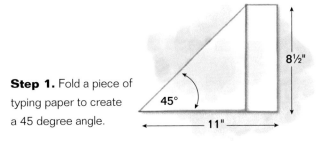

Step 1. Fold a piece of typing paper to create a 45 degree angle.

45°

8½"

11"

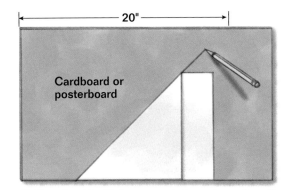

20"

Cardboard or posterboard

Step 2. Transfer this 45 degree angle to a piece of cardboard.

Step 3. Use a see-through ruler to draw a parallel line 1 inch from the first line.

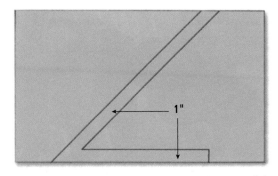

1"

Step 4. Draw another line 1 inch above the bottom of the cardboard and cut out the shape. Now you have an angle keeper that will make 45 degree diagonals 1 inch apart.

159

Step 5. Position it in the corner of the border, as shown. (You may want to try this on a large piece of paper first before you mark your quilt.)

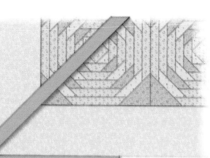

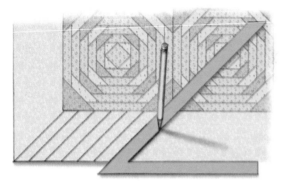

Step 6. Mark the first line and move it along the border, marking successive lines. You will notice that any discrepancies can be seen immediately and corrected with a slight adjustment.

The specific angle is not important and neither is the width between lines. These can vary and you may want to experiment with different angles and different widths between the lines.

Remember: As you mark your quilt, slight inconsistencies are nothing to worry about. They won't be noticed, and they are a natural part of everything that is made by hand.

Gwen Marston

Other Marking Options

Karen Bolesta and Ellen Pahl

Try as many marking devices as possible to see which ones work best for you. You may need to mark differently for hand quilting than for machine quilting. Here are some additional marking tools and methods you may want to try:

Hera Marker. A hera is a Japanese tool that scores a distinct crease in fabric when pulled across it. It is ideal for marking long straight lines with a ruler, or for gentle curves and freehand design.

The creases remain visible for a long period of time and will not show at all in the finished quilt. Incorrect marks are easily removed by spraying with a fine mist of water. Creases are even easier to see if you mark your quilt after layering and basting. The loft from the batting lets the hera sink in more, emphasizing the creases.

Tailor's Chalk. These triangular or rectangular pieces of compressed chalk have sharply honed edges that leave a very fine line on fabric. They come in white and darker colors.

Chaco-Liner. A thick, pencil-like barrel holds loose chalk, which is deposited as the tip is rolled across the fabric. Refills are available in white and a variety of colors.

Soapstone Marker. With a "lead" of natural soapstone, this marking tool looks similar to a mechanical pencil. Sharpen the soapstone to a point with an ordinary pencil sharpener, taking care not to splinter or crack the point, then insert the soapstone stick into the protective metal housing, leaving just the point exposed. Hold the marker like a pencil to draw thin lines on your quilt top; the lines rub off easily without leaving residue. Since soapstone is cream in color, it is ideal for darker fabrics. For lighter fabrics, use the lilac-colored chalk refill that is packaged with the soapstone marker.

Tear-Away Quilting Designs. Designed for machine quilting, these preprinted quilting designs are available on opaque paper in sizes to fit both blocks and borders. Pin them in place on the basted quilt top, quilt on the lines, and tear the paper away. Blank tear-away papers are available for making your own designs.

Freezer Paper. This inexpensive and readily available grocery store item can be used for drawing or tracing quilting designs. Draw on the dull side, and cut out your designs with sharp scissors or an X-Acto knife. Press the plastic-coated side to the quilt top with a medium hot iron, quilt around the shape, and peel off the paper. It can be re-used several times elsewhere on your quilt. This works best for hand quilting.

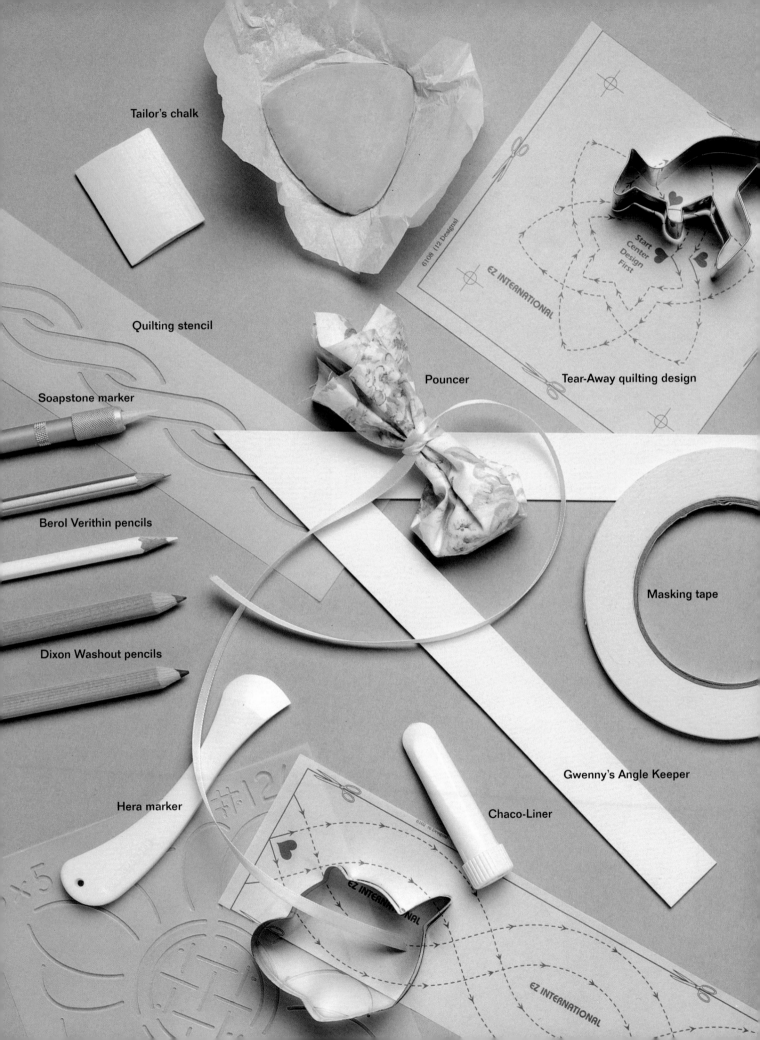

Tailor's chalk

Quilting stencil

Soapstone marker

Berol Verithin pencils

Dixon Washout pencils

Hera marker

Pouncer

Tear-Away quilting design

Masking tape

Gwenny's Angle Keeper

Chaco-Liner

MEDALLION QUILTS

"Another Day in Paradise," 80" × 80", by Karen Kay Buckley. This medallion quilt won Best of Show at the National Quilting Association in 1995 and won awards in several other shows.

point or straight. If set on point, corner units are generally added before the border designs.

The round robin quilts that are becoming popular with guilds are really medallion quilts. You can learn a lot by participating in one of these group efforts.

ON-POINT MEDALLION QUILT

The hallmark of a medallion quilt is the large central motif or focal point, with surrounding blocks and borders accenting and complementing the center design in color and theme.

The medallion quilt is one of the earliest quilt styles. In colonial America, quilters followed the tradition of English quiltmakers to begin with a central motif and work out from there. Most often the center was appliquéd, but fabric mills began printing panels specifically for medallion quilts. As patchwork caught on, quilters often arranged their blocks to form a central pattern or design in the quilt. The center design can be set on

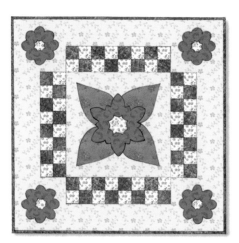

STRAIGHT SET MEDALLION QUILT

Designing and Planning a Medallion Quilt

The balance and radiating symmetry of medallion quilts make them a favorite of mine. Here's how I plan one.

For inspiration, I look for ideas in books, mainly those about art, art history, and architecture. I start sketching my design on oversized paper. When I get the basic concept down, I make templates for each shape. I cut every piece from fabric, and put it on the design wall before I start to sew. I generally try to include the borders in this planning phase as well.

I work with 100 percent cotton fabrics and often use a multicolor fabric that I love as inspiration for color combinations. I put it up on the design wall and work from those colors when I do my design. I may or may not include that fabric in the final quilt. If it doesn't end up in the quilt top, I may use it on the back. I always like to challenge myself to work in different colors than I have used previously.

Karen Kay Buckley

MINIATURE QUILTS

Today, making miniature quilts has become the preference of many quilters, and respect for the diminutive works is growing steadily. Some quilters enjoy the challenge of reducing a traditional block and sewing its pieces together accurately at 3 inches, or even smaller. Others like the fact that miniature quilts don't take as long to complete as bed quilts do.

What is a miniature quilt? If you ask ten people that question you might get ten different answers. We sometimes think all miniatures are made at a 1:12 ratio, where 1 inch of the miniature equals exactly 12 inches in the original piece. This scale is commonly used for dollhouses, but don't be intimidated by it. Unless that's how your quilts will be used, it doesn't apply to you. My own definition is that a miniature quilt is any smaller version of an original piece. Just how large or small your quilt should be depends on how you plan to use it.

If you're making a quilt to enter in the miniature category at a quilt show, be sure to read the show rules carefully. The rules pertaining to miniature quilts vary from show to show. The maximum block size is often 4 inches square, and the maximum quilt size is often 24 inches on a side. If you're not ready to work that small, make a slightly larger quilt for the wallhanging category, where the rules are usually more flexible.

The final determination of quilt and block size is up to you. Do you need a wallhanging that must be seen from a distance? If so, perhaps a slightly larger block or quilt dimensions would work best. Will your quilt be draped over a miniature rack, or must it fit a specific decorative hanger? In that case, the blocks and overall dimensions should be in scale with the accessory. Will your quilt be a miniature version of a historical piece?

"Red Arrowroot of Madness," made by June Kempston, measures 17½" × 17½". It was machine pieced with traditional ¼-inch seams and hand appliquéd. "Madness" comes from the length of time it took her to complete the quilt—one week!

TAKING THE TROUBLE OUT OF
Accuracy in Miniature Quilts

Accuracy is one of the most important aspects of miniature quilt construction, and the smaller the block, the more important it becomes. Even a $\frac{1}{32}$-inch variation can create problems in miniatures, especially if it occurs in many seams. There are several ways to improve accuracy:

- Use the same brand of rulers throughout a project. I prefer rulers with very thin lines because there's less "guessing" space hidden under the line itself.

- Make sure your sewing machine is set up to sew an exact ¼-inch seam allowance. (See "Seam Allowance" on page 215.)

- Press fabric thoroughly before cutting. I like to use spray starch to stiffen the fabric slightly; it helps me to cut more accurately.

- To avoid stretching, pay attention to fabric grain. All outer edges of the block should be cut on the straight-of-grain.

- Press seams carefully and thoroughly as you work.

Choose fabrics appropriate to the period, and be sure all prints are in scale with the reduced size of the quilt.

Don't be apprehensive about trying a miniature of your own. Choose a size that is most comfortable to you, and forget about the "rules." The satisfaction you feel when completing a beautiful quilt is the same, no matter what its dimensions.

Janet Wickell

How to Make a Successful Miniature Quilt

by Tina M. Gravatt

Equipment. Your equipment should be the best you can afford. Protractors and compasses should be of artistic or engineering quality. The better your tools, the more accurate your results.

Templates and Accuracy. Since the introduction of rotary cutters and rulers, accuracy has been much easier to achieve; however, certain quilt patterns are best created with traditional templates. I use gridded template plastic to make mine. The plastic is easy to see through and allows the quiltmaker to accurately place the template over a specific fabric image.

Mark on the plastic with an ultra-fine-line mechanical pencil or permanent marking pen. If the template has straight lines, cut it out with a knife, not with scissors. When cutting curves, use embroidery scissors. *Use equipment in scale with your project.* Large equipment is harder to keep steady and can produce shadows that make it hard to see the cutting line.

Fabrics. Often the charm of an old quilt lies in the variety of patterns and colors of the fabrics used in its construction. Try to do the same in a miniature quilt. Use stripes, geometrics, small- and large-scale prints, plaids, checks, solids, and meandering patterns. These can be in contemporary colors and motifs or any of the hundreds of reproduction eighteenth-, nineteenth-, and early twentieth-century prints available today. It is easy to reproduce a very old look in a miniature quilt.

Paper Mockup. Draw your planned quilt on graph paper to actual size. Choose the fabric you intend to use for your quilt. Cut out the fabric in the shapes needed (without seam allowances) and paste them onto the drawing. Often, doing this for only one quarter of the quilt is enough to give you an idea how the completed quilt will look. It is much easier to remove and replace fabric from paper than to unstitch an actual segment of a quilt top.

Construction. Use ¼-inch seams on both piecework and appliqué. After assembly, grade seams only where too many come together to lie flat.

Appliqué. When you are ready to appliqué a piece to the quilt top, trim 1/16 inch from the seam allowance and try sewing. If the seam allowance still seems too stiff or will not fold under smoothly, carefully trim another 1/16 inch and try appliquéing again. It is a good idea to do a test sample of each fabric using the actual templates needed for the quilt. Not all fabrics turn under easily. If you find that one you have selected is too difficult to work with, choose an alternate fabric. It is much easier to make changes *before* you are halfway through a quilt.

Alternative techniques. When reinterpreting a full-size quilt pattern in miniature, it is often wise to consider alternate construction techniques. For example, when a ⅛-inch wide bias strip is needed, try embroidery instead; use stuffed and unstuffed yo-yos as flowers, or quilt a motif instead of appliquéing it. Use your imagination and skills to their best advantage.

Batting. There are many thin and medium-weight cotton and polyester batting products on the market. Sample a few and determine which is right for the style of miniature quilt you are making. No one batting is right for all projects!

Quilting. Use a square or rectangular quilt frame. Ovals or round hoops will pull the quilt off grain and result in a lopsided quilt. The thinner the batting, the easier it is to make small stitches. Be sure to use quilting motifs that are simple enough to allow you to successfully complete them. When an area is too small to quilt inside, quilt in the ditch. Do not skip "large" areas on a miniature; it will cause the quilt to buckle and hang crooked.

Finishing. All of the styles of edge finishing on large quilts can be used on small ones. Piping, lace, prairie points, and scallops add an extra special finish to a miniature quilt.

Binding. Use a ¾-inch-wide bias strip long enough to go completely around the quilt. Sew to the quilt top in a ¼-inch seam. Trim the seam to ⅛ inch, and trim the points off the corners. Hand sew the binding to the back. This technique will produce a lovely narrow binding.

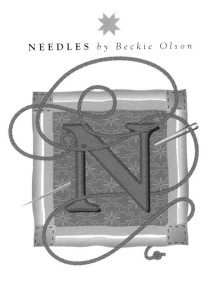

NEEDLES

The very earliest needles were fish bones or sharpened thorns with holes, with pieces of tough animal sinew for thread. Over time, crude bronze needles and then sharp steel needles took the place of bones and thorns. It's evident that advances in basic sewing tools go hand in hand with fine sewing skills.

Needles for Hand Sewing

The common household needle, called a "sharp," came about with the advent of steel needles. Bronze was too soft to grind to a sharp point; needles made of this metal had blunt tips. They were used by young girls to stitch needlework samplers and by tailors and shoemakers because of the strong, stout shafts.

Quiltmakers required a needle in between the stoutness of the bronze "blunts" and the longer, fine steel sharps. The "in-betweens" for quilting had the strength to go through many layers of fabric and a sharp point for piercing. This early categorizing of needles carries over in the name we now use for quilting needles, "betweens."

Today, both sharps and betweens are made from fine steel wires with a hole punched in one end and the other end sharpened. (If you are having trouble threading a needle, turn the needle around to the other side of the hole. You may be going against the punched area.) A needle is only as good as the steel it is made from. England and Japan are both known for quality steel products. The finest needles are made of smooth, highly polished steel that is without burrs, of small diameter, and sharpened to a nicely tapered point.

When choosing a between or a sharp, determine the qualities that are important to you. I prefer a needle with a nice large eye for easy threading. The needle should be strong enough so that it won't bend easily, thin enough to slip easily through the fabric, and sharp enough to pierce between the fibers of the fabric rather than snag them. The sizing rule is that the higher the number, the finer and shorter the needle will be.

For quilting, the shorter the needle, the smaller the stitches will be. Beginners should practice with a size 9 or 10 and work toward smaller needles. Betweens made in Japan tend to be a bit stronger and shorter than those made in England. This makes them perfect for me. I do not bend as many, and I can use a size 10 when I can't see well enough to thread a 12 and still have a short needle. Both Clover and Piecemakers are Japanese needles. For tying quilts with the Decatur Knot, I like a Piecemaker 5-inch needle.

For appliqué, use a long, thin needle, beginning with a number 10 sharp and working toward an 11 or 12.

For hand piecing, always use a number 10 sharp. An 11 or 12 would be so fine that it would bend too quickly. When I hand piece, I require a needle that can be pushed easily through the fabric. For this, I prefer a Hemmings number 10 sharp, which is less likely to bend with pressure.

You'll know you have the right needle for the task if the finished product looks nice and the needle was comfortable to use.

Beckie Olson

Machine Needles

Throw away those old machine needles! We purchase the best machines we can afford and spend our valuable time making wonderful quilts. Using old needles is not the place to scrimp. Dull needles can cause skipped stitches, a burr can snag your fabric, and a bent needle can damage the bobbin case.

Sewing machine needles are cut from various diameters of steel wire, measured in hundredths of millimeters. The eye and scarf are then stamped out. This process requires 45 production steps and 100 different machines.

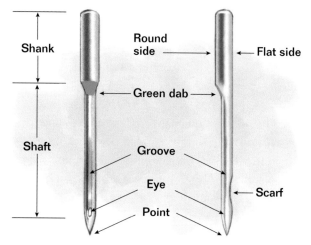

The shank is flat on one side so that it can be held tightly in the machine. Make sure it is pushed all the way up into the machine. This brings the needle closer to the bobbin hook to prevent skipped stitches.

The eye is highly polished and smooth to prevent breaking and wearing away the thread that passes back and forth many times while forming a stitch.

The groove allows the thread to lie close to the needle on its way through the eye. If the thread is too thick, it will not lie close to the shaft and will result in skipped stitches.

The indented part of the needle on the opposite side of the groove, directly above the eye, is called the scarf. A major engineering innovation, it allows the bobbin hook to pass closer to the needle to pick up the loop of thread and to prevent skipped stitches.

The point makes the hole through which the thread passes—the smaller the better.

Choose the correct size needle for your project by first matching the thread thickness to the fabric, then

to the needle. Size 75/11 is suitable for nearly every part of the quiltmaking process: piecing, machine appliqué, and quilting. If a slightly heavier thread is used for quilting, such as 40 weight or metallic, a size 90/14 needle may be used. For a thicker thread, try using a size 100/16 in the 130/705 H-J system.

Change the needle if you hear a "tick-tick" sound. This means that there is a burr on the point. Sewing over pins can cause this. A blunted point can damage your fabric or cause skipped stitches. Man-made fibers in fabric and batting will dull needles quickly, so change needles frequently when sewing on synthetics. Wipe needles occasionally with rubbing alcohol to remove synthetic fibers that may cling.

To test the straightness of the needle, draw a line on a piece of fabric and feed it through the machine without touching the fabric. A bent needle will veer to one side.

When sewing, make sure that the needle is completely down in the fabric when changing direction. Avoid pulling the fabric through or putting a drag on it, which will bend the needle. Remove work from the machine toward the back, or from the side to the back, toward the flat portion of the shank. *Never* pull it toward the front. Allow the feed dogs and presser foot to work together by making sure that the fabric lying directly beneath the needle is always relaxed. This will not only help to protect the needle but will also produce a nice, even stitch.

Try This If your machine does not have a built-in threader, try threading the needle by placing the freshly angled-cut thread between the index fingers of both hands. Wetting the eye of the needle may help you to pull the thread through.

Jeannette T. Muir

NEEDLES FOR QUILTERS

Sharps

Used for:
General sewing	Sizes: 5–10
Hand piecing	Size: 10
Hand appliqué	Sizes: 11–12

Keep an assortment of sharps on hand. Some have a gold coating at the eye to help prevent fraying thread. On some brands this makes the eye larger than the shaft, causing the needle to drag when pulled through fabric. Some have elongated eyes for easier threading without the drag.

Milliner or Straw

Used for: Hand appliqué — Sizes: 9–10
Smocking — Sizes: 9–10

Milliner needles have the same fine shaft as sharps but are longer to allow for easier control of the needle while doing needle-turn appliqué.

Betweens

Used for: Quilting   **Sizes: 9–12**

A size 10 between made in the United States is generally slightly thicker and longer than a size 10 made in England. The size 10 made in Japan will be just a bit shorter than the English needle. The general rule is the smaller the needle, the shorter the stitches.

Other Useful Needles

Quilters often use crewel or embroidery needles (sizes 8–10) in embellishing or decorative stitching. Chenille needles (sizes 18–22) are used for silk ribbon work or sashiko. Many quilters like to use darning needles to make basting a quilt easier.

Machine Needles

Quiltmaking has become so popular that the manufacturers are listening to us. Schmetz has developed the 130/705 H-Q system specifically for us. The "H" stands for *hohlkehle*, the German word for scarf, and "Q" for *quilting*. It is similar to the 130/705 H-J system ("J" for *jeans* and colored blue), but it has a slimmer point and a bright green dab just below the base at the top of the shaft. The needles come in a package containing three size 75/11 and two size 90/14. The top of the package serves as a magnifier, showing the size printed on the round side of the base.

Universal needles in size 80/12 are also fine for general piecing.

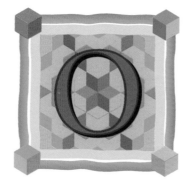

ONE PATCH QUILTS

A One Patch quilt is exactly what its name implies, a quilt made of one patch repeated over and over. One Patch designs have been popular for centuries in tiles, mosaics, and architectural adornments. Grandmother's Flower Garden is a traditional One Patch quilt design made of hexagons. Thousand Pyramids is made up of rows of equilateral triangles that point either up or down. Other shapes include clamshells, diamonds, and the apple core (also known as Spool, Double Ax, or Double Hammerhead).

Contrast between different elements is an important factor in any quilt, since it determines the overall visual design we perceive. Traditional pieced blocks provide many natural lines to emphasize specific portions of the quilt. In a One Patch quilt, only one shape is used. No predetermined divisions exist, so the final design is a result of our own creativity.

Another important difference between block quilts and many One Patch quilts is the way they are assembled. When stitching a quilt from individual blocks, the blocks are usually assembled first, then arranged into a pleasing setting, and finally sewn together to complete the quilt top. Although some One Patch quilts can be made in the same manner, it's common to first establish the entire layout by arranging single patches on a design wall or other flat surface. Only when the layout is complete are the patches joined together into larger units or directly into rows.

This assembly method is especially helpful to distribute patches in charm quilts, where no fabric is

"Natural Balance" is an original quilt design by Shelly Burge of Lincoln, Nebraska. The pinwheel effect in this lap-size quilt comes from careful color placement in each Four Patch block. In addition to being a One Patch quilt, this is also a charm quilt—the fabric in each patch is different throughout the quilt.

168

used more than once, and for scrappy quilts, where many fabrics are used but the "one-time" rule does not apply. In nearly all cases it's a good idea to cut more patches than you actually need. The extras will allow you more design options as you arrange and rearrange the patches.

One Patch quilts often contain irregularly shaped pieces that make them well suited to hand piecing, although most could be machine pieced if you don't let set-in seams and curves intimidate you. Grandmother's Flower Garden is usually done by hand using English paper piecing.

There are many commonly used layouts for traditional One Patch quilts. A few variations of the Tumbling Blocks design are shown here and illustrate how changing the contrast between patches changes the overall character of the quilt.

When you make a square or rectangular One Patch quilt, the patches will likely result in a quilt with jagged outer edges. While you may leave the quilt that way and bind the pointed or curved edges, some quilters prefer to use variations of the original patch to fill in the gaps. In Grandmother's Flower Garden, shown below, partial hexagons can be placed around the outer edges of the quilt to square up the sides. Pieces that are one-half or one-quarter of the original shape can fill in the sides so that borders or binding can be applied to straight edges.

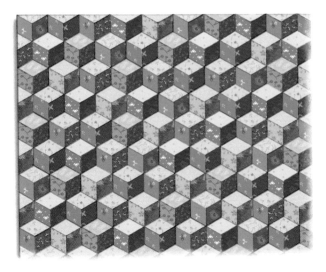

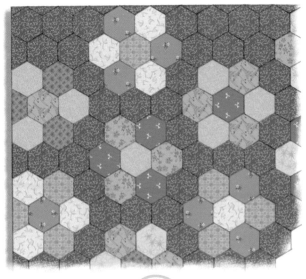

Janet Wickell

169

PINS

When shopping in a notions department of a fabric store, the selection seems to get larger by the day! Pins are no exception—with so many types and sizes, it can be confusing to know what to buy.

The very first implements that served as pins were made of bone. Later they were made of sharpened ivory. Today, most pins are made of coated, anodized steel. Even though they have this material in common, there are a number of distinguishing characteristics among types of pins. To make the right selection, you need to think about how you will be using the pins. There are differences in quality among various brands of pins; look for pins that glide easily through the fabric without catching on the fibers or leaving a large hole.

Many quilters and sewers, in general, prefer pins with a ball head since they are easier to handle. These ball heads may be plastic or glass. Be aware that if you iron a project with a plastic head pin, you could melt the plastic. Glass heads are heat resistant. The choice may depend on whether you will be pressing with the pins in or not.

When machine piecing, you should use a pin that will cause the least disruption or "bump" within the seam and lies as flat as possible on the bed of the machine. For this reason, silk pins are wonderful when sewing with quilting-weight cottons. They are so fine that they cause hardly any bump, and they lie virtually even with the bed, allowing the machine to stitch as smoothly and consistently as possible. Some quilters prefer the flat flower-head pins for the same reason, although they are slightly heavier and longer.

Pin Care and Maintenance

The ideal place to store pins is in a pincushion. If you keep them in a box or jar, they will be jumbled together and bump each other, creating burrs and dulling the points. The rubbing together can also chip the nickel plating, and rust will occur.

The tip of the pin is actually ground to a point, so this is where the nickel plating can wear off with use, causing the pin to rust. You can buy brass straight pins, although brass safety pins are more common. Brass will not rust, which is a definite advantage if you live in a very humid area.

The best pincushions are those made from wool that is rolled into a wide, flat cylindrical shape. These pincushions are wonderful because they contain lanolin, which helps to prevent rust. They also do a very good job of protecting the points of your pins.

If you use a magnetic pincushion, you should be aware that your pins can become magnetized and that some electronic sewing machines are sensitive to them. Magnetic "wands" or "pin grabbers" are helpful for picking up dropped pins.

Use the emery "strawberry" on a tomato pincushion (or they can be purchased separately) to remove any superficial burrs from pins and needles. It resharpens the point and cleans off any buildup of dirt, rust, or oxidation on the shank. Push the pin into the middle and twist it a few times.

170

Quilting Pins

These pins are much longer than other types, usually $1\frac{3}{4}$ inches long with the shank being slightly heavier like a dressmaker pin. They may have a large ball head, although many are made with flat flower heads. These flower heads allow the pin to lie as flat as possible on the bed of the machine when stitching.

The primary purpose of quilting pins is to easily hold the bulk of a quilt top, batting, and backing in preparation for basting. If the project is small, many quilters use these pins in place of basting. If you do that, however, you need to be very careful that your threads don't become caught on the pins as you are quilting. Many quilters prefer these pins when binding a quilt. The pins are long enough to go through all the layers and are easy to grasp when working on the binding.

Dressmaker Pins

These pins generally are sized from $1\frac{1}{16}$ inches to $1\frac{3}{8}$ inches long. The shank of the pin tends to be a heavier and slightly coarser type of steel with the tip ground to a point. Many of these pins have glass or plastic ball heads, which allow easier handling. This type of pin is meant to be used as an all-purpose pin, as it will work well with a variety of fabrics.

Silk Pins

These pins are longer than dressmaker pins and generally measure $1\frac{1}{4}$ inches in length. Silk pins were originally designed to be used with silk and other delicate types of fabric. They are extremely smooth and fine with a 0.50 millimeter shank diameter and have super-sharp points. The best brands are nickel plated, hardened steel that resist rust. These pins are especially nice as they won't leave holes or bend out of shape. They are available with either a flat or ball head and are wonderful to work with on all but the very heaviest fabrics.

Ballpoint Pins

These pins also have a heavier and coarser shank and come in a variety of lengths from $1\frac{1}{16}$ inches to $1\frac{3}{4}$ inches. Their ball point means that they should be used primarily with knit fabrics. The rounded point separates the threads in a knit rather than piercing them. This helps to prevent "runs" in the knitted fabric. However, unless you are working with knits, these pins are usually not sharp enough to do a nice job on woven fabrics and may, in fact, cause "runs" in woven fabric, since they don't pierce the threads as easily.

Appliqué Pins

These are sometimes called "sequin pins" and are the shortest of the straight pins. They are generally $\frac{1}{2}$ inch long and are available in dressmaker-type shanks as well as silk-type shanks. Their shorter length is often preferred for appliqué because the thread doesn't get caught as easily as it may on a longer pin. Also, if working with very small pieces, as is common in appliqué, a longer pin may be too cumbersome and not allow enough flexibility of the fabric when stitching. These pins are very tiny, but they are available in both flat and ball-type heads.

PIPING

Special trims, such as piping, can give a quilt, pillow, or other quilted accessory a professional finishing touch. Sometimes just the smallest amount of a contrasting color or print can make a dramatic difference in the overall design. I always enjoy discovering any unusual sewing detail upon close look at a handcrafted piece.

There are generally two types of piping: flat and filled. Flat piping can frame a simple block, serve as a tiny border between areas on a quilt, or accent and outline shapes and boundaries. I prefer flat piping to filled when using it within a quilt. Flat piping does not add too much bulk to seams. Filled piping is best used on pillow edges, or on the edges of a small quilt.

To determine the width of your piping, experiment a little with your project. Sometimes the color will determine how wide the piping should be, but the scale of the overall project will ultimately determine the finished width of the piping. For filled piping, the diameter of the cording will also be a factor to consider.

Flat Piping

Step 1. Determine the width of piping you desire. I often cut strips 1¼ inches wide. These are folded in half and stitched with a ¼-inch seam allowance to produce a narrow ⅜-inch flat piping when finished. Always test a sample.

Step 2. Determine the total number of inches you will need for your project, and divide by the width of your chosen fabric to determine how many cross-grain strips to cut. Cut cross-grain strips and piece, if necessary, using a diagonal seam. Trim the seam allowances to ¼ inch.

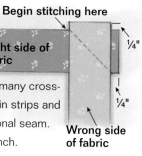

Step 3. Press the piping strip in half lengthwise with wrong sides together.

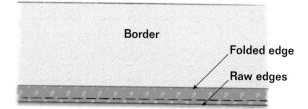

Step 4. When using flat piping as a narrow border, attach the flat piping to the border piece and treat it as one unit. Align the raw edges of the piping with the raw edge of the border piece, having the right sides of the border together with the piping. Machine baste the raw edges together with a scant ¼-inch seam.

Filled Piping

Filled piping, or cording, is made by covering cable cord with bias strips of fabric. The covered cord is inserted in seams to add a decorative edge. I feel the best use of filled piping is on a pillow edge or combined with a ruffle. The same principles would apply, however, when attaching filled piping to a quilt edge.

The size of cording determines the width of the fabric strips. Allow enough width to wrap around the cording, and leave at least a ½-inch seam allowance. For filled piping, use bias strips. They are more pliable and easier to handle.

Step 1. Determine the length of the piping and the width of the strips you will need. Allow at least an extra 6 inches of length. Cut the strips on the true bias. For help in calculating how much fabric you'll need, see the Try This box on page 41.

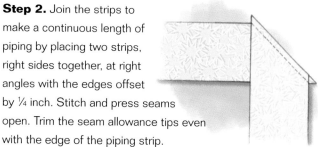

Step 2. Join the strips to make a continuous length of piping by placing two strips, right sides together, at right angles with the edges offset by ¼ inch. Stitch and press seams open. Trim the seam allowance tips even with the edge of the piping strip.

Step 3. To cover piping, place the bias strip right side down. Lay the piping cord in the middle of the bias strip. Wrap the strip around the cord, aligning the raw edges.

Step 4. Machine stitch, using a zipper foot; carefully stitch close to the cord without catching it.

Step 5. At this point, the piping is ready to insert into a seam. You may need to trim the piping seam allowance to match the seam allowance of your specific project.

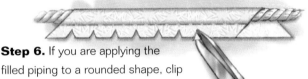

Step 6. If you are applying the filled piping to a rounded shape, clip the piping seam allowance to allow the piping to follow the curved shape nicely.

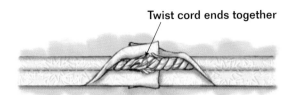

Twist cord ends together

Step 7. To join the cording ends, trim off the extra length. Remove stitching a few inches back from one end of the stitched piping. Fold under the diagonal raw edge of one end of piping fabric ½ inch. Overlap the adjoining end approximately 1 inch. The edge folded under will look just like the other diagonal seams in the piping. Cut the cording to meet. Unravel each end a little, and gently twist together the cording strings to make a continuous cord. Fold over, and restitch the fabric next to the cording.

Lynette Jensen

PLAIDS AND STRIPES

Plaids and stripes are often neglected by many quilters who feel that they are too much of a challenge to incorporate into a quilt. They are wonderfully versatile, however, lending an extra bit of personality to any quilt. Don't be intimidated by them!

Stripes have bars of color going in one direction while plaids have bars of color going in both directions—lengthwise and crosswise on the fabric. A woven directional fabric has the pattern in the threads so the pattern is of equal brightness on both sides and is reversible. If the pattern is printed, the image will be bright on one side, and pale on the other. This printed fabric has the advantage of having both a louder and a more quiet side.

Plaids and stripes share characteristics with other patterned fabrics. The larger scale patterns are busier than the smaller patterns.

Higher contrast in color value makes a pattern more obvious and thus busier. The more colors that are used, the busier the result. Plaids and stripes that feature an ikat look (change of color along one thread) or have slubs (thicker, uneven places in the threads) will appear busier than those fabrics that are more plainly made.

Ikat fabrics read as busy.

Calmer

Busier

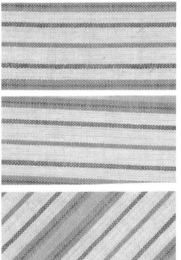

Fancy weaving patterns that feature slubs and different thicknesses of threads (novelty yarns) read as busy.

It's up to the quiltmaker to choose the correct grain line for a specific piece of fabric or for a whole project. When either calmness or control is the goal, work on-grain. When excitement is needed or you desire a primitive folk art look, work off-grain. Another choice is "casually off-grain," which means however it happens to come out. This approach gives a relaxed "real-life" look to a project.

Plaids and stripes can be used many ways in a quilt. Most times we need a quiet fabric to serve as a background in a quilt block. Quilters need to recognize that calm plaids or stripes can serve admirably as background fabrics because they're not eye-catching (the whole point!). Low value contrast between the parts of the pattern is important if the fabric is to serve as a muslin replacement. Think more of texture than pattern. Remember that this fabric will usually be light in value. Think how light muslin is!

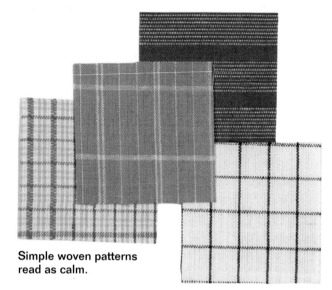

Simple woven patterns read as calm.

Grain line is the most controversial aspect of directional fabrics. Suffice it to say that plaids and stripes used on-grain are quiet, and those used off-grain are busier.

On-grain: Maximum control, maximum calmness

Uses: Borders, binding

"Casually off-grain": Relaxed feeling, slight visual activity

Uses: Scrap quilts, folk art quilts

Bias: Maximum activity

Uses: Binding

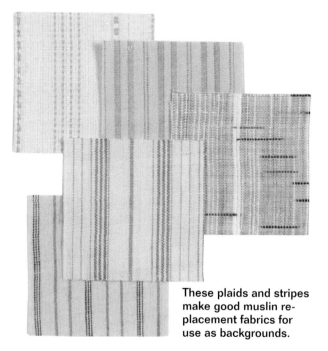

These plaids and stripes make good muslin replacement fabrics for use as backgrounds.

Plaids and stripes also make great border fabrics. Strong, medium and large scale, bolder patterns should be selected. If the quilt top is busy or visually needs to be pulled together or unified, make sure you work on-grain. The parallel lines will give you the control that you need.

When selecting a binding fabric for a quilt, consider a plaid or stripe. For a quiet look, place the lines parallel or perpendicular to the quilt edge. When more excitement is necessary, place the fabric on the bias. If the border is also a plaid, place the binding with the grain line going in the opposite direction for visual contrast.

Plaids and stripes can be used with other plaids and stripes, or they can be combined with other patterned fabrics. Contrasts show best, so combine small with large scale, calm with busy, and dark with light. In general, plaids and stripes will appear boring and uninteresting when placed next to other patterned fabrics. This is a very important relationship. Plaids and stripes allow the other patterned fabric to show better. This is their traditional role in antique quilts. When auditioning a plaid or stripe with a patterned fabric, always lay the directional fabric parallel to the other fabric so that you can see its quiet quality.

Roberta Horton

Stripes

I define stripes as a linear pattern made up of more-or-less straight lines running more-or-less parallel to each other. Today fabric manufacturers are producing lots of wonderful fun-to-use stripes that can enhance your quilts, but they need to be cut to see just how wonderful they are.

Fortunately, stripes can be efficiently cut with a rotary cutter and gridded ruler because it is easy to line up the lines of the stripes with the lines of the ruler. I cut stripes either perpendicular, parallel, or diagonal to the edge of my pattern pieces. To control the stripes, I cut strips from a single layer of fabric and then trim it into smaller units. (There is some waste involved when groups of pattern pieces are cut to be alike, so allow for extra fabric.)

When selecting stripes for your project, you'll discover that it is best when all your stripes aren't equally important and demanding of attention. Some stripes are "stars" because they are bold or unusual and demand attention. They make good sashing. Other stripes that are less dramatic and more supportive "bit players" are perfect for the star points or centers.

Scale, contrast, number of colors used, and uniqueness of the pattern all help to determine the importance of a stripe.

Stripes in a Friendship Star Sashing

A Friendship Star sashing, or lattice, pieced in stripes will enhance a set of pieced or appliquéd blocks. This is a good way to use and experiment with stripes. I usually cut strips that are 2½ inches wide, resulting in a 2-inch finished sashing. Determine how wide you would like the sashing to be by auditioning your blocks on a design wall.

Try This Make a template for the angled sashing piece if you want the stripes to repeat in a certain pattern. Mark the center of your template so you'll know where to align it with the design of your fabric. Use a triangular ruler to cut the triangles for the star points individually. This way you will be aware of how the stripe will look in the star.

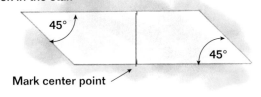

To form an ordered, repeating, all-over sashing pattern, you will have to decide which direction to cut your stripes for each pattern piece before you begin. It's a good idea to view the stripes through windows cut in graph paper. Then mark the position of the stripe on your plastic template as a reference when cutting. Begin by selecting one option for each of the pattern pieces. (Sashing usually shows off best in the perpendicular, or "piano key" position.) Study the following examples to learn how you can use a wide variety of stripes in sashing.

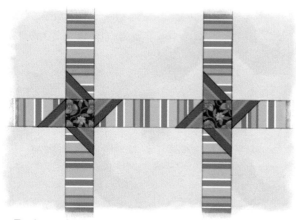

Traditional stripe sashing, "marker-drawn" stripe star points, and floral star centers

Traditional stripe sashing, wavy stripe star points, and conversation print star centers

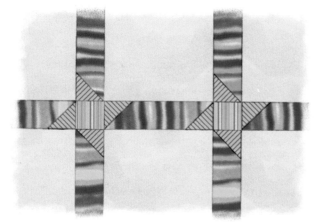

"Water color" stripe sashing, small, ordinary stripe star points, and multicolor stripe star centers

Free-form, novelty stripe sashing, "marker-drawn" star points, and abstract print star centers

PRAIRIE POINTS

On the prairies of northeastern Colorado in the early 1900s, Mary Stanley and her circle of quilting friends used small scraps of fabric folded into triangles to finish the edges of their quilts. This was much more economical than cutting up whole cloth into long bias strips for binding.

These triangles, later named prairie points, have also been called Sawtooth Edging, Dogtooth Borders, and Cats' Ears in different parts of the country. Individual points can be made of a variety of fabrics for a scrappy look and the points can be of varying heights. Prairie points are a very easy and fun way to add a special touch to any quilt by giving it extra edging attention.

Making Prairie Points

Each point begins as a square and finishes as a triangle. The raw edges that align along one side after folding will later be encased in a seam.

Determine the size of the squares to cut. You can experiment with different sizes to see what works best with the scale of the quilt. Prairie points that are too large tend to overpower a quilt top composed of many small patches, and finished prairie points taller than 2¾ inches may flop over because of their weight.

Try This

Here is a handy formula to determine the size of the square you'll need to cut for any size prairie point:

Height of finished point × 2 = _____ + ½"

For a 2-inch-tall prairie point,

2 × 2 = 4 + ½" = a 4½-inch cut square.

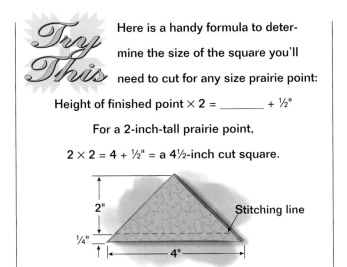

Also, the length of the finished base will equal the finished height × 2.

Cut a square of fabric and fold it one of two ways. The first method allows one prairie point to nest inside its neighbor, making it easy to adjust distribution of the points to match the length of the borders.

FOLDING NESTING PRAIRIE POINTS

"Gemstones" is a full-size scrap quilt made by Jeanne Jenzano as a wedding gift for her son and daughter-in-law. The prairie point edging highlights the angles and diagonal lines within the quilt.

The second folding method creates the same size prairie point, but the fold that shows along the center of the triangle provides a decorative addition to the edging. Triangles can be overlapped to adjust their overall length along the edge of the quilt.

FOLDING OVERLAPPING PRAIRIE POINTS

Overlapping Prairie Points

There are several advantages to overlapping or nesting prairie points: The added thickness of overlapped triangles gives more support to the edging, the area of overlap adds a continuous narrow border of color, and subtle adjustments can be made to equalize spacing along the length. A prairie point can be overlapped as much as halfway into the neighboring one, so you will need approximately twice as many triangles as you would if they didn't overlap at all.

Finishing the Edges

Prairie points are usually sewn to the edge of the quilt after it has been quilted. When quilting, leave at least 1 inch all around the outer edge unquilted.

Step 1. Trim the batting and backing even with the edge of the quilt. Fold the backing away from the edge, and pin.

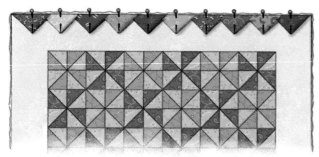

Step 2. Beginning at a corner, with right sides together and raw edges even, place the prairie points along the edge of the quilt. Adjust or ease as needed, and pin in place.

Step 3. Sew the individual points to the top and batting with a ¼-inch seam, removing pins as you go.

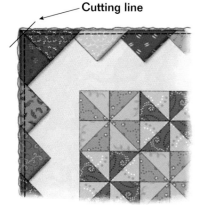

Step 4. Trim off the point of the seam allowance and the batting at each corner. Remove pins and turn seam allowances toward the back of the quilt. The prairie points will fold out along the edge.

Step 5. Fold the backing under ¼ inch and finger press. Pin in place over the base of the prairie points, just covering the previous stitching. Whipstitch in place. Continuing in this way, sew the backing in place all around the quilt.

Step 6. Complete quilting out to the edge, if necessary.

How Many Prairie Points?

If you want the prairie points to line up next to each other with no overlap, you'll need to determine a length for the *finished* triangle base that divides equally into the measurements of the quilt sides. You will be most successful with this if the quilt's dimensions are evenly divisible. For a 60-inch length, you may want a 2-inch-tall prairie point that has a 4-inch finished base.

60" divided by 4" = 15 Prairie Points
Length divided by Finished Base = Number of Prairie Points

You'll need to cut fifteen 4½-inch squares for this side. When positioning these triangles along the edge of the quilt, each base point will overlap its neighbor by ¼ inch so that when they are sewn down, all points will turn to the outside with no overlap.

POSITIONING PRAIRIE POINTS

178

PREPARING FABRIC

Today's fabrics purchased off the bolt are treated with protective coatings, sizings, and other chemicals. Some quilters routinely prewash all of their fabrics; some do not. The coated fabric has a crisp, starchy feel, which makes it easy to handle during either the marking process or rotary-cutting tasks, but there are some things to consider before you decide whether or not to wash your fabric before using it.

Exactly what's in the coatings that were used? The answer to that question likely differs from manufacturer to manufacturer. Some of the chemicals will inevitably flake off during handling, which means the residue will be on your hands and may be floating around in the air you breathe. This may not be of concern to you, but those with breathing problems or allergies to certain products should consider it carefully before working with unwashed fabric. If you like to work with a slightly stiffer fabric, you can prewash, then use a bit of spray starch before you actually begin to use a fabric in a project. You'll be putting a chemical back on the fabric, but you're in complete control of the quantity applied, and you can refer to the can for the list of ingredients.

How much will the fabric shrink? Will all fabrics in a project shrink at the same rate? All 100 percent cotton fabrics shrink when washed, in part because natural fibers like to remain in a relaxed position. When cotton fabric is produced, the warp and weft threads are pulled taut in the loom, stretching the fibers into an unnatural, straight position. The coatings used by manufacturers further stabilize the fabric, helping threads retain their rigid positions in the cloth even after it's removed from the loom.

When you wash and dry the fabrics at home, most of the restrictive coatings are rinsed away. The movement fibers undergo in both the washer and dryer and their wicking action in water help them relax and allow them to return to a position more like that in which they grew. This relaxation results in what we see as shrinkage, although the amount of shrinkage varies from fabric to fabric. If you prefer not to be surprised by just how much shrinkage will take place, prewash all of your fabrics. Use warm water and a mild soap, such as Orvus, to help keep colors bright.

If you want a new quilt to have the look of an antique quilt, assemble your quilt with unwashed fabrics, saving the first wash until the entire piece is complete. Shrinkage takes place during the wash, and causes slight puckers to develop around the quilting stitches, giving the appearance of an antique. If you are using a wide variety of fabrics, some more loosely woven than others, remember that shrinkage rates may vary.

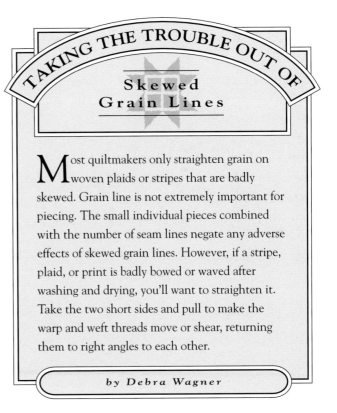

TAKING THE TROUBLE OUT OF
Skewed Grain Lines

Most quiltmakers only straighten grain on woven plaids or stripes that are badly skewed. Grain line is not extremely important for piecing. The small individual pieces combined with the number of seam lines negate any adverse effects of skewed grain lines. However, if a stripe, plaid, or print is badly bowed or waved after washing and drying, you'll want to straighten it. Take the two short sides and pull to make the warp and weft threads move or shear, returning them to right angles to each other.

by Debra Wagner

Pretreat Fabrics

Whether you prewash fabrics or not, be sure to test them for colorfastness, especially those containing deep reds, purples, and blues. Cut a small piece of fabric, and submerge it in hot, soapy water. Let it sit for a while, then inspect the water. Is it still clear? If it is, the fabric passed the first test. Remove the swatch from the water and place it on a white paper towel. If no color seeps onto the towel, the fabric is safe to use in your quilts.

If the fabric does bleed, the safest option is not to use it, especially if you are making an heirloom quilt or one that will get repeated washings. Another option is to purchase a dye-setting solution, such as Retayne, and follow the instructions on the bottle.

Avoid Wrinkled and Twisted Fabrics

To help avoid wrinkles:

- Shake out your fabrics and place them loosely in the washer.

- Use a gentle cycle to help eliminate twisting and raveling.

- Keep smaller pieces of fabric intact by placing them in a mesh lingerie bag before washing, or wash them by hand in a sink of sudsy water.

- Shake out each piece of fabric before transferring it to the dryer. A balled-up, wrinkled piece of fabric will likely come out of the dryer the same way it went in.

- Clip off clumps of thread that formed during the wash, and straighten any puckering that may have occurred at cut edges.

- Don't overload the dryer. Fabric that is able to fall freely is less likely to wrinkle. It's also a good idea to check the dryer after it's been running for ten minutes or so. If pieces seem to be stuck together and falling in one big heap, shake them out a bit before allowing the cycle to continue.

- Remove the fabric from the dryer while it's still slightly damp, and press it with a medium hot iron. If you can't press right away, leave the fabric in the dryer until it's just dry, and be sure to remove it *immediately* when the dryer stops. Use your hands to smooth away wrinkles, and store each piece with the fewest number of folds possible.

 As you remove fabrics from the dryer, use clothespins to clip pieces onto hangers. By hanging the fabric, you'll avoid many of the wrinkles that form while pieces are stacked up, waiting to be pressed. To guard against stretching, don't leave the fabric hanging for long periods of time.

Janet Wickell

PRESSING

Pressing is one of the most controversial subjects for quilters. You read books, you take classes, you ask fellow quilters, and you find the quilt world split about 50/50 on whether to finger press or use an iron during construction of a block and whether or not to use steam in your iron when you press.

There is division on this issue because pressing can be a problem. Pressing *can* cause stretching and distortion to the fabric if not done correctly. You must remember, you are handling fragile pieces of fabric, not a man's shirt. If you run the iron recklessly across the surface of the block, you will have a problem. Both sides of the pressing issue are presented here so you can try different methods and decide for yourself which to use. Armed with knowledge, you'll have even greater success during the piecing process of quiltmaking.

Steam Versus No Steam

Some experts feel that steam causes shrinkage and distortion when pressing because the fabric gets wet. If you then *shove* the iron along the surface of the fabric when it is wet, that indeed could cause it to distort. The shrinkage factor could also be governed by whether or not the fabric is prewashed. Washed fabric is not going to shrink when steam is applied, but unwashed fabric might shrink.

Most quilters who use steam in their iron do so because it does give the fabric a firmer, smoother finish. If used wisely, the steam iron will not distort the fabric or the pieces you are working on. It is easy to assume that once you experience a problem with steam, discontinuing its usage will eliminate all the problems. This is not necessarily so.

The Tools

The iron and ironing surface you are using can make a difference. Purchase a good quality iron, and take the time to keep it working properly. An iron should uniformly dispense steam, rather than spit water out. Using hard water in an iron may cause rust spots on the fabric through the mist of steam. If you are in an area with exceptionally hard water, consider using distilled water.

The ironing surface is normally the traditional ironing board. The cover consists of some type of padding and a fitted cover. That fitted cover can be cotton, teflon, or one of the foam or fiberglass specialty covers. The reflective heat properties of Teflon and fiberglass covers tend to press both sides of the

fabric at the same time; with these, use a medium setting on your iron. With a cotton cover, you will probably have to use a slightly hotter iron.

PORTABLE PRESSING BOARD

If you don't have room to set up a traditional ironing board, you can make a lightweight portable ironing surface by using an empty cardboard bolt from fabric, which most quilt shops are more than happy to give you. Wrap cotton batting, an old cotton terry towel, or needle-punched batting around the bolt, then cover with cotton fabric and tape to the underside of the board. For very little time and money, you have a pressing board that's lightweight, inexpensive, and extremely durable.

Finger Pressing

Finger pressing is becoming increasingly more popular with quilters, as it eliminates the constant darting back and forth between sewing machine (or chair for the hand piecer) and ironing board. Finger pressing can be every bit as effective as the iron if done correctly. It doesn't present the problems with distortion and heat setting that one can experience when using an iron. Finger pressing is most successful for the small units in a block, such as two triangles sewn together to make a square or simple Four Patches.

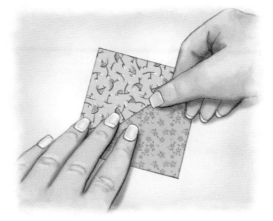

Finger pressing does not mean you take the pieces between the soft pads of your fingers and softly "smush" them. Finger pressing is done on a hard surface using the underneath side of a thumbnail. Firmly, but gently, run the thumbnail along the ridge of the seam on the right side of the pieced unit to press it. You can also finger press by holding the pieces in the air and running the thumbnails from the center out. Thumb-nails are nice because they are attached to the body, and you will not waste time looking for them!

If for some reason thumbnails don't work for you, a hera marker works quite well. (See "Other Marking Options" on page 160.) There is another quilter's gadget called a Little Wooden Iron, which is a cut and shaped rod of wood created specifically for finger pressing. Other tools that you might consider trying include the underneath edge of your rotary cutter (be sure to tighten the safety down securely first) or a stiff plastic template.

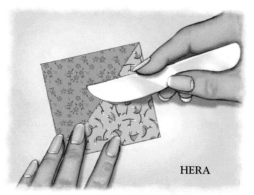

HERA

LITTLE WOODEN IRON

The important thing to remember when finger pressing is that the pieces should remain pressed to one side. They should not bounce back. If the seams do not lie flat, then you have not finger pressed securely enough.

Avoiding Distortion When Using an Iron

The same iron that can distort and heat-set units if used incorrectly can indeed prevent distortion if used correctly. If you iron the units first in the *closed* position, you will set the stitches firmly into the fabric. Open the pieces and carefully glide the iron across the seam allowance. You'll get a much better press when you set the seam this way.

Pressing Strip Sets

Step 1. Position the sewn strips on the ironing board with the sewn edge away from your body and the darkest fabric on top.

Step 2. Carefully lift and set the iron up and down along the entire row of strips to set the stitches.

Step 3. Go back to the beginning of the strip set. Lift up the top strip. Position the iron on the lighter strip (the one closest to your body). Glide the iron across the seam edge from the lightest strip to the darkest strip. Repeat along the entire strip set. The resulting strip set should be pressed firmly and aligned straight. Heat setting the stitches first helps eliminate waviness along the outer edges.

Pressing Block Units

In making any pieced block, there are units that are made first. These must be accurately pressed before proceeding. Using a simple Churn Dash block as an example, you must sew four pairs of triangles together and four pairs of rectangles together before the final block can be sewn.

Step 1. Position the sewn pair of patches on the ironing board with the seam edge away from you and the darker fabric on top. Press in the closed position to set the stitches.

Step 2. Open the unit up and glide the iron across the sewn seam—*not* up and down the length of the seam, but across the seam.

Pressing Pieced Blocks

Step 1. Place the block on the ironing board with the wrong side up. This will prevent slight pleats or "S-style seams," which can occur if the final pressing is done only from the right side. I like to use steam in the iron for this guidance. When pressing on the wrong side, the iron barely skims the surface of the fabric. You do not want to apply pressure with the iron at this stage or you will run the risk of pressing in glitches or pleats, which are difficult to remove. Just make sure the seam allowances are guided in the right direction.

Four Patch Trick

This is a trick you are going to love! It works on Four Patches, Nine Patches, and basically anywhere squares are joined in straight seams where you end up with bulky seam allowances at the intersections.

After you have sewn a Four Patch block, position the fleshy pads of your thumbs on the dark seams with one on either side of that seam intersection.

"Tweak" the allowances toward the lighter square on either side. This will cause the two stitches at that point to release and the strips to lie down.

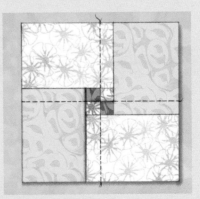

A perfect little Four Patch is formed. Bulk is reduced and the block lies beautifully flat!

Step 2. Turn the block right side up, firmly press, and heat set.

When attaching border strips to a quilt top, press the border together with the quilt top before pinning and sewing. Slippage between the two layers during sewing will be greatly reduced. It is that property of heat setting at work again. The borders should still be pinned every 5 or 6 inches prior to sewing. It is not a permanent bonding of the layers, but a temporary clinging effect, which allows the border strip to be sewn to the quilt without ruffling.

TAKING THE TROUBLE OUT OF

Distorted Blocks

Press border strips to the quilt tops

The iron can be used effectively to "block" your square and eliminate minor edge distortions. Pin the block to the ironing board cover, and use a ruler to make certain it is square. Gently manipulate the block with your iron. I like to use the steam setting for this. Use the iron wisely. Remember, you are not ironing an article of clothing. Treat the block with respect and you will not have problems with distortion or stretching.

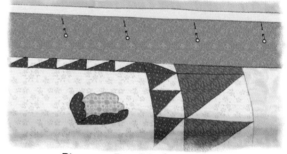

Pin every 5 or 6 inches and sew

QUILT CARE AND STORAGE

Quilt care is really about preventive maintenance. Most problems can be avoided by providing the right environment for your quilts, since environmental influences are the major factors affecting quilts.

Light

The greatest threat to your quilts will likely come from light. Just as sunlight can damage and age your skin, it can do the same to your quilts. Be sure your quilts, whether on a bed or a wall, are not getting too much sunlight from windows, glass doors, or skylights. Check those light levels and angles in the morning, midday, and afternoon. A cherished Baltimore Album quilt that's safe at breakfast-time may have a beam of light hitting your favorite block at teatime. Curtains, shades, and blinds can all help to block sunlight. Bright fluorescent light bulbs and hot incandescent ones can also damage your quilts, so be sure they're not too near.

Climate

If it's too hot or cold, dry or humid for you, it's probably the same for your quilts. Avoid extreme climate fluctuations. If your home is centrally heated and air conditioned, the climate is probably stable enough for your quilts. Good air circulation is important and becomes more so as humidity rises. Fans can keep air moving and reduce the chance of molds or mildew forming.

Pollution and Dirt

Air pollution, dirt, and dust can damage fabric in your quilts. Open windows increase the possibility of air pollution. Central air and heat offer some filtration and allow you to keep windows closed, but filters should be cleaned or replaced regularly. Normal housecleaning is sufficient to keep most dust and dirt in the air under control.

Pests and Pets

Good housekeeping will keep rodents and insect pests such as moths, silverfish, cockroaches, or scorpions under control. If you're in an area where they are prevalent, however, you'll need to be more vigilant. Simply vacuuming thoroughly can help eliminate insects and their larvae. You can discourage these pests by airing quilts regularly and storing them properly.

Pets can sometimes be pests, too! If they are allowed on quilts covering your beds, they can deposit fur, fleas, flea larvae and droppings, saliva, furballs, and the results of housebreaking lapses. Claws can snag threads and fabric. You must decide whether or not to share your quilts with your pets.

Storage

There are really only two options for storing quilts—folding or rolling—since most of us cannot keep our quilts flat and unstacked. Air your stored quilts at least twice a year and examine them at that time for any problems needing attention. Refold the quilt on different lines. If you store your quilts on wooden shelves in a closet, wardrobe, or cedar chest, place a barrier between the wood surfaces that touch your quilt or acids in the wood can leach into it. The barrier can be several layers of washed cotton sheets, muslin, or towels, or it can be special barrier paper.

You can also place the quilt in special acid-free boxes with reinforced corners (see the Resource Guide on page 274). The reinforced corners will allow you to stack boxes to save space without having them compress and crush the stored quilt inside.

Folding. You will need neutral pH tissue paper, acid-free tissue paper, and barrier paper.

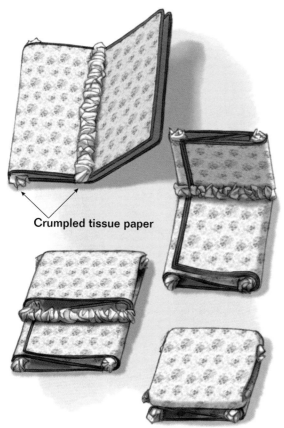

Crumpled tissue paper

Step 1. Pad each fold generously with the tissue, as shown above. Use acid-free tissue for cotton quilts and neutral pH tissue with silk or combination quilts such as crazy quilts. Don't press the folded quilt to flatten it.

Step 2. Wrap the folded quilt with more tissue and place it in an acid-free box.

Try This

If you run out of special tissue paper and boxes to pad your quilts and store them, here's an alternative. Make several bolsters quickly from leftover lengths of cotton muslin and quilt batting scraps. Roll muslin around the batting, and tie the ends of the bolsters with cotton twill tape. Make enough to pad your quilt. Slip the quilt into a large cotton pillowcase. Then slip another large cotton pillowcase over the open end. Place a cotton sheet or towel on any wood surface on which you plan to store the quilt.

TAKING THE TROUBLE OUT OF Quilt Storage

If you brought your grandmother's quilt home safely sealed up in a plastic garbage bag, take it out right away. A plastic garbage bag can ruin your quilt! If any dampness was sealed up with it—from the air on a humid, rainy day—that warm, moist environment could result in mildew on your heirloom. And mildew is virtually impossible to remove. At the very least, leave the plastic bag open so your quilt can breathe. Use the plastic bag only as a temporary means to transport your quilt. And always use see-through plastic bags, with your quilt's top folded to the outside. Don't take a chance that someone will put your treasure out with the trash!

Rolling. Don't roll fragile quilts or those with designs in high relief, such as trapunto quilts. Rolling can put too much stress on them.

You will need an acid-free tube several inches longer than the quilt and 4½ inches or more in diameter. You can also use a long tablecloth tube from a dry cleaner, pad it with acid-free tissue or quilt batting, and secure a washed cotton sheet around it.

Step 1. Place a washed cotton sheet on the floor. Put the quilt face down on the sheet. Put the tube on the quilt and sheet.

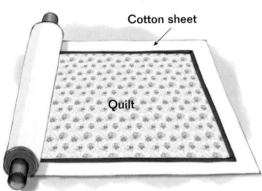

Cotton sheet

Quilt

Step 2. Begin rolling with the back of the quilt inside the roll and the front facing out. This puts the strain and possible wrinkling on the back of the quilt. Do not roll tightly.

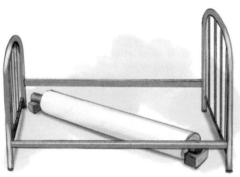

Step 3. Cover with acid-free tissue, muslin, or the sheet. Tie the ends with cotton twill tape. Suspend on the diagonal under a bed with the ends of the tube supported on blocks of wood or bricks. The blocks must be big enough so the quilt doesn't touch the floor.

Step 4. Check frequently to see that the location stays pest- and dust-free.

Cleaning Options (Other than Laundering)

No cleaning procedure for quilts is quick, trouble-free, or 100 percent safe, so you should avoid cleaning when possible. Don't sacrifice the enjoyment of your quilts just to keep them clean. Instead, divide your

quilts into those you want to use every day and those you consider heirlooms. Quilts used daily will need more cleaning and will wear out sooner. An heirloom quilt displayed on the bed for special occasions, hung on the wall as art, or stored much of the time will very seldom need cleaning.

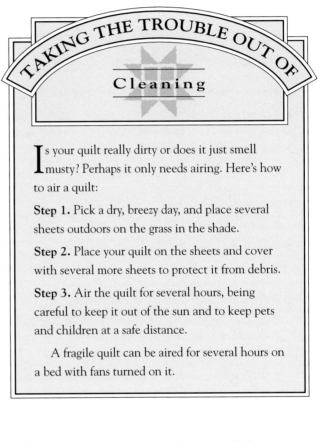

TAKING THE TROUBLE OUT OF Cleaning

Is your quilt really dirty or does it just smell musty? Perhaps it only needs airing. Here's how to air a quilt:

Step 1. Pick a dry, breezy day, and place several sheets outdoors on the grass in the shade.

Step 2. Place your quilt on the sheets and cover with several more sheets to protect it from debris.

Step 3. Air the quilt for several hours, being careful to keep it out of the sun and to keep pets and children at a safe distance.

A fragile quilt can be aired for several hours on a bed with fans turned on it.

When you must clean a quilt, first stabilize any holes, rips, frays, or tears, so the cleaning process doesn't make them worse.

Vacuuming. Vacuuming is the least stressful way to clean a quilt and removes a great deal of dust and dirt. If your quilt is fragile, vacuuming may be the only method of cleaning it can stand. Almost any quilt can be vacuumed successfully, if proper steps are followed.

Step 1. Spread the quilt out on a bed or table. If it's hanging on the wall, you can vacuum it there.

Step 2. Prepare a square of fiberglass or nylon screening (about 2 × 2 feet) by covering the rough edges with cotton twill tape or silver duct tape. Place the screen over the quilt.

Step 3. Use a hand-held vacuum or a regular vacuum with an upholstery attachment. Cover the opening of the attachment with several layers of cheesecloth, single-filament silk fabric, nylon tulle, or old pantyhose.

Step 4. Hold the screening down securely so the quilt isn't sucked into the vacuum. Vacuum both sides thoroughly using the lowest suction setting.

Dry Cleaning. Wool, silk, and combination quilts (such as crazy quilts) should be dry cleaned only if they are so soiled that you cannot enjoy them. The strong solvents and agitation used make dry cleaning quite risky. If you feel you must dry clean, seek a cleaner experienced in preparing items for museums. If you can't find one, look for a cleaner who preserves bridal gowns and ask for references. Be sure to check those references! Specify that you do not want your quilt marked in any way, or it may come back with a permanent laundry mark. Also, specify that you want fresh solvent used on your quilt, because solvent is often reused and can contain dyes and smells from previously cleaned items. Never attempt any type of dry cleaning yourself.

QUILT SIZES

Use this handy reference to help you determine the size quilt you need to make and the batting size to purchase. It will also help you visualize how a specific quilt size will fit your bed.

Quilts to be used with a dust ruffle (with the exception of crib quilts) include a 12-inch drop on the sides and bottom of the quilt. This size is designed for a dust ruffle, and no extra length is added for pillows. Use pillow shams or coordinating pillow cases.

Quilts that cover the box spring (except crib quilts) include a 16-inch drop on the sides and bottom and an extra 10 inches for pillow tuck. The quilt does not reach the floor, but it covers the mattress and box spring, making a dust ruffle unnecessary.

IDEAL QUILT MEASUREMENTS AND BATTING SIZES (IN INCHES)					
	Crib	**Twin**	**Double (Full)**	**Queen**	**King**
	27" × 52"	39" × 75"	54" × 75"	60" × 80"	76" × 80"
Quilt Used with Dust Ruffle	30 × 45	63 × 87	78 × 87	84 × 92	100 × 92
Batting Size	45 × 60	72 × 90	81 × 96	90 × 108	120 × 120
Quilt to Cover Box Spring	36 × 54	71 × 101	86 × 101	92 × 106	108 × 106
Batting Size	45 × 60	81 × 96	90 × 108	120 × 120	120 × 120

QUILTING DESIGNS

A look at nineteenth-century quilts offers ample evidence that the quilting was taken as seriously as the designing of the quilt top. It is my feeling that extensive quilting can elevate a common top and that a lack of quilting can diminish a grand quilt top. Any quilt top benefits when the quilting is taken seriously.

How to quilt your quilt is always a big question and one that has been largely ignored. What designs to use, how to draft them, and how to mark them on the quilt top puzzles many quilters. As you review the options for possible quilting designs and for design sources, you will be amazed and delighted by the number of exciting possibilities available to you.

Purchased Stencils and Tracing Patterns from Books

Commercial stencils and templates have long been used by quilters. You can buy them at a quilt shop in a wide variety of styles and sizes. There are a growing number of books on the market that contain collections of quilting designs, and quilt magazines also publish quilting patterns for your convenience. These sources will provide you with a wealth of possible designs to grace your special quilt. You can simply trace these quilting designs directly from a book or magazine and transfer them to your own quilt. You can redraft them to fit your specific quilt, or you can use them as a springboard for your own unique quilting designs.

Drafting Your Own Designs

Learning to draft your own quilting designs is the most effective way to make sure your design fits your quilt exactly and that you have the specific design you want. It is also much more economical. For me, it is rewarding because it is another way that I can personalize my quilts and make each quilting design unique.

Quilting designs should fill the area for which they are intended. Select a design that will fill the area, but also stay about ¼ inch away from the seams so you don't have to quilt through the extra layers of fabric.

Outline Quilting

Outline quilting is simply quilting around a shape, either pieced or appliquéd. The blocks that make up a pieced quilt are made of geometric shapes—squares, triangles, rectangles, diamonds, and other shapes. These shapes are often outlined with a quilting line on the inside of the shape.

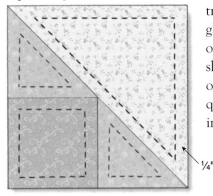

¼"

OUTLINE QUILTING

I used outline quilting on the pieced sawtooth border of my "Cherries" quilt, shown below. Notice that I quilted around every red and white triangle. The quilting line usually runs about ¼ inch away from the seam line so that the quilter can avoid quilting through the extra layers near the seam. I use the seam line as my guide and do not mark outline quilting.

"Cherries," 34" × 34", was made by Gwen Marston in 1991. This quilt features the ever-popular feathered vine on the border, outline quilting around the triangles in the sawtooth border, outline quilting around the appliqué patches, and freehand drawn leaves and vines as the background.

Outline quilting around the patches on appliqué quilts has always been common. The stitching varies just slightly from right next to the edge of the patch to about ⅛ inch beyond it. Sometimes on nineteenth-century appliqué quilts, both the outside and the inside of an appliqué shape were outline quilted.

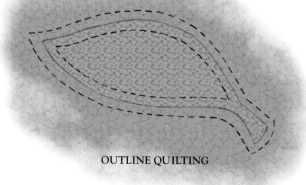

OUTLINE QUILTING

Quilting in the Ditch

Quilting in the ditch means that you quilt almost right in the seam line. The quilting line runs immediately next to the seam line on the side away from the seam allowance. By quilting right next to the seam, the stitches are hidden by the puffy seam on the unquilted side. Some quilters prefer this because they are not confident that their stitches look good enough. Others may choose to quilt in the ditch so the quilting does not interfere with the pieced design.

Cross-Hatching

Cross-hatching is one of many traditional straight line designs. It is a square grid created by 45 degree angles in both directions. The lines have to be marked at a 45 degree angle to the vertical and horizontal

CROSS-HATCHING

lines of a quilt to have a *true* cross-hatching design.

When the lines are closer to a 60 degree angle the result is a diamond grid, which is a very different look.

A slight variation on these two designs can be created by doubling every line.

The distance between the lines is optional. Generally the lines vary between ½ to 1¼ inches. Whether you are marking cross-hatching or a diamond grid, try using

DIAMOND GRID

an angle keeper to help you keep the lines straight and consistently spaced. (See "Marking a Quilt Top" on page 157.)

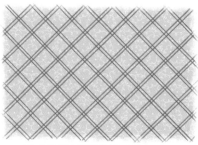

CROSS-HATCHING VARIATION

Cross-hatching is a design with many uses. It is often used as a background behind appliqué, as seen in my "Rose of Sharon" quilt, shown below.

"Rose of Sharon," 36" × 36", was made by Gwen Marston in 1987. Here the appliqué patches are outline quilted; cross-hatching fills the background along with shapes traced from cookie cutters. Echo quilting is used on the border.

Echo Quilting

Echo quilting is just what it sounds like—quilting lines that repeat themselves and echo the previous line. It is often used around appliqué motifs. Hawaiian quilters use it almost exclusively

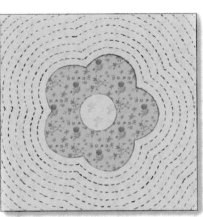

ECHO QUILTING

around their intricate appliqués. The effectiveness of echo quilting seems to depend upon the lines being no more than ½ inch apart, and usually they are closer than that. An advantage to echo quilting is that it does not need to be marked. Just echo the previous line, using it as a guide. I did echo quilting in the border of "Rose of Sharon," shown on the opposite page.

Ideas for Quilting Designs

Study photographs of old quilts, and scout out antique quilts at shows. There is a wealth of information in antique quilts. Nineteenth-century quilters showed great variation and imagination in the quilting designs with which they graced their quilts. You'll be inspired and feel a sense of freedom to create your own original designs.

You can also find inspiration on wallpaper, dishes, silverware, and in architectural design. It's everywhere, so start looking!

Meander and Stipple Quilting

Definitions for stipple quilting, meander quilting, and the older term, "seed" quilting, are a matter of interpretation. Depending upon whom you talk to, these terms may be interchangeable. This type of quilting consists of wandering lines that do not actually cross or touch each other. Stipple quilting lines are generally about ¹⁄₁₆ inch apart. Meander quilting lines are further apart than stipple quilting lines, but the lines still do not cross each other. Seed quilting consists of individual stitches going in all directions with no specific pattern. All of these quilting patterns produce a textured background that is quite beautiful.

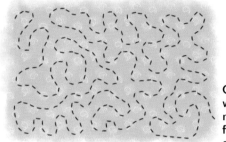

Quilting lines meander and echo each other and are very close together.

STIPPLE QUILTING

Quilting lines wander or meander, but are farther apart than stipple quilting.

MEANDER QUILTING

Individual stitches go in every direction with no constant patterning at all, resembling seeds cast on the ground.

SEED QUILTING

Feather Quilting

Feather motifs have always been one of the most graceful and elegant of all quilting designs. For that reason they have been, and continue to be, some of the most popular quilting choices. They come in many different shapes, sizes, and arrangements. They are useful for filling both plain blocks and borders and have even been used as all-over quilting patterns.

Let's begin by learning how to make the celebrated feather wreath. With these directions, you will be able to make a feather wreath template in any size you need for your quilt.

Step 1. The first step is to measure the block you want the feather wreath to fill. Let's say it is 4½ inches. Because you want to stay about ¼ inch inside the seam line, cut out a 4-inch circle.

Step 2. Fold the circle in half, in half again, and in half one more time. Now draw an ice-cream-cone shape across the top and cut along the line.

Step 3. Open it up and you should have a shape that looks somewhat like a flower.

Step 4. Draw curved lines and circles inside to create a wide variety of feather wreaths with this one beginning shape. This wreath will have eight feathers. For a larger wreath, you will need to draw in more feathers.

Make Your Own Feather Wreath Template

To make a feather wreath for a 9-inch block, begin by cutting an 8½-inch circle. Fold it in half four times. Cut an ice-cream-cone shape across the top, as shown in Step 2 at left.

Open it up and discover the beginnings of a 16-petaled feather wreath. Draw a circle in the middle and cut it out. By changing the size of the inner circle you can change the look of the feather wreath considerably. Experiment with this idea to create many different feather wreath variations.

To make a sturdy template, paste the paper pattern onto a piece of tag board or a manila file folder. Now you have a basic template.

16-PETALED FEATHER WREATH

Center the template on your quilt and draw around the outside and inside. Double the inner circle with a second line about ⅛ inch away from the first line. Now you can draw the feathers by eye, directly onto your top. Practice on paper first to see how easy this is to accomplish.

Border Designs

The three most common border designs, both past and present, are straight lines, cables, and continuous feathered vines.

Straight line designs work well on most quilts and are a good choice. Learning to use the angle keeper described on page 159 will make these designs easy to mark on your quilt. It is no surprise that the most common of all quilting designs for borders is also the simplest: single diagonal lines. Diagonal lines can be marked in one direction all the way around the quilt.

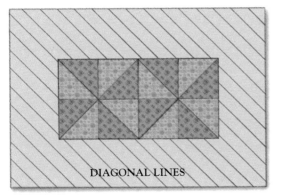

Most quilters today prefer a symmetrical approach, with all four sides being identical. Here are simple steps for designing a symmetrical diagonal border.

1. Place a pin at the center of each side.

2. Begin marking diagonals in the corners and mark toward the center.

3. When you reach the center, allow the lines to make "tents."

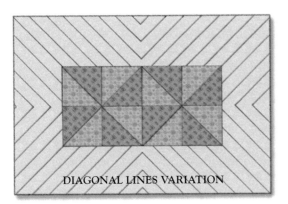

Look at the diagonal quilting on my quilt "Coxcomb," shown above at right. The appliqué patches are outline quilted and the backgrounds of the blocks are quilted in diagonal lines. Notice that all four corners of the borders are identical, and the quilting lines meet in the center of each side, forming tents.

Diagonal lines do not have to be symmetrical. In fact, most quilts made in the nineteenth century using diagonals did not have all four corners marked the same way. Take a look, and you will find that identically quilted corners are the exception rather than the rule. If you want an old-fashioned look to your quilt, consider this less than symmetrical corner treatment.

"Coxcomb," 73" × 80", made by Gwen Marston in 1984. This quilt is outline quilted around all the appliqué shapes and has diagonal line background quilting. The sashing is quilted in a lovely feather vine variation.

 Double or triple the diagonals for a surprisingly elegant effect. Another diagonal border design is made by first marking tents along the border and then filling each tent with additional tents or with straight lines.

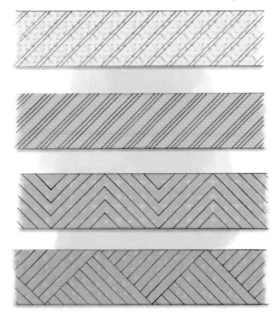

Hanging diamonds are less common and for that reason make an interesting choice. This design is made with a set of diagonal lines and a set of vertical lines. Notice that the diagonal and vertical lines do not line up with each other. Hanging diamonds also work well as filler quilting or an all-over pattern.

HANGING DIAMONDS

Cables come in a vast array of shapes and sizes. Single cables work well for sashing, or lattice, and narrow borders. Wider borders call for wider cables made with more strands. You can learn to draft your own cables to fit your quilts exactly, or you can purchase cable templates.

There are several traditional variations of a basic cable, all of which can be drawn with a single shape.

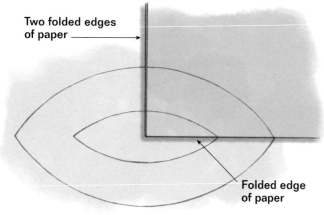

CABLE DESIGNS MADE FROM ONE SHAPE

Fold a piece of paper in half two times, draw the portion of the football shape indicated by the drawn lines in the illustration above, and cut it out to make a symmetrical shape. Trace the shape onto template material and use the template to make all the cable variations shown.

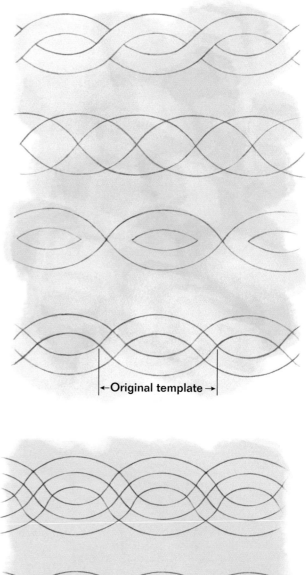

←Original template→

Erase portions of the lines to create this over/under cable variation

WIDER CABLE DESIGNS TO FIT WIDER BORDERS

Feathers are perhaps the most elegant of all border designs. Look at the feather variation in the wide sashing on my "Coxcomb" quilt, shown on page 193. A more common feathered vine can be seen on my "Cherries" quilt on page 189. It's not hard to design a perfectly symmetrical feathered vine that fits your quilt exactly. The general directions are given on the opposite page. Feel free to experiment on paper until you are happy with the results.

CONTINUOUS FEATHER BORDER

Step 1. Measure the sides of your quilt and divide it into equal units. To make a vine with a symmetrical curve, cut a piece of paper the size of one unit.

Step 2. Fold the paper in half across the border width. Keep the fold to the left and make a pencil mark 2 inches down from the top edge on the left and 2 inches up from the bottom 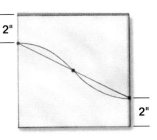 edge on the right. Find the center by folding the paper in half again, and place a dot at the center. Note that the 2 inches is an arbitrary measure. You may want taller or shorter feathers. Do some experimenting and decide how much space you need for feathers and mark a dot at that point.

Step 3. Now draw a symmetrical curved line connecting the dots. The curve should be very gradual and not steeply curved. Darken  the line so you can trace this curve on the other side of the paper. Unfold it, and you will have a nice, even curve as the basis for your feathers. Draw another line about ¼ inch away from the first line. Do this by eye. Some variation is natural and actually makes the finished design more pleasing to the eye.

Step 4. Draw the feathers on the paper freehand. This takes a little practice, but remember the feathers can vary. Work in pencil until you are pleased with your design. Then darken it with a felt-tip marker so it will be easy to trace.

Once you have designed one section of the feathered vine, simply move it along the border of the quilt, tracing it as you go. If the border fabric is light, you can slip the design under the top and trace it. If it is dark, trace it with the aid of a light table, or make a stencil. (See "Cut Your Own Stencils" on page 233.)

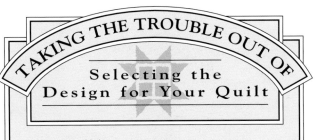

TAKING THE TROUBLE OUT OF

Selecting the Design for Your Quilt

Ask yourself these questions:
- Is my quilt formal or informal? Is it a country scrap quilt, an art quilt or an elegant quilt?
- Is there a lot of open space so the quilting will show up, or will busy prints obscure the quilting?
- What kind of overall effect do I want?
- Do I like to quilt?

If your quilt is formal, choose refined quilting patterns such as feathers, feather wreaths, or floral designs. If it is informal, consider an all-over pattern like cross-hatching, diagonals, or fans—so common on country quilts.

If it is an art quilt, look at other art quilts in books and magazines to see how they are quilted. You will see straight lines and curving lines, but most likely not feather wreaths and cables.

If you want to emphasize the quilting, plan for it to be an important element in your quilt. If you don't enjoy quilting, you will be wise to keep it simple and to make quilts that don't need elaborate quilting.

ROTARY CUTTERS

Rotary cutters were introduced to quilters in the early 1980s, and along with rotary rulers and cutting mats, they have become essential tools for many. When cleaning and changing blades, lay the parts down in the order in which you removed them to avoid confusion.

Rotary cutters have radically changed the way quilters cut fabric since they first appeared in the early 1980s. Resembling a pizza cutter, a rotary cutter uses a razor-sharp rolling blade to cut multiple layers of fabric with speed and accuracy. Different brands offer a choice of blade size, handle types, and locking mechanisms. Some offer a cutting guide arm attachment.

Blade Size and Use

All rotary cutters are available with a 45-millimeter blade, which can cut up to eight layers. Smaller 28-millimeter blades are often favored for cutting curves and by people with small hands. An extra-large cutter with a 60-millimeter blade is comfortable for larger hands and makes multiple-layer cutting even easier. Blades with pinked or waved edges are available for decorative and fun details or embellishments on

quilts. A double-blade cutter with an adjustable measuring bar will cut strips of pre-set widths. Cutters or blades can be reversed for left-handed use, and blades are interchangeable between brands.

Handles

Cutters are made with straight or curved handles. Some curved handles have molded finger-grips; one has a rounded, contoured shape that conforms to the hand. The blade is slightly more visible when cutting with a straight-handled rotary cutter, and some quilters feel they can control the pressure better with this type. Curved handles are often favored by people with carpal-tunnel problems or those who prefer to sit when cutting. All handles have protection to prevent the thumb from slipping onto the blade when pressure is being applied.

Blade Guards

To prevent accidents, it is essential to keep the blade closed when the cutter is not being used. The more convenient the guard mechanism, the more consistently it will be used. Most use a variation of a push-pull lock system, some work with the thumb, and others with a finger. One cutter has a two-step system, where the thumb rest releases the blade and a button on the handle retracts it. The most convenient is a spring-loaded guard that exposes the blade only when pressure is applied. Obviously, this feature is not recommended for homes with small children who might mistake it for a toy.

Changing Blades

A rotary cutter is only efficient and safe when the blade is sharp. A dull blade can require so much pressure that the cutter slips, causing damage to the fabric or the user. The length of time a blade remains sharp depends on how often it is used, how many layers are cut at a time, and the type of fabric being cut. Synthetics and specialty fabrics dull a blade faster than 100 percent cotton.

Change blades when they skip or cease cutting easily. Lay the parts down in the order they are removed to avoid confusion. Each time the blade is changed, clean and inspect the parts for wear. A worn pivot that holds the blade in the center can cause drag and make cutting more difficult. Wipe excess oil off the new blade before inserting it, and be careful not to over-tighten the retainer nut. Check that the blade rotates smoothly and the lock works easily when the cutter is reassembled. Dispose of the worn blade safely by placing it back in the original packaging; it can still cut!

Cutter Care

Between blade changes, periodically take out the blade and wipe off accumulated lint. Lint may mix with the oil on the blade and need to be removed with a piece of fabric saturated with sewing machine oil. If it becomes hardened, use nail polish remover. If high humidity has caused the blade to rust, remove the rust with very fine sandpaper. After cleaning the blade and holder, oil the blade and reassemble. This will extend the life of the blade.

Just remember, always consider your rotary cutter a rolling razor blade. Handle it carefully, and keep it well out of reach of children.

Dixie Haywood

ROTARY CUTTING

Rotary cutting made its debut in the quilting world in the early 1980s, radically changing the way quilts had been made for more than 150 years. The impact on quiltmaking has been phenomenal. This quicker, easier, and more accurate way of cutting patches for quilts gave rise to rapid growth in the quilting industry. More people than ever have taken up quilting as a hobby and as a profession.

Whether you're a beginner or advanced quilter, you'll have best results with a rotary cutter if you choose lightweight, closely woven, 100 percent cotton fabrics. The fabric should be preshrunk, color tested, and ironed before it is cut. (See "Preparing Fabric" on page 179 and "Pressing" on page 180.)

Straight Strips

The rotary method of cutting patches begins with cutting strips of fabric. Strips can be cut on the lengthwise grain (parallel to the selvage) or crosswise grain (perpendicular to the selvage). All strips are cut with the ¼-inch seam allowance included.

Step 1. To cut strips on the crosswise grain, fold the fabric selvage to selvage, aligning the cross and straight grains as best you can. Place fabric on the rotary-cutting mat with the folded edge closest to your body. Align a square plastic cutting ruler with the fold of the fabric and place a 6 × 24-inch cutting ruler flush against the left side of the square, making sure it is positioned far enough onto the fabric that a cut down its right edge will slice through all layers. When making all cuts, the fabric should be placed to your right. (If you are left-handed, work from the other end of the fabric, reversing the directions.)

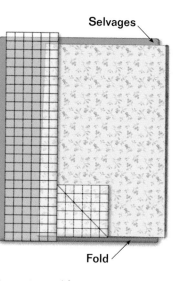

Selvages

Fold

Try This

If you don't have a square ruler, you can square up your fabric with just the 6 × 24-inch ruler. Align a horizontal line on the ruler with the fold of the fabric. The bulk of the fabric should be on your left. Make a

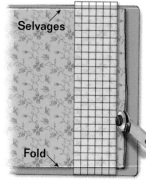

Selvages

Fold

straight cut through both layers. To continue cutting, move to the opposite side of the table, or rotate your cutting mat so that you can make your measured cuts with the bulk of the fabric placed to your right. This will ensure that you don't move the fabric and disrupt your squared edges.

Step 2. Remove the square ruler and hold the long ruler firmly in place with the left hand. Place the smallest finger off the ruler to serve as an anchor and to prevent slipping. Stand comfortably with your head and body centered on the cutting line. Make a rotary cut along the right side of the ruler. Use firm, even pressure as you cut. Begin rolling the cutter before you reach the fabric edge and continue across. The blade is very sharp, so be careful! Always cut away from yourself.

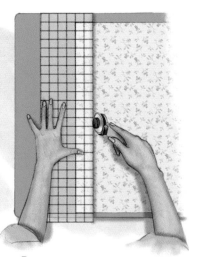

Tips for Rotary Cutting

- Be sure to hold the ruler steady.
- To keep the ruler steady on long cuts, periodically stop the cutter and move your left hand up so that it is even with the cutter. Make sure the markings remain properly aligned.
- For safety, always roll the cutter away from you.
- Keep your fingers away from the blade of the rotary cutter.
- Practice cutting on scrap fabric to get the feel for rotary cutting if you're new to the technique.

Step 3. Cut strips of fabric by aligning the vertical line on the ruler with the cut edge of the fabric. For example, if you need a 2-inch strip, line up the 2-inch line with the cut edge of the fabric and cut. Open the fabric strips periodically to make sure you are making straight cuts. If the strips are not straight, or if they have a bend in the middle, as shown above, the leading edge is no longer at a 90 degree angle to the fold. Use the square plastic cutting ruler to realign and square up the edge again.

Because the lengthwise grain holds its shape better than the more stretchy crosswise grain, it is better to cut borders, lattice, and other long pieces along the lengthwise grain. To cut strips on the lengthwise grain, fold the fabric so cuts will be parallel to the selvage. Trim away the selvage and make successive cuts, measuring from the first cut.

 Cutting accurate strips takes practice. Fine-tune your skills by practicing on pieces of scrap fabric, or cut shorter strips from an unfolded segment until you are comfortable with the technique.

To preserve the 90 degree angle of your edge, never cut a strip until one of the horizontal rules is aligned with the fold and the vertical line is aligned with the cut edge. Think of the ruler's lines as a two-way check system. If the horizontal and vertical lines are both lined up with the edges of your fabric, the strips will likely be accurate. —*Janet Wickell*

Squares and Rectangles

The strip method of rotary cutting squares yields a lot of squares of one fabric in a hurry.

Step 1. Cut fabric in strips the size of the finished measurement of the square plus ½ inch for seam allowances.

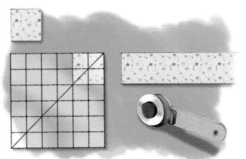

Step 2. Using a ruled square or other cutting ruler, align the vertical rule with the cut edge of the strip. Line up the top and bottom edges of the strip with horizontal lines on the ruler to double check that your square will indeed be square. Cut the fabric into squares the width of the strip.

Step 3. Cut rectangles in the same manner, first cutting strips the length of the rectangle plus seam allowances, then cutting to the proper width.

Cutting individual squares: When a strip of fabric will make more squares than you need, cut just a few patches using a ruled square. You can also cut one or two squares from several different fabrics at one time. Layer up to four different fabrics, and follow these steps.

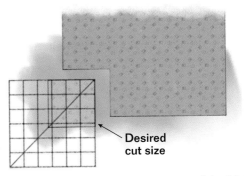

Desired cut size

Step 1. Position the square ruler on a corner of the fabric. Make two cuts along the edges of the ruler to separate the square from the rest of the fabric. The measurement used should be slightly larger than the desired cut size of the square.

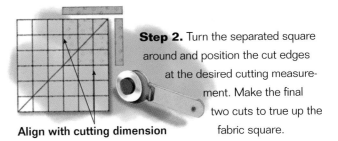

Step 2. Turn the separated square around and position the cut edges at the desired cutting measurement. Make the final two cuts to true up the fabric square.

Align with cutting dimension

Half-Square Triangles

To cut these triangles, cut a square, and then cut it in half diagonally. The resulting triangles will have short sides on the straight grain and the long side on the bias.

Step 1. Cut a square using *the finished measurement of the short side of the triangle plus ⅞ inch.* (Or, if you have a draft or a template, just measure the short side of the triangle you need to cut, including seam allowances, from corner to tip, to arrive at the proper size for the square.)

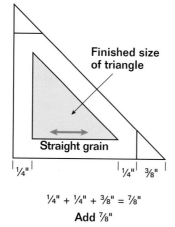

Finished size of triangle

Straight grain

¼" ¼" ⅜"

¼" + ¼" + ⅜" = ⅞"
Add ⅞"

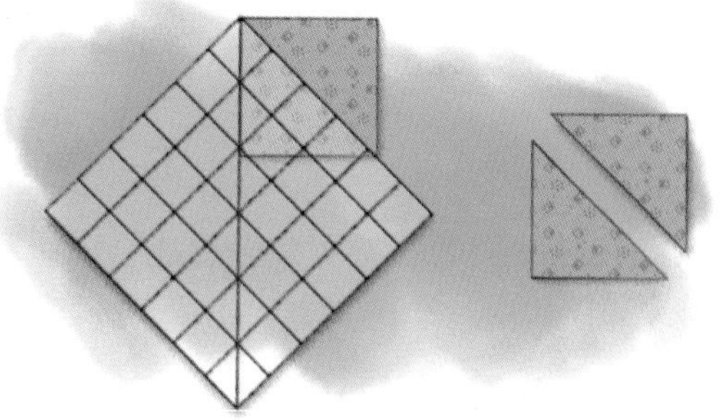

Step 2. Cut the square in half diagonally from corner to corner. Check the triangles to make sure they are the right size.

Quick-Cut Icons

Quick-cut icons are little pictures in many books and patterns that remind you how a triangle is cut. Half-square triangles are made from a square cut in half. Quarter-square triangles are made from a square cut in quarters.

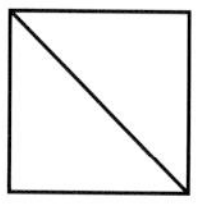

HALF-SQUARE TRIANGLES   **QUARTER-SQUARE TRIANGLES**

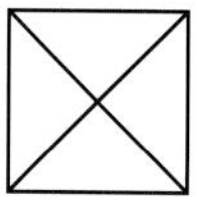

Quarter-Square Triangles

To cut these triangles, cut a square, and then cut it in half diagonally twice. The resulting triangles will have the long side on the straight grain and the short sides on the bias.

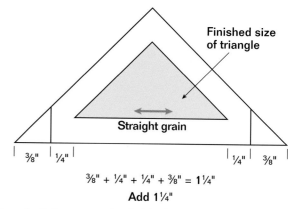

Finished size of triangle

Straight grain

⅜" ¼"   ¼" ⅜"

⅜" + ¼" + ¼" + ⅜" = 1¼"
Add 1¼"

Step 1. Cut a square the *finished measurement of the long side of the triangle plus 1¼ inches.* (Or, if you have a template or a draft of the triangle you need to cut, just measure the long side from tip to tip, including seam allowances, to arrive at the proper size for the square.)

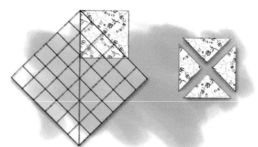

Step 2. Cut the square diagonally from corner to corner. Without moving the resulting triangles, line up the ruler and make another diagonal cut in the opposite direction. Each square will yield four quarter-square triangles.

Long Triangles

The long triangles that form the points of the Unknown Star can be rotary cut from rectangles. Note that in this pattern, the triangles must be cut as reverse, or mirror, images. The arrow indicates grain line.

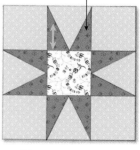

Reverse

UNKNOWN STAR

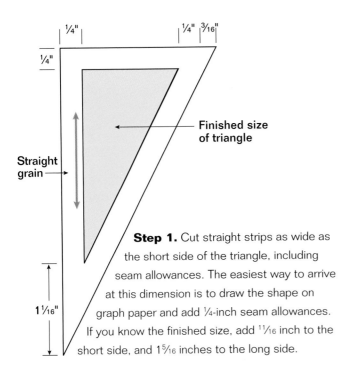

Finished size of triangle

Straight grain

1/4" 1/4" 1/4" 3/16"

1 1/16"

Step 1. Cut straight strips as wide as the short side of the triangle, including seam allowances. The easiest way to arrive at this dimension is to draw the shape on graph paper and add 1/4-inch seam allowances. If you know the finished size, add 11/16 inch to the short side, and 15/16 inches to the long side.

Step 2. Cut rectangles from strips, using the dimension of the long straight side of the triangle including seam allowances.

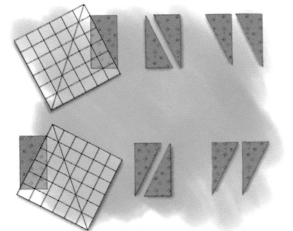

Step 3. Cut the rectangles from corner to opposite corner to yield two identical long triangles. To get reversed long triangles, cut the next rectangle diagonally in the opposite direction, or simply layer the fabrics, wrong sides together, when the rectangles are cut.

Diamonds and Rhomboids

Diamonds and rhomboids are similar shapes and are cut basically the same way. A 45 degree diamond has equal sides and equal opposite angles. It is symmetrical.

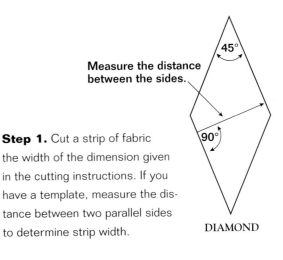

Measure the distance between the sides.

45°

90°

DIAMOND

Step 1. Cut a strip of fabric the width of the dimension given in the cutting instructions. If you have a template, measure the distance between two parallel sides to determine strip width.

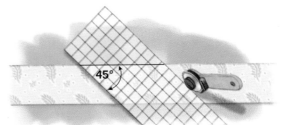

45°

Step 2. Make a 45 degree angle cut at one end of the strip, using the 45 degree angle line on the ruler.

Step 3. Make additional successive cuts parallel to the 45 degree angle cut, using the same dimension as the width of the strip.

Cutting rhomboids: A rhomboid is not quite a diamond because it has two long sides and two short sides. It is asymmetrical. When cutting, you are often instructed to "Cut 4, cut 4 reverse." (The latter is sometimes abbreviated to 4(r) or 4 rev.) This means to cut four of the shapes as the pattern is given, plus four more reversed. If you were using templates, you would simply turn the template over to cut the second set of four shapes or layer fabric with right or wrong sides facing before cutting. To cut rhomboids with reversals, follow these steps.

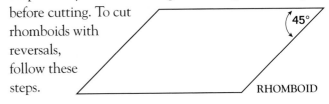

45°

RHOMBOID

Step 1. Cut two strips of fabric the width of the first dimension given in the cutting instructions. Measure from side to side if you have a template.

Step 2. Place the two strips of fabric with right or wrong sides together.

Step 3. Make a 45 degree angle cut at one end of the strip, using the 45 degree angle line on the ruler.

Step 4. Make additional successive cuts parallel to the 45 degree angle cut, using the second dimension (usually slightly larger than the first) as the length of each piece.

Paper Templates for Odd-Size Shapes

Often shapes and cut dimensions of pattern pieces do not correspond with markings on standard cutting rulers. Just because a square measures 4 5/16 inches does not mean it cannot be rotary cut.

To cut odd-size squares, rectangles, diamonds, parallelograms, and other shapes, first make an accurate paper template, including the 1/4-inch seam allowances. Carefully trace the shape on tracing or typing paper, cut it out, and tape it to the underside of your cutting ruler with removable tape. You will then have the proper guide for cutting your shape.

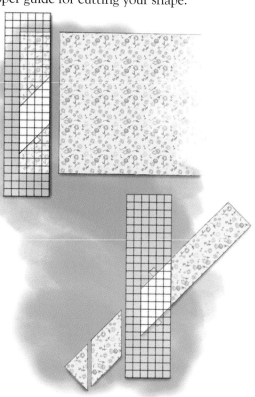

CUTTING PARALLELOGRAMS

Shapes such as trapezoids and octagons start out as triangles or squares and then have corner triangles trimmed away. The corner that is cut off is called a cutaway triangle.

Octagons

Octagons are squares with the corners cut off. To determine the size of the cutaway triangles at the corners, draw the square and octagon on a piece of graph paper. Add a 1/4-inch seam allowance around each shape. The triangle to be cut off is the difference between the two shapes with the seam allowances taken into consideration.

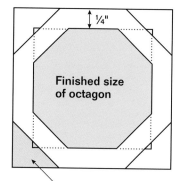

1/4"

Finished size of octagon

Cutaway triangle

Step 1. Cut a square the width of the octagon including seam allowances.

Step 2. Cut out a paper triangle template of the cutaway triangle, and tape it to the underside of your ruler. Position the ruler as shown, and trim off the four corners. Compare the cut octagon to your drawn pattern for accuracy.

Trapezoids

Rotary-cut trapezoids are based on triangles. Small cutaway triangles are trimmed from the 90 degree corner to create the trapezoidal shape. To determine the size of the cutaway triangle, draw the finished-size triangle and trapezoid on graph paper. Add a 1/4-inch seam allowance around each shape. The triangle to be cut off is the difference between the two shapes with the seam allowances taken into consideration.

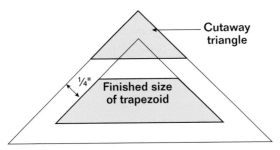

Step 1. Cut half-square triangles if the straight grain on the trapezoid should be on the short side; cut quarter-square triangles if the straight grain should be on the long side.

Step 2. Cut out a paper template of the cutaway triangle and tape it to the underside of the ruler. Position the ruler as shown and trim off the 90 degree corner of the large triangle. Compare the cut trapezoid shape to your drawn pattern for accuracy.

Other Shapes

Kites, equilateral triangles, or any shape with straight sides can be cut with the rotary-cutting techniques described here.

Make a draft for your block design, as described on page 90. Base your template and cutting dimensions on the shapes in the draft.

Make paper templates for shapes and dimensions that do not coincide with ruler measurements. Play around with it and you'll be able to figure out how to cut any shape.

CUTTING UNUSUAL SHAPES

Rotary Cutting with Templates

When working with a quilt pattern that provides templates but not rotary cutting directions, place your rotary-cutting ruler on top of the templates to measure them. Include seam allowances. If the templates don't have any seam lines, draw them. If the lines on the rotary-cutting ruler don't line up with the edges of the template, modify the ruler by taping a paper template to the underside of the ruler. Or, simply "eyeball" the cutting line; for example, align the edge of the fabric halfway between the ⅛-inch markings.

RULERS

Having a suitable ruler for rotary cutting is as essential to the process as having a sharp blade in the cutter. The ruler must be thick enough to guide the cutter blade along its edge accurately, be easy to read, and be a convenient size for the shapes being cut.

Rulers for use with a rotary cutter are made of thick acrylic with numbers evenly spaced across them. Some have a minimum number of lines both horizontally and vertically, some combine many solid and dashed lines, and a few have a ⅛-inch grid throughout. On some rulers, the numbers run in both directions, making it easy for both right- and left-handed quilters to use. A few have numbers extending on either side from a center zero. Most of the rulers have at least a 45 degree angle line, and many have 30, 45, and 60 degree angles, sometimes running both right and left. Most have holes for hanging.

Generally, rulers are accurate, but check a new one against a ruler you know is accurate. It's a good idea to use the same brand of ruler for cutting all the pieces of a quilt.

If you are just starting out or need to limit yourself to one or two rulers, the 6 × 24-inch ruler is a must. Then I would recommend a 3 × 18-inch ruler and either a 6 × 6- or 12 × 12-inch square.

Many specialty rulers, especially those for cutting 45 and 60 degree angles, can be used for a large number of patterns, and their use is explained on their packages. Others are designed for use with a specific type of pattern. These may be sold in conjunction with one or more books, although there are usually basic instructions in the package.

In addition to rulers, there are cutting guides, essentially templates, for particular patterns impossible to cut with a rotary cutter using a standard ruler. Examples are patterns such as Double Wedding Ring and Drunkard's Path that require both concave and convex curves. Unlike specialty rulers, these templates cut only one size. Other one-size cutting guides come in template sets containing shapes that can be combined to cut a variety of patterns.

Ruler Choices

Choosing a ruler that is easy to read depends both on what shapes and sizes the ruler will be used to cut, and the quilter's visual ability to select the desired lines on the ruler. Some quilters are confused by too many lines; some are annoyed by too few. The ruled lines come in a variety of colors, with varying thicknesses. Different colors may be more visible on some fabrics than others; for this reason some rulers have two-color lines.

With a little practice, a standard rectangular ruler with angle lines can be used to cut a wide variety of shapes. Still, many quilters are enthusiastic about specialty rulers designed for a specific shape. These rulers make cutting more routine by simplifying the process and eliminating errors. Most have the seam allowance built into the cutting system and will cut several sizes of the same shape.

Ruler Care and Use

Acrylic rulers are long lasting, although they will scratch. Markings can wear off with heavy use or if rubbed against other tools. Store them to minimize abrasion, either by hanging them or standing them on edge in a letter or napkin holder. Use a mild detergent to clean your rulers.

Learn to use your rulers, whether standard or specialty, efficiently. Practice cutting until you are familiar with how to hold the ruler, how to measure accurately, and how to guide the cutter along the edge. When cutting is routine, you will save both time and fabric, not to mention aggravation.

See also "Rotary Cutting" on page 197.

Dixie Haywood

RULERS AND USES COMPARED

Ruler	Use
24" and longer rectangles	Initial cuts from yardage; cutting long strips and borders; squaring quilt top.
18" and shorter rectangles	Secondary cuts; cutting sashing and smaller borders.
12" and larger squares	Squaring blocks and checking angled seams; use with rectangular rulers to extend width or length.
6" and smaller squares	Secondary cuts; cutting and squaring small blocks.
45° triangles	Cutting half- and quarter-square triangles; mitering corners; some designed for cutting diamonds and parallelograms.
45° diamonds	Cutting diamonds and parallelograms.
60° triangles	Cutting equilateral triangles, diamonds, and hexagons.
Other angles	Specialty rulers for cutting fans, arcs, Five-Pointed Stars, Dresden Plates, and Kaleidoscope patterns.
Curves	Specialty rulers and templates for Double Wedding Ring and Drunkard's Path; other curved designs.

SAMPLER QUILTS

"No Hands Sampler," 42" × 60", was made by Susan Stein.
It was constructed entirely by machine. It is a sample for a
class Susan teaches called "No Hands Allowed."

A sampler quilt is one in which the quilt blocks are each a different pattern, set together into a unified whole. A typical sampler quilt contains pieced blocks, sometimes with a few appliqué blocks included in the mix. A sampler made entirely of appliqué blocks is often referred to as an album quilt.

Sampler quilts have long been a popular project for teaching quiltmaking, as they are a great way for beginning quiltmakers to learn many quiltmaking techniques. They incorporate a wide variety of block styles and introduce many piecing skills. Strip piecing, chain or assembly-line piecing, bias edges, set-in seams, curved piecing, and even appliqué can all be included in one quilt top.

Sampler quilts also offer an introduction to quilt design, color planning, and fabric selection. Sampler color schemes can range from two colors (such as a red and green Christmas sampler) to a multicolor scheme that revolves around a theme fabric. But here's a tip—choose the sashing fabric at the start of the quilt. You'll have so many styles of blocks, plus a variety of fabrics, that you need to be sure that your sashing, whether pieced or plain, will help unify the quilt top.

Consider this quick and easy color recipe: Select one main print fabric as a theme fabric, and buy about 3 yards. It should have a variety of colors or at least a variety of shades in two or three colors. Then choose seven fabrics to coordinate with the main print—three dark, three light, and one bright. Buy at least ½ yard of each. Mix the scale of the prints (large, medium, and small) and type of prints (floral, geometric, stripe, and tone-on-tone.) for best results.

In short, sampler quilts offer it all, and they remain one of the most popular ways to learn how to make a quilt and express your creativity.

Karen Costello Soltys

SASHIKO

Sashiko is a true Japanese art form, originally a commoner's way to decorate a garment. It was also a beautiful method of repairing and disguising normal wear and tear, extending the life of a well-worn garment. It later became a more artistic endeavor of the elite as well. The origin of this stitching dates back as far as the 1600s.

Indigo fabric became popular throughout Japan during the Edo period of the early 1600s through the mid-1800s. Indigo is actually the plant from which a dark blue dye is obtained. When cotton was dyed with indigo, it was found to make the cloth much stronger and resistant to moths, making this fabric extremely versatile. The dark blue color made it ideal to display decorative stitching, and so the stitching of sashiko really caught on.

The word *sashiko* basically means "little stabs," which translates to be the running stitch that we are familiar with. This type of stitching was used not only for ornamentation but also to hold several layers of fabric together, which made sturdy and warm clothing. Decorative sashiko stitching was lovingly done mostly by the wives and mothers of working-class men in Japan.

The original patterns often reflected

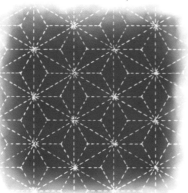

ASA NO HA, HEMP LEAF

MATSUKAWA-BISHI, PINE-TREE BARK

shapes or designs found in nature or in Japanese culture. There are overall geometric designs, such as hexagons and diamonds; overall curved designs, such as waves and interlocked circles; asymmetrical designs, such as ribbons and fans; and many other designs including cranes, butterflies, and flowers.

Present day sashiko stitching may be done on any color or type of sturdy-weave fabric, using any type of thread. It may also be done either by hand or machine! No matter which way you choose to stitch your design, first you need to transfer it to the fabric. If the design is drawn on paper, it could be placed under a light-color fabric and traced. If the fabric is dark, you could place it over a light box or other similar light source and then trace.

These examples of sashiko illustrate the potential design possibilities of this beautiful, time-honored Japanese quilting/embroidery technique. The two dark blue pieces were made by Susan Faeder. The white piece is a decorative sampler. The drawstring bag was made by Kazuko Yoshiura.

You can purchase plastic stencils or cut your own. (See "Stencils" on page 232.) Trace through the channels with a pencil, chalk, or a hera marker. (A hera is a plastic wedge that marks by creasing the fabric and making those threads light-reflective. See also "Marking Quilt Tops" on page 157.) You can also make a "pouncer" from a small piece of muslin (6 to 8 inches square). Place a small amount of powder or cornstarch in the center. Pull up the sides and tie or close with a rubber band. Now you can "pounce" the powder over the channels in the stencil, and they will be marked quickly and easily.

KIKKOU, TURTLE SHELL

KIKU, CHRYSANTHEMUM

even flannel. If you are hand stitching, specific sashiko thread is available, although pearl cotton or candle-wicking thread are also good choices. Sashiko stitches should be seen clearly; thus, a heavier type of thread is used. Sashiko needles are available, but a number 24 chenille needle will also work well. These needles are heavier and have a large eye.

SHIPPOU, SEVEN TREASURES

SEIGAIHA, WAVES

If you are simply embroidering for a decorative effect, you do not need any filler or batting. However, if you wish to actually quilt as you stitch, you may want to choose a lightweight filler, such as Thermore or

The Stitch

Begin stitching as you would when quilting or doing embroidery. Backstitch at the beginning, leave a knot on the bottom, or bury the knot between the layers of batting for hand stitching. Tiny stitches are not a concern with sashiko, as the goal is five to seven per inch. Practice so that you feel comfortable stitching both straight and curved designs. Continuous line quilting designs geared for machine quilting are good for practicing sashiko, since they have very few, if any, stops and starts.

If you are machine stitching, choose buttonhole or cordonnet thread with a 90/14 or 100/16 topstitch needle. Use a longer stitch length (six to eight stitches per inch) than for normal sewing. You may also wish to experiment with decorative threads for their effect.

Sashiko is a very easy and flexible form of stitching, so have fun!

Cyndi Hershey

SCISSORS

Scissors and shears are the workhorses of the sewing room. Quiltmakers reach for these to cut templates and fabric pieces, to clip into seam allowances, trim off points, and snip threads. Scissors are smaller and shorter, making them appropriate for lighter cutting tasks. Shears, used for heavier cutting tasks, are larger, with a more generous finger ring to accommodate several fingers and provide better control.

In quiltmaking, we rely on scissors and shears to provide good, smooth cutting action and control. Check that the blades meet at the point when fully closed. The blades of the scissors should not trap the fabric between them or cut unevenly.

Most quilters designate a pair of inexpensive scissors or shears exclusively for cutting paper and plastic template material. Others are reserved for thread and fabric only. Since quilters face several cutting tasks, most own, at minimum, a pair of paper scissors, a small pair of scissors, and a larger pair of shears.

 To test the effectiveness of scissors, cut a single layer of fabric using only the tip, the weakest point. The cut should be clean, and the tips should not separate.

The Correct Scissors for You

It is important to select the correct scissors for the intended purpose. A pair of 8-inch shears would be too cumbersome to cut delicate appliqué pieces or snip threads. Using a small pair of scissors to cut several layers or large fabric pieces would not give you the control you need and would weaken the scissors.

It is also important to choose scissors or shears that are comfortable. As length increases, so does handle size. An individual with a small hand will find the smaller 6-inch size more comfortable to use, while a person with a larger hand will prefer the 8-inch size. A left-handed person will favor scissors made especially for lefties. Lighter-weight scissors may feel comfortable to hold, but they must be strong enough to

cut through several layers of fabric if that is your intended purpose. People who experience weakness in their hands might find scissors with long cushioned handles and a spring action to be more comfortable.

Care for Your Scissors

As with any tool, protect and take care of your scissors to ensure long life and good performance.

- Clean the blades of the scissors occasionally with soap and water. Dry them thoroughly.
- Oil the rivet joint occasionally.
- Avoid cutting any needles or pins with your scissors.
- Use the proper scissors for the job.
- Protect sharp points of small scissors by placing them in a sheath. Avoid dropping scissors on the floor.
- Do not set your scissors down in an open position.

How to Hold and Cut Correctly

Since the size and shape of the finger loops vary with the scissors, there are several ways to position your fingers, depending upon the size of the scissors.

Larger shears, 9 inches and up. Place four fingers in the larger bottom loop. Your thumb should always be placed in the top loop.

Scissors or shears, 7 to 8 inches. Place three fingers in the bottom loop and place the index finger under and in front of the handle.

Smaller scissors with circular loops. Place your middle finger in the bottom handle, place the index finger in front and outside the bottom loop, and place the remaining fingers behind the loop.

To cut, hold the scissors upright. Open the scissors as wide as possible in a way that is still comfortable to cut from the pivot point to the tip. When cutting forward, cut away from yourself. When making angular cuts, cut counter-clockwise if you are right-handed, clockwise if you are left-handed.

SCISSORS COMMONLY USED BY QUILTMAKERS

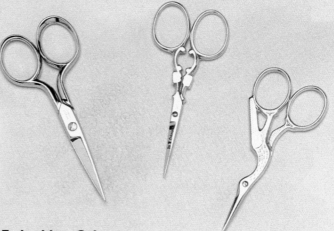

Embroidery Scissors
These 3½- to 4-inch scissors are for thread cutting. Both blades are pointed. They come in a variety of styles from plain to quite ornate.

5-Inch Craft Scissors and 6-Inch Knife Edge Straight Trimmers
These scissors are used for cutting thread and trimming fabrics of most weights.

Appliqué Scissors
These 6-inch knife edge scissors are used for close trimming with greater protection to the fabric.

Spring Action Scissors
These scissors come in both small and large sizes. They are ideal for those who experience weakness in their hands. They can be used by both right- and left-handed people.

6-Inch, 7-Inch, 8-Inch, and 10-Inch Knife Edge Bent Trimmers

These scissors are for general sewing and quilting with natural and synthetic fabrics of all weights. They provide accuracy when cutting fabric on a flat surface.

Thread Clippers

These scissors are for clipping threads only.

SCRAP QUILTS

The notion of scrap quilts historically being made from cutting snippets of fabric and old clothing is probably just a romantic myth. In any case, today scrap quilts are seldom made out of economic necessity. The term "scrap quilt" has come to mean a quilt made of many different fabrics, from a dozen to several hundred. They are made quite simply for their beauty, uniqueness, and for the sheer joy of the process.

Some quilters make scrap quilts to recreate the look of beloved antique quilts. In all probability, the old scrap quilts themselves were made and appreciated more for their graphic and expressive qualities than for their economy.

Scrap quilts have heart. When patches are cut from old clothes, they conjure images of the people we remember wearing those clothes. Even without these sentimental associations, scrap quilts move us. We pore over antique scrap quilts and imagine the people who put these fabrics together with the work of their own hands. We reinvent their lives and times. The juxtaposition of myriad colors and prints in a scrap quilt adds surface interest and speaks volumes about the personality of the individual who collected the scraps and pondered their placement.

Collecting Fabrics

Most quilters today collect new yardage for their scrap quilts. Fabric received as a gift or purchased as a souvenir of a trip can provide the same rush of memories as scraps from old clothes. With the plentiful supply of suitable and inspiring fabric now available for quilts, many quilters have significant stashes of new materials.

Collecting fabric for quilts is not a recent development. Quilters used to swap scraps with friends to improve the mix for a quilt. As early as 1850, when yardgoods became more affordable and plentiful, quilters purchased fabric expressly for quilts. Then, as now, quilters wanted to make their quilts as artful as possible, considering the time and attention that would be invested in them.

A good way to start a scrap collection is to buy more than you need for any given project or to buy specifically for your collection. Remember that collecting fabric is every bit as valid as collecting stamps. The cardinal rule is that you must not use up your fabric if you want your collection to grow. Don't feel guilty when you don't use a fabric in the project for which it was intended. Simply add it to your collection.

When I was starting out, I used to buy 3 yards if I liked a fabric and 1½ yards if I didn't! Twenty-six years later, I have so much fabric that finding a place for it is getting to be a problem. Now I buy only what I positively cannot resist, usually in ½-yard lengths. (I still seem to buy a lot of fabric, though.)

I sort my fabric by background colors for storage. Most of the time, the background color of the fabric determines how it will read and how it will be used.

"Feathered Log Cabin," made by Judy Martin for *Pieced Borders*. This bed-size quilt calls for two contrasting values and a solid accent color. I used a color scheme of red, blue, dark pink, and brown darks contrasting with white, gold, baby blue, light pink, cream and tan lights. The color scheme was inspired by a photo of an antique quilt.

Planning a Scrap Quilt

One of the beauties of a scrap quilt is that the different fabric pairings blur the shapes in one place and define them in another, adding interesting nuances and dimensionality. My favorite scrap quilts are made from blocks that call for just two colors, a light and a dark. I can sort scraps loosely, including medium shades in place of some of the lights and darks, for the most interesting scrap effects.

I don't interpret these two-color blocks in just two colors, however. Sometimes I'll choose two contrasting colors, such as red and white, and dance all around them, including red oranges, red violets, cream, and ecru. Occasionally I'll use multicolor scraps for the dark and a single solid for the light.

Selecting Fabrics

I select fabrics to correspond to my color plan. Then I fan out my folded fabrics in two long lines to preview the whole array. I keep the lights and darks separate, but within a category I mix hues and values. Here, I mixed red, blue, pink, purple, and green for the darks. I included pink, yellow, white, cream, light blue, light green, and lavender in the lights. I made a point of including some decidedly medium values in both the dark and light lines. At times, in fact, I include the same medium fabric in both the dark and light lines.

In order to maximize the scrappy effect, I prefer to rotary cut individual patches rather than strip piece units. This can still be quick and efficient, and it gives me perfect freedom in my fabric pairings.

I usually take a casual approach to fabric placement in a scrap quilt. Some people audition each patch on a design wall before joining them. I don't. I simply have stacks of patches next to the sewing machine. I pick up the top patch in one pile and pair it with one of the first few patches in the other pile. I make a quick judgment and try another combination if the first one doesn't wow me. If one or two fabrics seem to be difficult to pair with the others, I pair them first, while I still have a variety of partners from which to choose. This almost random approach is a wonderful opportunity for learning about fabric combinations. Even after all these years, I continue to discover lovely pairings that I might never have tried otherwise.

Color schemes may also be drawn from the colors in a favorite painting or a piece of fabric. I make a list of the colors included in the painting or fabric to help me notice every detail of the color scheme.

In a Log Cabin quilt, the block is usually half dark and half light. The light and dark blocks are arranged to form an overall pattern. Neighboring logs can blend together in a general swath of color. It is not necessary to define the edges of each patch. I like to blend log colors in some places and abruptly change colors in others. This allows both the overall pattern and the individual logs to be seen.

Judy Martin

Three Steps to a Scrap Quilt

For a simple scrap quilt, I follow three basic steps: first is choosing a pattern, second is making color decisions, and third is organizing and placing the scraps.

Choosing the pattern depends not only on selecting one I like but also on deciding the placement of values (the lights and darks) within that pattern. Essential to this is working first with black and white to get the desired effect and to see any secondary designs that emerge. I make a sketch on paper and shade it with a pencil. If I am combining more than one pattern, it also helps determine the way patterns blend and influence each other.

Once I have a black and white plan, my next step is to make color decisions. There, even if my overall color scheme is limited (to two colors, for example), I want the print scraps I use to include other colors within the prints.

Finally comes placement of the scraps into the design. To accomplish this, I first sort them by value, usually just lights, mediums, and darks. The original black and white design is then my guide for placing the different values of scraps into the basic scheme. I like to do this on a design wall to be sure everything blends well and there are no obvious problems.

Recipe for Scrap Quilt Memories

Organizing fabrics for a scrap quilt can be approached in many ways. In the past, scrap quilts were often utilitarian quilts, made to simply use up scraps. It is, however, very enjoyable and creative to gather scraps for a "planned" scrap quilt that will blend into a beautiful array of colors and prints.

I like to gather fabrics that have a similar color value. (Value refers to the darkness or lightness of a color.) I think all colors will work together if they are of a similar value. Look for fabrics with some variety in scale of prints to add surface interest to the quilt.

Rotary-Cutting Tips for Scrap Quilts

by Judy Martin

To create a scrappy look and still take advantage of rotary-cutting techniques, I cut just one or two strips from each of my selected fabrics. To allow more variety, I cut my strips lengthwise from ¼- or ½-yard pieces. Because they are just 9 or 18 inches long (instead of 44 or 45 inches), I won't have to cut too many patches alike. Cutting strips parallel to the selvage also takes advantage of the more stable lengthwise grain and the better alignment of prints.

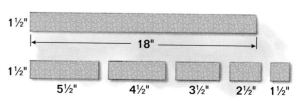

If I need to cut triangles from a 2⅞-inch strip and squares from a 2½-inch strip, I cut a strip of each width from each fabric. If I want more variety, I cut a 2⅞-inch strip and cut triangles until I have used half the strip. Then I cut the strip down to 2½ inches and cut squares from the rest of its length.

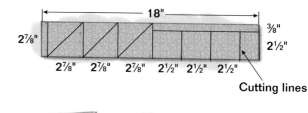

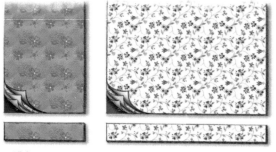

9"-long strips   **18"-long strips**

I layer four fabrics to cut at one time, so I group my ½-yard pieces with other ½ yards and my ¼-yard pieces with other ¼ yards. It is more efficient to cut fabrics of similar lengths together. For longer pieces, I cut off ½ yards, which can then be layered with other ½ yards.

If my pattern calls for numerous shapes to be cut from one strip width, I cut a single strip and cut it down into various patches. For a Log Cabin, I might cut a 1½-inch strip and cut that further into logs 5½, 4½, 3½, 2½, and 1½ inches in length.

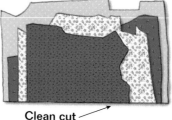

Clean cut

I sometimes use cutting remnants that are irregular in shape. To use these, I first make a clean cut along the lengthwise grain. I align this straight edge with the clean-cut edges of three fabrics of similar length and cut strips and patches through all four layers.

Tuck in a few plaids, a few stripes, and some geometric designs. Even if you would not choose a print to use in a large border or as a main part of another type of quilt design, it might be just the print needed to add spark to a scrap quilt.

Start gathering your scraps, and add to the selection as you encounter new exciting colors and prints. Purchase fat quarters in colors that you don't have, and soon you'll have the makings of a fabulous scrap quilt!

My favorite scrap quilt was made by my grand-mother for my son, Matthew, when he was born. She had painstakingly collected fabrics with recognizable images on them—fabrics referred to as conversational prints. At bedtime and naptime, Matthew and I would look over his quilt to find his favorite blocks. He learned his first words from the scrap quilt made for him by his great-grandmother.

SEAM ALLOWANCE

The seam allowance in quilt piecing is traditionally ¼ inch. This is enough to hold the seams securely without adding thickness to the piecing. Hand piecing and machine piecing have differing approaches to seam allowance.

For hand piecing, the seam allowance doesn't have to be extremely accurate. The seam lines of the individual pieces are marked on the fabric, and the seam allowances are cut "by eye" to be approximately ¼ inch. To join the pieces, you stitch the pieces together, lining up the marked seam lines. The seam allowances do not affect the fit or outcome of the block.

For machine piecing, the seam allowance must be accurate. The seam lines are not marked on the fabric; the only guide is the seam allowance. The correct placement of the seam lines depends on the ¼-inch seam. The seam allowance must be accurately maintained through the four steps of pattern making, marking, cutting, and stitching. A mistake in any of the four steps can quickly multiply and have a major impact on the finished block.

Ensuring Accurate Seam Allowances

Marking and cutting with templates. To improve seam allowance accuracy, use plastic templates, not cardboard or paper. Also, use a fine-point marking pen or pencil to trace around the templates. When cutting out the pieces, cut directly on the line or cut off (just inside) the marked line. Whichever cutting method you choose, be consistent. Whether you remove the marked line or cut on it, the secret is cutting all edges the same way. The width of a marked line can affect the fit of a complex block.

Cutting with rotary methods. Use high quality rulers. Frequently, inexpensive rulers are inaccurate on the ¼-inch measure on the ruler's edge. Some rulers don't even have the same size ¼-inch measure on different sides of the same ruler. To ensure accuracy, always use the same edge of the ruler to cut all the pieces for the project.

Stitching the seam. Most accuracy errors occur during stitching. Two things can go wrong. A common problem is careless stitching, caused by speed or inexperience. A more insidious problem occurs when the stitched ¼ inch does not match the cut ¼ inch.

Check Your Sewing

There are many ¼-inch presser feet available, and most machines have a ¼-inch guide on the needle plate. The problem arises in guiding the fabric under the foot. If you have a ¼-inch foot, is the true ¼ inch when the cut edge of the fabric just peeks under the right edge of the foot? Or is the true ¼ inch when the cut edge is under the presser foot? How you guide the fabric will depend on how you're viewing the foot. To be accurate, it is important to check the cut seam allowance against your stitched ¼ inch.

Rotary cut three $6 \times 1\frac{1}{2}$-inch strips of fabric. Stitch them together with your normal $\frac{1}{4}$-inch seam. Press open the seams and measure the width of the middle strip on the right side of the strip set. The middle strip should be exactly 1 inch wide. If it is not, cut new strips and repeat, adjusting the way you guide the fabric as you stitch the seam. This method will show you the correct way for *you* to guide the fabric as you stitch.

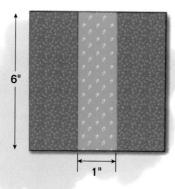

6"

1"

It is equally important to check your seam allowance when you use templates. Place the original paper pattern under the presser foot and observe where the seam allowance line falls in relation to the edge of the foot. Guide your seams accordingly.

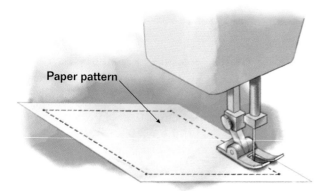

Paper pattern

Use a $\frac{1}{4}$-inch foot when possible. If you don't own one, substitute a straight stitch foot or a regular sewing foot. Frequently these feet have toes wider than $\frac{1}{4}$ inch. A common practice is to move the needle position to change the relationship between the right edge of the foot and the needle. In many cases this will give a true $\frac{1}{4}$-inch edge to the foot, but I don't recommend this. The sewing machine sews straighter and more evenly with the needle in the center position. The fabrics will be easier to guide with the needle position in the center.

Debra Wagner

Make a Temporary Seam Guide

I recommend using a temporary seam guide to ensure a true $\frac{1}{4}$-inch seam allowance if you do not have a $\frac{1}{4}$-inch foot. This method is accurate and fool-proof for even novice quilters.

You will need small pieces of vinyl tape and $\frac{1}{4}$-inch graph paper.

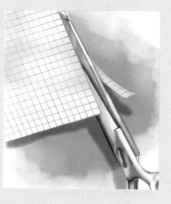

Step 1. Cut the $\frac{1}{4}$-inch graph paper on one of the lines. Place the paper under the presser foot.

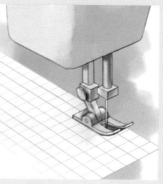

Step 2. Lower the needle and adjust the paper so that the needle pierces the first line to the left of the cut edge (your $\frac{1}{4}$-inch seam allowance). Lower the presser foot.

Step 3. Stack three or more pieces of vinyl tape to make a $\frac{1}{8}$-inch-thick layer. Place the tape on the bed of the machine directly in front of the presser foot toes. Line up the tape edge with the edge of the graph paper. Remove the paper from the machine.

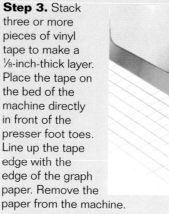

Step 4. Use the raised edge of the tape as a guide for your $\frac{1}{4}$-inch seam allowances. Check the accuracy of the seam allowance using the stitching test in the previous section.

This method is great for speed sewing like strip piecing. It is extremely easy to stitch a true $\frac{1}{4}$-inch by guiding the fabric edges against the tape guide.

SEMINOLE PATCHWORK

"Seminole Sampler with Five Leaves," 28" × 40", made by Cheryl Greider Bradkin in 1995. This is a stunning example of Seminole patchwork incorporated into a quilt. The quilt is machine pieced, machine appliquéd, and machine quilted.

southern Florida can find new Seminole patchwork clothing and gifts at shops on the reservations and along the Tamiami Trail.

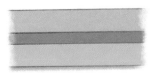

Without the facts of a written historical record, there are a variety of theories about the origins of Seminole patchwork. Some say the Seminoles, driven deep into the swamp by pressure from farming settlers, were reduced to using even scrap strips of fabric for their clothing. Others say the tartans of Scottish settlers in southern Florida inspired the Seminole tribe to create complex and colorful patterns. We know that runaway slaves found protection with the Seminole people, and perhaps one of them carried the concept of strip patchwork into the Everglades.

Whatever its origins, Seminole patchwork is an ingenious technique for creating machine sewn patchwork designs that appear deceptively complex. The design possibilities are unlimited, but even the simplest combinations make effective accents on clothing, accessories, decorative items, and quilts. Design and color choices can work together to achieve a range of effects, from traditional quilting patterns to high-energy contemporary images.

The Seminole Indians worked only with scissors, but the tools available now, such as rotary cutters and clear rulers marked for cutting angles, make the work faster and more precise.

The basic steps begin with sewing strips of fabric together to create a strip set. This strip set is cut into pieces. The pieces are offset and sewn together into a band of patchwork.

Variations are created by changing the number and widths of the strips, the angles of the cuts and widths of the pieces, and the way the pieces are sewn together.

In the swampy isolation of the Florida Everglades at the close of the nineteenth century, Seminole Indians developed a strip patchwork technique to produce striking and intricate designs. Trading furs and alligator skins for hand-cranked sewing machines and fabric, the Indians were machine sewing cotton fashions with contrasting ruffles in the late 1800s. By the early 1900s, the women's skirts and men's "long shirts" were decorated with horizontal bands of machine-sewn patchwork designs in brilliant colors. As Seminole women developed new designs, they were shared with admiring friends. Today lovely though faded early patchwork garments are found in museums throughout Florida and many other states. Visitors to

Seminole Guidelines

- All seam allowances are ¼ inch, so it is helpful to use a presser foot with edges that are ¼ inch from the needle. A tape line on the sewing machine bed ¼ inch from the needle is another way to sew precise seam allowances. (See also "Seam Allowance" on page 215.)

- Press only the completed strip set and the completed patchwork band. Pressing before all the seams are sewn can stretch the unsewn raw edges.

- Use the grid lines on your rotary ruler as a guide to cut pieces all the same width and on the same angle.

- Pieces are offset, and depending on the difficulty of the offset, held in position for sewing with just the fingers or with pins.

- Pieces are sewn together using continuous sewing, or chain piecing, to economize on time and thread.

Basic Seminole Piecing

For guaranteed success and authentic style, use 100 percent cotton, quilting weight fabrics in solid colors. Once the technique has become familiar, you may want to experiment with prints and different fabric fibers and weights.

Seminole patchwork begins with fabric strips cut with the straight grain. For efficient construction, cut strips crosswise (from selvage to selvage) from the different fabrics, and they will all be about the same length (42 to 44 inches). (See "Rotary Cutters" on page 196 for additional information.)

Here are the steps, with construction details, for creating a simple, basic design. The illustrations show what the segments would actually look like with seam allowances included.

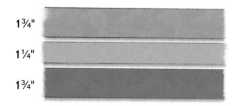

Step 1. Cut strips of three different fabrics. Cut two that are 1¾ inches wide and one that is 1¼-inches wide.

Step 2. Sew the strips together using a ¼-inch seam allowance and 10 to 12 stitches per inch, enough to hold the cut edges secure during handling.

Step 3. Press on the right side of the fabric whenever possible. Use the point of the iron to smooth the fabric along the seam lines, making sure they are flat and without pleats. Use your free hand to push the seam allowances on the back into place as you press. Press all seam allowances in one direction.

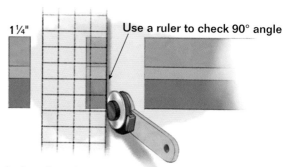

1¼"   Use a ruler to check 90° angle

Step 4. Cut 1¼-inch pieces from the strip set. Place the ruler grid line on the seam line to check the 90 degree angle.

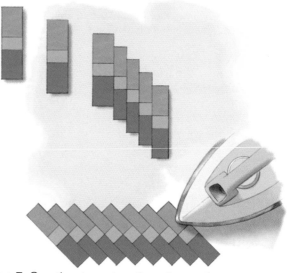

Step 5. Sew the pieces together, aligning the seams as shown. Use ¼-inch seam allowances. Press on the right side with all seam allowances going the same direction.

The raw edges of Seminole patchwork bands are finished off with edging strips. The number, widths, and colors of the edging strips are design decisions that depend on the space to be filled and the desired effect. While single, wide edging strips make a simple frame, many narrow edging strips can appear more complex. The pointed raw edges of the patchwork band are trimmed off, guided by the ruler grid laid on top of the design. The trimmed edges should be parallel, so the finished patchwork is even along its length.

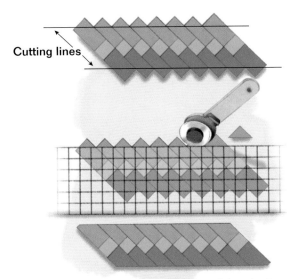

Step 6. Trim the points off the patchwork band using a rotary cutter and ruler. Place the ruler grid lines parallel to the design. Repeat on the other side of the patchwork band. The two edges should be parallel.

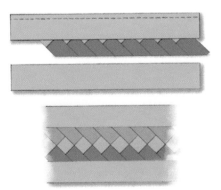

Step 7. Sew the edging strips on with a ¼-inch seam allowance. Point the patchwork band seam allowances toward you so they will run smoothly between the feed dogs and the presser foot. Press on the right side with the seam allowances toward the edging strips.

Variations

Variations in cutting and sewing create new designs from the basic strip set.

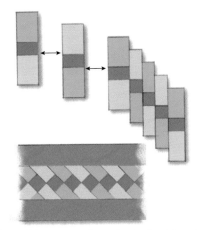

Variation One. Use pieces from the basic strip set and alternate them up and down. Align the seam lines as shown above.

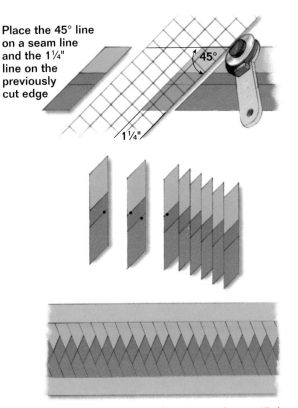

Place the 45° line on a seam line and the 1¼" line on the previously cut edge

45°

1¼"

Variation Two. Cut pieces 1¼ inches wide at a 45 degree angle from the basic strip set. Match the seams ¼ inch in from the cut edges to account for the angled cut.

Cheryl Greider Bradkin

219

SETTINGS

A setting is the way you arrange blocks into a quilt design. When you begin planning a quilt project and choosing a quilt block, think ahead to the overall design of the quilt and how the blocks will be set together. There are many alternatives to choose from and many possibilities that will help you achieve your desired results. As you look at quilts in books, magazines, and quilt shows, pay attention to the many innovative ways that other quilters have chosen to set their blocks together. There are endless ways to set blocks into a pleasing quilt design.

HORIZONTAL

The following categories are intended to help you understand the basic types of settings, what blocks are enhanced by each setting, and what design challenge they solve, such as what to do with blocks that aren't quite the same size. Be aware, however, that not all quilts fit neatly into one of these categories, and some fall into more than one.

DIAGONAL OR "ON POINT"

Within each of the setting categories, blocks can be set horizontally or diagonally (also known as "on point"). Some blocks, such as house blocks and basket blocks, are usually set one way or the other, while blocks such as stars can be set either way and take on a different look each way.

HORIZONTAL

ON POINT

Diagonal sets require side and corner triangles to complete the top. (See page 227 for a guide to cutting these triangles.) Diagonal sets are a good solution when you have an odd number of blocks, such as 5 or 13.

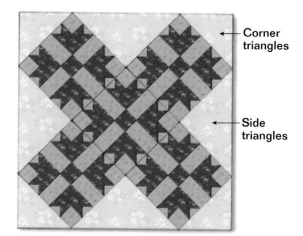

Corner triangles

Side triangles

DIAGONAL SET OF FIVE BLOCKS

Repeating the Same Block

There is a humble sweetness to lining up the same block, one after another, like books on a shelf. Many blocks gain an unexpected graphic punch when set side by side. Look for secondary patterns that emerge as the boundary of one block blurs together with the neighboring blocks, causing new and unexpected designs to appear.

WATER WHEEL BLOCKS

Try changing the colors in the blocks from the center to the edges of your quilt (light in the center to dark at the edges, creating a border). Or, change the background fabric in each block to set each one off. Many delightful scrappy quilts are made this way, letting the fabric changes add their own texture to the quilt.

Alternating a Main Block and a Plain Block

Combining your main block with a plain block gives some breathing room to your design and makes a bigger quilt from a smaller number of blocks. Keep in mind that all those plain blocks will probably require a greater amount of quilting. The time you don't spend piecing additional blocks will be spent quilting later. No free lunch, as usual!

Look for blocks—such as a simple Nine Patch—that connect visually at the corners and add diagonal movement to a quilt when alternated with a plain block. When you use the same background fabric for the plain block as you do in your design blocks, the design blocks appear to float on the surface of the quilt. Audition contrasting colors and prints with your blocks and see what happens.

NINE PATCH

If a block is asymmetrical—that is, a mirror image side to side or corner to corner, such as Log Cabin, Rail Fence, or Buckeye Beauty—turning the blocks in different directions creates some exciting design options. Combine this idea with changing the colors in the blocks for endless possibilities.

One block

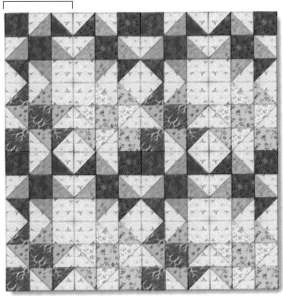

ASYMMETRICAL BLOCK: DARTING BIRDS

The designs in appliquéd blocks appear to "float" on the background fabric when set side by side. If you are considering this setting, try placing your blocks on the diagonal and see how this changes the look of your blocks. Many blocks take on a new and dramatic look when set this way.

Remember, when you are using alternating blocks you will want an odd number of blocks in each row and an odd number of rows so that you end up with the same type of

SISTER'S CHOICE

block in each corner. This is another good way to set odd numbers of blocks, such as 5, 7, 17, 31, and many more.

Many lovely appliqué blocks are set with alternating plain blocks. Elaborate quilting enhances the plain blocks, and this can be a stunning combination.

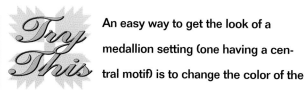 An easy way to get the look of a medallion setting (one having a central motif) is to change the color of the alternating plain block from the edges to the center.

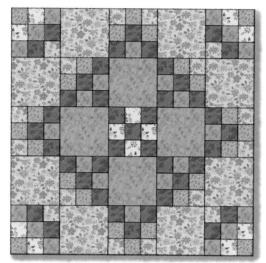

NINE PATCH "MEDALLION"

UNDERGROUND RAILROAD BLOCKS
WITH SNOWBALL BLOCK

If you are setting an appliqué quilt, try using a simple pieced or appliqué design that relates to the main block.

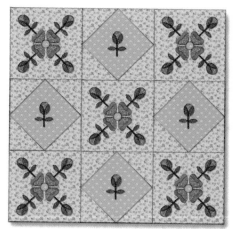

ALTERNATE BLOCKS WITH A COMMON MOTIF

Alternating Blocks

Many interesting combinations happen when two different pieced or appliqué blocks are combined. Usually one of the blocks is more complex than the other. For pieced blocks, both blocks should have the same divisions (such as 9-patch, 16-patch, or 25-patch), so that some of the intersections line up and carry the eye across the quilt. This gives a design diagonal movement that is so appealing in quilts such as Irish Chain, without using complex piecing techniques.

Below are some simple alternating blocks that can be combined with a variety of main blocks.

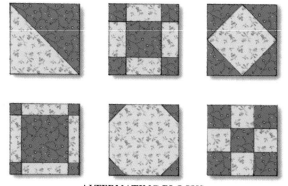

ALTERNATING BLOCKS

Simple Sashing

Adding sashing, or lattice, to your quilt design allows some elbow room between blocks so they can stand on their own without crowding their neighbors. At the same time, blocks that don't hold together on their own, such as sampler blocks, friendship blocks, or scrappy blocks, benefit from

MOUNTAIN STAR BLOCK
WITH NARROW SASHING

sashing that adds a unifying fabric to the quilt.

Try experimenting with the width of sashing—narrow sashing lets the design jump easily from block to block, while wider sashing allows each block to speak for itself. Wider sashing can also stretch a limited number of blocks into a larger quilt.

Changing the color of the sashing fabric is also a design consideration. Using sashing that matches the background in the blocks causes the blocks to float on the surface of the quilt. Using printed sashing helps to blur the seams, while a solid fabric shows off a beautiful quilting design. Remember that the sashing will make up a large percentage of the surface area of your quilt and can easily overpower your blocks if there is a lot of color contrast with the blocks. Save the shocking pink for a narrow accent border outside the sashing!

MOUNTAIN STAR BLOCK
WITH WIDE SASHING

Try This When you are cutting your sashing, first cut the long sashing strips that will join the rows together, then cut the short strips the same size as the unfinished size of your blocks. Unless you are using a directional fabric, cut your sashings along the lengthwise grain. You will find that there is less stretch in the lengthwise grain, and your sashing will be less likely to sag and stretch. Also, you will have longer strips, minimizing the need for seams.

Sashing and Setting Squares

Adding sashings and setting squares opens up a variety of design possibilities to complement your blocks. Setting squares, also called corner squares, are made of either a single piece of fabric or a pieced or appliquéd square design. Setting squares team up with sashing to connect blocks while creating interesting secondary designs at the intersections.

Consider a sashing that uses the same fabric as the background of the blocks with a contrasting setting square, so that the blocks appear to float.

MOSAIC TILES WITH SETTING SQUARES

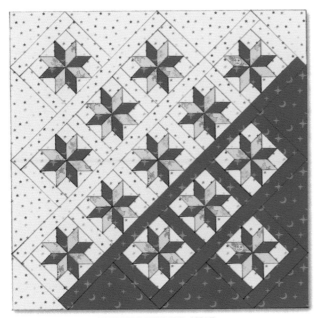

EIGHT-POINTED STAR

A sashing made up of three strips of fabric, as shown below, opens up the visual space around each block. Add Nine Patch setting squares to complete the design.

VARIABLE STAR WITH PIECED SASHING
AND NINE PATCH SETTING SQUARES

Include a design element from the block, either pieced or appliquéd, in the setting square. Repeat it in the original size or reduce to a smaller scale.

UNION BLOCK WITH PIECED SETTING SQUARE

One Directional and Zigzag Sashing

With this setting, the blocks touch each other in one direction and are separated by sashing in the other direction. For horizontally set quilts, the sashing can run either crosswise or lengthwise. If the sashing runs crosswise, it creates a landscape for houses, cats, rabbits, boats, cars, trains, or other objects in your quilt. Your sashing could become grass, flowers, sidewalk, highway, water, or a train track.

CROSSWISE SASHING

Flying Geese often have sashing running lengthwise. Keep your eyes open for lovely vine-type floral prints that lend themselves well to vertical sashings.

FLYING GEESE WITH VERTICAL SASHING

When this idea is carried over to a diagonal setting, it produces a zigzag effect with filler or side triangles becoming the sashing. To do this, move up every other row half a block, and use an odd number of rows to balance each side. This is a good way to set an odd number of blocks, such as 7 or 11, or a number that is hard to work with, such as 18.

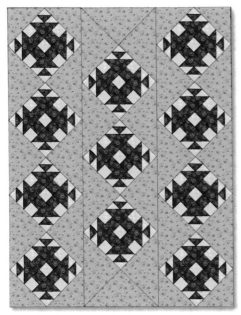

MONKEY WRENCH IN ZIGZAG SETTING

Combining vertical sashing with side triangles creates yet another setting.

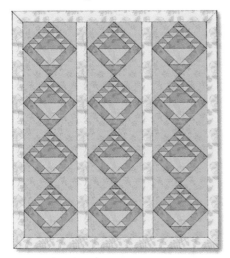

FRUIT BASKET WITH SIDE TRIANGLES
AND VERTICAL SASHING

Framing Blocks

Framing blocks in settings is an ideal solution to that age-old problem of what to do with blocks that don't measure quite the same size (especially common

with sampler or friendship blocks). You can standardize the size of blocks by adding an oversized frame to each block, then trimming them all down to the same size. The width of the frame may vary slightly, but it most likely won't be noticeable. The important thing is that the blocks will be easy to join and your quilt top will be flat. There are several frame variations from which to choose.

MITERED   ATTIC   OVERLAPPED
FRAME   WINDOW   FRAME

ATTIC WINDOWS VARIATION

By varying fabrics and values you can create endless variations in your quilts. Try framing half your blocks with one fabric and the other half with another fabric, then alternating the blocks when you join them.

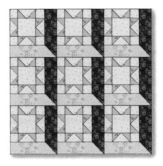

Use a dark fabric for two adjoining sides and a light fabric for the remaining two sides. This requires that you miter the corners, but when all the blocks are put together, it creates the illusion of light shining on your quilt. Attic Windows are a variation of this idea with the frame on only two sides.

Add a frame and setting squares to each block, again, using one color combination on half the blocks and another combination on the other half. When these blocks are joined, a Four Patch is created at each intersec-

tion. This option is less successful for controlling unequal block sizes.

Add triangles to each side of your blocks to frame them. You could, again, use one color combination on half the blocks and a different combination on the other half. Adding triangles can change the orientation of the blocks from horizontal to diagonal or the other way around.

DOUBLE PINWHEEL BLOCK WITH SIDE TRIANGLES

Try using one of the straight framing styles on some of your blocks and the triangle framing style on the remaining blocks. You will end up with some of your blocks set horizontally and some of the blocks set diagonally. This gives you the option of combining horizontal blocks, such as house blocks, and diagonal blocks, such as basket blocks, in the same quilt.

HORIZONTAL AND DIAGONAL BLOCKS

Medallion Sets

This setting has many different variations, but usually one or more blocks serve as a central focus. From there, borders, complementary blocks, and other elements are added. These can be pieced or appliquéd, or a combination of both. Often the various elements switch from a diagonal setting to a horizontal setting, creating the illusion that one part is placed on top of another. This is a good option for a large central block or if you don't want to make the same block over and over. When switching from horizontal to diagonal orientation, it is helpful to add a framing border, which I call a "coping strip." This helps you "cope" with the change in orientation by giving you a strip that can be trimmed down so things fit properly.

Coping strips

MEDALLION SET

Inspiration for Settings

These are the basics, and there are endless variations on and combinations of these themes. As you look at quilts take note of unusual block arrangements and settings. Clever quilters come up with ingenious ways to solve various dilemmas that you may be faced with someday. Start a file of creative settings that you come across to get you started designing your own show-stopper quilts.

226

SETTING TRIANGLES

Straight grain

Diagonally set quilts are made with blocks that are turned "on point" so that the straight of grain in each block runs diagonally. Quilt blocks set this way need setting triangles, sometimes called filler triangles.

When this type of quilt is hung, it has a tendency to sag. To help control this, cut the filler triangles that surround the blocks so that the straight of grain runs up and down. These triangles give support to the blocks and help the borders go on more smoothly.

Arrows indicate straight grain

Side Triangles

Side triangles are made from a square cut diagonally in two directions so that one square yields four side triangles. To calculate the size of the square needed, multiply the finished block size by 1.414 and add 1.25 inches for seam allowances. Round this up to the nearest ⅛ inch. To match, align the right angle of the triangle with the edge of the block.

$$10" \times 1.414 = 14.14" + 1.25" = 15.39", \text{ or } 15\frac{1}{2}"$$

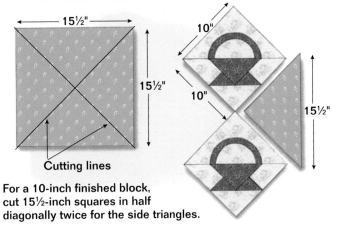

Cutting lines

For a 10-inch finished block, cut 15½-inch squares in half diagonally twice for the side triangles.

The table below gives the square size needed to cut filler triangles for common block sizes. You may overcut squares by ½ to 1 inch and trim the triangles down after your top is pieced together. Many quilters do this to ensure that the triangles will be big enough.

Corner Triangles

Corner triangles are made from a square cut diagonally in one direction so that one square yields two corner triangles. To calculate the size of square needed, divide the finished block size by 1.414 and add 0.875 inch (⅞ inch) for seam allowances. Do all the math on a calculator, then round the number up to the nearest ⅛ inch. To match corner triangles to the quilt blocks, fold the triangle in half to find the center. Match this to the center point of the block.

$$10" \div 1.414 = 7.07" + 0.875" = 7.95", \text{ or } 8"$$

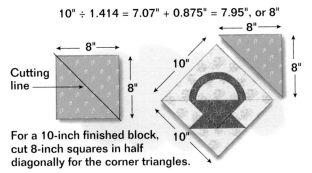

Cutting line

For a 10-inch finished block, cut 8-inch squares in half diagonally for the corner triangles.

TRIANGLES FROM SQUARES		
Finished Block ◆	Square for Corner Triangle ◧	Square for Side Triangle ⊠
4"	3¾"	7⅛"
6"	5¼"	10"
7"	5⅞"	11¼"
8"	6⅝"	12⅝"
9"	7¼"	14"
10"	8"	15½"
12"	9⅜"	18¼"
14"	10⅞"	21¼"
16"	12¼"	23⅞"

Joan Hanson

SEWING MACHINE

A sewing machine in good working order is an essential tool for quiltmaking. Before you begin to stitch, it's a good idea to insert a new needle in the machine to ensure smooth, even stitches. Clean the machine by brushing away all the lint from the feed dogs and bobbin case area. Check the owner's manual for information on oiling your machine. Many new machines require only a few drops of oil in the shuttle race; older machines may require oil throughout the machine.

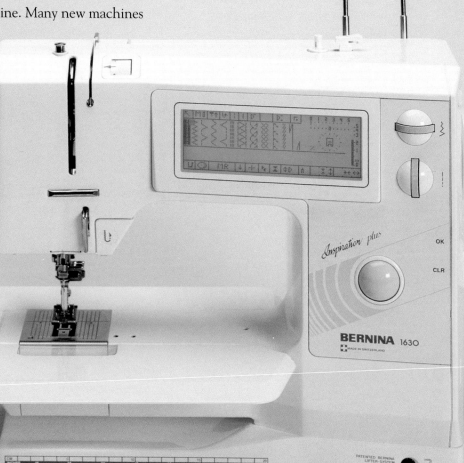

Features for Quiltmaking

Your machine should have these basic features:

- A dependable straight stitch and reverse sewing capability
- A large flat sewing surface like a slide-on table for portable machines, or a cabinet
- A good machine light that illuminates the presser foot and stitching area
- A two-speed motor with excellent speed control on slow speed
- A selection of feet designed for quiltmaking—a ¼-inch foot, a walking foot, and a free-motion quilting foot or darning foot

Newer machines offer other features that are advantageous to the machine quiltmaker.

Needle down. This feature ensures that the needle stops, lowered in the fabric, when you stop stitching. Use the needle down feature for both piecing and quilting. It keeps the stitching lines straight and uniform.

Auto knot. This feature makes a secure knot at the beginning and end of lines of stitching. Unlike reversed stitches, a machine knot is made with small straight stitches. The knot is very flat and extremely secure. Use this with piecing and machine-guided quilting.

Electronic motor and control. An electronic motor and control give you stitch-by-stitch accuracy. With electronic controls it is unnecessary to use the handwheel to encourage the machine to begin stitching. With a slight tap on the foot control, you can raise or lower the needle a half stitch at a time.

TAKING THE TROUBLE OUT OF Jammed Threads and Thread Tension

Correct thread jams or thread tension problems using the rule of TNT—Thread, Needle, and Tension. Surprisingly, most problems are caused by the thread, not the machine tension.

Thread. First, rethread the machine through both the needle and bobbin. Check to make sure you have the bobbin turning the right way in the case—usually clockwise.

If your machine has a two-sided needle tension assembly—and most machines do—try rethreading on the opposite side of the tension disk. Tension disks can fill with lint or glaze from poor-quality thread. When tension disks become clogged, they will not work as well. Often, using the opposite side of the disk will temporarily correct the problem.

Make sure the thread is pulling smoothly from the spool or bobbin. Occasionally a spool or bobbin can become "bruised" by rough handling. The bruise occurs when the threads on the outer layer of the spool or bobbin are forced into the inner layers. The threads become wedged together and stick or pull as the thread unwinds from the bruised area.

Needle. If you are still having problems, check the needle. Make sure the needle is smooth and straight, without any burrs. You may need to replace it. Choose the needle according to the thread and fabric. Size 12/80 or 14/90 are average-size needles. Check to make sure you have the needle in the needle clamp correctly. Is the flat side of the shank facing the correct direction? Is the needle all the way into the clamp? If the machine is skipping stitches, try a new, larger-size needle.

Tension. Third, adjust the needle tension, if required. When the needle thread appears on the bottom layer of the fabrics, you should tighten the needle tension. When the bobbin thread appears on the top layer of the fabrics, you should loosen the needle tension. Adjust only the needle tension dial. Turn the tension in small increments and always write down the starting location of the tension dial before making adjustments.

Electronic controls run smoothly, and unlike the older thermal controls, remain cool to the touch. (If you have ever noticed the foot control becoming warm as you stitch, your machine has the older, less effective, thermal control.) An electronic motor and control are a necessity for machine quilting and make machine piecing much easier.

Bobbin thread indicator. This little feature may seem like a frill, rather than an important feature for the quiltmaker, but it is indispensable for machine quilting. The indicator warns you when your bobbin thread is running low. The feature can help you avoid running out of bobbin thread in difficult parts of a quilting design.

Using Your Machine

Here are the key elements to successful use of your machine:

1. Always hold on to the top and bobbin threads when you begin a line of stitching. This prevents jams and thread snarls.

2. Always raise the presser foot before you thread the machine. The presser foot must be raised to place the thread in the tension disks. Threading the machine without raising the foot will cause thread jams.

3. Always lower the foot before you begin to stitch.

4. Use matching thread in the bobbin and top when possible. Using the same thread will make the best stitches and will result in the best tension.

Debra Wagner

STENCILED QUILTS

The fashion for stenciled quilts and coverlets was popular in rural America from approximately 1825 to 1845, mostly in the East. Stenciled walls, floors, and furniture were also in vogue. The stenciled bed coverings were more decorative than utilitarian. Few examples of fully quilted coverings remain today. Flowers, birds, baskets, and fruit were the most popular motifs, usually in an overall placement with stenciled borders around the edges and requiring many hours of tedious work. Some blocks were combined with a Nine Patch block or sashed with a lovely red calico.

For today's quiltmakers, stenciling on fabric is a wonderful way to incorporate the art of stenciling with the art of quilting. It opens many doors of creativity and can add a delightful new aspect to your quilts.

Supplies

Fabric for blocks

Stencil design

Stencil paint for fabric

Stencil brushes

Soft paper towels

Sandboard

Black, fine-point, permanent felt-tip pen

Note: You can purchase a sandboard or make one by gluing sandpaper to Masonite or cardboard.

Stenciling Quilt Blocks

Determine how you will incorporate your stenciled blocks into a quilt. First make a rough sketch of the setting, and then decide on the fabrics to be used—both for the blocks to be stenciled and the fabrics for the remainder of the quilt.

 Instead of using plain, off-white fabric, consider using a beige-on-beige print or a soft pastel for the stenciled blocks. Your block will look more attractive if the motif fills most of the area of the block.

Step 1. Cut fabric for the stenciled blocks to the required size. Remember to allow a ¼-inch seam allowance on each side.

Step 2. Mark the center of each square by folding the fabric in half both ways. Mark the center of the stencil by using a black, fine-point, permanent felt-tip pen.

Step 3. Place the fabric block on top of the sandboard. This will prevent any slipping of the fabric while you are working. Place the marked center of the stencil on the center of the fabric. Secure with masking tape.

Note: Every purchased stencil comes with specific instructions for that stencil. Be certain to read the instructions before beginning, to make sure you understand where each piece will be placed.

Step 4. Place two or three sheets of soft paper towels in a serving tray and dip the brush into the paint, picking up a small amount of paint on the bottom. Push the paint into the brush by pressing down and using a back-and-forth motion on the paper towels.

Step 5. Hold the brush straight up and down. Starting on the plastic, right next to the opening, use a circular motion to fill in the opening with paint. The opening can be lighter in the center, but not white or blank. If it's not filled in, this creates the illusion of a hole in the opening.

Step 6. Let the blocks air dry according to the instructions on the paint. Set the paint by ironing on both sides. The longer you iron, the better the paint will set. Place a piece of scrap fabric or paper over the stenciling to protect it from scorching. Now the blocks are ready to be incorporated into your quilt.

Each block will look a little different while you are working, but once you have them in place in the quilt, they will all look the same. Don't try to be perfect—each block will have its own personality and will add to the charm of the overall quilt.

 Use a darker color of paint to shade around the outside edges of the stencil middle.

Stenciled Wallhanging

For a small wallhanging, use a stenciled square for the center block. Use coordinating fabrics for the borders, or add a lovely pieced border. The stenciled blocks can be any size or shape. Just be careful not to have a small stencil on a large block. The size of the stencil should determine the size of the center block.

 To add the finishing touch to a diminutive quilt, embellish with buttons, charms, lace, or ribbons. Sew buttons and charms onto the quilt top before layering with the batting and backing. (You can also glue these on later with fabric glue.)

Ribbon glued on

Other Stenciling Ideas

Try stenciling techniques with your appliqué for a different look. Stencil some leaves and small flowers among the appliquéd designs to add another dimension to your work. You can also stencil some of the details in landscapes, rather than appliquéing all the small bits and pieces.

It's exciting to think of the many options for incorporating stenciling into quiltmaking. Don't be afraid to try something new and different—you might be surprised with what you can do with a little paint and thread!

STENCILS

Modern stencil manufacturing methods have given quilters hundreds of designs in an easy and economical form for marking their quilts. These precut stencils allow an accurate transfer of a quilting design to the quilt top, where they can then be quilted by hand or machine.

A stencil is a design created by a series of narrow slots cut into plastic, cardboard, or other stiff material with bridges between the slots to hold the design in place. The slots must be narrow ($\frac{1}{16}$ to $\frac{1}{8}$ inch), yet wide enough to allow the point of a pencil or other marking device to fit into the slots and mark the design on the fabric or quilt block.

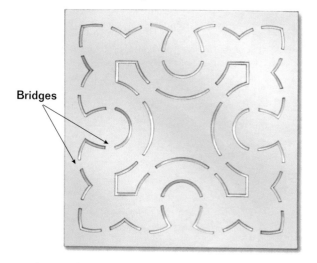

Bridges

A template, sometimes used to transfer the design, is a shape cut from plastic or cardboard, with minimal detail inside the design. Because a slotted stencil allows for greater detail in the quilting design, it is usually the preferred method for transferring the design to the quilt top.

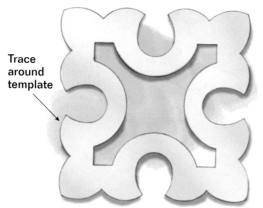

Trace around template

Selecting Designs

Stencils are available for blocks, borders, and large open background areas. They are also available in a range of sizes to fit most any space on the quilt top. Special designs are made for Double Wedding Ring and Giant Dahlia quilts, to name a few. There are also continuous line designs especially for machine quilting, which require minimal starting and stopping.

The selection of the quilting design can sometimes "make or break" the quilt. It should be compatible with the patchwork or appliqué and provide a unifying element to the finished quilt. Selecting the design early in the quiltmaking process will often ensure the desired harmony of the finished product.

An elaborate feather design (normally considered traditional) might not be compatible with a more contemporary patchwork or appliqué design. The selection of the quilting design should be made carefully, keeping the overall appearance of the quilt in mind.

The size of the design in relation to the area it is to fill is another important consideration. The design should fill but not crowd the area being quilted. A good rule to follow is to select a design that, when marked, will leave $\frac{1}{2}$ to 1 inch between the design and the seam line. For example, a 10- or 11-inch design should be used in a 12-inch finished block area, and a 2- to $2\frac{1}{2}$-inch-wide border design should be selected for a 3-inch-wide finished border.

Too small   **Too large**   **Correct size**

Marking the Design

Step 1. Position the stencil over the area to be marked and hold firmly with your hand or secure it in place with masking tape. Small circles of sandpaper are available, which can be placed on the reverse side of the stencils to keep the plastic from slipping while you mark.

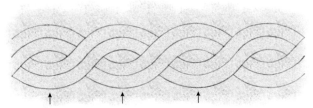

Lengthen or shorten at these points. Make adjustments consistent all along the border.

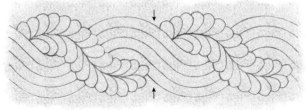

Lengthen or shorten border designs at these points.

Step 2. Using a very sharp pencil, mark lightly through the slots in the stencil, following each line until the design is completely marked. If possible, mark consistently on the same side of the slot. The mark should be distinct and just dark enough to see. Try not to mark with a heavy line. The more you mark, the more you'll have to remove after quilting.

Step 3. Remove masking tape. Reposition the stencil and continue to mark until the complete design has been marked. A series of short lines will make up the complete design. You may either join these lines with your marking pencil to make a continuous quilting line, or join the lines during the quilting process. Remember, the "bridges" hold the stencil design together; they are not to be skipped over in the quilting process.

Join

Other Sources for Quilting Designs

Quilt books and magazines usually print designs specifically for the patterns that are also in the books. In most cases these are printed in the exact size required for the project. A printed design can either be traced directly from the book or duplicated on a copy machine.

Holice Turnbow

Adjusting Designs

Designs often need to be adjusted to avoid crowding or getting lost in the space. Echo quilting around the outer edge of the design can sometimes be added to increase the size. Or, draw the design on paper and reduce or enlarge it on a copy machine. Trace on the fabric with the use of a light box or make a new stencil from the drawing.

When shortening or lengthening border designs, the adjustment should be made consistently at several places along the design to give uniformity to the overall appearance of the design.

SKILL BUILDER

Cut Your Own Stencils

A stencil can be made using a double-blade craft knife (X-Acto leaded glass cutter) and flexible plastic such as DBK brand plastic. These are available in quilt stores. Freezer paper will also work if you are unable to obtain the DBK plastic. Practice with the knife before cutting your design. Try some straight cuts and right and left curves.

Step 1. Trace or duplicate the design onto paper. Add bridges so the design will not fall apart when slots are cut.

Step 2. Place the design under the plastic and on a rotary cutting mat. Tape down the layers so they will not move.

Step 3. Cut slots using the double-bladed knife, leaving the bridge sections uncut. Do not cut more than 2 inches without leaving a bridge.

STRING PIECING

"Christmas Stars," a wall quilt designed and made by Eileen Sullivan, is a striking example of what can happen when one simple string-pieced segment is repeated.

"What's in a name?" No great mystery here—the name says it all. String piecing is a technique that utilizes strips or strings of fabric sewn together on a base or foundation to create quilts, garments, or other items. Developed as a utilitarian method to make use of what was on hand, early examples were made from garment fabric leftovers, outgrown clothing, and household fabrics—a tribute to the waste-not spirit of our ancestors. Foundations used to "string on" were muslin, ugly fabrics, pages of old catalogs, newspapers, and magazines. Antique quilts and blocks may have foundations still intact to help date them.

Fabrics were used randomly, without regard to color. Strip width was based on whatever was available. Simple base shapes, such as squares, were covered, then joined together for an overall scrappy effect. As quiltmakers began to explore more visually exciting and controlled images, combinations of pieced designs with string elements could be found. Examples of Eight-Pointed Stars, each star segment being a string

unit, or triangle wedges done in the same fashion, resulting in the well known Spider Web pattern, attest to the creative spirit of many early quiltmakers.

Foundation Choices

For today's quiltmaker, the approach remains the same. The foundation used can be permanent (muslin or other fabric) or temporary (various papers or removable stabilizers).

Permanent foundations add an extra layer to the project and are best suited to quilts intended to be tied or machine quilted. Choose temporary or removable foundations if the project is to be hand quilted. Among the most common are lightweight papers, such as typing paper, clean newsprint, or freezer paper.

The paper is perforated by the sewing machine needle as each string is added, making it easy to tear away after the project is completed. Freezer paper has the added benefit of adhering to fabrics, eliminating the need for pins to hold strings in place when they are opened and ironed.

Working with Different Foundations

Permanent foundations should be cut to include the seam allowance for joining blocks together. For example, a finished 6-inch square would require a 6½-inch square foundation. Strings are sewn to the foundation, and the excess is trimmed even with the foundation edge. Permanent muslin foundations are often used for garment construction with the muslin cut according to the pattern, seam allowances included.

Paper or other foundations that will be removed after the blocks are joined together should be cut the desired finished size. Strings are added, extending beyond the paper. They are then trimmed to ¼ inch beyond the edge of the foundation to allow for joining. The edges of the foundation become the sewing lines for joining the blocks. This avoids sewing the paper into the seam allowance, which is difficult to remove.

Fabrics can be cut into random widths as desired (include seam allowance). They should be long enough to cover the entire length of the foundation.

Piecing

When using a removable foundation, set your machine for a shorter than normal stitch length to help perforate the paper and add strength to the seam.

Step 1. Place the first string on top of the foundation, right side up. It can be placed in the middle, or elsewhere, and built upon from either edge. Pin the first strip in place. If using freezer paper, simply iron in place on the coated side of the paper.

Step 2. Place the second string on top of the first, right sides together, aligning raw edges. Pin in place, if desired. Sew the entire length of the seam through the fabrics and foundation, using a ¼-inch seam.

Step 3. Open and press in place. Continue in the same manner until the entire foundation is covered.

Step 4. Trim the blocks in the appropriate manner for the foundation used, and join together. (Trim even with permanent foundations and trim ¼ inch out from the edges of temporary foundations.)

Creative Variations

There are almost limitless options to expand the visual impact of this technique. There is only one basic rule: *Each new string must cover a previous raw edge, or several previous raw edges, if changing direction.*

Consider the following possibilities, and soon you'll be designing your own wonderful string-pieced quilts.

Option 1. Vary the strip widths.

Option 2. Vary the strip widths and angles.

Option 3. Vary the foundation shapes.

Option 4. Another possibililty is to use more than one direction within the same foundation. Draw a line to divide the foundation into two sections. Work first with the section that has its strings running perpendicular to that line. Add all strings going past the line.

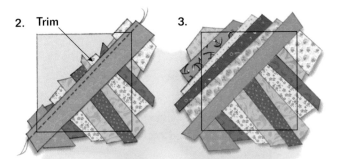

Add the first string that runs parallel to your line. It should cover the ends of the first set of strings. Excess ends can be trimmed after sewing. Cover the remainder of the foundation.

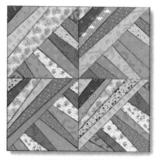

BLOCKS SET STRAIGHT

BLOCKS SET ONE QUARTER TURN

Experiment with settings. Try blocks set straight or blocks set one quarter turn.

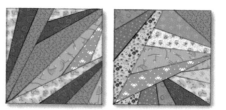

Try your own variations on this idea.

Option 5. Use wedges instead of strings, following the same principles.

Note the secondary patterns that develop with various arrangements. Preplanning color placement can help to emphasize the design elements.

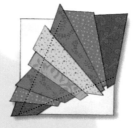

Option 6. Divide your foundation into three segments. String the perpendicular section first. Complete remaining sections, adding strings over the ends of the first section.

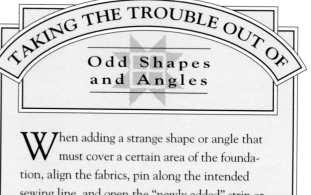

TAKING THE TROUBLE OUT OF

Odd Shapes and Angles

When adding a strange shape or angle that must cover a certain area of the foundation, align the fabrics, pin along the intended sewing line, and open the "newly added" strip or string to be certain it will cover all of the intended area (and beyond, if needed). This quick extra step can save a great deal of frustration by avoiding having to rip out a misjudged addition.

String-Pieced Elements

Combine this technique with others for exciting variations. A simple heart-shaped foundation can be treated with string piecing, then appliquéd onto a project. Consider making elements for pieced borders in the same fashion, as well as entire borders for quilts or wallhangings. Use delicately colored string-pieced blocks as the background for appliqué designs, rather than one large piece of fabric. In other words, let the technique work for you to explore your creativity!

Eileen Sullivan

STRIP PIECING

Strip piecing is a contemporary quiltmaking technique that relies on rotary cutting and machine piecing to yield fast and accurate results. This is the best technique to use for simple designs of squares, rectangles, or diamonds.

Basic strip piecing involves simple straight-sewn cut strips. Strips sewn and cut on a 45 degree diagonal will result in sets of diamonds that can be used for blocks like the Lone Star. Half-square triangles can be made from strips cut on the bias. (See "Triangle Squares" on page 251 for the bias strip method.) Fabric strips can also be sewn together to make yardage rather than a special pattern.

Spray starch all your fabrics prior to cutting. It makes the fabric easier to cut and stitch accurately.

Basic How-To for Strip Piecing

Step 1. Use a rotary cutter and ruler to cut fabric strips quickly. Most directions are based on cutting the strips of fabric cross-grain and across the full 44/45-inch width. As in all rotary cutting, the strip should be straight and accurately measured. (See "Rotary Cutting" on page 197.)

Step 2. Stitch the strips together using a straight stitch and a ¼-inch seam allowance. Choose a slightly shorter than average stitch length, since pieces are cut from the strips. Short stitches will prevent the stitching lines from pulling apart.

Step 3. Press the seams. Traditionally, quilters press seams toward the darker fabric. I press the seams open. Open seams result in flatter strip sets that are easier to match and stitch.

Step 4. Cut the pieces from the strip sets using a rotary cutter and ruler or a template and scissors. Stack them in piles of like colors. Stitch the blocks together.

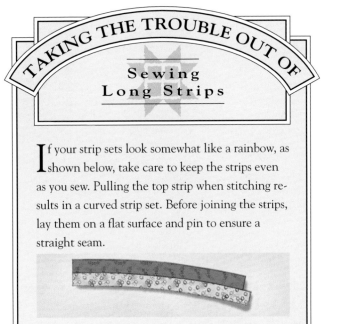

TAKING THE TROUBLE OUT OF
Sewing Long Strips

If your strip sets look somewhat like a rainbow, as shown below, take care to keep the strips even as you sew. Pulling the top strip when stitching results in a curved strip set. Before joining the strips, lay them on a flat surface and pin to ensure a straight seam.

Nine Patch

The Nine Patch is made of nine equal squares. In traditional piecing, each square is individually cut and stitched. Strip piecing constructs the block as three strip-pieced units of three pieces.

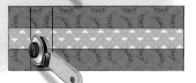

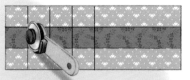

Step 1. To make the units, stitch together long strips of fabric, alternating colors. Then cut the strips into the units.

Step 2. Join the three units to make the block.

Debra Wagner

TEMPLATES

A template is a tool that quilters use as an aid in cutting the various fabric pieces needed for either patchwork or appliqué blocks. Templates can vary, depending on whether you are hand or machine piecing, rotary cutting, or cutting with scissors. The materials used to make templates may also be different depending on whether this is a one-time-only usage or a shape you will want to use repeatedly. Templates that will be used many times should be made of a stronger, more durable material.

Templates for Machine Piecing

Templates for machine piecing must always include the ¼-inch seam allowance. You will need a pattern piece that you have either drafted yourself or have obtained from a pattern, book, or magazine. This pattern piece is usually a flimsy piece of paper that is very difficult to cut or trace around. You need to stiffen this pattern piece so it can be used effectively as a tool.

You may want to blunt the long points of pattern pieces such as triangles and diamonds before making the templates. This removes the tips that extend beyond the seam and makes matching easier. I normally blunt the point using the graph paper lines, ¼ inch from the finished shape,

TEMPLATE FOR MACHINE PIECING

whenever the piece is identical side to side and will remain identical with the blunting. For a diamond, blunt the point ¼ inch from the finished tip, perpendicular to an imaginary line that would run from tip to tip on the diamond.

If you plan to use the template just once, glue the paper pattern piece to a sheet of heavyweight template plastic, and cut carefully through the two layers with paper-cutting scissors. This template can be traced around, or if you are extremely careful, you can even cut around this template with a rotary cutter. (See "Templates and Rotary Cutting" on the opposite page.)

If you want to make more permanent templates, make that same paper pattern piece even more durable by adding extra layers. Think of this process as making a template "sandwich." You will need heavyweight template plastic (preferably without grids) plus a sheet of heavyweight, fine- to medium-grit sandpaper and glue. I use a Dennison or Avery brand glue stick because they don't get hard or dry out easily. Glue the template plastic to the top side of the paper pattern piece, and glue the sandpaper (rough side out) to the back side of the paper pattern piece. Allow the three layers to dry completely before taking paper-cutting scissors and cutting through all three layers at once to create very sturdy templates. The sandpaper helps to grip the fabric during the cutting or marking process.

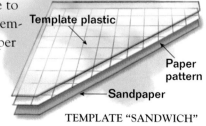

TEMPLATE "SANDWICH"

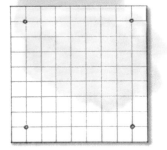

You can use a ¹⁄₁₆-inch paper hole punch to punch holes in your templates at the seam intersections. Use a pencil to mark dots on the fabric for situations when extra care is needed to match up points.

Some quilters like to add an extra layer of cardboard to their template sandwich. (The back of a tablet of paper works well.) The layers from the top down would be: template plastic, paper pattern piece, cardboard, sandpaper. If the paper pattern piece is in a book or magazine that you prefer not to cut up, an easy solution is to photocopy the pattern pieces at *100 percent*.

Another wonderful material to make your own templates from comes in a Cut Your Own Template Kit produced by John Flynn. The material is a plastic laminate backed by a material that grips the fabric in a manner similar to sandpaper. The beauty of this material is that it absolutely cannot be cut with your rotary cutter, so there's no chance you'll shave some off by accident! To create the templates, cut out your paper pattern piece and glue it to the colorful side of the laminate material. The kit comes with a special cutter and complete instructions on usage. Once the template is prepared, you are ready to cut fabric. This template material is particularly useful on shapes you will use repeatedly. (You will not be able to punch holes in it for matching points.)

Templates and Rotary Cutting

If you are like most machine piecers today, you usually cut patches with a rotary cutter and ruler. You most likely wouldn't trade these tools for all the templates in

the world! There are a myriad of rulers made for use with the rotary cutter but can rotary cutters ever join forces with the templates you have made? The answer to that question is unequivocally "Yes!" Just follow a few simple guidelines to rotary cut using templates.

When marking around templates, be sure to use a fine line marker or a very sharp pencil. A dull pencil will make for less than accurate lines and dots. Do not let the marker slip. Keep it snug against the template. If you have punched holes at the seam intersections, mark the dot exactly in the center of the hole.

—*Debra Wagner*

Step 1. Cut a strip of fabric from selvage to selvage, and cut off the selvage edges. To determine the width of the strip, position the template on the ruler and measure it. Be careful to take into consideration where you want the straight of grain.

Step 2. Once the strip is cut, position the template on the folded strip, beginning at the cut edges. Carefully cut the template shape with your rotary cutter. (If you have a problem doing that, place a ruler exactly over the edge of the template as a cutting guide.) Or trace around the template and position a ruler exactly over the drawn lines. You will be cutting two layers at a time. Depending on the shape, up to three edges of the template may already be aligned with the edges of the strip, which means you will only be cutting one edge. Reposition the template on the strip, and continue cutting the required number of pieces. For easier matching, you may want to cut the points off after cutting the basic shape.

Note: Be sure that your rotary cutter blade is sharp and that it is loose enough to glide along easily. Add a drop of oil when cutting with the templates to help the blade turn smoothly.

Write information on a Post-It and attach it to the right side of the template. Include the strip width, number to cut, how many of each fabric, and yield per strip. This can save you a lot of thinking time in the long run!

Templates for Hand Piecing

Hand piecers traditionally use templates without the seam allowance. Make templates the same as for machine piecing, but make them the finished size. Position the template on the wrong side of the fabric, and draw around the template with a marking pen or pencil. The ¼-inch seam allowance is frequently only eyeballed as the fabric is cut out with scissors. Sewing is done on the drawn line.

Templates for Appliqué

Appliqué templates do not include seam allowances. Usually you would only make a permanent template for appliqué blocks when making several with the same image.

Easy temporary templates can be made from freezer paper, available in the grocery store near the aluminum foils and plastic wraps. Freezer paper is paper with a plastic coating on one side. The paper side is perfect for drawing on with a pencil. Since you can see through the freezer paper, position it on top of the pattern and trace each shape you need.

For the single usage freezer paper template, position the freezer paper shiny side down on the right side of the fabric, and iron with a hot, dry iron. The heat will allow the freezer paper to bond to the fabric temporarily. (You only need to hold the iron down for about two seconds.) Using scissors, cut around the shape, adding the ¼-inch seam allowance by eye. Use the freezer paper as a guide for turning under the seam allowance, or trace around it and peel the freezer paper off, using the pencil line as a guide as you appliqué.

If you want the pattern pieces to be permanent, here are two easy solutions. First, take the freezer paper template you just cut out, and iron it to a piece of cardboard or tagboard (such as an old manilla folder). When ironing the freezer paper to the cardboard, make sure you have a *dry* iron (not steam) and position the freezer paper with the paper side toward the iron. Ironing causes the plastic-coated side to bond to the cardboard. You can then cut out the shape to trace around on your fabric.

A second option for appliqué templates is plastic template material. Position the template plastic on top of the pattern design, and trace the required shapes. Cut them out and you are ready. An advantage to template plastic is that you can see through it. This is helpful in situations where you are looking for a particular print placement on the fabric. Templates cut from plastic are good for repeated usage and can be traced around as many times as necessary.

Storing Templates

The key is to store templates so that you can find them easily, should you ever want to use them again. Try one of the following storage options.

- Plastic see-through boxes
- Plastic zipper bags
- Zipper pouches that fit into a notebook
- Top loading page protectors, stored and labeled in a notebook
- Manilla file folders in a hanging file box
- Secured together on a metal shower curtain ring and hung from cup hooks

If you roam through one of the home or office supply stores, you're likely to discover all sorts of storage solutions and ideas. Once you are through using the templates, the thing to remember is to *put them away*. Being consistent about how and where you store your templates will definitely make finding them again later much easier.

Sharyn Craig

THIMBLES

For many quilters, young and old, using a thimble can feel like having a brick on the end of your finger! As a result, some quilters learn to quilt by pinching the needle between their fingers or developing a callous on their "pushing" finger, which, in fact, acts almost like a thimble. While these methods may work well for some, most quilters try to use the "rocking stitch" for hand quilting, and this requires a thimble.

When using the rocking stitch, it is critical to achieve the proper leverage so that the needle is as perpendicular as possible to the quilt layers each time it enters the fabric. This method helps to achieve a small and even stitch on both sides of the quilt. Using a thimble to push the needle makes it easier to gain this leverage. When pinching the needle, it enters the fabric at an angle, most often resulting in different size stitches on the top and bottom of the quilt.

Finding a thimble that is comfortable requires some trial and error. There are many different types and just as many different opinions on what works well!

Metal Thimbles

These have always been the most familiar but seem to be the most difficult to get used to. However, there are many different styles, one of which may work well for you. Look for a thimble with a deeply dimpled top, which helps to hold the needle in place.

Some thimbles have deeply grooved sides, which may feel more comfortable depending on the angle at which you push the needle. Some thimbles have a recessed top, which helps keep the needle in place and prevents it from sliding off the thimble. There are open-top thimbles, commonly called tailor's thimbles. With these, you need to push from the side. The open top also helps to keep the finger cooler. Other open-ended thimbles allow space for the fingernail to extend.

Leather Thimbles

Leather thimbles have gained popularity since they allow the quilter to "feel" the needle, giving a greater sense of control. Some of these thimbles cover the length of the finger, while others are shorter. Simple leather thimbles are nice, but they tend to wear thin with extended use, sometimes allowing the "eye" end of the needle to pop through and into the finger. Goat leather thimbles tend to be much thicker and have more of a cushion. Also available are leather thimbles with small metal plates layered inside. These metal plates allow you to push the needle without worrying about the needle popping through, but they still give a sense of flexibility and control. There are several styles of metal plate leather thimbles, each with their own slight differences.

One particularly nice style is a thicker leather that wraps around the finger and is secured with Velcro. It also has a flexible metal pad that you can bend to whatever angle feels comfortable on your finger. This thimble accommodates any size finger and can adjust if your finger swells at all during the stitching process.

Plastic Thimbles

Most basic styles of metal thimbles are also produced in plastic. While plastic is lightweight, it tends to be slippery in comparison to metal. There is a simple open-top plastic thimble that conveniently adjusts to finger size and also allows for a longer fingernail. A lightweight, plastic thimble may feel the least "foreign" to a new quilter.

Paddle Thimble

There is a unique "paddle" style thimble that is gripped in the hand and not worn on the end of the finger. This sturdy metal thimble allows the quilter to stitch using the wrist and forearm muscles instead of pushing with the fingers. This style is especially nice for those quilters affected by arthritis or other conditions that limit dexterity. It takes some practice to get used to, but many quilters swear that they'll never use a traditional thimble again!

Thimble Fit

To determine whether a thimble fits your finger correctly or not, consider the following hints: Your finger should just touch the end of the thimble without forcing it. If your finger does not reach all the way to the end, you will find you have less control when manipulating the needle. In the case of enclosed metal or plastic thimbles, it is very common for the finger to swell after stitching for some time. Keeping that in mind, it is better to start with a thimble that has a comfortable but not tight fit. A leather thimble will conform to your finger if it swells. Open-top and open-ended thimbles allow for longer fingernails and let air circulate more freely.

Thumb Thimbles

Yes, there are thimbles specifically designed to be used on the thumb! They are great if you are a "thumb pusher!" These thimbles are usually leather or soft plastic, which helps to grip the needle as you stitch. Most thimbles meant for fingers are too small or not shaped to feel comfortable on the thumb, so these were developed to offer an alternative.

Cyndi Hershey

Metal
Thimbles

Paddle
Thimble

PAT. NO. 4534495

CLOVER

Plastic
Thimble

Leather
Thimbles

Thumb
Thimble

242

THREAD

Quilters use thread for every phase of quilt-making—piecing by hand or machine, appliqué, embellishment, and of course, quilting itself. Today's quiltmakers have a huge, sometimes overwhelming, variety of threads to choose from.

The Low-Down on Thread

Thread is twisted from strands of fiber that are spun from silk, cotton, wool, or synthetic material. Generally, the more tightly twisted the thread, the thinner it will be in diameter. *Denier* is a term referring to weight, but think of it as the diameter (thickness) of the thread strand. Thread is numbered according to thickness—the lower the number, the thicker the thread.

Thread may be plied; that is, several strands are twisted together to form a single thickness. Plying two or more strands together will increase a thread's strength; however, fewer strands twisted together will make the thread smoother. Cotton threads are often labeled with two numbers. The first number refers to the size thread (denier), and the second refers to the ply, or how many strands are twisted together.

Some threads are manufactured by wrapping one thread around a filler core of a different fiber content. Many of the special-effect metallics are made in this manner. The filler core is normally a stronger fiber than the wrapped thread and increases the strength of the prettier but weaker thread on the outside.

Threads that may be used for quiltmaking are available in cotton, rayon, and silk, as well as numerous synthetic fibers, such as metallic, polyester, and acrylic. The fiber content itself will help you evaluate the strength as well as the physical characteristics of a particular thread. As a general rule, man-made fibers are stronger than natural ones. Therefore, thread with a polyester, acrylic, or nylon content will be less apt to fray and break than a cotton thread. A synthetic thread is ideal for stitching through heavy and bulky materials when maximum strength is required.

The thread you choose must be compatible in strength to the technique employed. If you are quilting by hand, the thread must be strong enough to withstand repeated needling through the layers of the quilt sandwich without fraying and breaking. If you are machine quilting, you must determine which thread and needle combination will be most successful. (See also "Machine Quilting" on page 150.)

Compare the color, sheen, and texture of the different types of threads to determine the effect that you desire. Metallics will provide a shiny, sparkling look for machine or hand quilting. Rayon will produce a high sheen, and cotton will give a lovely matte luster.

Consider a thread's visual attributes, and weigh these against its strength. Natural fiber threads have characteristics that may make them preferable over synthetic ones, even though they may not be as strong. For example, although it is not especially strong, 100 percent cotton Cotona thread is ideally suited for machine stipple quilting. Because of its hair-like fineness, this 80 weight thread seems to melt into the background to enhance the "shadows and valleys" of stipple quilting.

Decorative Threads for Machine Quilting

Quiltmakers have learned that by using a decorative thread for the quilting stitch, they may embellish their quilt as they secure the layers together. Quilters are enchanted by the dazzling lure of decorative threads, and manufacturers are responding by churning out new products every season.

With so many different decorative threads to choose from for machine quilting, you need to have a good understanding of how to adjust your sewing machine to achieve the best results. Tension is critically important in the needle and bobbin. The stitch should hold the quilt sandwich layers together firmly without causing puckering or pulling on the bobbin thread. The perfect machine stitch will show only the top decorative thread on top and only the bobbin thread underneath, while maintaining a straight, firm depression. You will probably need to adjust the upper tension so that it is in correct balance with the bobbin tension.

THREADS FOR QUILTMAKING

Rayon Thread

Often referred to as "machine embroidery thread," 100 percent rayon thread may be used for nearly any type of machine application, including quilting. It is strong, shiny, beautiful, easy to use, and widely available. Rayon thread comes in a variety of spool sizes and weights; 30 weight rayon is heavier than 40 weight, and using it will create a more pronounced line of quilting. The finer 40 weight rayon produces gorgeous stipple quilting, especially in one of the many variegated shades.

Nylon Thread

Nylon, or monofilament, thread remains very popular among machine quilters. It is very easy to use and is widely available. It leaves a nice crisp indentation for the quilting line, and the stitch itself is nearly invisible, making it especially appealing to beginners whose stitches are less than perfect. Nylon thread comes in two colors: clear for light to medium fabrics and smoke for dark fabrics. Since nylon is a strong, man-made fiber, the quilting lines may cut into the weaker fibers of the cotton fabric over time.

Cotton Thread

Cotton seems to be the thread of choice for quilt-makers. It has earned its reputation as a good quality workhorse thread. It is inexpensive, relatively easy to find, and well suited for piecing, machine quilting, and hand quilting. Cotton has little to no stretch, so the quilting line will remain crisp and not lose its definition years later. Cotton is the thread that "was good enough for grandma and is good enough for me!"

Cotton is available in many grades. Use only a high-quality cotton for quiltmaking. To compare the quality, pull out a long strand, and hold it up to the light. Inferior thread will have "fuzzies," or lint, protruding from the edges of the strand, while the premium grade thread will be noticeably smoother.

Polyester-wrapped cotton thread is stronger than cotton, but the wrapping process also produces a more abrasive thread with a rougher texture. Cotton and cotton-wrapped polyester threads are not exceptionally beautiful or unusual, but they are very easy to use and are readily available.

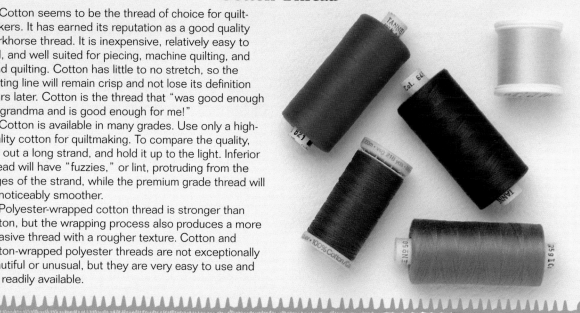

Mylar Metallic Thread

Mylar threads are flat in shape and aluminized to highly reflect light. They add a brilliant, almost transparent shine to a quilt's surface when used for hand or machine quilting. Use a Metafil needle or large-eye needle when machine quilting, and use a stronger thread, such as the cotton Tanne, in the bobbin.

Because of the flat surface of the Mylar, these threads are best pulled from a vertical pin to minimize "coiling" that will twist the thread and cause it to snap. If your sewing machine does not have a vertical thread pin or a vertical thread attachment, you can easily rig one up by taping a slender dowel rod to the top edge of your sewing machine.

Silk Thread

Another natural fiber, silk is very strong and will withstand brutal treatment. This makes it useful for machine quilting, which may put a lot of stress on the thread. Silk is the most lustrous thread available; its sheen has a highly polished luster that beautifully enhances any quilting design. It comes in many sizes and weights and absorbs dye beautifully for the most brilliant colors imaginable.

Metallic Thread

Quiltmakers have long been tantalized by shimmering metallic threads that reflect light to add movement and sparkle to a quilt's surface. However, using them successfully requires certain precautions.

Always use a large-eye needle manufactured specifically for metallic threads, such as Metafil, made by Lamertz, or Metallica, made by Schmetz. These needles have an elongated eye, extra sharp point, and a groove in the front of the needle to help reduce friction against metallic threads.

Lower the top tension setting slightly and sew at a slower speed to reduce stress and friction on the thread. Always use a good quality thread in the bobbin; my favorite for machine quilting is the 50 weight cotton Tanne, which is the perfect balance with the weaker metallic on top. Although using metallic threads does require more "kid-glove" treatment than other decorative threads, I feel they are well worth the extra effort.

To test your machine tension, prepare a practice sample using the same fabric, batting, and threads that you plan to use for quilting. Set the sewing machine for free-motion quilting, or engage the feed dogs for machine-guided quilting, exactly as you plan to quilt your project. Quilt a straight line about 3 inches long, then examine the stitches to test the tensions. If you see the bobbin thread being pulled to the top surface, that means that the top tension is too tight, so lower it slightly. If you see the top thread being pulled to the underneath side, that means that the top tension is too loose; tighten it slightly.

THREADS FOR QUILTERS

Thread Type	Tension Setting	Needle Type
Cotton	3 to 5	Universal
Cotton/Polyester	3 to 5	Universal
Metallic	2 to 3	Metafil or Topstitching
Mylar	2 to 3	Metafil or Topstitching
Nylon	3 to 4	Machine Embroidery
Silk	3 to 5	Machine Embroidery
Rayon	3 to 4	Machine Embroidery

TAKING THE TROUBLE OUT OF Tension

Thread tension should be tight enough to hold the quilt layers together snugly to form a depression. The texture that results is commonly referred to as the "hills and valleys" of quilting. It is possible to achieve a quilt stitch that is perfectly balanced but that is too loose to form this nice depression. First tighten the top tension until this pretty depression occurs, then tighten the bobbin tension, if necessary, to balance the stitches.

It is important to use the correct needle when machine quilting with decorative threads. Decorative threads may have special considerations, depending on their fiber content. For example, rayon threads are loosely spun and slippery, metallic threads are more fragile, and Mylar threads cause more "drag" through the upper tension disc.

Fortunately, special sewing machine needles are manufactured to accommodate these variations. Large-eye and Metafil needles have an elongated eye and a deepened groove on the front of the needle to help reduce friction when using metallic threads, and machine embroidery needles have slightly rounded points to prevent damage to rayon threads. Always select the needle type to best suit your particular specialty thread, and choose the needle size according to the weight of the fabrics that you are using. Heavier fabrics require a larger needle size.

Refer to the chart above to help select the needle type and tension setting for your particular decorative thread. I prefer to use 100 percent cotton thread in the bobbin, no matter what I use on the top. Cotton is trouble-free thread that ties off easily, doesn't come undone, doesn't fray, and has almost no stretch. It is the best thread to use with other, more troublesome threads. Use a 30 weight heavier thread if you want the stitching to show up more. Use 50 weight if you want the thread to blend in. The 50 weight is more readily available and comes in more colors.

Occasionally you may need to adjust the tension of your bobbin in order to achieve a pretty stitch, especially if your top thread and your bobbin thread are different in weight and type. Check your manual for instructions on loosening the bobbin's tension if your sewing machine has a

A

Loosen   Tighten

built-in bobbin case. If you have a separate bobbin case, remove it and turn the tiny screw that is located next to the thread opening. Turn the screw to the right to tighten the bobbin tension, and turn the screw to the left to loosen it.

Sharee Dawn Roberts

TRAPUNTO

"April's Promise," 19" × 21", was designed and made by Hari Walner in the spring of 1995 when the irises were in full bloom. This miniature whole-cloth trapuntoed quilt was done completely by machine.

The terms trapunto, Italian trapunto, cording, stuffed work, and stuffed or padded appliqué are commonly used interchangeably, although there are differences in the way they are created. They all refer to the technique of stitching a design and stuffing it for a padded, sculptural effect. The play of light and shadow created as a result of the high relief patterns can be stunning!

Trapunto is the process of outline stitching a motif and stuffing the resulting areas of the design with cotton, wool, or polyester stuffing material. Traditionally, this painstaking method was accomplished by gently spreading apart the threads of the coarsely woven quilt backing and inserting bits of batting until the area was raised. A stiletto was the tool often used for this task, as it aided in working the holes closed after each area was filled.

Corded trapunto is used in narrow areas such as stems, vines, cables, or channels. After stitching parallel quilting lines, a blunt tapestry needle threaded with lengths of cotton or synthetic yarn is inserted between the threads in the back of the quilt and run through the channel to raise the motif.

Stuffed work involves stitching individual fabric appliqué designs to a quilt top and filling each with batting, tufts of polyester fiberfil, cotton, or wool.

The instructions here will guide you through my methods of trapunto. At first glance it may appear that I am creating more work for myself, but quality control and my level of patience inspired me to develop this approach for trapunto and corded trapunto.

Using a coarse backing fabric for my quilt wasn't appealing to me, and I usually ended up with ugly, undesirable holes in the backing along with a high level of frustration! This led me to stitch a lightweight "inner layer" to the wrong side of the quilt top. I stuff this before layering the quilt sandwich, resulting in a lovely front as well as back.

Trapunto and Corded Trapunto

Step 1. Trace the quilting design onto your quilt top. (See "Marking Quilt Tops" on page 157.) Thread or pin-baste a lightweight piece of fabric, such as voile or thin muslin, to the wrong side of the quilt top. If your design has a central motif or only a few scattered patterns to be stuffed, you may baste the voile behind those areas only, rather than the entire quilt top. Voile or thin muslin must be basted to any area to be stuffed.

Voile or thin muslin

Step 2. From the right side, sew a running stitch just inside the marked outer areas of each trapunto design, using a contrasting thread. Some motifs may have additional lines within the main design to further define the pattern. You'll need to stitch along one side of the design lines to help define each of the sections to be stuffed. After the area is stuffed and quilted, this thread will be pulled out, so you want it to be easily seen.

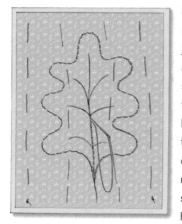

Step 3. This step is optional. Working from the reverse side, trim away sections of voile that are outside the design areas to be stuffed. This will reduce bulk for hand quilting. For corded trapunto, skip to Step 6.

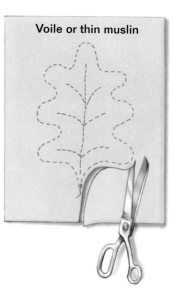

Voile or thin muslin

Step 4. For trapunto, working from the back, use small, sharp embroidery scissors to cut a small slit in the voile or muslin, taking care not to cut into the quilt top. Complicated designs may require slits in each section of the design to make it easier to stuff.

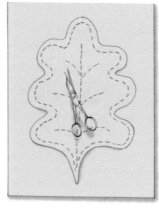

Step 5. Insert a small amount of your stuffing material with a blunt tapestry needle, crochet hook, or stiletto. Stuff small bits in at a time to achieve lump-free trapunto. Continue until the motif is lightly but evenly filled. Do not overstuff! Overstuffing causes the adjacent background around the design to distort and pucker. Whipstitch the opening closed.

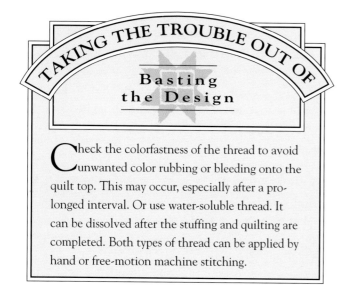

TAKING THE TROUBLE OUT OF
Basting the Design

Check the colorfastness of the thread to avoid unwanted color rubbing or bleeding onto the quilt top. This may occur, especially after a prolonged interval. Or use water-soluble thread. It can be dissolved after the stuffing and quilting are completed. Both types of thread can be applied by hand or free-motion machine stitching.

Step 6. In corded trapunto, the space between two lines of stitching is stuffed. Work from the back, and carefully insert a blunt tapestry needle threaded with yarn into the voile or muslin (do not poke through the quilt top). Leaving a 2-inch tail, start at the beginning of the design between the two lines to be filled. Work the needle

through the design by gathering the fabric as you go. Bring the needle out where the design turns or when it becomes difficult to proceed. Pull the yarn through the channel, leaving a slight slack to ensure pucker-free lines, and return to the same hole to continue. Adjust the slack in your strand of yarn, and trim ends close to the fabric at the start and finish, working ends into the holes. Wider channels may require several runs through the design to fill in the entire area.

 I use a variety of thicknesses of yarns or double the strands of one yarn, depending upon the design to be filled. I also attempt to match the color of the yarn with the quilt top to prevent shadowing.

Step 7. After all the trapunto work is completed, baste the quilt top to the batting and backing. Quilt in the usual manner, quilting on the original marked design lines, just outside or to the side of the previous stitching of the trapunto areas. Remove the contrasting temporary threads

by clipping and pulling out. Wait until the quilt is bound before washing if you used water-soluble thread.

Stuffed Work

Stuffing can be done using a stiletto, crochet hook, the blunt end of a small scissors, or even the slightly sharpened point of a chop stick. Be extremely cautious not to poke a hole into the appliqué fabric. *Do not* overfill. It will cause puckering! There are two methods you can use to fill appliqué areas.

Method 1. Partially stitch the prepared appliqué design onto the quilt top, leaving a small section open. Keep the needle threaded, and move it out of the way. Through the opening, lightly fill the appliqué area with stuffing material of your choice. Continue stitching the appliqué into position.

Method 2. Stuff the appliqué design from the wrong side after it has been completely stitched to the quilt top. Cut a slit in the background fabric behind the appliquéd shape, creating an opening. Lightly fill with stuffing material of your choice and whipstitch the opening closed.

After all the appliqué and stuffing are complete, layer and baste the quilt top with the batting and backing. Quilt as desired.

Mary Stori

Machine Trapunto

The word trapunto comes from the Italian word, *trapungere,* meaning "to embroider." The traditional method of doing trapunto is a very time-consuming process and often leaves traces on the back of the quilt where the holes were. Thanks to modern tools and technology, it's possible to do trapunto by machine with a technique that is easy to learn and quick to execute, and you won't have a single hole in the back of your quilt!

Supplies

Water-soluble basting thread
Regular machine quilting thread
Piece of thick polyester batting
Piece of cotton batting
Your favorite marking device
Pair of blunt scissors
Container of water large enough to hold your project

How to Do Machine Trapunto

Select a quilting design that is suitable for trapunto. The designs must have enclosed areas where you want the raised look. Many designs cannot be stuffed because there are open lines. Free-motion quilting skills are most often used for this technique, but you can also incorporate straight-line quilting. Follow these steps to achieve a wonderful stuffed effect.

Step 1. Use your favorite method of marking and mark the complete design on your quilt top.

Step 2. Put water-soluble basting thread in the needle of your sewing machine. Use regular sewing thread in the bobbin. It should be a light-color thread that matches the color of your batting. Drop or cover your feed dogs and put on a darning or quilting foot.

Step 3. Layer the thick polyester batting directly behind the area you want stuffed and pin with safety pins or straight pins. Do not add the backing fabric yet.

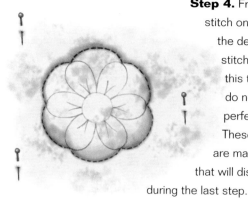

Step 4. Free-motion stitch on the outline of the design. Do not stitch the details at this time. Relax and do not worry about perfect stitches. These initial stitches are made with thread that will dissolve in water during the last step.

Step 5. Turn the quilt top over and, with your blunt scissors, trim away the polyester batt from the areas that you do not want to appear stuffed. Trim very close to your line of stitching, but be careful not to cut the quilt top. If you accidentally cut some of the basting stitches, do not worry. Just as long as there is enough stitching to hold the thick batt in place you will be all right.

Step 6. From this point on, you can proceed with your quilt top as you normally do. Layer your quilt top with the regular batting and the quilt lining. Pin-baste very securely, especially next to the areas with the additional batting. These areas tend to pucker, and a little extra pinning helps to eliminate these puckers in the quilting.

Step 7. *An important tip:* Rethread your machine with the thread you use for machine quilting. Continue to use the darning or quilting foot and keep the feed dogs down or covered.

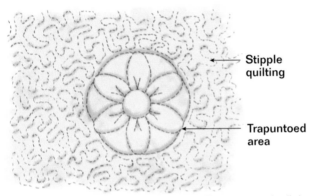

Stipple quilting

Trapuntoed area

Step 8. Free-motion quilt your design. This time, quilt all the lines, including the details of the design. Sometimes you will

be stitching on top of stitching lines that you made previously with the water-soluble thread. Don't fret if your new stitches are not exactly on top of the older stitches. The first stitches will be removed later. If you want to make your design stand out even more, do some background or stipple quilting next to the trapuntoed areas.

Step 9. When all of your quilting is complete and you have attached the binding, immerse your quilt in clear (no detergent or soap), tepid water. Wait a minute or two, and then agitate it by hand for a few seconds. This immersion will dissolve the water-soluble thread. Allow your quilt to dry, smooth the edges, and pat into shape, as needed.

TRIANGLE SQUARES

These humble building blocks of quiltmaking are known by many names—pieced triangle squares, triangle-pieced squares, half-square triangles, split squares, squares with two triangles, two-triangle squares, half-of-a-square triangle units, and bias squares. Whatever you call them, they are simply patchwork units made of two triangles stitched together to create a square, and there are many ways to make them.

Bias Strip Method

This method for making squares of two triangles is actually a form of strip piecing. Strips of fabric are cut on the bias and sewn together. The squares are then cut from the bias strip set with a square ruler. The 45 degree line on the ruler is aligned with the seam line to make the cut. The resulting cut squares have the straight grain along the outer edges. Triangle squares made with this bias strip method are extremely precise and accurate.

Step 1. Layer your two chosen fabrics with right sides together, and cut a square that measures anywhere from 6 inches to 15 inches. Use a large square rotary-cutting ruler to cut both squares at the same time. See the table on page 253 to estimate the size square you need to cut.

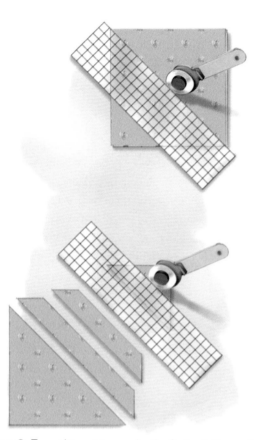

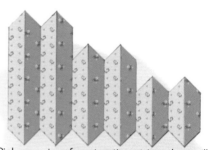

Step 3. Pick up pairs of contrasting strips; they will be right sides together and ready to stitch. Sew them together on the long bias edge, using a ¼-inch seam allowance, and press. Press seams open for triangle square units that are 1¾ inches or smaller. Press seams toward the darker fabric for larger squares. There will be strip pairs of varying lengths. Sew the longest strip pairs together, then the next longest, and so on. The most efficient configuration for sewing them together is shown here. Keep the Vs along the bottom edge even. The corner triangles left over after cutting the bias strips from the large square can also be sewn together.

Step 2. To cut bias strips, make the first cut diagonally corner to corner across the squares. Measure the desired width of the bias strip from the first diagonal cut, and cut again. Continue until the whole square has been cut into bias strips.

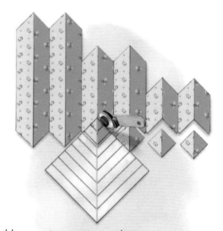

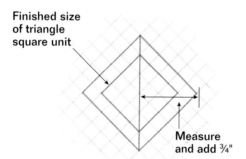

Finished size
of triangle
square unit

Measure
and add ¾"

Note: To determine the proper width of the bias strips, draw the cut size (finished size plus ½ inch for seam allowances) of the triangle square unit on graph paper. Draw diagonal lines from corner to corner. With a ruler, measure the distance from the center to a corner of the square. Add ¾ inch to this dimension for a workable strip width. The number won't always be one that is easy to measure, so round the dimension up to a number that can be cut easily using the markings on your rotary-cutting rulers.

Step 4. Use a rotary cutter and a square rotary-cutting ruler marked with a 45 degree diagonal line to begin cutting at the lowest points. Place the diagonal line on the ruler on the first seam line. Cut squares slightly (a few threads to ⅛ inch) larger than the desired cut size of the two-triangle unit. Two cuts are required to separate the square from the sewn strips. If you have joined two or more sets of strips, continue to cut squares from alternate seam lines working across the strips from one side to the other.

Tip: Let your rotary cutter go a few threads beyond the seam line on each cut to cleanly separate the square without leaving a maddening two threads uncut.

TRIANGLE SQUARES: STRIP WIDTHS & YIELDS OF COMMON SIZES

Finished Size of Triangle Square	Cut Size of Triangle Square	Strip Width	Yield from 10" Squares	Yield from 13½" Squares	Yield from 15" Squares
1"	1½"	2"	35	61	84
1½"	2"	2¼"	23	43	53
2"	2½"	2½"	13	30	36
2½"	3"	2⅞"	10	20	27
3"	3½"	3¼"	7	16	19
3½"	4"	3⅝"	7	11	16
4"	4½"	4"	5	7	9

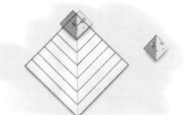

Step 5. Turn each square so the two sides that were just cut are pointing toward you. Align the diagonal line of the square rotary-cutting ruler with the seam line of the square and the exact dimension on the ruler with the cut sides of the square. Make the final two cuts.

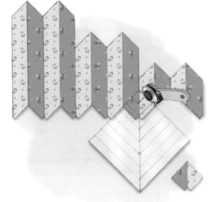

Step 6. After cutting the first squares, go back and cut from the skipped seam lines.

Try This

To get a random scrap look when piecing triangle squares with the bias strip method, cut small beginning squares, 6 to 9 inches, from a variety of prints. The more fabrics used, the scrappier it will look. Cut all the squares into identical bias strips. Mix and match the strips before sewing them together for the greatest variety of combinations.

Use the handy table above to determine strip width of common sizes of triangle squares and to estimate how many two-triangle squares you can get from 10-, 13½-, and 15-inch squares of fabric. The 13½-inch square is an efficient size to cut since you can cut three of these across the width of your fabric.

Marsha McCloskey

Slice and Sew Method

This is a good technique for quilters comfortable with piecing accurate ¼-inch seams and manipulating pairs of triangles through the sewing machine. This method requires the least amount of cutting and sewing, and it works well for scrap quilts that need triangle squares of many different fabrics.

Step 1. Cut two squares of contrasting fabric ⅞ inch larger than the *finished* size of the desired triangle squares. Place squares right sides together and press. (Pressing helps the layers "grip" each other for more accurate cutting and sewing.)

Two fabric squares, right sides together

Step 2. With a rotary ruler and rotary cutter, slice the squares in half once diagonally.

Step 3. Without peeling apart the layers, feed the triangle pairs through the sewing machine, stitching an accurate ¼ inch. Be careful not to tug or distort these bias edges while sewing. Beginners may find it helpful to pin at each tip of the triangle pair. As you gain experience, you may find it unnecessary to pin. To chain piece, feed pairs of triangles one right after the other without stopping to clip threads in between.

Step 4. Press the squares open with seam allowances toward the darker fabric. Trim off the triangle points.

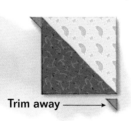

Trim away ⟶

Draw, Sew, and Cut Method

With this technique, you piece slightly over-size triangle squares, which you then trim down to the desired size. This helps guarantee that the units will be perfectly square, which can be very appealing for quilters who are not avid or accurate piecers. The drawback is that there is a little more work involved. For anyone who has struggled with triangle squares, this nearly goof-proof method makes perfect piecing a breeze. It also makes scrappy fabric combinations easy to do.

Step 1. Cut two squares of contrasting fabric 1¼ inch larger than the *finished* size of the desired triangle squares.

Step 2. Place squares right sides together and press, if desired. With a mechanical pencil or extra-fine point fabric pen, draw a line from corner to corner on the lighter fabric. If you don't have a ¼-inch presser foot, draw a line ¼ inch away from this line on both sides as sewing guides.

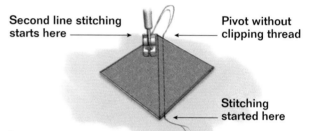

Second line stitching starts here ⟶

Pivot without clipping thread

Stitching started here ⟶

Step 3. Stitch ¼ inch along *each side* of the drawn line, beginning on the left side of the center diagonal line. At the end of the seam, lift the foot and pivot the square without clipping the threads, so that the unsewn side of the center diagonal is under the needle. Finish sewing this side.

Step 4. Cut along the marked center diagonal line with scissors or a rotary cutter. Press seams toward the darker fabric.

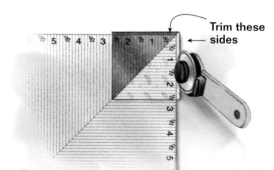

Trim these sides ⟵

Step 5. Trim each triangle square to the size needed (finished size plus ½ inch for seam allowances). Line up the 45 degree line on a square rotary-cutting ruler with the diagonal seam. Trim just enough from the two sides farthest away from you to square up the pieced unit. Make sure the measurements for the size needed fall inside the fabric square.

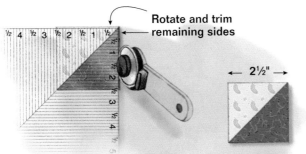

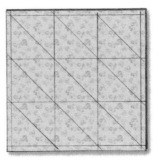

Step 5. Draw diagonal lines through all the squares in the grid.

Step 6. Lift the ruler and pivot the square so that the two trimmed sides are closest to you. Match the diagonal on the ruler with the diagonal seam. This time, align the measurement for the size needed (2½ inches for this example) with the edges that were just trimmed. Trim the two remaining sides. What you have left is a perfect triangle square.

Grid Method

This technique offers the twin advantages of accuracy and mass production. By drawing a grid of squares on large pieces of fabric, sewing, then cutting along marked diagonal lines, you end up with lots of triangle squares in the same two contrasting colors. This is an advantage for quilts with a planned color scheme.

Step 1. Determine how many finished triangle squares you need for your project. Divide this number by 2. The result is the number of squares you will need to draw in your grid.

Step 2. To determine the square size for your grid, add ⅞ inch to the size of the desired *finished* triangle square.

Step 3. Decide how you will arrange the grid on your fabric. It's usually most efficient to make the grid as close to a square as possible. (If you need 40 triangle squares, draw a 4 × 5-square grid to get the needed 20 squares.) The fabric should be at least ½ inch larger than the grid on all sides.

Step 4. Place the two fabrics right sides together, with the lighter fabric facing up. Use a rotary-cutting ruler and extra-fine point fabric pen to draft the grid onto the fabric, beginning ½ inch in from the edge of the fabric. Draw parallel lines, using the size of the square as your spacing guide. Mark parallel lines across the fabric, and then add the perpendicular lines.

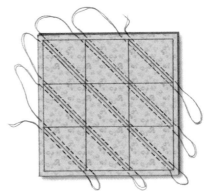

Step 6. Stitch ¼ inch along each side of the marked diagonal lines. To save time, don't cut the thread at the end of each stitching line. Lift the needle and presser foot, pivot and reposition the fabric, then begin stitching the next side of the line.

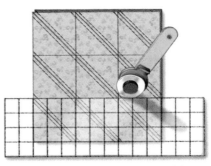

Step 7. Cut the grid apart along the sides of the squares, working row by row. Use a rotary cutter and ruler. After the squares have been cut apart, cut along the diagonal lines. Remove the stitches at the tip of each triangle.

Step 8. Press the squares open with seam allowances toward the darker fabric.

TYING

Quilters continually debate about whether you tie a comforter or tie a quilt. Purists maintain that it's not a quilt unless it's quilted. I use the term coverlet because it defines a broader type of bed covering that includes fabric and batting held together by knots rather than by a pattern of quilting stitches.

Tying has provided a way to have warm coverings for beds and cribs with less time and effort. I can appreciate the convenience of tying and still admire the beauty and usefulness of quilted projects.

Yarn, pearl cotton thread, and ⅛-inch ribbon are the most common materials used for tying. Ribbon can be used, but the ends will need to be treated to keep them from fraying after the knots are tied. Use a needle that is big enough to put a hole in the fabric and batting to allow the thread, yarn, or ribbon through without pulling batting to the surface. Needle size is determined by the type of thread or yarn used.

It is easier to tie a coverlet when the pattern repeated in the fabric or patchwork forms 3- to 4-inch squares or when the top is marked in squares or diamonds.

Names for the tying methods vary in different parts of the country, but those included here are the most common ones I have seen used.

Race Horse Stitch

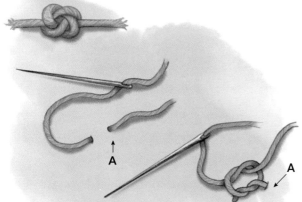

Step 1. Use a single strand of yarn 3 to 5 feet long. Take a small ¼-inch stitch at a 45 degree angle at point A. Work down and up through all the quilt layers. Leave a 2-inch tail of yarn, and use this to tie a square knot with your fingers.

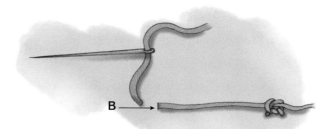

Step 2. Tie a second square knot 3 to 4 inches to the left of the first by first taking another ¼-inch stitch at point B.

Step 3. Loop the yarn that is in the needle over, then under the yarn that is strung between the first and second knots, and pull the yarn tight.

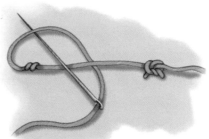

Step 4. Tie a second loop by again bringing the needle yarn under the yarn that is strung between the first and second knot back over, then under the yarn from the second knot. Pull it tight to secure the knot.

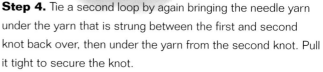

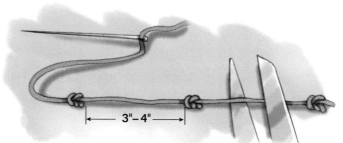

Step 5. Without cutting the yarn, repeat the stitch at each of the next points. You will have a row of square knots. When the row is finished, cut the yarn to the desired length.

256

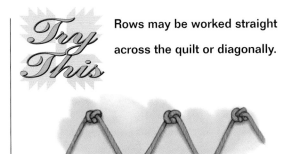

Rows may be worked straight across the quilt or diagonally.

Popcorn Ball Stitch

After the coverlet is laundered, this stitch looks like a popcorn ball!

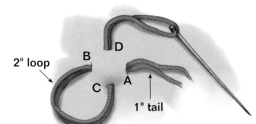

Step 1. Use a 3- to 5-foot strand of yarn, doubled in the needle. Insert the needle through the three layers, and take a scant ¼-inch horizontal stitch from point A to point B, leaving a 1-inch tail.

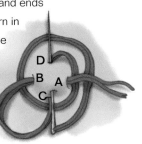

Step 2. Take another stitch at a right angle, from point C to point D, using a scant ¼-inch stitch, leaving a 2-inch loop of yarn.

Step 3. With one hand, hold the loop and ends firmly together. With the needle and yarn in the other hand, circle the yarn loops one and a half times, tightly, and then take a stitch from point C to point D. Pull tightly, centering the loops and tail over the center of the stitch. Clip yarn ends ½ to ¾ inch long.

Crow's Feet Stitch

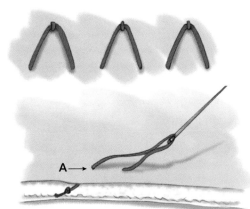

Step 1. With one strand of knotted pearl cotton thread in the needle (a straight 5⅛-inch doll needle is preferred), pull the knot to bury it in the batting. Pull the needle up at starting point A.

Step 2. Looping the thread, insert the needle through all layers of the quilt at point B and out again at point C, making a ⅜- to 1-inch stitch.

Note: The size of the crow's feet is determined by the weight of the fabric. On lightweight fabric, make the stitch approximately ⅜ inch long.

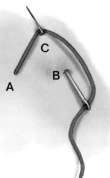

Step 3. Make a small catch stitch over the thread, entering the top fabric and batting only, then go between the fabric layers to the next area to be worked.

Working diagonally to the left creates a connected chain of crow's feet stitches. You won't need to go between the fabric layers to the next starting point because you are already there!

Carol Johnson

The Decatur Knot

Not every quilt needs to be quilted. If I can piece a quilt top quickly and tie it quickly, it will get on the bed. At the same time, I am too vain to take a top that I have pieced and hide it under yarn strings. The Decatur Knot satisfies my need to finish a quilt but it does not detract from the visual impact of the piecing. Only a ¼-inch stitch is visible on the back and just a twisted cross stitch is seen at each intersection on the front. The thread tails are on the inside.

I discovered this hidden knot in 1985 while at the National Quilting Association show in Decatur, Illinois. I was unable to find the source of the knot, and since that time, I have called this method the Decatur Knot. I use number 8 pearl cotton thread and a 5-inch doll needle. It will take two balls of thread to complete a queen-size quilt.

Step 1. Cut a piece of thread about 45 inches long and tie a single knot in one end. Leave a tail of 1 inch beyond the knot. Insert the needle into the top fabric of the quilt about 3 inches below the lower right-hand corner of the intersection where you want your first knot to be.

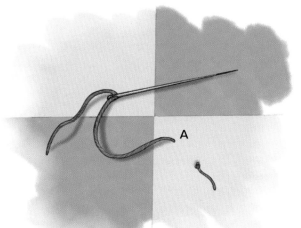

Step 2. Bring the needle up at the lower right-hand corner of the intersection, point A. At this time, leave the knot and tail at the end of the thread exposed on top of the quilt.

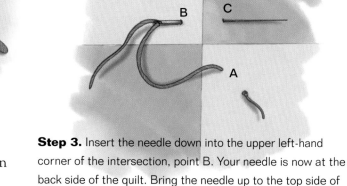

Step 3. Insert the needle down into the upper left-hand corner of the intersection, point B. Your needle is now at the back side of the quilt. Bring the needle up to the top side of the quilt in the upper right-hand corner of the intersection, point C. You have almost made a cross stitch. There is a short stitch on the back of the quilt.

Step 4. Bring your needle up and around counterclockwise to form a loop. Slide the needle under the first stitch between points A and B.

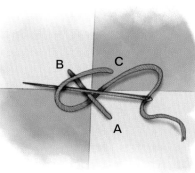

Step 5. Insert the needle back through the loop as shown. Pull the thread up until you have a small loop. Insert the needle through this loop to make the knot. Pull the thread tight. You may need to hold on to the starting tail while you pull the first knot tight.

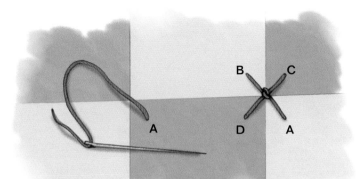

Step 1. Begin by stitching "in place" for three or four stitches, then sew about four zigzag stitches right next to each other. Make another "knot" by stitching in place again.

Step 6. Insert the needle into the batting again at the lower left-hand corner, point D. Slide the needle through the batting to the next point A, the lower right corner of the next place where you want a knot. Be careful not to pull the thread tight.

Step 7. After you have made a few knots, go back and bury the starting tail and knot by sliding your needle between the quilt top and the batting and pulling the knot with the tip of the needle.

Step 8. To end, just exit about 3 to 4 inches from your last intersection and tie a knot. Bury this knot the same way that you handled the starting knot.

Note: Point A may not always be at the lower right-hand corner of the intersection, but B will always be diagonally across from A. Positioning of A will depend on whether you are working from right to left or from left to right.

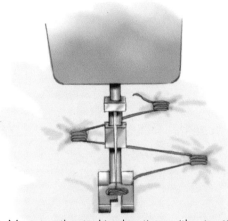

Step 2. Move to other tacking locations without cutting the threads.

 Use quilting thread to tie the Decatur knot on a small wallhanging or miniature quilt. The knots will stabilize the center and yet not be noticeable. Quilt the border to give the impression that the quilt is quilted.

Beckie Olson

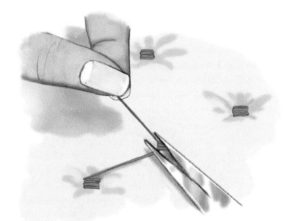

Step 3. When you have finished tacking a section, pull the quilt out from the machine and trim threads close to the stitching on both the front and back.

For cozy, warm, and quickly finished quilts, tie them and wrap them around someone you love.

Machine Tacks

Another quick way to tie your quilts is with the zigzag stitch on the sewing machine. Choose thread colors that either complement or contrast with the fabrics in the quilt top and backing.

Caroline Reardon

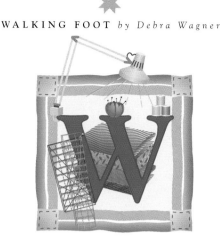

WALKING FOOT

A walking foot is helpful when doing machine-guided quilting and when attaching the binding to a quilt.

The walking foot, or even feed foot, is a sewing machine accessory that provides uniform feeding of multiple layers of fabric. The design of the foot provides an upper set of feed dogs to match the lower feed dogs. The upper feed dogs sit in special slots cut into the presser foot sole and sit directly over the lower feed dogs.

Feed dog widths and placement can vary for each machine, so it is important that you buy the correct walking foot for your make and model of machine. The foot is slightly larger than a traditional foot. The walking foot is wider, and there is a small box behind the foot that accommodates the mechanism that operates the upper feed dogs. Usually this foot has a lever that hooks around the needle clamp. The lever moves up and down with the needle. The motion of the needle controls the upper feed dogs and synchronizes the movement of the two sets of feed dogs.

Synchronization of upper and lower feed dogs

On some brands of machines, the even feed system is one of the built-in features. The system is located directly above and behind the presser foot ankle. To use the system, simply lower and snap the upper feed dog in place behind the regular presser foot. The built-in even feed system is smaller and easier to engage and disengage than the separate walking foot.

The walking foot or even feed system is recommended for machine-guided quilting. Using this feature when quilting prevents many common machine quilting problems. It reduces fabric pleats on the front and back of the quilt and ensures that the quilt finishes square and flat. The walking foot is also helpful when attaching binding by machine. This foot prevents the binding from twisting or stretching while you stitch it to the quilt.

Debra Wagner

WHITE WORK

This is a close-up of a 90" × 108" white work whole-cloth quilt. It was purchased as a new quilt by Doris Adomsky in 1990 in a shop in New Holland, Lancaster County, Pennsylvania. The design, "Queen Anne Star," was quilted by an Amish woman, one of the shop owner's best quilters.

were among the more popular subjects, sometimes with the addition of birds and animals—or even human portraits! By the late nineteenth century some quiltmakers experimented with machine-stitched white work or quilt-as-you-go, block-style white quilts.

In designing white work, keep in mind that the important parts of your design will stand out better if surrounded by a background that is more closely quilted. Remember, it's the *unquilted* sections that will be highlighted.

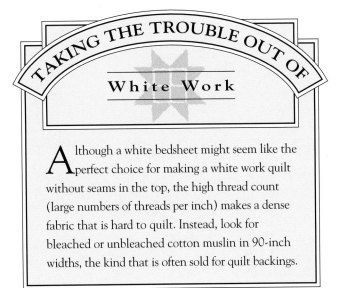

TAKING THE TROUBLE OUT OF
White Work

Although a white bedsheet might seem like the perfect choice for making a white work quilt without seams in the top, the high thread count (large numbers of threads per inch) makes a dense fabric that is hard to quilt. Instead, look for bleached or unbleached cotton muslin in 90-inch widths, the kind that is often sold for quilt backings.

White work can refer to any textile in which white fabric is embellished with white thread or yarn. Different types of white work include quilting on a plain white background, stuffed or corded work (which is also called trapunto, or Italian quilting), candlewicking or tufting, various types of embroidery, and even some types of woven bedspreads.

White work, then, is more of a "look" than a particular technique. White work was popular in Europe for centuries, not only for bedcovers but also for petticoats, babies' caps, waistcoats, and table covers. In America, white work bedcovers enjoyed widespread popularity in the late eighteenth and early nineteenth century.

Traditional white work bedcovers typically display a prominent central motif—such as a vase of flowers or a wreath—surrounded by smaller figures and one or more borders. Trees, flowers, and graceful grapevines

For a whole-cloth quilt, you will need to mark your entire design on the quilt top before layering the top, batting, and backing. Use a marking method that will remain visible during the whole quilting process. Many quilters have had success using water-soluble pens, while others prefer the traditional pencil. Choose a hard pencil, a number 3 or 4, and keep it sharp to achieve a thin, light line that will become invisible after quilting. (See also "Marking Quilt Tops" on page 157.)

White work lends itself to either hand or machine quilting. Traditionally, quilters have used a thin batting layer for white work in order to make small stitches.

In white work, the quilting *is* the design. Anything you can draw or trace can become the design of your quilt. Today's quiltmakers can re-create historic masterpieces or go wild with new interpretations of white work. White work can be as simple as a feather wreath quilted in the plain blocks of a pieced or appliquéd quilt or as complex as an elaborate design for a whole-cloth quilt.

See also "Trapunto" on page 247 and "Whole-Cloth Quilts" below.

Laurel Horton

Try This

Do you want the elegant look of a white work quilt but don't have time to make one? Find a quilt, new or old, that has beautiful quilting and a plain back, and display it wrong-side up! Or design your next quilt to be reversible, with a patchwork side and a plain side to show off the quilting. —*Laurel Horton*

WHOLE-CLOTH QUILTS

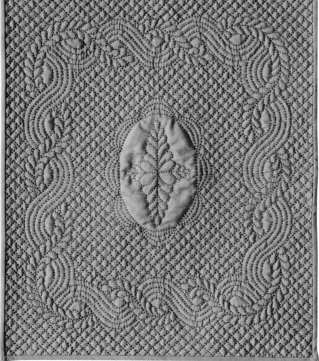

This charming miniature whole-cloth quilt, 15" × 18", was made by Martha Fraxer of Hollis, New Hampshire, in 1993 and was purchased by Carol Doak at a benefit quilt auction.

The purest definition of whole-cloth quilt is a quilt made of a single length of extra-wide fabric in which the quilting stitches themselves become the design. Since early colonial days, these solid-color quilts displaying intricate and finely stitched patterns have been highly prized.

History teaches us that early whole-cloth quilts were commonly called linsey-woolsey, a name derived from the village of Lindsay in Suffolk, England, where fabric consisting of linen warp and wool weft was first made. Often, early American quilts of this type were actually made of strips joined together because their makers didn't have home looms wide enough to weave an entire quilt top. Even though the fabric was rather coarse, colonists favored linsey-woolsey for its strength and warmth. The earliest Amish quilts were whole-cloth and quite striking because of the glowing colors of cloth that showcased their fabulous quilting designs. Another popular material for the whole-cloth quilt was calmanco, an imported fine worsted fabric that was sometimes glazed.

The whole-cloth quilts of the nineteenth century became more refined with the availability of better material and improved living conditions. Wealthy women had the time and resources to pursue their needlework skills. Quilts created with white cotton fabric and white cotton thread became known as "white work quilts" or "white on white." These elegant quilts—featuring elaborate quilting motifs, abundant with feathers, leaves, baskets, and flowers— were created more for their decorative application than for utilitarian function. The finely hand-stitched designs often displayed trapunto or stuffed areas that were further highlighted by closely stipple-quilted backgrounds. Such quilts often took years to complete and were generally attempted by only the most experienced stitchers.

Age-old quilting lore has maintained that a well-prepared young lady was expected to have made 12 quilt tops for her trousseau. The 13th, designed by the bride but quilted by family and friends, was often an all-white whole-cloth quilt. Stitching hearts on the wedding quilt was common practice, although superstition held that too many on a quilt was sure to result in a broken romance!

Today the whole-cloth quilt is still held in high regard. There are a myriad of quilters who dream of creating the ultimate hand-stipple-quilted, trapunto whole-cloth quilt as the master work in their quilting career.

Mary Stori

WORKSPACE ORGANIZATION

A hundred years ago, organization was probably not a problem for quilters. A sewing machine, a well-supplied sewing box, a bag of scraps, and a frame for quilting were about all that was needed. Quilters today can easily become overwhelmed with tools and supplies. Besides a sewing machine and basic sewing supplies, there are specialized rulers and threads, cutting mats, hoops, gadgets, patterns, drafting supplies, and, of course, *fabric!* We often see pictures of the studios of famous quilters and we may yearn for similar ideal workspaces. But the truth is, they are unrealistic for most of us. How then can we organize what we have and make the best of the space available?

Organizing will depend on the kind of quilter you are, the space that can be made available in your home, the tolerance of your family, and safety considerations for small children. Your workspace may be nothing more than part of a closet from which you get what you need for a particular project, or if you are lucky, you may have a whole room to work with. No one can tell you how to organize your particular workspace. Pick and choose from the following ideas to organize your space to suit your individual style.

The Basics

Lighting: One universal need is good lighting, so plan for it. Swing-arm and small halogen lamps are both good.

Sewing Machine: Only those who make quilts totally by hand have no need for a sewing machine. A cabinet or sewing table for your machine will give extra workspace and keep the machine easily available at all times.

Iron and Ironing Board: Though these may be stored, having them set up next to your machine removes the hurdle of having to haul out and set up your ironing board and iron. This makes it easy for you to sit down and sew, even if only for a few minutes.

Work Surface: If you're fortunate, you'll always have a large table available. Alternatives for those with more limited space are card tables, lightweight folding tables, dining room or kitchen tables, Ping-Pong tables, or as a last resort, the floor.

Fabric

Bookcases or closet shelves, plastic storage and shoe boxes, blanket chests and old suitcases all work to hold your fabric stash. Fabric can be rolled to stand on end in a box or basket.

Organizing fabrics by color or value makes using them easier. Avoid bags since they cause excessive wrinkling, and keep lids loose on plastic boxes to allow fabric to breathe. Think about fading since clear storage boxes or open shelves may let sunlight reach the fabric.

 Protect fabric stored on shelves with a piece of fabric hung at the top with Velcro. It can be removed easily while you are working and put back in place quickly afterwards.

Velcro strips hold fabric

Wall Space

If you are lucky enough to have a large wall available, you can hang flannel or lightweight batting to make a design wall. If not, a large sheet of Styrofoam or plywood covered with flannel, felt, or batting can stand in a corner and serve the same purpose.

Trays

I have a limited work area. My ironing board and sewing machine cabinet are my main work surfaces, so trays are real life savers for me. I use two constantly. One tray contains all the small items I need at the machine or ironing board. When I use the ironing board, the tray is easily moved to the machine; when I use the machine it goes back to the board. There is no bother about moving lots of little things, and everything is at my fingertips.

WORK AREA TRAY

I also use a small tray when I quilt. It contains just what I need for the particular project I'm quilting and keeps all my quilting tools ready to use in an instant. A small, shallow box could substitute for a tray. It could be covered and put away to keep it out of reach of children.

Storage Ideas

Boxes have endless uses. Place one on its side to hold oversize books. Magazines can be organized in special purchased boxes or in those made by cutting diagonal slices off detergent boxes. Shallow, stackable boxes or purchased stackable drawers are good for thread and other small items. Shallow boxes are better than deep ones, where items may get "lost" or damaged. Be sure to label closed boxes so that you know without opening them what is inside.

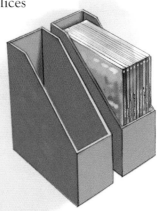

BOXES FOR MAGAZINES

Hardware storage has many possibilities for quilting and sewing supplies. A set of multiple small drawers sold for storing screws and bolts is an excellent answer for pins, tape measures, needles, and other small items. Tool and fishing tackle boxes can be used. A carpenter's chest has multiple possibilities for thread, shears, rulers, markers, or any flat items. Again, label the front of the drawers for easy identification.

CARPENTER'S CHEST

Plastic zipper bags work well for organizing patterns and templates. They can be labeled and put into looseleaf notebooks or stored in a box. They can also be used to keep patchwork pieces organized after cutting and before sewing them.

Peg-Board is wonderful for anything that can be hung, including quilt hoops, rulers, and numerous small items. A bag clip hung on the board can hold a sketch of what you are working on. Hanging Peg-Board on the inside of a door keeps tools out of the way.

Try This Drill holes in large rulers or cutting mats so they can be hung on hooks and attached to a wall or Peg-Board to keep them handy but out of the way.

Bookcases or closet shelves can hold fabric, and they are an obvious answer for books, magazines, tools, rulers, and boxes.

A small chest of drawers is good for items that need protection, such as shears, scissors, rotary cutters, and drafting tools. Since the drawers may be too deep for easy organization, it helps to use small boxes as dividers within the drawers.

A filing cabinet can be a real friend. It can hold patterns, templates, stencils, notebooks, certain tools, magazines, books, and even fabric. Depending on the dividers used, it has almost unlimited possibilities. Be sure to label things well.

However you choose to organize, browse through home supply and hardware stores and check out the storage products in discount and grocery stores to get many helpful ideas. Use your imagination and you can organize even a small space to make your quilt-making life easier.

Becky Herdle

Compact Work/Storage Area

by Karen Kay Buckley

The best way to economize on space is to combine ironing, cutting, and storage areas. My cutting and ironing surface was created from a hollow door. Cover a portion of the door with some old wool blankets (look for good buys at yard sales or flea markets). Purchase a piece of cotton drill, which is similar to muslin, but heavier, and wrap it around the wool blankets, then staple it to the door. Determine the height needed to be comfortable for cutting and ironing, and purchase two small bathroom cabinets for the ends that will give you that height. I store a portion of my book collection in the cabinets, which gives the cabinets extra weight and stability—another good reason to purchase more quilting books! I filled the space between the cabinets under the ironing and cutting area with a pair of two-drawer filing cabinets for additional storage. I love this work area, and the cost was minimal!

Organizing Multiple Projects

If you quilt a lot, you probably have several projects in progress at the same time. To keep all of your projects ready so that you don't have to waste time looking for their various parts, keep separate boxes on a shelf with the necessary materials for each project inside. If you have clear boxes you can see what is inside easily, but be sure to keep them in indirect light so that the fabrics do not fade. If you use cardboard boxes, use labels to identify each project. When you are heading to a quilt group meeting, it's easy to grab a box to ask for input from your friends on how to proceed.

The Office/Sewing Room Dilemma

My office at home doubles as a sewing area, so space is limited. An antique, binned kitchen cabinet provides decorative storage for some of my fabrics and tools, but since it became full ages ago, a variety of small rubber and plastic storage bins with lids are the best solution for the overflow. The bins are just right for holding fat quarters and other small, folded, or rolled pieces of fabric. I keep tools and other items in see-through bins, but to help eliminate fading, I usually keep fabrics in opaque bins. I label and stack bins one on top of the other to help keep my overworked room from getting entirely out of control.

Plastic zipper bags come in a variety of sizes and make wonderful little storage compartments for quilting paraphernalia. I like to keep tools and other items in plastic bags inside see-through plastic sweater boxes. I keep these boxes stacked on shelving units. The small items can become an unorganized mess if they're not stored separately. Snack-size bags are great for lumping together things like thimbles, packaged needles, rotary blades, needle pullers, and threaders. Larger bags make handy, inexpensive storage bins for specialty threads, marking pens, and cut patches. Decorative rubber stamps and those used to print foundation blocks can be popped into a bag to keep ink residue from rubbing off on their neighbors. By sorting with plastic bags, I can place more items in each sweater box and still find things quickly when I need them.

YARDAGES

Most quilt patterns include recommendations for required fabric yardages, but there may be times when you alter fabric choices in a way that makes the provided calculations meaningless. There may also be times when you choose to design your own original quilt. In either case, follow the easy steps below to calculate yardages.

Rotary-cut pieces are normally subcut from strips of fabric cut selvage to selvage along the crosswise grain. Patches cut from templates are marked side by side on fabric before being cut out. Yardage calculations are made the same way, no matter which method you are using. For 44- to 45-inch-wide fabrics, use a strip width of 42 inches for your calculations to allow for shrinkage and trimming the selvages from each side.

Step 1. Determine which pieces will be cut from the same fabric. List them in the first two columns of a table similar to the one on page 268. Then calculate the total number of each of those pieces required, and enter it in the third column.

Measure here

Step 2. Determine the cut size of each piece in the quilt, and enter it in the fourth column. Sizes are usually given for rotary-cut pieces. If templates are used, measure them along their outer edges. Measure irregular shapes at their widest points.

Step 3. Select one of the dimensions as the strip width, then divide the width of the fabric (usually 42 inches) by the other dimension to calculate the number of pieces that you can cut from one strip of cross-grain fabric. Round the answer down to the nearest whole number.

Step 4. Divide the total number of pieces needed by yield per strip to get the number of strips to cut. Round the answer up to the nearest whole number.

Step 5. Multiply the number of strips needed by the strip width, and divide by 36 inches per yard. This will give you the number of yards needed. Always round up when calculating yardages to allow for shrinkage and the cutting errors we all seem to make at times.

 As an example, let's say that you need forty-eight 2½-inch squares of Fabric A. The 2½-inch squares can be cut from a 2½-inch wide selvage-to-selvage strip.

42" ÷ 2½" = 16.8 squares/strip

From each 42-inch strip, the yield would be 16 full squares plus a leftover scrap. Now you need to determine how many strips are required to cut 48 squares.

48 squares ÷ 16 squares/strip = 3 strips

To get total inches, multiply 3 strips × 2½ inches. You'll need 7½ inches of Fabric A. Calculate yardage by dividing 7½ inches by 36 inches, resulting in 0.21 yards, which we round up to 0.25, or ¼ yard. If Fabric A will be used for additional pieces, calculate the total inches required in the same manner as for the square. Add up the totals before figuring the final yardage.

CALCULATING YARDAGE FOR VARIOUS FABRICS

Fabric	Piece	Number of Pieces Needed	Dimensions (Cut Size)	Yield per Strip (42" ÷ Length of Cut Piece)	Number of Strips to Cut (Total Pieces Yield/Strip)	Total Needed
Red	A	48	2½" × 2½"	16	3	7½"
Red	B	50	1½" × 4"	10	5	7½"
Blue	C	66	4" × 6"	10	7	42"

To determine total yardage needed for a fabric, add total inches and divide by 36.
For example: 7½" red fabric + 7½" red fabric = 15" ÷ 36 = ½ yard.

Make a table similar to this one to help you determine yardages.

If a fabric will be used for just a few pieces, it's simple to keep a running total of the inches required as you make calculations. For fabrics that will be used extensively, I suggest you use graph paper to make a cutting guide, as shown below, to help you plan the best use of your fabric. If you intend to cut one-piece borders or sashing on the lengthwise grain, remember that cutting wide sashing or borders will shorten the length of selvage-to-selvage strips.

Borders

← 42" →

CUTTING GUIDE

 To double-check your figures and to guarantee you've added enough "insurance" fabric, multiply the calculated yardage figure by 36 inches. For instance, if you need 2¾ yards of fabric, multiply 2¾ × 36. Compare the answer, 99 inches, with the total number of running inches shown in your original calculations. Is it enough? Most cottons shrink from 2 to 5 percent, so keep that shrinkage in mind. In this case you could lose 2 to 5 inches from the length in shrinkage alone.

Cutting to Conserve Fabric

Since squares are equal on all sides, there is only one dimension to consider when determining strip width. For rectangles or other objects with unequal sides, evaluate the shape before deciding which way to cut.

For instance, 2½ × 4½-inch rectangles can be cut from strips that are either 2½ inches or 4½ inches wide. The difference in the resulting rectangles is which grain runs along their sides.

Nine rectangles can be cut from the 2½-inch-wide strips, with a 1½ × 2½-inch scrap left over. Or, you can cut 16 rectangles from a 4½-inch-wide strip, with a 2 × 4½-inch scrap left over.

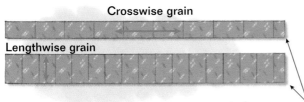

Crosswise grain

Lengthwise grain

Leftover scraps

Before deciding which strip width to use, consider the total number of rectangles you'll need and the dimensions and number of leftover scraps those strips will generate. Your goal is to conserve fabric, unless specific sides of a patch should be cut on the lengthwise grain to add stability to the block.

DECIMAL TO FRACTION

Decimal	0.125	0.25	0.375	0.5	0.625	0.75	0.875
Fraction	⅛	¼	⅜	½	⅝	¾	⅞

YARDS TO INCHES

Yards	⅛	¼	⅜	½	⅝	¾	⅞
Inches	4½"	9"	13½"	18"	22½"	27"	31½"

TAKING THE TROUBLE OUT OF

Irregularly Shaped Patches

Appliquéd quilts and quilts with many curved patches often contain irregularly shaped pieces that cannot be placed side by side for cutting. Be sure to purchase additional "insurance" yardage for those quilts. To determine the best way to arrange the patches for cutting, tape newspaper together to achieve a width of 42 inches. Trace the shapes (plus their seam allowances) onto the newspaper to see how many can be cut from a given strip width. Use the results to determine yardage in the same manner used for symmetrical patches.

Janet Wickell

YO-YOS

Yo-yos are whimsical, decorative flower forms that create a textural effect. They are made from fabric circles that are hemmed and gathered into small rosettes. Yo-yos can be stitched together to make a bedcover or a vest or appliquéd as an embellishment. Yo-yo quilts were very popular as scrap quilts in the 1930s. Even though we say yo-yo "quilts," there is no batting or backing involved. Households used those quilts in the warm summer months as a bed adornment with a white or colored broadcloth sheet underneath that peeked through the spaces between the yo-yos.

Step 1. To make a yo-yo, draw a circle for a pattern at least twice the size of the finished yo-yo onto cardboard, and cut it out. The end of a large spool of thread makes a good pattern for a small yo-yo.

Step 2. Trace the circular shape onto the right side of the fabric, and cut out the fabric ¼ inch from the line.

 Raid your kitchen for lots of ready-made patterns. Jar lids and mouths, lids to plastic tubs, glasses, and other objects make great patterns. Tracing around these items saves the effort of making a pattern. Plus, it's easy to trace around the hard edges, and it's less likely that you'll lose your pattern.

—*Suzanne Nelson*

The search for the perfect yo-yo quilt ended when quilt book editors and copy editors at Rodale Press whipped up this scrappy blue table runner. It contains 304 yo-yos.

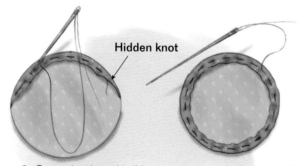

Step 3. Since the thread will have to support the tension of the fabric, use quilting thread or regular sewing thread doubled. Holding the circle wrong side up in your hand, turn in the edges of the circular piece on the line so you see it appear as you stitch. Make sure the hem falls over the wrong side of the fabric. When you begin stitching, bring your needle up from the underside of the ¼-inch seam allowance so the knot will be hidden when the yo-yo is completed. Using a short running stitch, sew on the folded edge all the way around. Your stitching must be continuous, with no backstitches.

Step 4. The yo-yo is formed when you pull on the thread, forcing the edges of the circle to pull together and leaving a hole in the middle. Stitch evenly around the perimeter and then pull smoothly to gather the circle into a yo-yo. If the hole is too big, try taking larger stitches.

Step 5. Arrange the folds evenly and fasten with a few backstitches. Finger press and primp the yo-yo to flatten it. The yo-yo can now be appliquéd or sewn together with others.

To make yo-yos into a quilt or a vest they need to be accurate for joining into even rows. Join the circles together in strips or blocks in the desired color sequence by holding the circles with their gathered sides together and taking several overcast sewing stitches close together. Open this unit flat, and add another yo-yo to the opposite side. Continue in this manner to make a row of yo-yos. When the row is the desired length, add yo-yos to the other side.

Appliqué Yo-Yos

Yo-yos of any size can be used as appliqués. They can be grouped together as berries, used as flowers on a stem, put into an appliquéd basket, or stacked in various sizes with buttons for embellishment.

Appliqué the yo-yos with a hidden stitch, a decorative blanket stitch, or a feather stitch. Use embroidery floss or pearl cotton (size 5 or 8) when attaching the yo-yos with the blanket or feather stitch.

Blanket Stitch. Bring the thread up from the underside of the background fabric. The tip of the needle should come out exactly at the edge of the yo-yo. Insert the needle down ¼ inch into the yo-yo. Bring the needle back up through the base fabric ¼ inch away from the first stitch. The needle should come out at the edge of the yo-yo, over the thread. Pull up the stitch to form a loop, and repeat around the yo-yo.

Try This Use a little dab of fabric glue stick to hold the yo-yo in place as you stitch. A pin can "warp" the yo-yo, making stitching tricky. —*Suzanne Nelson*

Feather Stitch. Work these stitches with the left half of the stitches placed on the yo-yo and the right half of the stitches placed on the background fabric. Bring the needle out at the top center, going off the yo-yo. Hold the thread down with the left thumb and insert the needle a little to the right on the same level and into the yo-yo. Take a small stitch down to the center, keeping the thread under the needle point. Next, insert the needle a little to the left on the same level and take a stitch to the center, keeping the thread under the needle point. Work these two movements alternately.

Judy Murrah

271

YUKATA

Yukata is a lightweight, flat-weave fabric used for casual summertime kimonos. This 100 percent cotton fabric is widely sought by many American quilters, decorators, and sewing enthusiasts. Like other traditional Japanese fabrics made to sew a kimono, it comes 14½ inches wide with 12½ yards in a standard bolt.

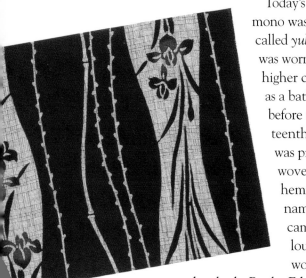

Today's yukata kimono was initially called *yukata-bira* and was worn in a tub by higher class samurai as a bathing robe before the fourteenth century. It was probably woven with hemp. The name gradually came to include lounge-wear worn after a hot bath. By the Edo Period, in the beginning of the seventeenth century, it spread widely to commoners and became woven with less expensive cottons. It was then often worn as an in-house summer kimono. It was only in the late nineteenth century that yukata made its first public appearance on hot, humid summer days. As more of them were worn in the open, elaborate weaves including *chirimen* (creped weave), *ro* (open variegated weave), and *koubai-ori* (a variegated yarn flat weave) were incorporated. Deep indigo-dyed designs and motifs, reflecting refreshing indigo color to alleviate summer heat, became a standard for today's yukata fabrics.

Yukata is traditionally dyed, not printed, with a katazome technique in which resist made from rice bran flour is squeegeed to both sides of the cloth through the cut openings on a stencil paper. Care must be taken to match the designs from one side to the other. A medium-length stencil paper called *chugata* with one complete design, or one repeat, measuring about 39 inches, is used.

The resisting was done on a long wooden board called *nagaita*, but a vacuum table is used today. A bolt of fabric 12½ yards long is folded into 12 layers 39 inches in length on a vacuum table, sandwiching paste resist between all layers. A dyer pours dye and solvent through unresisted areas from the top as a vacuum table sucks dyes through all the layers. Thus, both sides are dyed and the fabric has no right or wrong sides. A printed "yukata" fabric with a definite wrong side is used in Japan only to make inexpensive hotel pajamas, and is *not* a kimono yardage.

The designs in yukata run both ways because the fabric is folded as the images are transferred to the fabric. A yukata kimono is sewn unlined and without shoulder seams using continuous fabrics. Many yukata motifs are planned so that a design mirrors the adjacent panel when sewn in a kimono.

Traditionally, young girls wore larger and brighter floral designs on white, and as they matured, the designs became smaller and the color more somber. However, the women's yukata is rapidly changing to reflect the cosmopolitan outlook of today's Japanese women. Bolder and nontraditional colored motifs are now dyed on colored and textured backgrounds with increasingly Western flavors. But men are still wearing the traditional geometric designs in blue and white or in other darker colors.

For use in quiltmaking, preshrink yukata, if desired, without soap in warm water. Machine wash and dry, but remove it from a dryer while still damp, and iron until dry for the best result. Iron with a pressing cloth over a dark indigo-color area, since indigo color may develop a shine with high heat.

Debby Wada

ZIGZAG STITCH

This back-and-forth stitch is used in machine appliqué to create the satin stitch. It is also used for embellishing and couching decorative yarns and braids. Using different threads on the top, such as metallic, rayon, or machine embroidery thread, will give you different effects with varying amounts of sparkle. Experiment with the width of the stitch and with different threads to discover how you can creatively incorporate this stitch into your quiltmaking.

Adjusting Tension

You may need to adjust your tension, but do a test on a sample first. Always make any adjustments on the top tension first.

Draw lines about 1 inch apart on fabric similar to the kind you will be stitching. Mark the spaces between the lines from 1 to 9. Set your tension on 1 and start stitching in the first section, marked 1. When you reach the line, change your tension to 2. Continue until you reach 9. Check the front and back of the sample to determine which tension setting is the best.

If all adjustments to the top tension fail, the screw in the bobbin case can be adjusted. (If you have a Bernina sewing machine, try taking the thread through the finger of the bobbin case first.) Never play with the bobbin case that comes with your machine. Use a spare bobbin case and mark it with nail polish so you know which case is the one you can play with. Pretend the screw on the bobbin case is a clock and turn it in five-minute increments. This is a very short screw, and you do not want it to fall out because you may never find it again!

See also "Machine Appliqué" on page 17 and "Couching" on page 96.

 Have you ever tried machine quilting using a zigzag stitch? You may be surprised at how much fun it is and how it can make machine quilting more interesting.

Karen Kay Buckley

RESOURCE GUIDE

SOURCES FOR PRODUCTS AND SUPPLIES MENTIONED IN THE BOOK

CONTRIBUTORS

Elizabeth A. Akana is a teacher, lecturer, author, and quilt historian. She has been demonstrating the art of Hawaiian quilting since 1972 and has taught and lectured about the subject throughout the United States and in New Zealand, Japan, Scotland, and England. Her quilts are included in many private and corporate collections and have been accepted in numerous juried and invitational exhibits throughout this country and in Japan. She was the instructor for a Hawaii Public Television series, "Hawaiian Quilting." She is currently working on a book about Hawaiian quilting.

Karen Bolesta began sewing in the fourth grade and made her first quilt, a king-size Dresden Plate, at the age of 17. Her early exposure to fabric and thread developed into an undeniable passion and led to an editing career in needlecrafts. She was an editor at *McCall's Needlework & Crafts* magazine and is currently a senior associate editor for Rodale Quilt Books.

Cheryl Greider Bradkin began sewing Seminole patchwork in 1977 and happily found that it combined a scientific education with her love of color and textiles. She published her first book of Seminole patterns in 1978. She has led workshops in the United States, Canada, and Japan and uses Seminole techniques to create ocean, feather, and botanical designs. Her third book, *Basic Seminole Patchwork*, gives full-color patterns for over 56 Seminole designs along with great ideas for using the patchwork. Cheryl and her husband live in Coupeville, Widbey Island, Washington. Cheryl continues to play with Seminole patchwork possibilities.

Karen Kay Buckley resides in Carlisle, Pennsylvania, with her husband, Joe, and their dog, Samantha. Karen graduated from Lock Haven University with a degree in education. She has been quilting for 13 years and teaching quilting for 10 years. She has over 200 quilts to her credit, and they have won numerous national and regional awards.

Her first book, *From Basics to Binding: A Complete Guide to Making Quilts*, was published in 1992, and her second book, *Above & Beyond Basics*, was published in 1996.

Doris Carmack is a quilting teacher who first published *Easy Biscuit Quilting* in 1985. She lives in Fountain Valley, California, with her husband, Bob, and she teaches this technique and many others in the southern California area. She likes to include machine embroidery techniques in her quilts and is a member of several machine arts organizations. She has taught at seminars in various parts of the country.

Sharyn Craig began quilting in 1978 by taking a local adult education class. By 1980 she was teaching quiltmaking on her own through that same adult education system as well as in local quilt shops. In 1984 she took her classes on the road. She has written three books: *Designing New Traditions in Quilts, Drafting Plus,* and *Twist 'n Turn.* As a regular contributor to several quiltmaking publications, she is probably best known for the "Design Challenge" column she writes for *Traditional Quiltworks* magazine. Through that column she sends out her message of encouragement to all quilters to do their own thing.

Mimi Dietrich lives in Catonsville, Maryland, with her husband and two sons. She has a degree in American Studies from the University of Maryland Baltimore County. Mimi specializes in teaching Baltimore Album Quilt classes using dimensional appliqué techniques. Mimi offers a "Home Town" tour of Baltimore, taking visitors to monuments and places that have been stitched into album quilts. Her latest project involves quilt research at the Smithsonian Institution's National Museum of American History. She is the author of *Happy Endings: Finishing the Edges of Your Quilt, Handmade Quilts, Baltimore Bouquets, The Easy Art of Appliqué,* and *Quilts from the Smithsonian.*

Carol Doak is an award-winning quiltmaker, designer, teacher, and author of several books, including *Quiltmaker's Guide: Basics & Beyond, Easy Machine Paper Piecing, Easy Reversible Vests, Easy Paper-Pieced Keepsake Quilts,* and *Easy Mix & Match Machine Paper Piecing.* Carol travels nationally and internationally to share her quilting "Tricks of the Trade." Carol's quilts have been widely published in books and national quiltmaking magazines.

Philomena Durcan has been involved in quilting for over 20 years. She introduced Celtic design to the quilt world in 1980 with the publication of her first book, *Celtic Quilt Designs.* Since that time she has presented lectures and workshops throughout the world on her interlace and spiral designs as well as on the Bias Bar technique of appliqué. More recently her fascination with floral art has led to the technique of "painting" with fabric. Her work has been exhibited nationally and internationally in numerous museums and shows. Philomena lives in Sunnyvale, California, where she owns and operates the Celtic Design Company and continues to explore new horizons of Celtic design.

Lynne Edwards has been making quilts both by hand and by machine since 1970. She specializes in the development of Cathedral Windows, using a variety of shapes and fabrics to create original and exciting designs. Lynne writes, teaches, and lectures internationally on all aspects of quiltmaking. In addition to her Cathedral Windows book *Through the Window & Beyond,* she has produced a video on machine patchwork and has just completed a book on her sampler quilt course for an English publisher.

Anna Eelman's fascination with women's nineteenth-century diaries led her to quilting, blending her long-standing interest in history and the needle arts. Anna currently does freelance writing and publishes a bi-monthly newsletter for the Feedsack Club. She has four grown children and two grandchildren, tends a home and husband, holds a job outside the home, runs a quilt guild, and chairs an annual community quilt show. She is a Christian, sports fan, and cat lover. She specializes in finding and finishing old quilt tops and blocks and loves to make scrap and charm quilts.

Marianne Fons and partner, **Liz Porter,** have been quilting and working together since 1976 when they met in a beginner's quilting class in Winterset, Iowa. Well known to quilters across the country for their down-to-earth and practical style of teaching and writing, their joint efforts also include lecturing, designing fabrics, and most recently, hosting a public television series called *Sew Many Quilts.*

Gladys Grace has more than 20 years of experience in stenciling and quilting. She combines her expertise as an artist with her talents as a teacher to make stenciling easy to learn with wonderful results. Her knowledge of the history of stenciling, her innovative approach, and her love of teaching have led her to be in demand as a lecturer and designer. She has taught seminars throughout the country, and she travels to quilt shows to market her products. She has her own line of stencils, paints, and brushes.

Tina M. Gravatt is known for her heirloom miniature quilts. Each quilt she makes represents a fad or fashion from American or European quilting tradition. Her quilts are known for their attention to detail, excellent scale and proportion, as well as technical excellence. Tina has also become involved in collecting old and new doll beds upon which to display her quilts. Since the full-size quilts she copies were meant as functional items, she likes to see her miniature quilts used in the same way. Tina is the author of three books on miniature quilts.

Jane Hall and **Dixie Haywood** are award-winning quiltmakers who are known for adapting traditional designs using contemporary techniques and innovative approaches. Their quilts have been exhibited throughout the country and are in private and public collections. Both have been teaching and judging quiltmaking for over 20 years. They have a strong commitment to provide students with well-grounded and creative information so they can make their own unique quilts. They have co-authored *Perfect Pineapples, Precision Pieced Quilts Using the Foundation Method,* and *Firm Foundations.* Dixie is also the author of *The Contemporary Crazy Quilt Project Book,* and *Crazy Quilting with a Difference;* her articles appear regularly in leading quilt periodicals. Jane is a certified appraiser for old and new quilts. Long-time friends, Jane lives in Raleigh, North Carolina, with her husband, Bob, and Dixie lives in Pensacola, Florida, with *her* husband, Bob. They rely heavily on telephone, fax, and airlines to function as a team.

Joan Hanson began her life-long love affair with fabric at an early age, spending many happy hours stitching clothes for her dolls. She made her first quilt at the age of ten for her Barbie doll. She later earned her degree in home economics and taught for several years. She began quiltmaking in earnest in the early 1980s using up-to-date techniques and equipment to make her quilts. One quilt led to another and one class led to another, and before long, Joan was teaching classes on quilts that she designed herself. She is the author of *Calendar Quilts* and *Sensational Settings*. She is the co-author of *Quilters' Companion* and *The Joy of Quilting*.

Becky Herdle lives in Rochester, New York, with her husband, Lloyd. She started making quilts in 1977 after their family was grown. Her work and articles have been published in magazines, books, and quilt calendars. She has recently written a book, *Time-Span Quilts: New Quilts from Old Tops*. Though she is an author, workshop instructor, lecturer, and certified judge, she still actively pursues her two main interests: making new quilts and completing old quilt tops.

Tess Herlan, from Redmond, Washington, began her long association with English paper piecing 15 years ago when she was teaching the method to beginning quilting classes. Liking the more traditional patterns, she found it an accurate and portable way to make quilts. Ten years ago she launched her own company, Paper Pieces, and now designs patterns to use the large variety of precut papers they have available. She also teaches and lectures on this technique, traveling to meet quilters in the United States as well as in other countries.

Cyndi Hershey has been quilting since 1978 and began teaching quilting in the early 1980s. Her background is in interior design and textiles. The colors, patterns, and textures of fabric are still the things that interest her the most. Being able to combine so many different fabrics in one project is the primary reason that she loves quilting! She and her husband, Jim, bought The Country Quilt Shop in Montgomeryville, Pennsylvania, in 1988. Her favorite part of owning the shop is that it allows her to teach as often as possible, helping other quilters to learn and grow.

Laurel Horton discovered quilts in 1975 while studying for a master's degree in folklore. Since then she has been active as a quiltmaker, teacher, lecturer, and researcher. Her favorite quilts are those that combine many different fabrics to create striking visual designs. Her research interests focus on regional variations and traditions in the southern states. Since 1983, she has been an active member of the American Quilt Study Group, a national organization dedicated to encouraging and publishing research on quilts, textiles, and quiltmakers. She received a travel grant from the National Endowment for the Humanities in 1991 to study quilts in Ireland and Northern Ireland.

Roberta Horton has been a quiltmaker since 1970. She travels worldwide to lecture and hold workshops. She has authored five quiltmaking books, the most recent being *The Fabric Makes the Quilt*. She also designs plaid and stripe fabrics for Fasco/Fabric Sales of Seattle. Roberta's focus is the fabric from which quilts are made.

Lynette Jensen created her company, thimbleberries, in 1989 based on a love for the needle arts, fabric, color, design, and antique quilts. Her company is known for designing projects large and small that have a warm, inviting country look. The patterns are based on traditional antique quilts but with an updated, creative twist. She also designs fabrics for RJR Fabrics in rich shades of colors found in vintage textiles.

Carol Johnson has a graphic art and journalism degree from Utah State University. She belongs to local, state, and national quilt guilds, has taught quilting throughout Utah, and has written for books and quilting magazines. Her quilts have been exhibited in local, state, and national contests. She specializes in making and teaching how to make

tied coverlets and uneven curved pieced and quilted scenes from nature. She has worked as an editor and graphic designer and is at present a docent at the Nora Eccles Harrison Museum at Utah State University. She and her husband, a retired Air Force officer, live in Nibley, Utah, and they are the parents of six children.

Jeana Kimball's favorite quiltmaking medium is appliqué. Through it she has found the freedom to tell stories and portray ideas without being confined to geometric shapes. She is a prolific author of quiltmaking books, including *Reflections of Baltimore, Red and Green, Appliqué Borders, Loving Stitches, Fairmeadow, Rabbit Patch, Come Berrying,* and *Backyard Garden.* She has also designed fabric for Marcus Brothers Textiles and has done commissioned work for publishers. Jeana lives in Salt Lake City, Utah, with her family. She travels nationally and internationally, sharing her knowledge and love of quilting with her students through classes and lectures.

Betty Kiser, a resident of Carlisle Springs, Pennsylvania, learned machine sewing from her Grandmother Green by making Four Patches from flannel and quilt tying from her Grandmother Emerson. It was many, many years later while overseas with her husband, Walt, that she learned how to quilt. It became her number one craft choice, leading to research for and publication of *The Path Less Traveled: Variations on the Drunkard's Path,* intended to be a complete collection of the design's possibilities. She began a second book, *The Path Beyond: Exploring the Drunkard's Path,* almost immediately, as she didn't get them all in the first book!

Gwen Marston is a professional quiltmaker, author, and teacher who has written 12 books and produced a series of videos on quiltmaking. She has taught quilting across the United States and in Japan and has been a regular columnist for *Lady's Circle Patchwork Quilts* magazine for 11 years. Her recent book, *Quilting with Style: Principles for Great Pattern Design,* gives detailed information on how to draft most classical quilting designs. Gwen offers quilting retreats at her Beaver Island home on Lake Michigan, and her quilts have been shown in many exhibits throughout the United States.

Her work is represented by the Tamarack Craftsmen Gallery in Omena, Michigan.

Judy Martin has been designing and making quilts for 27 years. She is the author of ten popular quilting books, including *Scrap Quilts, Judy Martin's Ultimate Book of Quilt Block Patterns,* and *Pieced Borders.* For 8 years she was a designer and editor at *Quilter's Newsletter Magazine* and *Quiltmaker.* Now she and her husband own Crosley-Griffith Publishing Company. They have a new line of tools called "Judy Martin's Ultimate Rotary Rulers" that cut a variety of shapes from strips. Judy's tools will be featured in her forthcoming books and patterns.

Mary Mashuta has been quilting since the early 1970s. She is a professionally trained teacher and has taught on the national quiltmaking circuit since 1985. She bills herself as "the foremost buyer of stripe fabric in the United States." Her newest book is *Stripes in Quilts.* She also wrote *Wearable Art for Real People* and *Story Quilts: Telling Your Tale in Fabric.* Her informative articles on stripes, wearables, story quilts, and quilters' workspaces have appeared in *Quilter's Newsletter, American Quilter, Lady's Circle Patchwork Quilts,* and *Threads.*

Marsha McCloskey has been quilting since 1969 and teaching since 1975. She has taught throughout the United States, Australia, Holland, Belgium, France, Canada, Japan, Norway, and Denmark. Marsha was a graphic arts major in college, but she turned from printmaking to quiltmaking as motherhood made the messier media impractical. She published her first book, *Small Quilts,* in 1981; since then she has written or co-authored 15 books on quiltmaking. She has her own publishing company, Feathered Star Productions, and in 1995 she designed a new line of quilting fabric called Staples under the Clothworks label.

Roxanne McElroy was born and raised in Colorado, but if you ask where her home was, you may get for an answer Utah, Montana, Texas, California, Tahiti, Georgia, or Hawaii, because she lived in all those places. She specialized in Tahitian quiltmaking and appliqué. She was an award-winning quiltmaker, lecturer, teacher, and author with her own unique and successful method for teaching quilting techniques. Roxanne designed the very popular Roxanne's Thimbles and Quilter's Choice Pencils. Her patterns, products, and methods continue to be marketed and taught by her daugher, Dierdra McElroy, through her company Roxanne International.

Susan McKelvey discovered quilting in 1977, and since then her work has appeared in museums, galleries, quilt shows, and magazines. She is a quilt artist, teacher, designer, and author, specializing in color and writing on quilts. Her company, Wallflower Designs, sells her patterns, quilt labels, and fabric pens. Her books include *Color for Quilters II*, *Light and Shadows*, *Friendship's Offering*, *A Treasury of Quilt Labels*, *Scrolls and Banners to Trace*, *The Signature Quilt*, and *Creative Ideas for Color and Fabric*. Susan and her husband have two grown children and currently reside in rural Maryland with two rescued golden retrievers and two spoiled cats—quilt lovers all!

Penny McMorris is the corporate art curator for Owens-Corning Fiberglas Corporation and a private consultant to several contemporary quilt collectors. She has been an advisor on quilt exhibitions for The American Craft Museum in New York City and the British Craft Council in London. She has juried Quilt National '86, The American Quilter's Society Show, and Visions 1996. She has produced three PBS television series on quilts, most recently "The Great American Quilt." She wrote *Crazy Quilts* and *The Art Quilt* (co-authored with the late Michael Kile). She and her husband, Dean Neumann, are partners in The Electric Quilt Company.

Suellen Meyer writes about quilt history and teaches seminars in dating antique fabrics and quilts. Her work has been published in *Uncoverings*, the journal of the American Quilt Study Group, as well as in magazines such as *Quilter's Newsletter* and *Country Living*. With her husband, Richard, she has collected over 100 antique mid-American quilts. She lives in St. Louis, Missouri, where she is professor of English at St. Louis Community College at Meramec.

Jeannette T. Muir's involvement in quiltmaking began in 1975. She has earned teacher and judge certifications and has served as president of the Tri-State Quiltmaking Teachers and the Moorestown (New Jersey) Area Quilters. Her quilt-related experience includes teaching, judging, designing and making quilts, collecting and restoring antique tops, and writing. Her specialties are machine quilting, precision hand piecing, and precision machine piecing. She is the author of the book *Precision Patchwork for Scrap Quilts . . . Anytime, Anywhere*, and is a contributor to *Easy Machine Quilting* and *A Quilted Christmas*.

Debbie Mumm is a quilt and fabric designer, author, and illustrator. She runs a quilt pattern company, Mumm's the Word, from her design and production center in Spokane, Washington. Her country-style designs feature quick cutting and sewing techniques that appeal to today's busy quilters of all skill levels. Debbie has written three books, her most recent being *Quick Country Christmas Quilts*. She continues to design fabric and is now designing for home and gift products. Debbie lives with her husband, Steve, and son, Murphy, in a hilltop home overlooking Mount Spokane.

Judy Murrah received a B.S. degree in education and art from Southwest Texas State University in 1965 and taught her first quilt classes in Houston, Texas, in 1977. She wrote the best-selling book, *Jacket Jazz*, published in 1993. *Jacket Jazz Encore* was published in 1994 and a third, *More Jazz from Judy Murrah*, in 1996. Judy's growth as a professional instructor and author has paralleled her responsibilities as Director of Education with Quilts, Incorporated, which produces the International Quilt Festival held in Houston each fall. Judy resides in Victoria, Texas.

Suzanne Nelson is Managing Editor of Rodale Quilt Books. A love affair with fabric and the sewing machine began at the tender age of eight when she began stitching one-of-a-kind clothing for her Barbie dolls. Discovering quiltmaking in 1988 was like love at first sight. Since then, she has made over 40 quilts, ranging from miniature to queen-size. A fan of machine piecing, hand appliqué, and both hand and machine quilting, she makes it a point to spend at least 15 minutes every night working on one of many ongoing projects. She hopes her enthusiasm for quilt-making rubs off on her two young daughters.

Nancy O'Bryant wrote the first book on caring for quilts in the home in 1986, after coordinating the nation's first quilt conservation and restoration seminar. She founded and served as president of the Austin Area Quilt Guild, wrote its "Ten Steps to Save a Quilt," and chaired its successful effort to produce the first video on quilt care, "Quilt Care in the Home." Nancy is co-founder of the American International Quilt Association, the Alliance for American Quilts, and the Texas Sesquicentennial Quilt Association. She helped plan and direct the Texas Quilt Search and co-authored two books on historic Texas quilts.

Beckie Olson started quilting in Berkeley, California, in the early 1970s. While living in Lexington, Kentucky, she owned a quilt shop for ten years before moving to Paradise, Utah. Beckie is a quilter, author, teacher, and lecturer, and she chairs the board of the American Heritage Quilt Festival. She teaches both nationally and internationally and has written *Quilts by the Slice*, a variety of patterns and kits. She is writing a second book, *Hand Pieced Heirlooms*.

Ellen Pahl learned to love working with a needle and thread as a young child. Her resourceful and creative mother, her grandmothers, various aunts, and neighbors taught her everything from darning socks to smocking and making yo-yos. She made her first quilt while majoring in biology at Kent State University. Her passion for quilts and sewing as a hobby eventually led to a career editing for Rodale Quilt Books. Her husband, Gary, is an artist who understands her need to collect fabric.

Karen Phillips is a self-taught fiber artist and has had a needle in her hand since age ten. She first began by sewing and embroidering beautiful clothes for her dolls. This led to designing clothes for several leading doll artists. When she married and moved into a 200-year-old farmhouse with five children and many rooms to decorate, she began to design original quilts, pillows, dolls, and dimensional embroidery

projects that won many blue ribbons in competitions. Requests began to pour in for classes and workshops featuring dimensional embroidery. Since then she has been teaching in her home studio, "The Quilted Heart," and throughout the United States.

Toni Phillips and **Juanita Simonich**'s partnership combines a diversity of background, experience, and education with a common love for creating, teaching, and encouraging their customers in the art of quiltmaking. Toni first learned needlework through embroidery and cross-stitch, but once she was introduced to quilting it became her passion. She has been writing patterns and teaching for the past 15 years. Juanita learned to sew as a child and continued her sewing education in college, majoring in Clothing and Textiles. Juanita's love for color and design shows in her quiltmaking style.

Toni and Juanita met in 1990, formed a pattern company called "Fabric Expressions," and soon the creative juices were flowing. Toni and Juanita wrote the books *T.L.C.: Tender Loving Covers* and *Quilt-A-Saurus* and contributed to Rodale's *Fast, Fun, and Fabulous Quilts*. In 1994 they opened a retail quilt shop in Littleton, Colorado, with the motto: "Give the customer more than she expects."

Caroline Reardon was 10 years old when her mother helped her cut patches for a Sunbonnet Sue quilt that she completed 14 years later for her own daughter. Her love of quiltmaking flourished, and after 13 years as a middle-school language arts teacher, she joined Leman Publications. She is now Managing Editor of *Quiltmaker* magazine. Caroline enjoys designing and using traditional patterns or pictorial appliqués to make quilts with a new look. Her work has appeared in magazines and in numerous shows, including the American Quilter's Society show in Paducah, Kentucky; the American International Quilt Association show in Houston, Texas; and Quilts '93 in Louisville, Kentucky.

Sharee Dawn Roberts received her Fine Arts Degree in Textile Design from San Diego University. She is well known for her high-fashion quilted clothing and special machine art techniques. She has received numerous awards, and her clothing has been shown in galleries and exhibitions in the United States, Japan, and Europe. She has taught throughout the United States and in Japan and Australia. Sharee wrote *Creative Machine Art* and has been a contributing editor for several sewing and quilting magazines. She has designed a line of appliqué patterns and is the owner of Web of Thread, a mail-order and retail business specializing in decorative threads for the needle artist.

Virginia Robertson comes from a family that includes five generations of quilters. She has been in the fabric and quilt business for 26 years, owning a quilt shop for 12 years, teaching college-level quilting, and for the last 15 years, operating the Osage County Quilt Factory, a quilt pattern publishing business in Overbrook, Kansas. She also designs her own line of fabrics for Fabri-Quilt. Virginia's strength is in color and design. She has written a color workbook for quilters called "If Monet Were a Quilter."

Marie Shirer is a former quilt-shop owner and has worked for Leman Publications since 1982, where she has been an editor for *Quilter's Newsletter Magazine*. Marie is the author of *Quilt Settings: A Workbook* and *The Quilter's How-To Dictionary*. Marie reports that she owns both a rotary cutter and a sewing machine and knows how to use them, but her true loves are hand piecing, hand appliqué, and hand quilting.

Karen Costello Soltys, a senior associate editor for Rodale Quilt Books, has been active in the needle arts since childhood. An early love of embroidery, crocheting, and knitting soon gave way to a passion for sewing. After earning a degree in marketing from Penn State University, Karen took her first Sampler Quilt class in 1979 and was hooked. Her sewing room is now bursting at the seams with fabric, and her hobby has become her career. Karen has edited numerous quilt books, including six books in Rodale's *Classic American Quilt Collection*.

Susan Stein succumbed to the quilting obsession in 1977. Since then her work has been built on traditional designs used by generations of quiltmakers. The use of solid-color fabrics, especially in hand-dyed gradations, lends a contemporary look to the wallhangings and liturgical pieces that are her focus. The use of texture and multiple layers, machine quilting, sampler quilts with unique settings, and Double Wedding Ring quilts with innovative backgrounds and embellishments are current interests. Susan writes and designs for publication and teaches nationally. In the fall of 1995, she opened a contemporary quilting store in St. Paul, Minnesota.

Mary Stori is a lecturer, teacher, author, Fairfield designer, and quilter whose work has appeared and won awards in numerous national shows. She has written articles or been featured in several quilting and sewing magazines. Her book, *The Stori Book of Embellishing*, guarantees inspiration for embellishing ideas! Mary loves the challenge of creating one-of-a-kind fashions and quilts. Her work is often humorous and frequently features a method of three-dimensional stuffed appliqué that has become her specialty. Traveling throughout the country to present lectures, workshops, and fashion shows of her wearables keeps her busy and motivated.

Eileen Sullivan has been working exclusively with foundation piecing since 1988, in what she describes as a "sew and flip" or "beyond string piecing" technique. Her quilts utilizing this method have appeared in numerous books, magazines, and a Fairfield advertisement, as well as in the permanent collection of the Museum of the American Quilters Society. An active quilter since the late 1970s, she currently resides in Alpharetta, Georgia, where her time is divided between teaching, quilting, and maintaining The Designer's Workshop, which distributes patterns of her designs throughout the United States and abroad.

Jane Townswick has been a quiltmaker since 1983. She is the former owner of Quilter's Cupboard quilt shop in Rockford, Illinois, where she taught beginning quiltmaking and advanced appliqué classes until 1990, when she began her career as an editor at Chitra Publications' *Traditional Quiltworks* magazine. She is currently an editor for Rodale Quilt Books and the editor of Rodale's Creative Needlecrafts Book Club.

Holice Turnbow began quilting in the early 1970s. Since that time he has lectured and conducted workshops throughout the United States. His area of specialty is in quilting techniques related to the development and use of quilting designs. He designs quilting stencils for The Stencil Company and whole-cloth designs for Spartex, including those adapted from quilts in the National Museum of American History, Smithsonian Institution. He is a quilting consultant to Benartex Fabrics and regularly contributes articles and designs to *Quilt Craft* magazine. He has appeared with Kay Wood on her popular PBS series and is a National Quilting Association certified quilt teacher and judge.

Debby Wada has been a co-owner and manager of Kasuri Dyeworks, a retail store specializing in Japanese textiles and folk crafts in Berkeley, California, for the past 11 years. Through her importing business, she has personally come to know many dyers and weavers in Japan. Today she shares her accumulated knowledge of traditional Japanese textiles with many quilters, designers, and seamstresses here in the United States through workshops and lectures in her store.

Debra Wagner considers herself a traditionalist in design, if not in technique. Her main interest is in developing machine methods for traditional quiltmaking. In 1992 her quilt *Rail through the Rockies* was designated as a Masterpiece Quilt by the National Quilting Association. Her quilts "Floral Urns" and "Sunburst" won the Bernina Award for Machine Workmanship at the 1993 and 1995 AQS Show and Contests. Other works have been displayed in Europe and Japan. She is the author of *Teach Yourself Machine Piecing & Quilting, Striplate Piecing,* and *All Quilt Blocks Are Not Square.*

Hari Walner and quilting were introduced to each other in 1987, when she was hired by Leman Publications as a designer and illustrator. The talented editors, artists, and quilters she worked with shared techniques and ideas. Soon she was hooked. She began staying up late at night to sew, design, and work on developing her own techniques. Hari now owns her own company, Beautiful Publications, which publishes her continuous-line machine quilting designs.

Jean Wells has been quilting and teaching for over 25 years. She is a designer, author, and for the past 22 years, owner of The Stitchin' Post, a nationally known quilt shop located in Sisters, Oregon. She has written numerous books and magazine articles in her helpful, inspirational, and down-to-earth style. She has been on the Home and Garden Network's "Simply Quilts" series and has designed a line of fabric called Pinebrook with P&B Textiles. She continues to teach in her shop, across the United States, and abroad.

Janet Wickell is the sponsor of Minifest, an annual event designed especially for miniature quilt enthusiasts. Top instructors from across the United States teach at a three-day seminar held in conjunction with the Minifest quilt show. Janet teaches quilt construction and hand marbling of fabric. Her marbling specialty includes small, intricately combed patterns that are easily incorporated into both traditional and contemporary quilts. She is fascinated by quilts and fabrics from past times, particularly those made during the last half of the nineteenth century. Home life includes husband, Dale, daughter Carly, and a menagerie of animal friends.

Darra Duffy Williamson is the author of *Sensational Scrap Quilts* and numerous magazine articles on the subject of quiltmaking. In 1989 she was named Quilt Teacher of the Year, and she has traveled extensively, teaching and lecturing at guilds and quilt events. Although no longer teaching full-time, she remains active by quilting, designing, exhibiting, judging, collecting, and writing about quilts. She has served as a technical writer for various Rodale publications and is currently at work on a second book for the American Quilter's Society. In addition, she is an avid and knowledgeable baseball fan and maintains a notable collection of outrageous socks.

INDEX